Praise for *Blackthorn's Protection Magic*

"You can never be too safe! *Blackthorn's Protection Magic* is an informative guide for anyone who has ever felt vulnerable. Each section of the book covers a different topic relating to self-defense providing readers with insightful information on protecting oneself from emotional, physical, and even psychic attacks. Amy's straightforward style makes it easy to read and understand but still provides enough depth to hold the interest of seasoned practitioners who are sure to learn some new tricks and techniques to add to their toolbox. *Blackthorn's Protection Magic* is an excellent addition to any library."

—Mat Auryn, author of *Psychic Witch*

"What you have working for you in *Blackthorn's Protection Magic:* the focus of a martial artist, the wisdom of an elder, the keen eye of a sharpshooter, the disciplined mind of an investigator, and the compassion of a counselor. Amy Blackthorn is all of these things, and her latest magical manual is a practical, realistic, and trustworthy guide that will help you prepare for any kind of attack—Amy will show you that *you* are your best defense."

—Natalie Zaman, author of *Magical Destinations of the Northeast* and *Color and Conjure*

"*Blackthorn's Protection Magic* is a book I wish I'd had when I was young. For those under the gun, it provides clear, actionable advice to immediately improve your situation. For beginner magicians, it offers a coherent introduction to sensible protections. For experienced practitioners, there's a variety of fun and fascinating spells in many different styles to whet the imagination and inspire your own work. 10/10 recommend."

—Sara Mastros, author of *The Big Book of Magical Incense*

"Protection magic is one of the most popular reasons for spellwork, and few people know as much about it as Amy Blackthorn. *Blackthorn's Protection Magic* explores spellwork and ritual, much of it drawn from the author's own experience, that will help keep you safe in an unsafe world. From simple actions like planting protective herbs or carrying a crystal to ward off psychic attack, to awareness of PTSD responses, evasion tactics, and mundane methods of staying safe, Amy blends her knowledge of witchcraft with her background as a protection specialist creating a magical and ethical manual for personal safety. *Blackthorn's Protection Magic* is the self-defense handbook you didn't know you needed."

—Patti Wigington, author of *Herb Magic*,
Witchcraft for Healing, and *Badass Ancestors*

"A treasure-trove of practical protection magic, *Blackthorn's Protection Magic* is a must-have addition to any witch's magical library. This guide is filled with invaluable information for any level of practitioner. Amy's writing is open, easily accessible, and engaging."

—Rhonda Alin, founder of the Northern New Jersey Tarot Meetup

"In a world that makes us constantly feel unsafe, we can easily be riddled with anxiety about even leaving home. Amy Blackthorn offers us a way to overcome fear by choosing to be proactive about our personal safety. Casting a protective circle around the reader, she offers her knowledge, practical advice, and magical techniques for how to avoid harm, minimize risk, and navigate the ever-present threats. Blackthorn brilliantly weaves her background in executive security with her witchery, while adding well-researched psychological constructs and emotional considerations into her formula for keeping us safe. I've already implemented parts of the book. *Blackthorn's Protection Magic* should be part of our libraries and our emergency preparedness kits."

—Cyndi Brannen, author of *Entering Hekate's Garden*
and *Keeping Her Keys*

"*Blackthorn's Protection Magic* is like sitting down with the kind of experienced, wise-witch aunt I think we've all wished for when trouble comes a-knocking. You know the kind of person I mean: the one who invites you in, makes you a cup of tea, and then helps you work through whatever challenges you're facing in a clear and down-to-earth manner. Amy's approach is refreshingly holistic, covering everything from shielding, wards, and hex-breaking to physical home protection and how to deal with a whole range of self-defense scenarios. The section on boundaries, trauma, and mental health is also invaluable. Above all, *Blackthorn's Protection Magic* is an affirming, empowering work that not only gives readers concrete steps they can take to stay safe, but also reminds the reader that they are worth the fight and to never give up."

—Cat Heath, author of *Elves, Witches, and Gods*

"The world can be a beautiful place but it can also be a threatening one at times, and *this book* offers you the spiritual tools to change your reality so that you can stand strong, thrive, and feel the deep sense of peace that is your birthright. With dozens of spells, checklists, practical advice, and reference guides, I know *Blackthorn's Protection Magic* will be the first book I grab when I need inspiration to weave some powerful protection magic myself."

—Madame Pamita, author of *Madame Pamita's Magical Tarot*
and *Baba Yaga's Book of Witchcraft*

BLACKTHORN'S
PROTECTION
MAGIC

BLACKTHORN'S
PROTECTION
MAGIC

A Witch's Guide to Mental & Physical Self-Defense

AMY BLACKTHORN

WEISER
BOOKS

This edition first published in 2022 by Weiser Books, an imprint of
Red Wheel/Weiser, LLC
With offices at:
65 Parker Street, Suite 7
Newburyport, MA 01950
www.redwheelweiser.com

ISBN: 978-1-57863-761-4
Library of Congress Cataloging-in-Publication Data available upon request.

Cover and interior design by Kathryn Sky-Peck
Typeset in Minion

Printed in the United States of America
IBI
10 9 8 7 6 5 4 3 2 1

This book contains advice and information for using herbs, essential oils, and
incense for your safety and protection. It should be used to supplement, not replace,
the advice of your physician or other trained healthcare practitioner. Readers are
cautioned to follow instructions carefully and accurately for the best effect. If you feel
you are in danger, please consult your local police or available security team. Readers
using the information in this book do so entirely at their own risk, and the author
and publisher accept no liability if adverse effects are caused.

Dedication

To the fierce and beloved protectors in my life, body, mind, and spirit.
Everyone needs a little backup sometimes.

"Most people are good and occasionally do something they know is bad.

Some people are bad and struggle every day to keep it under control.

Others are corrupt to the core and they don't give a damn,
as long as they don't get caught.

But evil is a completely different creature.

Evil is bad that believes it's good."

—Karen Marie Moning, *Shadowfever*

Contents

Contents

What Is Protection?
What Is Magic?

This book, like many, is a labor of love. I have spent a goodly number of
years spreading the word of our botanical allies. Writing this book was
a chance to blend my longtime love of weaving botanical lore into our
collective unconscious and to reawaken our symbiotic relationship with
flora. However, in the past part of what makes me Amy wasn't included
in my work. The part of me that wasn't previously included is my professional background in private security and executive protection.

What Is Protection?

Protection isn't only the ability to keep yourself safe from curses, hexes,
or jinxes. It also encompasses our ability to set the energies in our homes
to *safe* and feel that security in our bones. I've devoted a decade and a
half to the service of protecting those around me professionally. I was
the head of security for a top real estate firm in the state of Delaware,
and I have also worked to protect public personalities, CEOs, CFOs,
and senior executives. I volunteer to act as escorts for women under-
going sensitive medical procedures, divorce decrees, and court appear-
ances for domestic violence cases. I may have lived a security mindset,
but my heart will always be with green, growing things.

I have worked with plants since I was in the second grade, mixing potions in the back yard and using fallen feathers to cross-pollinate the flowers in the garden, hoping to create my very own plant minions. However, as some children do, I learned all too young that our world isn't as safe as it should be. I spent my formative years protecting my friends from schoolyard bullies and potential threats that only an elementary school-aged child really understands. As the tallest kid in the first grade (head and shoulders above the tallest boy) I felt the weight of protecting those smaller, weaker, or more shy than I. I carried these ideals with me into middle and high school when friends started making romantic groupings, and I was on the lookout for dating violence and pressure to engage in sexual activity. My need to protect myself and those close to me drove me to join the local dojo the moment I had my own money and could drive myself. These desires to keep myself and loved ones as safe as possible are pretty universal, but they affect us all in different ways.

After my first Saturn return, my previous job experience seemed like another lifetime ago. I had been working in executive protection, but I missed my tarot clients and the holistic atmosphere of working around witchy people every day. I was in the broom closet and had little time for covens, Pagan conferences, or even my own spirituality. That is until one day, one of the security officers that reported to me came up to me, before my shift to say, "So, you're a witch, huh?" Suddenly, I was aware again just how thin the veneer of my compartmentalization was. "Who have you been talking to?" I asked with a half-hearted chuckle. The next thing I knew, my entire staff knew. The guy in charge of watching all the security cameras called to ask if I *magically* changed the colors of the orchid display behind me. The patrol officer stopped by to see if I went to the same school as Tabitha from *Bewitched*. While I don't believe this person had malicious intent, he had no idea that by merely making this information public, without my consent, he exposed me not only to personal ridicule, but also potentially life-threatening hazards.

Blackthorn's Protection Magic

> **Saturn Return: The Quarter Life crisis.**
> This refers to Saturn coming back to the place it held at the moment of your birth, which falls somewhere between twenty-seven and twenty-nine and a half years of age. This is a life-changing and potentially difficult period where we move into who we are supposed to be for the next thirty years. It's also potentially the reason for the 27 Club of celebrities who died in their twenty-seventh year.

This is why—out of all the magical disciplines—protection magic is among the most important. It is crucial to be well-versed and experienced in protection magic and to have a personal safety practice that is ongoing, rather than based only on emergent need. Our understanding of personal protection needs to extend beyond curses, hexes, and jinxes to include real-time monitoring of your personal bodily, home, and psychic security.

What Is Magic?

First, let's discuss some terms.

Magic—Magic is a set of coordinated actions such as lighting candles, singing songs, or burning incense performed to create intentional change. These actions may involve candles, herbs, stones, poppets, gardens, tarot cards, meditation, potions, essential oils, incense, and other physical items, although these are not required. Magic can also manifest in prayer, rituals, magical motions, dances, music, chants, or stories.

Although usually intended beneficially, magic can take harmful forms:

Curse—This is a magical, ritual action intended to cause magical harm to a person, persons, corporations, public figures, or governments, usually because of perceived (or actual) wrongdoing on the target's part. This may entail a plea to gods, spirits, saints, or other nonhuman entities or it may involve any of the tools, actions, or motions used in magic. It may also entail seeking help from external sources.

Hex—This is a ritual action announcing to the universe, god, goddess, spirits, or others the practitioner's own desire to manifest harm to another person, persons, corporations, public figures, or governments because of perceived wrongdoing. It can involve any of the above tools, actions, or motions. Statement of intent to render action on behalf of themselves or others, handled by the practitioner, via their own will or intent.

Jinx—This is a *low energy,* usually passive, harmful energy that can be directed consciously or unconsciously toward someone because of perceived wrongdoing. For example, cutting someone off in traffic—whether or not the cutting off was intentional on your part, if they were to make a rude gesture toward you, it could carry the energy of a jinx. That gesture could result in something mildly inconvenient, such as being late for work, a paper cut, stubbing a toe, or spilling coffee you were looking forward to.

• • •

It is also important to note that, as magical practitioners, we have a tendency to take on responsibility for so much more than could ever be our *fault* that it is crucial to note:

No spell is foolproof. Sometimes, we could have been distracted, the magic wasn't 100 percent our business so the spell was half-hearted at best, and sometimes, it isn't our job to fix whatever this situation is. That happens, too.

If your spell fails, there are a myriad of reasons why it could have happened.

If your protection magic was not enough, and you or someone you love was harmed or hurt? It is never the fault of the person who was harmed. That blame lies squarely at the feet of the person who did the harm. If Sandy did a protection spell to keep burglars away when she bought her house, and fifteen years later someone steals her television, it doesn't mean her magic failed. She is not to blame. The burglar is. Magic isn't an everlasting gobstopper, and long-term spells need refreshing from time to time. It doesn't matter who you are, what your job is, how you dress, whether or not you ingested a substance that altered your perception. You matter, and you should be able to live your life without someone hurting you because they decided to do so. Accidents happen, but that is not the fault of the person who was harmed. It isn't karma—karma is a religious concept deriving from Eastern religions, such as Buddhism and Hinduism. Karma is not Pagan, Wiccan, Heathen, or under any of these Western umbrellas. It isn't part of your *soul contract* and though the people making these comments may think they are helping, they aren't. Victim blaming isn't okay and we don't do that here.

PART I

MIND

(Psychic Security)

1

Practical Considerations (Before You Start)

Witchcraft is a practice of discernment. In judging well our surroundings, compatriots, and how we spend our time, we can head off many of life's foibles and traps. Sadly, no matter how shrewd a judge of character someone may be, no person and no witch is immune to the pitfalls of life. This is never the fault of the victim, whether perpetrated by hateful people, circumstance, or the will of the gods. We have very specific thoughts and feelings around the need to be protected; it's a very human desire to want to feel safe. What does that mean to you? Examining your own fears is the first step to understanding protection magic. Addressing these fears is how we build a sense of safety and security.

- Do you feel unmoored if your pantry isn't full?

- Can you not sleep if your checking account is below a certain amount?

The things that we need to meet our comfort threshold are usually linked to a sense of safety and security. Throughout this book we will examine the things that give us a sense of peace and security, and how to maintain them.

Ethics

One of the first things we need to discuss is our own morals and ethics. By journaling about these ideas, as you proceed through this book, you'll better see the evolution of your thoughts over time and be better equipped to maintain your own ethics and morals with healthy boundaries if they are listed in writing where you can refer to them in times of moral or ethical crisis. All emotionally evolved people allow themselves to grow and change over time; that maturation is an important piece to understanding where your heart lies and where your safety begins.

When we are first exploring the idea of protection, it is important to outline those places where our boundaries currently reside.

With your journal, I'd like you to ask yourself some questions, and write out the answers for yourself. No one will see these, and no one is grading you or judging you. No one else has lived your experiences, and as such, they have no power over your thoughts and feelings.

- Do you believe in magic?

- How might you use your magic?

- Do you believe in magical harm?

- What would constitute harm done to someone else?

- How do you define self-harm or harm to yourself?

- Are those two things different?

- How do you feel about curses, hexes, and jinxes?

- Do you practice spellwork already?

- Under what situations do you practice or utilize spells?

- Under what situations would you *not* use spells?

Blackthorn's Protection Magic

- How do you feel about physical violence?

- Have you ever felt the need to use physical violence?

- How might you deal with a physical threat as opposed to a magical threat?

- How do you feel about magical consent? Is it a requirement for spellwork?

We need to consider these questions before there is a possibility for an ordered response to these events, so we know how we might respond. This the first step in your foundation for your own protection.

THE IMPORTANCE OF GOOD BOUNDARIES

For those who weren't taught or shown how to maintain healthy boundaries and emotional stability, it may be harder to exhibit those patterns in their adult years. However, it can be done, but this means examining where those sensitive spots are and working to correct disordered thinking or reactions.

Examples of Healthy Boundaries

- Ability to say "no"

- Sticking to a budget

- Self-care rather than self-destruction

- Allowing yourself to take control of your happiness

- Ability to examine your feelings before committing to someone else

- Saying "yes" to enjoyable things for yourself, without obligation

- Capacity for exploring negative thoughts without fear
- Having your own opinions rather than mimicking those around you
- Setting a limit on television viewing
- Admitting you are not responsible for others' happiness
- Stating your needs
- Understanding your own values
- Limiting caffeine intake
- Strength in pursuit of your goals
- Belief that debate is healthy and having the capacity for disagreement without catastrophic thinking

MY OWN VIEWS

My own answers will likely change on some things. That's okay, I feel this way at the time I'm writing it. But who knows how you or I will feel in five years, or even ten.

Do you believe in magic?

I do. I believe in the magic of liminal spaces. I was raised by a musician in a family where music was everything from a barometer to a nurse. I believe that liminality is reflected all around us. I find magic in the deep breath of a vocalist before they burst into song, and in the quick inhale between lyrics. I see the threads of the universe in the squeak of guitar strings, when fingers move between frets. Spells are a projection of our will, our thoughts, and our feelings in a particular time, the same way that a vocalist is projecting their thoughts and feelings into the universe.

How might you use your magic?

It's a simple thing to light a candle for a friend in need or to cast a healing glow around a friend who has been under the weather. I might work a woven tapestry of light to guard a friend in a fragile place. I have divined a healing bath for a friend suffering an unimaginable loss. I have prayed for the safe capture of a violent criminal. I have sat up at night on the other end of the phone with someone who didn't know what to say, but just needed to know someone was there for them. These things may not seem like a big thing. Magic isn't all *Charmed* reruns and artful special effects. It is found in the small, quiet hours of the night, in another hand being there for you when you reach out. And at that time in that place, that may be no small feat.

Do you believe in magical harm?

I believe harm can be done magically. I know that my magic has probably caused harm, even if it wasn't intended. The example I often give is a job spell. If Joan needs a job to feed her family, to see that they are taken care of and have food to eat, is it ethical for her to do a job spell? Many people say emphatically, yes. Consider that there are other people also applying for that job. Those other people applying most certainly have bills to pay and mouths to feed, and even if they don't, it doesn't mean that they are any more or less in need of a job. When we look at all the sides of the issue, there is often a wealth of understanding that needs to take place. You can word your spell in a number of ways: "If this job is right for me . . ." or "That everyone applying for this job get the job they deserve . . ." You see, while harm and intention aren't the same things, it's important to examine the repercussions of magical workings before we set our wands to that aim.

If you're asking about hexes?

I do those too. I live every day with the aim to try to be the very best person I can. Do I always make it? No, but that's okay, no one does. Part of my aim to do the best I can for all the gods' creatures includes hexing child predators so that they are caught by the police and are unable to harm anyone ever again. Will everyone agree with me that this is good? Likely not. And that's okay. Because while the Wiccan Rede*—"an' it harm none, do what thou wilt"—doesn't apply to everyone (not even all Wiccans!), I still try to inflict as little actual harm as I can each day. I ask, "Who does it serve?" and go from there.

What would constitute harm done to someone else?

Sometimes I think harm is a really vast subject. There are of course degrees of harm. A paper cut isn't the same as a stab wound, even though they both hurt. By the same token, a stab wound isn't the same as surgical removal of a malignancy. Just causing harm to people for the fun of it is not ethical in my book. Some magical practitioners feel that harm done for money is the debt of the person who paid or hired, not the actual practitioner, and so there is no cosmic justice for them, as they were merely the instrument. It's not my place to say, as I'm not doing magic for money—not that it's my job to judge how someone else makes their rent. It isn't.

How do you define self-harm or harm to yourself?

Harm to yourself includes negative self-image, or self-talk. "I'm (fill in the mean word)." That is definitely harm. Literal and physical self-harm also count. From eating things that will intentionally hurt you, to self-injury. Are they harm, yes, but notice I don't say that it's good or bad. We all have scars from our past; some are visible, and some aren't.

Are those two things different?

They are. I can consent to things involving my own person. I can't give consent for someone else, so it takes more thought for me.

---

* The Wiccan Rede, while compared to the ten commandments of the Christian faith, is a statement of intent. Rede means advice or counsel, not law.

How do you feel about curses, hexes, and jinxes?

As stated above, I'm for them. Not the petty jinx because some-one cut me off in traffic, but those involving the larger things in life. Domestic violence, hate crimes, child harm, abuse of the elderly, and those sorts of things. Things done to those who cannot stand up for themselves are morally reprehensible to me. Remember, it is not our job to heal our abusers.

Do you practice spellwork already?

You bet I do. I found my first spell book at eleven years old and never looked back.

Under what situations do you practice or utilize spells?

In the '90s (when I started) all the books were lamenting *magic as a last resort* and while I agree that you must also act in the physical or mundane world—that's why I included a chapter on physical self-defense—I don't think that magic is something you set aside for special occasions, or never utilize for your own benefit. While I respect those that choose not to employ magic for their own gain, I never heard any-one state this "personal gain" clause before *Charmed* appeared on TV in the late '90s.

Under what situations would you *not* use spells?

This one is a little easier for me. I don't do spells if I'm not feeling well. Whether it is mental fatigue or physical illness, if I'm not feeling great that day, I'll guard my energies for a later date. That being said, as a chronically ill person, I will never say that you can't do magic if you aren't 100 percent. I don't think I've been 100 percent in the last twenty years. Ha!

How do you feel about physical violence?

It has always been a last resort for me. Working in executive protection for fifteen years means that my mantra is first and foremost "de-escalate, de-escalate, de-escalate." That being said, if I'm defending someone else, I stand ready to do violence on their behalf, should it come to that. I'm not eager to harm another person, but I cannot stand by and let someone else be hurt.

Have you ever felt the need to use physical violence?

Yes. In defense of my own life, and always the least amount required to get the job done.

How might you deal with a physical threat as opposed to a magical threat?

I got my black belt at the age of twenty-one. I spent years learning to de-escalate when possible, and to do the least amount of harm required to accomplish the goal. You won't see me casting a spell in hopes that someone doesn't punch me in the face. Either that person attempts such a thing, and I must defend myself, or they don't. I can utilize my protection magic to keep those things from happening in the first place and I can protect myself from magical malfeasance, but I'm pretty pragmatic about it.

How do you feel about magical consent? Is it a requirement for spellwork?

I'm also pragmatic about the need for magic in its time and place. I will ask for consent whenever possible. That being said, if I feel the need for binding, hexing, or the like, it is much more likely that the target of a hex is not interested in consenting to that. Outside of situations where life, limb, and safety are in jeopardy, I obtain the consent of the person or people involved whenever possible. The best of intentions can have harmful outcomes otherwise. Healing spells are usually regarded as benign, but if you're prolonging the suffering of someone in hospice because it hurts too much to let them go? That's harm, and that's why I talk about ethics in every class I teach. Just because magic makes you feel nice, doesn't make it good. Those terms are very subjective and much open to interpretation.

"Why Hexing Is the Answer"

Because it is our right to stand up to our abusers.

Because it is bullshit to tell people to just take the abuse.

Because it is not our job to heal the people that hurt us.

Because we should support self-defense.

Because pacifism is one belief that doesn't apply to everybody.

Because karma doesn't work the way you think it works.

Because sometimes, magic is the last recourse of the downtrodden and the hurt, the people who can't go to law enforcement, or the people who are alone in their struggles.

Because each person has a right to do what they want with their magic.

—*Unknown (Public Tumblr post, accessed February 11, 2020)*

TOXIC POSITIVITY

"Good vibes only!" is the rallying cry of many a witchcraft group today. Sadly, it is important to talk about this sort of behavior when engaging with protection work today. When we refuse to acknowledge that people are indeed human and have sad days, depressive episodes, and even tumultuous relationships, it can very easily turn into a toxic situation. People, especially witches, need the freedom to grow and experience the full range of human experiences, and sometimes those things are painful. Even the times that bring us emotional and physical pain can have a beneficial outcome. Understanding that we each have negative traits and past behaviors that were formed during times of stress, and though they protected us when they were needed, they may no longer be healthy to hold onto. To integrate the shadows of our past, it is important to bring them into the light of day and look at them for what they were. Only then can we incorporate the new positive behaviors that will benefit us, rather than harm us.

The first step to integrating those behaviors is to understand why we might have them, and what those behaviors protected us from.

- If your grownup or grownups (not everyone was raised with a parent) were overly critical, whether it was your grades, looks, taste in clothing, or friendships, you may have developed avoidant patterns revolving around making decisions, because someone in authority taught you that your choices weren't good enough.

- If your grownups' choices made you feel helpless or hopeless, you might have overindulged in food, drink, drugs, or escapist behaviors.

- If your grownups made sure that their gifts came with expectations attached, you may feel suspicious when good things happen to you seemingly out of nowhere.

- If your grownups had to be the most important person in the room, you might be wary of authority figures.

- If your grownups made sure you felt as though it wasn't safe to disagree with them, you might have a severe reaction to perceived criticism or confrontation.

- If your grownups repeatedly abused your trust, you might trust too quickly, or not at all.

- If your grownups belittled your feelings or thoughts, you may have a difficult time talking about your feelings.

The next step is to forgive yourself. It isn't your fault that your parents acted this way, it's theirs. Be gentle with yourself. You aren't perfect, and neither is anyone else.

- If you find yourself diminishing all you accomplished today, because you couldn't "do it all," remind yourself that you have tomorrow.

- If you find yourself berating yourself for not being able to save everyone, remember that is an insurmountable task and you're just one person.

- If you find yourself upset that you don't have all the answers, remember that perfection is an unattainable goal, and you are doing all you can.

- If you find yourself hesitating to set a healthy boundary with yourself or someone else, remind yourself that you are worth taking care of.

- You are enough.

John Welwood, the esteemed psychotherapist responsible for the term "spiritual bypassing," defined it as "spiritual ideas and practices to sidestep personal, emotional 'unfinished business,' to shore up a shaky sense of self, or to belittle basic needs, feelings, and developmental tasks" (Raab 2019). The long and short of this idea is that people strive to avoid the things that make them uncomfortable, and in many instances, the avoidance takes the form of devotion to spirituality, but as a means of avoiding any painful feelings. Outside of religious and spiritual communities, this avoidance can take many forms, gambling addiction, recreational drug dependence, binge eating, restrictive dieting, and even exercise to extremes.

As children we learn to cope with stress, abuse, and fear in a number of ways. These fall into four types of responses or defense mechanisms, fight, flight, freeze, and fawn. All humans do this; there's no shame in responding to stress, it's automatic. The problem occurs when reactions to perceived threat that are learned in childhood can cause harm or shame in adulthood. If someone challenges our beliefs, we can feel the need to fight them, whether in the comments section or in the street. In the heat of the moment, our brains may not be able to differentiate between a physical threat and a verbal one. That's why it is so important to assess our responses when they seem out of proportion.

Coping with a Perceived Threat

- **Fight**—This could be a physical fight, or even defending yourself verbally. Keep in mind, the physical response to a threat includes loss of fine motor skills as blood rushes to extremities preparing for a battle, even if you don't engage that threat. The adrenaline dump into your system may leave you feeling shaky, dizzy, nervous, anxious, sad, or any of the above. These feelings are natural and will subside after you sleep off the chemical imbalance.

- **Flight**—Everything in your system is telling you to run. Even if your body is not physically capable of running, your brain may send blood to the large muscle groups in an effort to flee the perceived threat.

- **Freeze**—I talk about this briefly in the section on Cooper's Color Code (p. 88). Freeze is condition black. The brain is so unprepared for what happened that it goes blank for a moment. Picture a cartoon character being shocked, the jaw drops, and the only thing you hear is, "Uhhh . . ."

- **Fawn**—This phenomenon, a more recent addition to the lineup, is the brain telling us to befriend the threat. It may sound counterintuitive, but these maladaptive appeasing behaviors are instinctual, especially with childhood trauma surrounding abusive parents. People-pleasing as a defense mechanism can lead to sacrificing personal boundaries and safety to please others.

It is an easy trap to fall into, to buy the shiny new rocks or the amazing new pendulum you spotted in your favorite shop rather than doing the emotional heavy lifting that can help us discern where our disordered responses lie. When that happens, we find ourselves chasing the next high of a new guru, a new modality, a new crisis, a new something, anything to distract us from ourselves. We cannot face the shadow and heal if we are so busy running from ourselves, that we never stop to rest and reflect.

Post-Traumatic Stress/ Complex Post-Traumatic Stress

Post-Traumatic Stress Disorder (PTSD) is a complex series of emotional and physical reactions related to a stressor, usually experiencing or witnessing a traumatic event. These learned responses stem from the body's attempt to regulate itself after exposure to a subsequent triggering event (that includes sights, smells, sounds, physical touch, and taste). These learned responses can present themselves for months or years after the inciting event but all involve a fear of death. The inciting trauma itself can be a single predominant event or a series of events with a smaller impact, though still traumatic. One in twelve adults will experience PTSD at some time in their life, with one third of those affected having symptoms that last over ten years (Zimbardo, Johnson, and McCann 2017, 623).

The significant difference between PTSD and Complex Post-Traumatic Stress (C-PTSD) is that C-PTSD is rooted in childhood, making it a long-term pattern of behavior, rather than a single inciting incident. It can result from misattunement, or a faulty bond between parent or caregiver and infant, that results in the infant not feeling heard, understood, or cared for. That pattern of neglect can include physical abuse, both physical and mental neglect, as well as medical neglect. The most prevalent type of C-PTSD both within the Pagan community and without is from children being raised in an abusive home situation. Current statistics posit that one in three girls have been sexually assaulted as a child, as well as one in five boys (Walker 2013, 2). By examining and understanding these behaviors and their origins, we can grow into more well-adjusted adults.

One of the results of this type of systemic, long-term abuse is toxic shame. It is the result of having self-esteem systematically dismantled by abuse or neglect. This usually occurs when there is a flashback to a specific time of derision, contempt, or vitriol. It can be created by parental neglect, internalized as a child being unworthy of love (Walker 2013, 5).

Affirmations to Fight Toxic Shame

(Repeat as needed.)

I am worthy of love.

I depend on me.

I am a good person.

I refuse to talk badly about myself.

Anger, fear, and sadness are all reasonable and natural responses to internal and external stimuli.

Neglect of Child Me is not my fault.

I can parent myself now.

My journey is my own.

Going through a terrifying ordeal can have lasting effects. It doesn't make you any less than you were before the incident. The abuse is never the fault of the victim. Ever. In spiritual communities, people have expressed the platitude that negative experiences are the result of a *soul contract* or "the Universe has a lesson for you." These things are not okay. It helps no one but the person giving these clichéd responses. *Your energy* didn't draw these things to you. The entirety of the blame rests with the perpetrator of that abuse. More often than not, when people share their vulnerability and receive comments such as this, they are the result of the discomfort on the part of the listener. They aren't sure how to make it better, but the truth is often that the person sharing this difficult truth wants to be seen, and heard, rather than helped by a platitude. These comments are not helpful, warranted, or needed. Abuse is not a spiritual test. Abuse is abuse.

It can happen that we feel we are fine in the moment, and the incident didn't have any lasting impact, and you may be right. Humans are resilient and our brains malleable. We can accept a lot. However, if you are experiencing some of the feelings or circumstances on the below list, and they are disruptive to your life, you may consider talk therapy with a licensed professional to sort out your feelings on the subject. You can search PsychologyToday.com for a therapist or a psychologist that deals specifically in trauma. There are charities that offer free help to victims of sexual assault, domestic abuse, those with income disparity, and a number of other situations. Don't let finances keep you from getting the help you need. Let us be clear, experiencing these symptoms after a traumatic event is normal, but if they disrupt your life, or persist after a year, it can be diagnosed and treated by a professional. A history of trauma does not guarantee feelings of trauma, but it is wonderful to know that there are professionals available to help.

Some Symptoms of PTSD

This is not a comprehensive list. Please seek therapeutic intervention for a more comprehensive discussion.

- Sleep disruption (sleeplessness, nightmares)

- Emotional flashbacks, unwanted memories

- Physical sensations of injury tied to memory

- Exaggerated flinch response to minor stimulus

- Negative self-image

- Hypervigilance, searching for threat

- Dissociative episodes

- Prolonged distress

- Isolation

- Memory problems

- Inability to look in a mirror or recognize the self

- Anger

- Blame

- Guilt

- Shame

- Intrusive thoughts

- Overly critical of self

- Social phobia

- Relationship problems

Blackthorn's Protection Magic

How to Tell if You're Cursed

First let me say that curses, hexes, and the like are intensive and require a lot of work. Because they take time, attention, effort, and occasionally supplies, they aren't as common as many people fear. They can require specialized supplies and a knowledgeable practitioner. They do *not* require that the practitioner be of the same religious practice as you. Some Christians pray for God's help while others, especially Catholics, may ask a Saint to intervene. The entire book of Psalms is used for spells from cursing an enemy's livestock to curing headaches. That being said, true curses are rare. It is much more likely that you have had a spate of bad luck, and you can work to change it.

That's the most important part of the topic, owning your magic. Your magic is yours alone, and no one else is entitled to it, so don't give it away. Don't tell yourself you have been cursed. You are not a victim. Stand in your power and recognize your strength. Laugh (yes, really) in the face of the mere idea of a curse. Laughter is the first line of defense in protecting yourself from the odd jinx. Laughter is sound waves that carry joy and mirth. By directing your laughter, joy, and mirth at a potential curse, you've already defeated nine out of ten magical threats.

Jinxes are small things, devoid of true intention or drive; they're often the result of petty jealousy. That is why the jinx has such small energy. It could be the result of accidentally cutting someone off in traffic who then makes an obscene gesture. It doesn't take any time to research magical methods—no tools are required. You didn't intend any malice in cutting it too close, and they may not have magical training. That doesn't mean you're in the clear as far as this wisp of magic is concerned. Laugh at it and move on.

Before you delve into the checklist to see if you might be cursed, ask yourself, "Who would want to curse me?" The answer is hopefully a simple one. If you think no one would want to curse you, you're either extremely blessed, or not very self-aware. We usually have one or two people whom we've had arguments with, but fear not, they are usually minor issues on the threat assessment.

Use this time to really reflect on whether you're being your best self. If you have a laundry list of people who hate you enough to hex you, it's time to re-evaluate your life. What are you doing that so many people are out for your metaphorical or physical blood? What do these people have in common? If they're all surface-level people whom you've engaged in social media bickering, perhaps you can consider if that is where your time is best spent. Perhaps instead of scrolling for stress relief that isn't forthcoming, you can find a new hobby, explore new genres of literary escape, or even detox from a certain platform altogether. If they are all people you've screwed over in the past, be honest with yourself; no one is checking your answers, but honesty is the only way you're going to move past a life of constant threat of curses, hexes, and jinxes. If these are people whom you've merely stated and restated your boundaries with, good for you! Boundaries are so important. Keep up the good work. Remember, the only people who hate healthy boundaries are the ones who benefit from your lack of them.

CURSE THREAT ASSESSMENT
(Check all that apply)

A run of bad luck	
Unexplained pain	
Perception of soul loss or soul theft	
A perception of people talking about you, especially disembodied voices	
Sudden clumsiness	
Feelings of someone standing on your chest or arms	
Being run-down without cause	
Nightmares (out of the ordinary)	
Feelings of being watched or followed	

Grading Your Assessment

One to three checks: Just a bit of bad luck. It's possible it is merely anxiety. Time to refresh your home's warding and protections. Remember when cleansing your home to utilize different methods in a regular cleaning schedule. For instance, this month you might asperge (sprinkle magically charged liquids) around your home with charged full moon water (water placed in the light of the full moon) and a pine branch, for example. Next month you might bang your pots and pans together until the space feels right. The month after that, try maybe burning some mugwort (*Artemisia vulgaris*) in your space.

You want to vary your practice for a few reasons.

- You don't want the magical equivalent of a resistant staph infection.

- Never show your true speed—you never know when a friendly glance is really a surveillance camera.

- Friends don't always stay in your life forever.

Four to six checks: Possible jinx. A salt bath or shower blessings with salt wouldn't hurt. Sound is a great cleansing tool (bells, tuning forks, or good, loud music all help). Remember to layer your home protections. No one method is proof against all comers, so keep the home secure by using three, six, or nine different types of magical barriers so that you know you're taken care of, and so is everyone in your home.

Seven to nine checks: Sounds like you might be cursed or hexed. Cleanse your home. Cleanse yourself. Work a curse-breaking spell. Start your personal cleansing with herbal washes or waters in a nice shower or bath. (Check out Essential Oils for Protection for ideas.) Once you're clear, go through the house and cleanse it several times, just to be sure. For instance, one round with smoke, one round with bells, one round with a spray or floor wash. Order them in the way that makes the most sense. For instance, if you're working with an herb bundle, do that before mopping the floor with a cleansing floor wash so you can get any ash that fell. Remember to leave offerings for your house spirit! They are your first line of defense, but you need to build a relationship with them. Ask for something to call them, or ask if you can make up something to call them. Listen to your gut. Leave them offerings of coffee or bread, porridge or wine. A cup of coffee a week can save you a *lot* of money in repair bills. They like to be remembered! (For more on this, see the Protection in the Home chapter.)

Ten checks: Seek help from a professional. Therapeutic and magical interventions go hand in hand. Clergy or talk therapy as well as magical help can be required. This is too much work for one person. Talk to a trusted friend and seek recommendations for an ethical practitioner from a local new age shop if you have one.

A Note on Curse Breaking from Mortellus:

Until death do us part . . .

A common piece of liturgy in the book of common prayer, and a phrase that often echoes through the mind of any who have found themselves caught in the web of an abusive partner. How do we extricate ourselves from these situations . . . and when we do, how does one break an unbreakable bond? The answer, of course, is simple. We don't. We die.

Breaking curses, bonds, and unwanted grasps someone might have made upon us, body and soul, is a thing often talked about and it takes no amount of work at all to find dozens if not hundreds of bits of instruction on "cutting cords," prayers and spells to break curses, and well-meaning advice to simply not believe in them. But how often do you hear someone say, "The curse has returned," "I cut the cord but found another," and so on? Too often. It may be because we don't fully understand the workings of these curses, or perhaps they are indeed unbreakable, but lucky for those of us handy with a bit of death magic, we have a stopping point. Until death do us part.

My favorite method of curse removal and breaking of bonds, and one I write and speak about often, is truly to simply "die." Just a little, and just for a little while. Utilizing one of my favorite magical tools, Corpse Water (simply water that the recently deceased have been bathed with), you are able to apply the qualities of death to yourself and then reenter the space of the living free and clear of any unwanted attachments. To apply this method is simple: consecrate yourself using Corpse Water and a black or alaea salt (or my preference, a Grave Salt —salt ritually and practically imbued with the qualities of death) with the intention of applying the qualities of death to yourself, taking as little or as long in that state as you like, and then, reconsecrating yourself with fresh water and clean mineral salt to remove those temporary qualities and reenter the spaces of the living free of those unwanted attachments. It will feel easy, and it is. There's no lightning bolt, no spell cost weighing you down; it's as simple as death itself.

"Until death do us part . . ." an ominous portent of things to come, a threat, "if I can't have them, nobody can" dressed in formal attire; but for us, let it be a tool. If death is the answer, let us claim it for our own.

Bio: *Mortellus is a Mortician, Medium, Necromancer, British Traditional Wiccan/Witch, Llewellyn author, and High Priestex of the Coven of Leaves, a Gardnerian training group who likes to say that they are a bubbling cauldron of bitter esoterica slithering their way through western North Carolina. Currently, Mortellus resides on three acres—that are becoming hastily overgrown—with their partner, adult child, and twin toddlers, wishing they had more time for Pathfinder RPG and playing around in the pottery shed.*

SPOTTING A SCAM ARTIST

An ethical practitioner will not charge thousands of dollars just to hand you a candle.

If the person you seek out tells you things like, they need large sums of money from you to *burn* the curse away, look for help elsewhere. Magic workers have bills just like everyone else, so they may charge you for their time and their work, but just like with any other service, the price has to be right for you. Reasonable rates are in the same realm as a massage therapist, one to two dollars per minute.

- If they keep you in fear, it's a scam—a professional wants to empower you to solve your own issues, even if you need help.

- If they come to you, rather than you seeking them out, it's a big indication of a scam, especially if they are asking for personal details.

- If they keep changing their story to manipulate you into extra services, it's a scam.

- If they tell you that they are the only ones who can save you, find your twin flame, return your lost heirloom, it's a scam.

2

Crystals for Protection

Working with stones and crystals for magical protection is a smart idea. This gives you the ability to personalize your protective field—carrying an object like a stone on your person gives you a physical reminder of the protection you have and the resources you possess. Having a literal touchstone reinforces your protections because it directs your attention to the working each time you reach into your pocket or see the stone you've chosen.

That being said, there are ethical choices to be made when working with stones. Child labor, destructive mining practices, and the like are rampant and not just in the diamond industry. If you choose to work with stones, talk to your local, independent shop owners. They choose all of their vendors, and an ethical shop will know who their vendors are and where their stones come from. Here in the United States there are some great vendors who supply witchcraft shops with stones they dig themselves by hand. No child labor. No big production involving earth-damaging excavation methods.

Myself, I live in an area known as Garnet Valley and you can find garnets in many places, including wading at the local creek. The house I lived in during my later high school years was a few miles from a stone quarry that supplied all the houses on our street with free gravel. You could find large chunks of green tourmaline in the gravel without trying. Stones are reaching out to work with us; we just have to know the way.

Protection Stones

Below are some of the best crystals for various protection needs.

Amber—Not a stone in the traditional sense of the word, amber is actually fossilized tree sap that appears in colors ranging from yellow and orange to green, red, and blue. It is very soft (2–2.5 on the Mohs hardness scale) and easily damaged. For protection magic, amber is associated with absorbing and transmuting negativity. Whether worn or incorporated into your home's protection system, amber is a great addition to your arsenal.

Amethyst—This gorgeous purple stone is aligned with psychic protection as it incorporates the energy of the third eye (the theoretical seat of psychic power) as well as beneficial shielding properties.

Black Tourmaline—A dark, opaque black stone with obvious cleavage (the planes of a stone). It commonly comes in log-shaped pieces, similar to selenite. If you have a crystal ball in black tourmaline, it'll have a

disco ball texture from each band cut. You will be able to see a matrix or inclusion of mica in every case, even if it's a small amount. Black tourmaline is a great stone to defend you from negativity. If you're looking for jewelry, the quartz with black tourmaline inclusions (small particulates within the stone's surface), also called tourmalinated quartz, is the perfect stone to reach for. It protects from negativity and has the added energy of the quartz, which acts like a magical battery.

Bloodstone—Bloodstone has a wide variety in color base, from greens to reds. The most common is a lustrous forest green with small spots of red jasper included, often seen in shops as a tumbled stone. This stone, known for protecting health and well-being, also repels evil spirits and nasty people. This stone's ability to push away negative energies makes it great for both personal wear and incorporation into your home's protective crystal grid. (Find more about this in Protection in the Home.)

Citrine—Gold is commonly associated with the sun and its magical affinities, so utilize this golden-hued crystal for protection in an active capacity. That protection is powered by the sun, leaving a cleansing swath of energy that blasts away negativity like power washing concrete.

Clear Quartz—Clear quartz is one of the most readily available stones on planet earth. Because of this availability the smaller "species" of quartz (broken down by color) are also readily available. If your working calls for a specific quartz that you don't have available, reach for a clear one. This stone can present as one large point, or other common shapes, and adds strength and power to other stones. It's a great magical battery for home protection grids as well as raising the vibration of your own personal energy.

Hematite—A personal favorite of mine, this iron ore looks silvery on the surface, like magnetite, however, when sliced thinly, the cutting wheel turns as red as blood, hence the name. This cold, dark stone is useful for grounding for ourselves, as well as grounding any negativity before it can enter your auric field. For those with anxiety, I've found a "strand of pearls" type necklace of hematite especially helpful for dissipating excess energy that can manifest as anxiety or mania. The cool temperature of the stones themselves brings the nervous system down to a manageable level the same way ice chips under the tongue or on the inside of the wrists do.

Howlite—This milky white stone has thin, faint gray veins and an incredibly calming presence. (Remember, this stone is often dyed to attract buyers. You can use those colors in magical workings; just check out the color section in Other Correspondences for Protection.) A bracelet of calming howlite is a great gift for a child going through a trying time (like puberty) and helps lessen the out-of-control feelings that arise during stressful times. Howlite soothes children's anger and temper tantrums. In adults it can transmute anger directed toward you that isn't yours and help it find a beneficial placement, such as back to the earth, where it can't hurt anyone else.

Jasper—Jaspers are a large gemological family with many subtypes. Jasper itself is a very nurturing stone. **Red Jasper** helps healers of all stripes give the needed healing, while reminding them to keep something for themselves. It is also useful for those in professions working for social change to avoid burnout. Boundaries are even more important in healing modalities. **Blue Jasper** can protect our spirits from magical attack. **Brown Jasper** can ground magical attack. **Green Jasper** can protect the heart from emotional attacks or anxiety. **Purple Jasper** is useful for protecting against psychic attack. **Yellow Jasper** can protect the self while astral traveling or on spiritual journeys. **Black Jasper** (basanite) is a superb stone to *scry* with as it protects and filters any negativity in the message.

Scrying is a meditative type of psychic visioning that relies on a physical object or objects. This divination style can be used to detect threats to yourself, home, family, and others.

For scrying, a candle flame, a bowl of water, a bowl of salt or a crystal, or incense smoke are all useful tools for scrying; try them all—you may get different results for each type.

Sitting in a darkened room with low music, enter a trancelike state. This is a great starting point for scrying. If you have trouble meditating, scrying is a great alternative. There can be movement, chanting, singing, humming, or rocking—all that is needed is you and the information. My first suggestion is a bowl of salt or sand. You can run your fingers over the sand, or gently toss it in the bowl until your thinking brain turns off and your symbolic understanding turns on.

Labradorite—This highly protective member of the feldspar group was first discovered in Labrador, Canada, and thus named for the region. It has blue, green, reddish, and brown flashes with blue and green being the most prevalent colors. Feldspars are the largest geological group of stones, making up more than 50 percent of the earth's crust. This showy stone is called the *teacher stone* as it is said to help people learn the mysteries of the universe. Wearing this stone helps to deflect negative energies aimed at the wearer as well as helping to maintain one's own energy within the aura. If you are in a place with high emotionality, labradorite is a great stone to keep your energy from leaking out or adding to volatile feelings. This stone is especially helpful for paranormal investigators.

Malachite—Don't let the marbled green appearance fool you; it's anything but healthy. This stone has enough copper to poison someone foolish enough to try to eat, drink, or breathe in the dust from this beautiful stone. It's okay to touch and to work with in magic, but I have seen people recommending some dangerous practices in relation to this stone. Don't grind it, carve it, sand it, or manipulate the surface in any way, and absolutely don't leave it in contact with your skin for long periods of time. It's adept at pulling energetic toxins from the air and your body (negativity doesn't stand a chance with this in your corner), but that copper content means that jewelry should be worn for short bursts, not as an everyday piece unless it's in a ring or necklace and out of direct contact with the skin.

Moonstone—Moonstone comes in many colors of the rainbow, even rainbow. Black, peach, yellow, blue, green, and more are favorites of the moonstone branch of the feldspar family tree. Moonstone aids in renewal, just the like lunar name implies. But the lunar associations don't end there; the moon's tie to psychic gifts makes this stone a clear help in the arena of psychic protection. Black Moonstone is doubly protective as it aids in banishing perpetrators of psychic intrusions.

Onyx—Onyx is a stone of many colors, from the marbled green and brown, to black as midnight. Each onyx has its own strength, but all of them lend to the magical strength needed to face any challenges that may lie ahead. It absorbs negative energies, but instead of negating them, they are transmuted into something beneficial. If used in a home grid, this stone is a great filter to take any negative thoughts or feelings aimed at residents of the home and put them back into making the grid stronger and the occupants happier and healthier. That transmutation of negative energies ensures the grid is functioning with renewed vigor for years to come.

Pyrite—Otherwise known as *fool's gold,* this golden stone is commonly seen in prosperity workings. Its common cluster formation is great for aiding the personal shield of the wearer or the home. Another easily obtained shape for this stone is the naturally faceted cube shape. The cubes come in all sizes, and, within the home grid, it is a great shape to add stability to the finances of those within the home.

Ruby—Ruby is a lovely helper for shielding the wearer against psychic attacks, or jinxes; however they should be worn only for the time of the upheaval, rather than daily armor for those that are highly sensitive to external stimuli as it is an energetic stone and can add to sensitization. Rubies are a fantastic armor against psychic vampirism, or energy being leached without consent.

Selenite—Incorporate selenite into your home grid to bar access from unhealthy energies (from negativity to hexes) from entering the home. Selenite bowls are perfect to use to keep daily-wear jewelry clean, vibrationally speaking. Worn on the body, selenite can act as a filter, asking us whether or not our choices are in our best judgment.

Shungite—This is carbon in its natural state. It grounds negativity headed your way and does not allow it into your energetic body. You will know real shungite from fake, as fake shungite has a dull, lifeless color and heavy feel. Because shungite is mostly carbon, it can leave faint black smudges on your skin when worn in direct contact with the skin. It isn't harmful, but can look off-putting. Real shungite in its natural state is quite shiny and is very light, even lighter than amber or jet.

Smoky Quartz—This is an incredibly accurate and easy-to-use stone for grounding harmful energies. Picture the smoke absorbing and transmuting the harmful energies into something useful and regenerative, rather than extractive.

Tiger's Eye—This is a perfect stone for protecting the psyche, most efficiently when asleep. It protects from harmful dreams, nightmares, and psychic attacks during sleeping hours.

Beware the Crystal Fakes and Other Cautions

Before rushing out to buy every stone on the protection stones list (I worked in a new age shop for many years, it happens), make sure that you know what you're looking for. *Fake stones* are on the market and there are always people looking to take advantage.

HOW TO RECOGNIZE FAUX STONES

Following are some of the more common crystal fakes.

Amber—Real amber doesn't float in water; if yours does, it's plastic, and the same goes for jet. Either way, don't let it sit in water, as it will dissolve.

Amethyst and Citrine—Keep an eye out, as amethyst is often exposed to heat (about 400°F or 204°C) until it changes to an orange hue, and is sold as citrine. True citrine doesn't grow in small geodes, it forms more as single points. Those single points often have flecks of black in it due to the hematite and goethite that give it the characteristic golden hue. Smoky citrine has an olive hue to it.

Dyed stones—Howlite, agates, and others are being dyed to resemble other, frequently more expensive stones. If the natural cracks in the stone surface are darker than the immediate surrounding stones, it's dyed. Big giveaways, fuchsia agate slices, dark, almost navy blue stones, and bright green agates are likely dyed. Dyed stones will be white when scratched with steel; a true stone won't have that issue.

Malachite—Real malachite stone has soft, muted colors, and unpredictable patterns of loops and whorls, while fake malachite (either reconstituted from offcuts or made from plastic) has darker colors, regular patterns, and very bold black bands. True malachite is heavier than it looks, as it has a high copper content. Keep in mind that certain stones like malachite, agate, chrysocolla, and others are poisonous, and stones should never be cut, polished, ground, or carved without proper protective equipment. Always do your homework.

Moldavite—The popularity of this stone has grown by leaps and bounds in the last twenty years. If you're looking for this beautiful, green space glass look closely. Real moldavite will have bubbles, inclusions, and texture. It will feel textured, rough, not smooth, but also not like fine sandpaper either.

Opals—A natural opal will have an organic flash with color, tone, and shape differences. Fake opals have a uniform flash that is exactly the same no matter the angle of observation. Note: Opalite is a man-made glass, not a crystal. Also called sea opal, opal moonstone, and other names.

Quartz—If it is named after a fruit (like cherry or strawberry) it's likely dyed glass. There's nothing wrong with using glass in magic, just know what you're paying for.

Turquoise—Howlite is much stronger than this water soluble mineral, so unscrupulous vendors have been known to try to sell dyed howlite and dyed magnesite as this watery blue stone. If your turquoise has deep cracks in it, it's magnesite. Turquoise is also gathered from grinders and offcuts and mixed into resin to make fake turquoise that looks real. If it is a fake it will fluoresce under UV light, so consider taking a black light key ring with you to shop for stones.

Anything with "Aura" in the name—These man-made stones are created by electroplating precious metals one atom thick onto (usually) quartz stones to make them rainbow flash. If you suspect that your stone has been treated, run your fingernail along one side of the stone; it won't have the texture of a natural quartz crystal. There's nothing wrong with enjoying the rocks you like, I just want to make sure everyone knows what they are buying.

Another good reason to know what's in your stones is that some are toxic.

NATURAL DOESN'T MEAN HARMLESS

Caution: As an instructor for over twenty years I must remind my readers to be cautious. New ideas surrounding the use of stones, crystals, and other magical tools come up frequently. Innovation in magic is a feature, not a flaw in the system. However, we must exercise extreme caution when doing so. In the last years I have seen numerous trends become popular in the magical use of stones. Many of these crystal fads were and are harmful and dangerous. People were grinding stones and adding them to face masks, to wall paint, and more to imbue the materials with energy. I have even seen crystal marital aids made out of poisonous stones. Yes, crystals hold a reserve of energy, but So. Do. You.

Please do your research before engaging in any practice. Do not place stones inside the body of a living person—it can cause toxic heavy metal poisoning, cancer, and even death. Always wear proper protective equipment when working with stones. Have adequate ventilation and particulate management. Practice the utmost of care with any ground, powdered, or sanded crystal. Some stones can poison you merely by touching eyes, nose, or mouth (mucous membranes) after handling the stone without gloves. (Stibnite comes to mind with actinolite poisoning.) Stones are magical, but so is every material on this planet. Some magic is helpful and life-affirming, some magic is not. Some weather is life affirming, some, such as hurricanes, perhaps less so.

Just because something is natural doesn't mean it won't kill you. Use your deductive reasoning skills.

Psychic Protection

Protection through Breath

Breathe. That is ritual. In this moment what you can do, what you can change, and what you can control is your breath.

Meditation is tricky for most people. We live in an active society that prizes overworking, undereating, and treating ourselves poorly. We as witches know that the fundamentals of breath work are important to a complete ritual practice, but it is much easier to remind ourselves of that, than to create and maintain a breath work practice.

What is it?

Breath work sounds pretty self-explanatory on the surface: it's the work of breathing. However, if we have active and passive breathing (controlled breath, and breath that happens as a part of respiration, or breathing we aren't actively controlling) we have more than one way to approach our breath. Breathing comes naturally to babies—no one taught them to push out their bellies, rather than puff out their chests. If we are breathing so that our chests rise, we are only using the top 10 percent of our lungs.

Let's start with the basics. Lie down. (We are starting from scratch.) Take a deep breath. Push your belly up toward the ceiling with each deep inhale. Your chest will naturally rise, but the diaphragm is the small muscle that is responsible for pulling air into your lungs, so that your body can extract oxygen from that air. (Only about 21 percent of air is oxygen, 78 percent is nitrogen. From there the percentages get infinitesimally small.) Notice your breath and how your lungs, belly, and torso feel. This is the basis for magic. You can have all of the pretty stones and baubles you like, but it all starts with you, with your breath and the ability to move on from there.

While meditation is usually depicted as someone looking serene doing nothing in a stark room, that image can be really daunting for neurodivergent people like myself. There isn't a wrong way of meditating, just different ones.

- Just breathe. For a moment or several. Find your moment, not mine or anyone else's. If that moment is when the baby is nursing, or when your boss leaves your office for the sixth time, or if it's in your car when you get home for the day. It doesn't have to be the same time every day, but it might help if it is. The only thing that exists in that moment is your breath.

- Invite yourself to notice the quality of your breath, but don't beat yourself up with words like "pay attention," because you might not be able to today, or ever. That's okay.

- Guided meditations offer a scenic view to watch as you concentrate on your breathing. The important part isn't what you see, or don't see, the important part is a slow, even, deep breath that renews you. Only you know what will make you feel the best you can.

- If left to your own devices, choose your own scenery. Building a *home space* within the confines of your mind is a very fulfilling meditation trick that allows you to decorate a space wholly your own where you feel safe, protected, and well.

- If you want a neutral space to return to, I suggest picturing a white room where there are acres and acres of nothing. You can use any color you like; I use white because it reminds me that there is nothing hiding in the shadows of this meditative space.

- If focusing on the physical sensations of breath is uncomfortable (no matter the reason) feel free to turn your attention to a part of the body that isn't uncomfortable. Perhaps noticing the way our breath affects the room around us is helpful. For days like this I do my breath work with a jar of bubbles. I breathe in gently through my nose and have a long, soft exhale out my mouth, which just happens to have a bubble wand in it. It still counts. You're still breathing.

Blackthorn's Protection Magic

- The important thing isn't nailing yourself to the floor and not thinking of anything; that's unrealistic and can be anxiety-producing. Rather allow thoughts that bubble to the surface to be acknowledged and released to flow on their way. By acknowledging them, they served their purpose.

- *Monkey mind* is a term borrowed from our Buddhist friends and refers to distracting thoughts, feelings, and actions that pop up when we are working hard to clear away thoughts and feelings for breath. Fidgeting, scratching your nose, wiggling your feet, these are all things that can indicate that we are nervous, worried we aren't doing it right, or any other number of reasons. Instead of worrying why they happen, just redouble your focus on your breath. The images in your mind will work themselves out. I promise.

- Some people aren't capable of creating the visuals experienced by others while meditating, and that's okay too. The important thing is giving yourself permission to not worry about work, kids, dinner, partners, or anything but your breath for a moment or two.

- If whatever type of meditation you've decided to try isn't working, that's okay. There are as many ways to meditate as there are people, and then some. Perhaps your meditative time is doing the dishes, or pulling weeds in the garden. Moving meditations are just as valid as those that require sitting still with candles or incense. You are valid. Everyone's personal neurology is different.

- Don't feel you have to time yourself, and don't set a timer on your phone or other device. The bells and alarms we experience in our day-to-day life are hard enough on our systems; don't make it harder. What if you feel like you're not really doing anything unless you're being timed? Good. Then leaving the timer off will allow you to experience the moment. What if that moment is thirty seconds because that's all the ability you have today? It's still valid. If one day it is five minutes and the next it's twenty-three, it's still valid. Every day is different and it calls for a different version of ourselves. If you are stressed, tired, emotional, or otherwise not your best, don't be hard on yourself for not having more to give your practice today.

- The only important part is continuing to breathe, because if you stop that, you stop everything.

Grounding during Protection Emergencies

If you're feeling anxious, one of the most helpful tools at your disposal is grounding. It gives some of that nervous energy back to the earth, where it isn't hurting anyone, rather than bouncing around inside of you where, maybe, it doesn't feel so great. Keep in mind that our bodies carry our feelings, just as much as our brains and hearts do. If you are feeling anxious you might bunch your shoulders up around your ears, like a turtle going back inside its shell. So somatic awareness (awareness of your body as a whole, rather than just pieces) is really vital to helping to process the impacts our emotions can have on us as people and practitioners.

WHAT IS AN EMERGENCY?

You are the only one who can answer that for sure. It could be a personal confrontation in the grocery store, or it could be witnessing an altercation between people unrelated to you. It doesn't have to impact you personally for your body to interpret your feelings as an emergency. Sometimes the wrong sight, sound, smell, or taste can convince your body that you are in an emergency situation even though your thinking brain knows that this isn't the case.

There are so many ways to ground your energies during an emergency:

- Wash your hands in cold water. On your hands and wrists the blood flows very close to the surface of the skin. Bringing those temperatures down quickly help reset your autonomic nervous system, which is currently overloaded.

- Light a candle. Small lights, pleasant smells, and warmth are all things that tell our bodies that things are going to be okay.

- Chew gum. If your body is telling you that you should fight, flight, freeze, or fawn, a quick way out of the loop is to grab some gum. Chewing gum signals to your body that you aren't in the peril that it perceives; after all, if you're fighting for your life, you don't have time to stop for a snack.

- Ice chips are a great way to shock the nervous system back into rhythm. Just let them melt on your tongue; there is a large bundle of nerves in the soft palate of the mouth that runs all over the place (hint: it's what causes *brain freeze* if you eat ice cream too fast) and helps calm an overactive system.

- Go for a walk, jog, or run to burn off some of those jittery feelings that can arise when faced with a stressful situation—this is why people pace when they are worried and can't do much about it.

Remember, all of these are ways of closing the loop on anxiety, rather than riding the wave from crisis to crisis. That can get addicting and we can come to rely on the high of the adrenaline and cortisol being released into the system. Instead, cementing an issue as resolved gives us a chance to relax and reflect on what happened rather than looking for the next high of adrenaline to make us feel vital.

Eustress (good stress) and distress (bad stress) both affect the body in the same way. Even happy stress is hard on the body. Moving to a better housing situation, buying a home, changing jobs, or even getting a promotion can be really stressful on a person, as well as everyone in a relationship with that person. Be gentle with yourself as well as your partner (or partners) if you have them. We often downplay our stress, anxiety, or other feelings for numerous reasons: disenfranchised grief (not feeling enough to have earned that grief experienced), trying to take care of loved ones, or even being so enmeshed in the situation that we don't realize just how exhausting it can be. Initiations of all kinds are stressful. Whether it's entering parenthood, transitioning from high school to college, moving away from home, or moving back home, all are new steps in our lives that need time, honor, and acknowledgment. You'd tell your best friend the same, right?

GROUNDED AND WHOLE

There is a wonderful practice of coming into connection with the ground underneath our feet that is exceptionally beneficial, whether you're in a crisis or not. Grounding is the act of connecting your personal energy with that of the earth under us. While it sounds like *earthing* (walking around barefoot to calm yourself, something that isn't advisable for many areas for so many reasons) you need not be in direct contact with the dirt to do so. These techniques are just as helpful in a third floor walk-up, or at twenty thousand feet in an airplane.

Rather than simply breathing, it's time to take it a step further and turn your attention inward. You can do this lying down, sitting, standing, or even on a merry-go-round.

- Turn electronic devices to *do not disturb* or related quiet settings, so they don't interrupt you.

- Close your eyes to block out external stimuli, clutter, chaos, and moving things as they can all be a distraction.

- Bring your awareness to each muscle group in the body starting at the bottom and working your way up visualizing large muscles and soothing them until they each feel relaxed. (Yes, this is a sneaky meditation trick. It works when I'm feeling too animated for a more neutral visualization for meditative space.) If you are more tactile than visual, feel free to soothe muscle groups with tapping, massage, or the simple warmth of your touch to bring your awareness to these pieces. As all bodies have different journeys, feel free to skip any areas of the body with troubling histories that could distract you from your main objective: centering and wholeness.

- Once you feel completely at ease (or a reasonable facsimile) visualize the scattered energies within your body; some see static, some feel a buzzing, and some imagine colors. Picture all of these excess, scattered energies coming into the center of your being as a whole, or as a ball of light in the center of your being. Keep whatever energies you need for yourself, and send the excess energy, that golden ball of light, into the ground. It'll make it there, whether you are close to the ground or not.

- Take a deep cleansing breath.

- Practice bringing the energy of the earth into your body and releasing energy from your body back into the earth. Energy in with every inhale; exhale energy out with each breath.

> If you are tired, drained, or depressed, or have very little energy to ground, feel empowered to bring some of the energy of our incredible planet into your being. This give-and-take means the world to your physical body, but as a person, you cannot drain enough energy to harm the planet in this reciprocal practice.

- The more you practice, the less ritual you need to accomplish your goal, until it becomes unconscious.

Psychic Exercises

In understanding your protection needs, it's important to take the time to protect your psyche from outside attack. We do this by building a projected psychic wall around ourselves and around our homes through wards, shields, and the like. These mental exercises are designed so that they can be built upon and adapted to fit a changing world.

Ward—This is an energetic shield that surrounds a building such as your home or workplace that is powered by an external source such as a crystal grid, designed to protect all those within those walls from harm.

Shield—This is an energetic barrier between a person and other people, powered by energy provided by the shield-ee, with energy drawn from the earth and other means.

Projection—This is a visual, auditory, or energetic emanation from one person to other people, powered by the witch or psychic sending the message. Can also be referred to as "sending energy."

FLEX THOSE PSYCHIC MUSCLES

Creating an Egg Shield

This is one of the first protection visualizations taught by many teachers. It takes the imagery of the eggshell and allows you to adapt it for your own use. It is a common item, so it's easy to visualize the white, blue, brown, or green surface of the egg, with its occasional dimple or imperfection and smooth, hard surface. You will notice that there are no holes in an eggshell, otherwise the yolk would leak out. I've had people ask me why their shielding isn't working, and in troubleshooting the issue, you might be surprised at the number of people who tell me they leave holes in their shield for love, or friendship, or the gods. The thing is, we are tuning our shield to block out harmful energies, and *harmful* is however you define it because it is your shield. We don't need to leave holes in it to keep love flowing in; it is one of the things we might set a filter on to let into your shield. But that's the next step.

First, we have to build your shield. Start with the breath. Remember, as long as you are a living being, breath is always going to be the first step, because if you stop breathing, everything else stops, too. Once you have calmed your breathing, close your eyes. When you have grounded your excess energy and feel centered, I want you to picture yourself from about ten feet (or three meters) away. I want you to be able to visualize the whole you, not the small bit you might see when brushing your teeth. I want you to see everything from the shape of your face to the style of shoes you do (or don't!) love to wear. The greater the detail you can visualize with your eyes closed, the better. Now, overlay the image of an egg over the image of yourself. The entirety of your body will fit inside the egg's shell. Thick, whole, and unbroken. The reason I love teaching the egg visual as a first exercise is that eggs are a commonly found item, they are whole to demonstrate the need for a complete visual, and they are concrete enough of a concept that even folks who don't eat eggs know what they look like. Sit with this visual for as long as you can. (Whatever that length of time, it is enough. We aren't judging ourselves, or our friends.)

Repeat this exercise as often as you can until it becomes second nature. Do this whenever you think about it during your day—if you're standing in line and reaching for a phone to scroll through the same few applications, practice taking down and putting up your shield. Put up your shield before leaving the house, and make sure to check the stability of that barrier throughout your day. It's common to feel like there might be some strengthening needed in different places at different times. Simply push a small bit of energy into that hole to fill it in, as you might with spackle to fill in a blemish on a wall.

Fine Tuning

Once you can bring up your shield in a second's notice, it's time to have some fun.

- If you are dealing with a particularly nasty person, feel free to add a layer of bricks onto the exterior of your eggshell.

- If you are dealing with a situation where your intuition is needed, add an antenna or cell phone tower to the exterior of your egg.

- The bland surface of an egg is the perfect surface to embellish with sigils (magical symbols).

- Feel free to change the surface of the egg when needed or desired. Crystal allies are a great visual as they are strong and inherently magical. Project the surface of a diamond for strength, rose quartz for love, or hematite to ground any potentially harmful energies. (Check the Crystals for Protection chapter for more ideas!)

- If you're feeling vulnerable, extend a bubble of barbed wire that sits just past your shell and adds a little extra cushion.

- Feel free to include plant allies as well. No one wants to tangle with poison ivy, rue, nettle, or thorns, and a border outside your shell will let people know to stay away.

- Try projecting a never-dry layer of hand sanitizer during cold and flu season to protect you from minor illness.

This exercise is infinitely variable and is easily started—no need to buy any specialized tools.

Comfort in the Memory

As we discussed earlier, understanding techniques of controlled breath, visualization, and grounding is a foundational skill needed to embrace the idea of psychic projections like our egg. In a discussion on psychic projections with Mat Auryn, author of *Psychic Witch*, in February 2019 at PantheaCon, we discussed the ideas of self-protection via psychic projection. We were discussing our favorite projections for our own personal security and he relayed a popular favorite projection, an angry barking dog—find this in his book under Exercise 91, "To Be Left Alone." He also shared his favorite for dealing with unwelcome crowds, which he shared in *Psychic Witch* in Exercise 76, "Clearing Out a Crowd." Mine is always an etheric copy of my leather motorcycle jacket, because

- I have a strong emotional connection to it.

- I have a history of favorable sense memories attached to it.

- I know the sight, sound, feel, and smell of this jacket.

- I feel safe with it on.

In order to make an etheric (of the ether, related to spirit, psychic, nonphysical) copy of my jacket I had to create a few steps, which you can do for yourself using a comfort object, a favorite cozy blanket, or other such item.

1. I sat with my jacket in my lap for a few moments, remembering the jacket with my senses. I examined the texture of the surface, the cool metal of the zipper, the heavy weight of it, and the feeling of safety that it gave me. I inhaled the musky dragon's blood scent of my perfume lingering in the liner.

2. I closed my eyes and pulled up each of these senses in turn and explored my sense memories of this jacket, times when I wore it in the sunshine, on my motorcycle, or the weight of it on my shoulders walking through my city. The more emotional connection you have to that item, the stronger your link will be.

3. I stood up, sat the jacket on the couch, and visualized putting on the jacket in my mind's eye. I recalled those feelings of safety and security that wearing the jacket produced. I projected the visual of the jacket and the surety that it represented.

4. Feel free to try this yourself with your favorite necklace or a cherished belt, pair of shoes, or a jacket of your own.

The Cat's Whiskers

This is a great addition to your psychic senses and can be done with or without external shielding. The Cat's Whiskers refers to your proprioception, the sense we have of where our bodies exist in any given space—yes, we have more than the five you learned in school. It's what allows us to know where our foot is, even if it's under our desk, and we can't see it. It's also the sense that allows us to know someone is standing behind us before they announce themselves, or that we are being watched). This isn't a psychic sense, so to speak, however it is connected to our unconscious, which is why you can feel someone watching you, even if you are asleep.

This exercise is designed to connect our proprioception to our extrasensory senses (clairaudience/clear hearing, clairsentience/clear knowing, clairvoyance/clear seeing, and the like) to enhance our personal protection.

1. Find a comfortable place and position to sit in, and relax your mind. Take a few deep breaths until you are ready for the work.

2. Picture yourself from that ten feet-ish distance. Rotate your vision of yourself 360° so you know you have the image firmly in place.

3. Imagine you have whiskers coming out of your face, the way a cat does. Look how dashing you are!

4. Picture them growing out until they extend past your shoulders by a comfortable margin. This is where your sense extends to, and it can be bigger or shorter, depending on the level of awareness that you are seeking. If you're in a crowded place and your whiskers are giving you more feedback than you'd appreciate, trim them a bit. Just picture them pulling themselves back into your face.

5. You might add a few longer hairs down the length of your spine for additional feedback.

6. Evaluate the length of your whiskers occasionally. I know that if I pull my whiskers in too close to my body, I tend to walk too close to corners and doorways, and bump into them.

HOW TO BE LEFT ALONE

Where Did You Go? (Invisibility!)

Everyone wants to know how to make themselves invisible, right? I've seen invisibility cloak spells for years, and I get asked about this sort of thing on the regular. After all, a problem can't find you if you're invisible, correct?

1. Find a comfortable place and position to sit in, and relax your mind. Take a few deep breaths until you are ready for the work.

2. Picture yourself from that ten feet-ish distance. Rotate your vision of yourself 360° so you know you have the image firmly in place.

3. Now picture yourself growing very, very small, shrinking your etheric body until it is the size of an ant or other small insect. Everything else seems so large, except you. This means it's pretty easy for things to pass you by, like people spoiling for a fight, hexes, and general trouble.

4. Once you have the feeling down, picture your etheric body growing. You grow so tall that anyone wishing you harm is as small as you were a moment ago. Now you're too big to feel the effects of whatever magic might have been headed your way. It's less than beneath your notice. You might notice when your spirit is taller, you stand straighter, or feel more grounded. Our energetic bodies have a great deal of effect on our physical bodies.

5. When you have the feeling down, return to your regular size. Use that allover visualization again to make sure everything is back where it belongs.

6. When you're sure that all is well, watch yourself be enveloped in a fog or a mist. You start to fade from view, until there's nothing but the outline of your body, and then even that is gone. Internet squabbles,

junk mail, and those pesky sales calls warning you that your car's extended warranty is about to expire—none of them can find you. You won't truly be invisible—this isn't the movies. However, you will be imperceptible as long as you don't attract attention to yourself. No trying to rob a bank, no crossing the street illegally—just move about as commonly as you can. It will help you blend into a crowd, or avoid the nosy neighbor who always wants to know what you are up to.

7. Practice it often; you never know when you might need to change your shape.

The S. E. P. Field (The Lesser Invisibility)

In his book, *The Hitchhiker's Guide to the Galaxy*, Douglas Adams invents the neatest gizmo for his universe. This small generator created a field that projected "Somebody Else's Problem" energy around an object that enhanced humans' natural tendency to not care about things that don't personally affect them. This is magical technology at its finest. By casting a small bubble around yourself and steadily projecting the energy of "someone else will deal with whatever is going on here," you can go on about your merry way, not invisible, but at least not bothered by people with no authority.

The Clipboard of Authority

Similar to the S. E. P. Field is the Clipboard of Authority. If you either carry a clipboard or just project the aura of your own clipboard when alone at work, in the field, at a park, or even on a busy street, people recognize you as someone "on a mission," and steer clear. Whether they think you're taking boring surveys and they don't want to be bothered, or they assume you're selling something and they *really* don't want to be bothered, your serenity is virtually guaranteed. If you doubt how effective this technique is, a furrowed brow does wonders to keep people from your path.

PART II
BODY

(Physical Security)

4

Protection in the Home

You deserve a home where you can feel safe. In this chapter we'll look at the home as a whole and make sure you are secure within those walls, whatever the shape.

Spells for Protection of the Home

Salt Spray

Salt is the tool of purification, and as such, we can use it to embody that within our homes. That purification can keep the home free of threats to our security. This will create a salt circle inside your home, without the damaging effects of salt outside the home.

You'll need:

- A clean spray bottle

- A handful of salt (table salt is fine)

- Water (tap water, moon water, or distilled—use what makes you happy)

- Optional: witch hazel or rubbing alcohol, essential oils

Water Version

Charge the salt with your intent to protect your home from any entities who do not have your highest good in mind: negative spirits, curses, hexes, and the like. Add it to the clean spray bottle. Add water, seeing the power of water empowering the solution. Circle the interior of your home, spraying the walls and envisioning any dangers to your home or family being washed away and building a salt wall around the interior of the home to deflect anything directed at your home.

Oil Version

Choose an essential oil that best represents your desire for the protection spray.

- Angelica (banishing, binding evil, protecting children, dispelling negativity)

- Cloves (hex breaking, dispelling negativity, protection)

- Frankincense (banishing, protection, blessing, consecration)

- Peppermint (consecration, good luck, uplifting, healing, purification, release)

Pour three tablespoons of witch hazel or rubbing alcohol into the clean spray bottle. Add three drops of your chosen oil (or oils) to the solution. (Remember, oil and water don't mix.)

Charge the salt between your hands by sending energy into it and seeing it driving away harmful forces. Pour the salt into the spray bottle and allow the solution to soak up the salt. Add water to the top of the bottle and see it washing away unhealthy energies. Circle the interior of the home spraying the walls (careful, oils could stain fabric) and building a wall of salt blocking any harm from entering your home.

Housekeeping tip! Washing your walls can be a chore; make it magical! Add a cup of vinegar and a cup of fabric softener to a mop bucket of *hot* water. Then add a handful of salt to purify the home. The vinegar will cut down on any oily dirt lingering on walls and baseboards, and the fabric softener will help the walls repel dirt too! Clean away and know you're cleansing at the same time.

Remember, just because it looked cool in a movie to create a salt circle outside doesn't mean that it isn't harmful to the environment. If you're working outside, consider a circle of native plants, leaves, flowers, crushed eggshell, or something else that will biodegrade and leave no trace.

Protection Crystal Grid

This is a layered approach (all of your protections should be—if one fails, you'll still have redundancies) so feel free to pick multiple stones to work together for your home. When we coordinate multiple stones (especially in a geometric pattern) we call this a crystal grid. My suggestion is to pick even numbers of stones for each job so that they can work together in harmony.

Example grid:

- Four small black tourmalines to be placed inside the home at the lowest level in the four corners of the home. They protect against attacks and negative entities.

- Four small hematite stones at the north, south, east, and west positions on the outside of the home, if possible, to ground any negativity directed at those living inside or the home itself.

- Four bars of selenite to shield the home from outside influence; they can be placed in four corners of an upper floor if there is one.

Keep this one inside the house, as it's a salt and will melt if exposed to the elements.

- A single quartz point positioned near the front door to anchor wards (see the next section for how to set wards) and to link the other stones together. Teamwork!

The goal of a grid is to choose stones that will work together for your goal. You can create them for love, prosperity, protection, and any intention under the moon. Listen to your higher self and choose stones that make sense for you. If you choose to lay your grid on a full moon, or some other astronomical event, it'll add some extra energy, but stones don't need a particular event to work best. They'll lend their soft glow any time.

Home Mirror Box

This is a fun project that can use as little or as much detail as you choose. Your box can be an elaborate jewelry box, or a cardboard box painted with mirror paint. The goal: protect the home. My mirror box is a jewelry box with mirrored sides that I found on sale during a store closing. Inside I have placed a copy of the blueprints to my home, as well as protective herbs, stones, and curios. It is renewed regularly. Magic is a sympathetic practice; by creating a mock-up of my home being protected on a micro scale, it helps my magic know what to do on a macro scale.

Supplies

- A box, any size—craft shops often have small cardboard or wooden boxes to decorate

- Craft mirrors, mirrored paint, or as a last resort, silver paint—the clearer the image reflected, the stronger the effect

- Symbol of your home—this can be a photo, a drawing, a copy of the plat of land, a printed photo from a map website, blueprints, and the like

- Herbs, incense, and stones of your choice

- Glue for mirrors if needed

Feel free to make your space as magical as you like while working. Work under a full moon, or listen to music that feels special—make an event of it.

Paint your box or cover it with craft mirrors, or both.

Once the outside of the box is ready to reflect any harm headed your way, it's time to make it nice and cozy inside for your home to rest in. You can add things like roving or cotton balls; they make a great bedding for protective oils as well. Sprinkle protective herbs inside like lavender, peppermint, or cloves before resting the representation of your home on top of the soft bed you've created for it. Once you've finished, close the box, name it with your home's name or address, bless it with incense or your own breath, and leave it in a safe place. Renew annually by replacing herbs, cleansing any stones inside, and empowering it again. PS: If stalking is something you are dealing with, please add mugwort to the list of supplies to keep the stalker from discovering your home address.

Setting Wards

Wards were mentioned briefly in the crystal grid section because I work with these two techniques in tandem. They are both beneficial on their own, but together they dominate any nastiness headed their way. Firstly, what is a ward? It is an energetic barrier blocking unwelcome energies from entering your space. These barriers can take many forms or shapes, and they are commonly layered to make a more substantial barrier. They are commonly constructed in geometric designs.

Tools: none

Instructions

This is a mental exercise, but feel free to add a crystal grid to anchor the wards and keep them energized. First take a look at your home and where it is situated. If it is inside of an apartment building or other shared space, you may need to employ a strategy that still allows your neighbors to come and go freely. If you live in an apartment, town house, or a row home you may want to protect the entire row or building from fire, so you are also protected.

Once you've outlined the boundaries for your warding, take another look at the surrounding area. In my area, there are many trees that could be dangerous in the event of a storm. You may wish to incorporate a layer of protection for dangerous weather; it isn't a curse or a hex, but it can be manipulated. A good strategy would be to have a simple shape guard the furthest boundary of your home. For example, if your home is in the middle of a small tract of land, we might set a cube ward over the entire property for harm from weather and any ills directed at the home or its inhabitants. A few feet inside that square might be an octagon protecting the home and property from theft or vandalism. These are three-dimensional shapes that encompass the entirety of the house, including under the ground where wells, water mains, electrical hookups, and cable wires run, as they are also vulnerable to attack. The more complex the shape, the stronger it is. An icosahedron is made of triangles and has twenty sides. I might put a shape like that directly over the exterior of the home.

Visualizing these shapes and projecting them (add texture for more oomph) is an incredible exercise in psychic witchcraft; they just need practice and repetition. Repeat the same techniques for creating your egg shield. Practice putting it up and taking it down a few times to get it just right.

For an apartment, the exterior ward could be a circle around your entire building, to protect everyone from fire. A smaller cube can border your apartment, to keep out anyone who doesn't have your best interest at heart, and another smaller delineation can protect your bedroom.

Check the Gardening for Protection section on page 65 for more suggestions on shapes and their magical uses.

Tarot in the Protection of the Home

Five Cards

Place four cards on four sides of a central card to protect from all comers. I love this for house protection. You could have a scale drawing of your home, and images from four tarot cards (or four copies of one tarot card) glued to the four borders of your drawing. Print images found online for long-term protection projects.

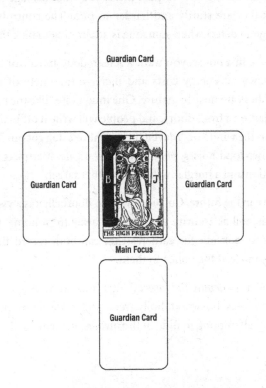

Guardian Card

Guardian Card

Main Focus

Guardian Card

Guardian Card

Suggested cards

- The High Priestess: divine protection, awareness of potential threats

- The Empress: protection of your income and loved ones

- Queen of Swords: help to overcome your enemies

- The Wheel of Fortune: protection through time

Physical Protection for the Home

- Seventy-five percent of new construction homes use Kwikset locks. Everyone knows how to pick these. You want Schlage or Medeco locks; they are sturdy and harder to pick. The controls are tight enough to detect when someone is attempting to pick them.

- If you're in a house, you want a screen door and a front door. It'll cut down on energy costs and increase the safety of the home. Neighbors are nosy by nature. One loud noise (like the breaking of the glass on a front door), and people will write it off in their mind, "It was the wind," or "Maybe the neighbor's dog got out." However, with two loud noises, people will investigate. It attracts too much attention and a burglar will seek another target.

- We live in the future. Consider a video doorbell; it is a visual deterrent as well as security when you're away from home. Criminals know to look out for cameras that can both record their illegal deeds and lead the police to them.

- Consider *hardening the target* that is your home. Aggressive plants such as roses, boxwood, holly trees, and more are inhospitable to anyone attempting to hide in the bushes. Remember, if a plant can protect itself, it can protect you. Rue's flowers and fruit can leave burns on exposed skin.

- When installing hardware such as a strike plate for a doorway, most kits come with a 2/3" long screw to attach the strike plate to the doorway. Instead replace these with 2" or 3" wood screws. They will dig into the framework of the house and make the door that much more kick-proof.

- Consider glass film. A few companies like adhesive giant 3M make a clear, sticky film that bonds with glass and makes it shatter resistant, so kids are safer and a *bad guy* can't just break the glass and let themselves in. That protection doesn't stack well, so a 7 mm film on one side of the glass is still stronger than 3 mm on both sides of the glass. I've seen a guy take an electric guitar to a glass door coated with this type of film—he still didn't get in.

- If you have glass in your front doors, consider dead bolts that are double-keyed rather than having a knob on the inside of the door. Once they're locked, someone needs the key to open it from the inside or outside. This is also helpful if you have a small child in their escape artist phase.

- If you decide to install a security system, make sure to place it on a wall that can't be seen from the front door windows. It makes it impossible for someone breaking in to know if the system is set by peeking inside. It also prevents someone from seeing what brand of security system you have in place. They may know how to circumvent Acme Home Security systems, but they don't know how to get around Brand X. This goes double for the small yard signs that advertise for that company. You can get a generic sign from a home hardware store that doesn't advertise the brand of service you have. Don't make their job any easier.

Can you ever be too safe?

If you start to notice things *just* outside your boundaries going haywire, with electrical outages, water problems, and the like, it's a good sign that someone is attempting to harm you or someone in the home, and it's time to strengthen your wards, shields, and do a cleansing just in case.

5

Gardening for Protection

Did you know that your home can be protected by the plants surrounding it? It's a method that's been used for thousands of years. Ancient temples of the goddesses Hestia and Vesta both had virgin priestesses as attendants within their walls. In this context virgin didn't mean "untouched by man" the way it is used today, it meant that these priestesses were servants of the temple and not beholden to anyone outside those walls. Offerings were made to these goddesses in homes at the hearth, as well as at the communal hearth in larger metropolises. This *house cult* was particularly important because in many areas only men were allowed to attend the communal offerings at the temple because it was so closely linked with the politics of the time. However, the allure of a temple filled with young women led to an ingenious burglar alarm within these communities. The exteriors of these temples were ringed with rue (*Ruta graveolens*). This succulent member of the same family as frankincense, citrus fruits, and mangoes has a particularly protective trick up its sleeve. This ornamental shrub produces a fruit as well as flowers that produce a strong smell, warning those nearby that if you brush up against it in the sunlight it can result in a nasty chemical burn. In an Ancient Greek or Roman town, these chemical burns might be interpreted as a punishment from the gods. The rue also served another purpose, as a powerful abortifacient.

Merely tending this protective garden on a regular basis would keep any woman from conceiving a child, much less carrying it to term. This protected any priestess from unwanted pregnancies as well. After all, the college of priestesses was (at least in the case of Rome) considered foundational to the security of the entire empire.

Outdoor Gardening

Let's start outside.

PLANTING FOR PROTECTION MAGIC

Growing the annuals (remember, plant annually), perennials (come back every year), or biennials (bloom every other year, usually live for two years) listed below can add to the magic that you are already making. There are pros and cons to each planting, and it's important to understand that when planning a garden. Annuals live only one year, but they bloom all season and often reseed themselves. Perennials seem to live forever, but they bloom only about two weeks out of the year. Biennials are tricky because they bloom for two weeks, but they don't last forever.

> For example, raspberry and blackberry cane bloom every other year, but are hard to get rid of if you ever change your landscaping design. In order to get more berries the second year, when the first two canes come up in the spring, I cut one off. This shocks the plant into thinking it might die any day, and it produces twice the number of berries. Since anything that can protect itself can protect you, I use the thorny canes for protection magic around the entrances of my home. I'll mount an X of crossed raspberry, blackberry, or wineberry canes over my threshold to make sure that no ill magic can enter my home.

Adding plants and flowers that attract pollinators will increase the energy put into your garden and your protection, so focus on pollinators first. These aren't traditionally associated with protection magic; however each of these plants has its own protective magic that it is happy to lend to you.

Butterfly weed (*Asclepias tuberosa*)—As a member of the milkweed family, it's a famous landing place for monarch butterflies and butterflies of many sorts, hence its common name. The sweet smell brings pollinators from all over and all of that natural attention is great for your magic.

Chaste tree berry (*Vitex agnus castus*)—This native to Croatia is very popular with butterflies, bees, moths, and hummingbirds. The plant is associated with Hera and the berries (which are really more like peppercorns, hence its other name, Monk's Pepper) have been used to bring on a missed period for thousands of years. Monks would grow this in the sheltered inner courtyard of monasteries to season food, as peppercorns were worth their weight in gold at the time. The smooth, white, featureless wood is reminiscent of holly's wood and is easy to carve. The monks would carve wooden handles for the small knives

they carried for eating with. They believed that keeping the wood close at hand would keep them chaste. They didn't know that the berries themselves were keeping them chaste as they had an estrogenic effect on the body and reduced their sex drive.

Sweet William (*Dianthus barbatus*)—This member of the carnation family has a beautiful clove scent, reminiscent of its cut flower cousins, and that scent attracts butterflies, hummingbirds, and more. They come back every year so their color lasts a few weeks, but they will spread in time to bloom again next year.

Here's a list of some other amazing flowers and plants that can make a magical addition to your protection garden.

Clover (*Trifolium repens*)—This is already in so many yards and gardens it seems redundant to add it, but this happy nitrogen fixer is a great companion for tomatoes, peppers, sweet corn, cucumbers, and squash. If you have vegetables on the mind, leave that clover in your yard, and consider adding it to your protection garden.

Lavender (*Lavandula angustifolia*)—Lavender is one of those incredibly versatile plants that is not only easy to find in garden centers, but also immensely useful in magical workings. (Chin up if you've been trying to start this plant from seed; it's a slow grower and needs just the right amount of water.) Those uses include sleep (it's famous for use in calming and sleep blends), protection, purification, divination, and so much more. It's almost as useful and popular as another member of the *Lamiaceae* family, rosemary.

Rose (*Rosa sp.*)—There are over a hundred species of rose shrubs within the Rosa genus, so just saying "rose" is about as helpful as saying "sage" (there are only 960 species there). With over 2,500 different species and ninety genera (the plural of genus) in the Rosacea family (including blackthorn, hawthorn, cherry, apricot, and many more) picking one variety is going to be difficult. For best results talk to local growers, garden centers, and aficionados for the best growing practices for your area's climate and soil content.

Vetiver (*Vetyveria zizanoides*)—This aromatic grass has a dark, resinous aroma in essential oil form, but that oil comes from the distillation of the roots. The green of the grass makes it a large, showy centerpiece in a larger area. This fragrant grass is similar to lemongrass, citronella, and others. It forms as a large clump as do other varieties of bunchgrass. With the bountiful showing you can dry it, chop up a good-sized handful, and ring your property with it. Rather than the fiery protection that solar herbs bring, this earthy grass grounds hexes, jinxes, and curses directed toward you or your home.

See Other Correspondences for Protection on page 169 for additional herbs and plants to add to your garden.

PROTECTING YOUR OWN HOME

While looking at our own homes, whether apartment, town house, condo, or standalone home, every living situation has its own security, as well as gardening, needs. In an apartment, there may or may not be a balcony or patio for that outside feel, but with many plants that are herbaceous, sun isn't the most important factor, as we aren't trying to grow fruits and vegetables. Whatever you decide to try your hand at, some sun will be needed, so if you're in an area with long winters, you might consider a UV lamp to make sure your plant friends will be getting enough light.

The great thing about magical gardening is that each garden has the ability to grow magical herbs, redoubling your efforts. For this example, you are growing magical plants for protection in a shape that aligns with your protective goals and imbues the plants with protection magic. You can then can dry the plants you grew in a protective garden to use in protection magic. Layer upon layer in your magical intention, and incredibly powerful ritual tools. You don't need a lot of time, energy, or even a yard to do this.

Now that you know which plants are and are not protective, I want to talk about shapes. We learned shapes in kindergarten; now I want to apply the same ideas to our magical practice.

Square—This is incredibly easy to create, as most home stores sell either wooden or stone borders that are all of equal length, perfect for creating a square garden. Square gardens are a perfect choice for protecting the home as they add balance and stability to the energy of the home (as all four sides are the same length, and four is an incredibly stable number). They then lend their energies to a stable home security plan. You can create a border of some brightly colored flowers to attract happy energies into the home. Squares are easily divisible, so they could be separated into smaller squares or triangles for plants that relate to each of the four elements, four greater or lesser sabbats, and so much more.

Triangle—This three-sided polygon is reminiscent of deities with three forms, three faces, or even three deities as a trinity. Planting a garden in this three-sided shape can allow for a further division into three smaller triangles, one for each face of a deity in a trinity, three phases of the moon (waxing, full, and waning—the new moon deals more with the unseen and relates to the crops grown beneath the soil, like potatoes, tubers, carrots, peanuts). You could place three window boxes end to end on a patio for a triangular garden.

Rectangle—This is the best for protection gardens that have to deal with binding someone from harming you—especially great if your gardens are prone to field bindweed, also known as *Convolvulus arvensis*. This shape allows you to harness the stability of four sides and the warding potential of the longer sides. Think back to our earlier discussion of rue fences around the temples of Hestia and Vesta. They were around the exterior of the temples, which often used straight lines rather than curved for their fortification. If you are able to border a home with gardens, you will have a great magical fence to keep your home in check and block out any unwanted energies.

Though bindweed is a member of the morning glory family, this invasive weed is quite happy to move into garden beds and choke the life out of anything growing there. It is the toughest weed to get rid of, trust me. It will eventually flower, but the flowers are white and aren't as showy or plentiful as our colorful, domesticated version. To be clear, this is an invasive weed and not moon flower or morning glory; they just happen to have a family resemblance. True morning glory is a part of the Ipomea (eh-POE-me-uh) family, along with High John the Conqueror root and the ornamental sweet potatoes that have been popular in landscaping for the last twenty years.

Circle—This popular (and easy to replicate) shape has a world of uses, pun absolutely intended. You can think of it as the world card in the tarot. In your protection magic, you are *casting* this circle on the ground to mark the achievement of your family, home, and self-protection. You are empowering the wheel to keep spinning in your favor and can even divide your wheel into smaller sections that get rotated each year to keep the energy moving. This circle can be used to illustrate the cycle of life, death, and rebirth. If you practice with other witches, your circle can include protecting the health of your coven as a whole, the group mind as well as the individual members. A circular garden is also the perfect place for a garden devoted to a particular deity. Simply fill that space with plants, flowers, vegetables, or combinations thereof that are associated with the deity you are choosing to honor. Your circle could also be reflective of the sun. Plant solar herbs for use in male mysteries or to represent male-aligned deities. For an extra solar twist, consider planting a circular bed of giant sunflowers, with a small doorway left unplanted. It'll make a nice summer shady spot that can be enjoyed by children, pets, wildlife, or yourself. I tucked a small Adirondack chair in mine so I can enjoy the cool shade and fresh air without the risk of sunburn. A dear friend did the same with her yard and planted sunchokes—they are related to the sunflower, but their roots are edible and resemble galangal, potatoes, and other root vegetables.

Wheel—Closely related to the circle is the wheel. Taking a larger footprint than the circle, this space can be divided into sections and planted with flora you associate with holy days, seasons, or individual spokes to represent the Wheel of Fortune in the tarot, especially if you think you've been hexed due to a run of bad luck. Use this wheel shape to change your luck for the better and keep it there. You can plant a sweet annual border with something useful like marigold (pinch the dead flower heads and dry them in a paper bag for a sweet steam facial that will unclog pores and kill pimple-causing bacteria!) to divide the circle into four parts and place herbs associated with an element in each of the four quarters.

> While poisonous plants and flowers are intimately associated with death for obvious reasons, I'd caution planting protection vegetables with poisons in different sections of the same small area. Popular vegetables like tomatoes, potatoes, eggplant, bell peppers, tomatillos, and cayenne are all closely related to datura and belladonna. All of these plants are found in the Solanum family, with over two thousand other plants, meaning they can cross-pollinate and breed. There are stories of people being poisoned by the resulting fruit of this union, so let's not tempt fate by planting them too close together. This isn't to say "don't grow poisons" because lots of incredible flowers are potentially toxic, even some states' signature flowers (I'm looking at you, bluebonnets).

The Moon—A crescent moon is a lovely devotional to the moon and can be filled with lunar flowers and herbs to be used in goddess rituals or mysteries. Since the moon is associated with intuitive ability, feel free to plant protective plants that are associated with psychic ability to protect your psyche as well. Psychic protection is just as important as physical protection.

Triple Moon—From the Northern hemisphere the waxing, full, and waning moon appear as)O(, however in the Southern Hemisphere the reverse is true (O). Even the constellations we are so familiar with could be reversed from our previous vantage point. Utilize this pattern to create waxing, full, and waning moon motifs as one larger garden or three smaller gardens. The waxing garden can be filled with herbs and plants to increase your personal, familial, or home's protection. The full moon is the union of the sun and the moon—as the sun shines on the moon, the moon reflects its light onto the earth. That's why lunar eclipses happen only during full moons. The earth is passing in between the moon and sun, casting a shadow on the moon. The full moon is a powerful time for magic because of the alignment of the moon and sun, so it's a great time to make your wishes known to the universe. Fill your full moon section with plants like angelica, rosemary, clover, and anise. They're great multipurpose plants and can help the multitude of your magical dreams come to fruition. The waning part of your triple moon is to banish anything that can negatively impact your safety. You can banish creepy people, unwanted attention from romantic sources, as well as professional ones, or even creditors. You can plant silver dollar eucalyptus (it won't get as large as a eucalyptus tree if you've got limited space), sunflowers, lilac, peony, rue, or any of the mints (seed catalogs have an abundance of varieties: peppermint, apple mint, chocolate mint).

Diamond—this simple take on the rhombus is ideally suited to protection in family situations. Whether it's an abusive family member who likes to pop up and cause trouble unannounced, or siblings who have no boundaries, this diamond-shaped garden can ward your home (as it grows, so do your protections), as well as restore and grow harmony within the home. This is especially helpful if there have been financial hardships causing tension in the home. It adds stability just like our square, but is focused on restoring balance and maintaining it. Magic is great for protection from outside forces, but if the danger comes from inside the home, I implore you to find someone safe to talk to and plan a way out. Check local listings for free services for domestic violence.

> For this garden in particular, I would try growing patchouli for soothing tempers and grounding anxious feelings. If your first reaction was, "Blech, I hate patchouli," no fear, the plant does not have the strength of smell you're remembering. The plant is fermented to strengthen the smell in the leaves before distilling, so you won't "smell like a hippie"; it will just have a soft loamy smell. It can be dried and sprinkled around the exterior of your home at the end of the growing season; repeat annually.

Star—This slightly more complicated shape is great with or without the circle around it. This can be a Witch's Garden, meaning anything grown inside is useful for magical ritual or spells. You can of course divide a circle into a pentacle, but keep in mind that plants need room to grow, so if you go that route, plan on making it bigger than you already have in mind. The points of the star can be used for the five points of a pentacle, earth, air, fire, water, and spirit, or the whole of the star can be assorted protection plants that strike your fancy. The shape of the star will imbue the plants grown inside it with the blessings of the elements. If you go the star-within-a-circle route, the blank spots can be universal plants that are good for a wide variety of magical uses like rosemary and mints.

Keep in mind that mint is invasive. Some gardeners caution growers to never plant mint directly into the ground because it spreads. If you're worried about the spread of mint, feel free to cut the bottom off of a five-gallon bucket and plant the bucket down two-thirds of the way into the ground. This will keep the runners to a minimum and make sure that the mint isn't extending its boundaries. I on the other hand plant mint wherever I can as it makes a great tea.

Hexagon—The sixes in the tarot are exploring our ability to arise from strife and conflict, and to embrace harmony and peace. To bring these calming feelings to your home, consider a six-sided garden spot. While a circle has no edges and allows energy to flow continuously, the hexagonal shape slows rapidly moving energies to still thoughts, feelings, and emotions.

Septagon—While an odd number of sides can make for a more difficult time plotting out the boundaries of the garden, it makes for an incredible protection garden. The sevens in the tarot can be topsy-turvy and they can disrupt spellwork aimed at you, your home, or your family. The seven-pointed star is associated with the fae, so once you've laid the groundwork for this seven-sided beauty, grab a premixed flower assortment that you can sprinkle over your new soil. A garden laid for the fae is a wild place, so no need to weed. Just place this wild place on the edge of your property and let this wildness disrupt any malignant magic headed your way. You can mow around this garden if you need to, but keep those nasty chemical sprays *far* away from this garden.

Octagon—While some things with eight sides are usually painted red and meant to stop you at important crossroads, in magic, the tarot, and numerology, the eight is about action, perpetuity, and longevity (an eight on its side is the symbol for infinity, after all). In your protection magic it can activate stopped or stagnant energy. If you feel like you've been stuck in a rut, an eight-sided garden bed can stir up the energies and keep them going. Your protective measures will get an extra boost if you use vine plants and creeping flowers, from Don Juan climbing roses to clematis or morning glory on a trellis. To let the element of air keep your protection energies going, absolutely consider adding a wind feature like a small windmill or colorful flags.

Indoor Gardening

The ability to grow something inside, where it isn't subject to the whims of Mother Nature, can be incredibly rewarding. Oddly enough, botanical acumen outside of the home doesn't guarantee success in growing things inside the house, and vice versa. There is an idea that having living plants in the home of magical practitioners is inherently protective, because being such a small life, they can more easily be affected by changes in nature and their surroundings. While the life and vigor of plants that are in our care can be incredibly soothing, they can also alert us to a larger magical threat. If you have taken all care to tend to the needs of plants in your care, and they seemingly die without reason or cause, it could be that this plant died in protecting you from a curse or jinx. That isn't to say that this is why we keep them; as any plant mom

or dad can tell you, these plants can give us more than we give them at times. They do make an effective magical barometer, however.

If you have thought about indoor gardening as a part of your protective plan, refer to the above list of shapes for possible containers for your plants, and depending on the plants that call to you, and the crystals you have available, consider decorating the soil with a protective stone or two to help establish your protection grid around your home. This is especially exciting for those without a yard to plant a protective garden in.

Indoor plants and their magical jobs:

- **Aloe** (*Aloe* spp.)—There are over five hundred cultivated aloe species that have reputed medical benefits, and more; however we are most interested in its reputation as a protection plant. The watery flesh of this succulent aligns it with the energy of the moon and the sign of Cancer. Think of it as washing away anything aligned against you. The gel of the aloe may wash away the pain of burns, but the prickly leaves mean that it is fully able to protect itself and your emotional needs.

- **Cacti** (spp.)—This is a family of plants, rather than a single genus and species of plant. While most cacti are succulents, not all succulents are cacti. (Just like frogs and toads.) This order Caryophyllales is vast and includes flowering species of carnations, beets, dianthus, and the Venus fly trap. They'd love a sunny spot (they are flowering plants, after all) and need very little water. How do you know when to water them if they need so little? Check in with them, tell them about your day. They will appreciate the carbon dioxide you are giving them, and you can keep a close eye and watch for a telltale shrinking, wrinkling, or drooping that says, "It is time for a drink of water." The spines, thorns, or needles of cacti place it under the auspices of Mars and therefore the plant itself has an active protective quality, rather than passive.

> Like dogs and crystals, I've found that plants flourish when given a specific task, rather than a general one. You might ask a cactus to protect the house from door-to-door salespeople, or to keep a specific person from contacting you.

- **Dracaena, Red-Edged** (*Dracaena marginata*)—The same genus that gives us the power and beauty of the dragon's blood tree (*Dracaena draco, D. cinnibari*) provides us this mini dragon with sharp, swordlike foliage. It still carries the protective Mars energy of its larger counterpart. They don't flower as such, so it doesn't have a particular need for bright, direct light, so feel free to supply diffuse light. It comes from arid climes, so it likes *dry feet* and isn't fond of overwatering.

- **Maidenhair Fern** (*Adiantum sp.*)—There are over 250 species of ferns that are generally viewed as being in the maidenhair family. These ferns are associated with banishing evil spirits, and protection magic, because they are well suited to grounding harmful intent, as well as being able to diffuse any ill will. Keep this one watered though; it can shed drastically if it gets too dry. Don't worry, it can still be saved, just keep an eye on it after you water it.

- **Pothos, Devil's Ivy** (*Epipremnum aureum*)—Ivy of all sorts is useful for protection magic. The vines can encase problem issues that arise, and their roots make it possible for them to cling to their support system and survive insurmountable odds. If they are cut off from their support system, they have the resources to take care of themselves.

- **Snake plant** (*Dracaena trifasciata*)—Another of the Dracaena family, this plant grows from a bunch, rather than a single stem, and has a sturdy growth habit and thick leaves. Think of them as the broadsword of the plant world. They're also called *mother-in-law's tongue* and can keep gossip from your door.

- **Succulents** (var.)—These strong, drought-resistant plants are great for people who work outside the home, go away on business, or frequently forget to water other plant species. They are hearty (though not as hearty as plants in the bromeliad family or even cacti; check those out if you're worried) and are associated with the magic of resilience and constancy in adversity. With the rising popularity of succulent gardens, there are cultivars with dolphin-shaped leaves, people-shaped foliage, and every color in the rainbow. Just double check the succulents purchased in larger chain stores, as they likely use plant spray paint to make a plant look more appealing. Plants purchased at big box stores may not look that way once they have grown out a bit. Check near the soil line to be sure.

6

Personal Security

I went back and forth over including a chapter on personal security in a book on protection magic, but I feel like if I don't include it, I'm doing a disservice to my community. You won't find a list of punches and kicks, as I want everyone to protect themselves in the best way they can, no matter their age, ability, health, or strength. I'm a black belt and can teach that class in person, but I can't supervise you at home to make sure you aren't hurt practicing. I fully believe in encouraging a society where instead of admonishing women not to be assaulted, we teach everyone consent. Sadly, that is not the world in which we currently find ourselves. If you can get away, do it. If you can escape and get other potential victims to safety too, do it. But get out so you can save yourself and call for help if others are affected. If it is only you, you are the only one who can make that decision, and whether or not you choose to report, I believe you. I see you. I stand with you.

Physical Security Secrets

Being out of the broom closet has been dangerous for me at times. I'm not saying, "Don't come out of the broom closet." That is an intensely personal choice, and one that can be made more than once.

Just because coworkers at "Job A" knew you were a witch doesn't mean when you move to "Job B" you have to disclose it. The same goes with family members, friends, and more. Healthy boundaries are helpful for everyone.

As someone who is public about my witchcraft practice, I've been threatened more times than I could count. I've been threatened with murder, stoning, sexual assault, bludgeoning, fire, hanging, and the murder of my family and pets. I had a man run me off of the road into oncoming traffic because I had a "Witches Heal" bumper sticker on my car. There are still countries with anti-witchcraft laws in effect. One of my most poignant fan letters when *Blackthorn's Botanical Magic* was released included, "I hope it is okay that I only bought your book on my Kindle," from someone who resided in a country where owning my book could get the letter-writer put to death. That has a weight to it that I never expected.

We can take for granted the ability to be open with our family, our friends, or our communities, but *both* being open and being closeted are valid choices, with their own risks and rewards that only you can weigh. My junior year in high school, my boyfriend's ex asked about a pendant I was wearing (a silver moon and star embellished with seashell): "Does that mean you're Muslim?" I stated that I was Wiccan (I eschewed the word witch, due to the stigma in our small, rural county). I wrote her a heartfelt letter explaining what that meant. Two weeks later, that same note was tossed onto my desk in history class by someone walking by (not the original recipient). It had been circulated through half the school and had cruel things written inside. My sincere words of faith were an olive branch to someone and that olive branch had been used as a torch to incite the villagers to violence.

I didn't back down, I doubled down. I chose to write about the similarities between Christian holy festivals and Wiccan ones in an assigned twenty-page research paper. I got death threats from "Billy," one of the popular kids in my grade, as well as others. My favorite English teacher warned me that he overheard girls in our class plotting against me because of my faith, and he went with me to the guidance office to figure out what to do about it. The guidance counselor even supported me. Later, in my senior year, that counselor came to me to ask questions about Wicca for another student. People can be supportive if you allow them the chance, but that chance should be your choice. My being dragged out of the broom closet wasn't okay. But I am okay. There are adults who were worthy of the trust of sixteen-year-old me. There are people who are worthy of your trust, too. And, I'm still friends with that brave English teacher.

Gods and Spirits of Protection

The best defense is a good offense. When looking for the gods and spirits of protection, you will largely find varied pantheons of (mostly) war gods. Defending your home and your person has long been considered a right, and the ability to protect oneself in one's home from outside trespass is considered a foundational right in some places. While the specific categories of actions that fall under protection are many, you'll find some examples throughout this chapter. Just remember, just because deities have similar affinities or are linked frequently (for example, Greek and Roman deities) does not mean they are the same deity. This isn't an equivalency. I am a hard polytheist; each god gets their own libation. Give each culture, people, and history their own respect and courtesy.

Having said that, most of the self-defense tidbits we tell people are not helpful and can, in fact, be downright dangerous at times. I'm from the old-school generation of the Internet and can remember the days before social media when it was just bulletin boards and email list groups. It was common to see the "Women's Safety" chain letters that have been forwarded so many times that the page is nearly illegible, with *facts* that were told to someone's aunt's hairdresser "by a cop" as though that gave it legitimacy. It included things like "Wear your hair in a ponytail," and "Always check your back seat before getting in the car." These tidbits have grown like wildfire and many people still recite them as fact when someone mentions feeling unsafe. "If you can't find pepper spray, wasp spray is just as good." No. It isn't. No, no, no. If you read the back of the wasp spray can, you will see a large federal warning label explaining that if you use this in a manner other than prescribed by the label, you can be subject to federal prosecution. Don't defend your life, only to end up in prison. (See the section on pepper spray on p. 112 for more help.)

Many of these tips are well-meaning, like "Park in well-lit areas," and "Don't flash valuables." By well-meaning I mean that people have been telling us these things since birth. We know. The harm comes from the advice like "Carry your keys between your fingers." Please never do this. Carry your keys in your hands, and be ready to quickly and efficiently enter your vehicle and lock the doors before driving away. It sounds plausible to rake or cause damage with keys, which is why the advice passes a cursory glance. However, using your key ring like that can very easily break your fingers with one punch. Then how will you fight back? If keys are your only defense (and in some places they may be) carry the ignition key or other large key between your thumb and index finger and attempt to use it as a hole punch.

I hope you never experience the scenarios I'm going to help you defend against. I'm experienced enough to understand that by the time this book finds you, you may have experienced one or more of them. I'm so sorry that happened to you, and please know that it is never the fault of the victim in these instances. Not ever. It doesn't matter what you were wearing, what you had to drink, what your job is, or how you transported yourself there.

SITUATIONAL AWARENESS

People are often taught to avoid eye contact, as if this will ward off an attack. It isn't so. However, if you notice that someone is giving you a lot of eye contact, it's a pre-incident indicator. This means that it is likely that either: (a) they have already chosen you as a target, or (b) that they are evaluating you as a target. Only two types of people give folks that much eye contact. Police and criminals.

Pre-incident indicator number two is speed matching. If you're out walking and you pass them, and they jog to catch up with you, that can indicate a potential threat. This isn't a guarantee, but it should evoke a response where you increase your personal awareness.

Another important tip, whether in a hotel getaway or a changing room trying out new duds, is to check out the mirrors around you. Touch your fingernail to the glass and observe. The depth in the glass is important in determining whether or not you've encountered a two-way mirror. If your nail doesn't touch the mirrored counterpart, congratulations, you've found a standard mirror, and there is nothing tricksy happening here. However, if your fingernail touches your mirrored counterpart, guess what: you have found a two-way mirror. Someone is spying on you and could be recording what you are doing. Remember, "No space, leave this place." It's not safe.

COL. JEFF COOPER'S COLOR CODE

Jeff Cooper developed a code of awareness that helps explain mental readiness in response to a threat, and how each scenario should affect it.

Code White—Completely unaware of your surroundings, unable to respond to a threat. This includes being asleep in your bed at home, texting, walking with head down, being lost in thought, and others.

Code Yellow—Aware of your surroundings, but not worried about any specific threat to your person. Engaged with your surroundings.

Code Orange—You've been alerted to a specific threat: this could be a car coming toward you, an angry dog coming your way, or a person invading your space in a threatening manner. Formulate your response now, before it's a threat to you.

Code Red—Immediate danger, requires active response. This could be running away, yelling, fighting, or more. Implement the plan you came up with in the previous step.

Code Black—This is a freeze response, and it is totally normal to freeze when faced with a potential threat. There is no shame in this. However, it is a learning experience. The way we can train ourselves out of a freeze response is to practice. If you can go over scenarios in your mind while out and about, it can help you plan your moves ahead of time. Remember, action is always faster than reaction.

Use Cooper's color code to do some candle magic for your protection.

White—Burn a white candle anointed with diluted anise oil to light the way for pleasant dreams, the best time to be unaware of your surroundings.

Yellow—Empower a yellow candle on a Sunday with sunflower oil to alert you to magical threats; think an early warning system. Repeat anytime you suspect something afoot.

Orange—Color magic tells us that orange is a combination of yellow (air/thought) and red (fire/action). Use an orange candle on a Wednesday (to speed action) to spur you into action to protect yourself, family, or home.

Red—Anoint on a Tuesday with jojoba (removes obstacles) to give you the strength needed to fight back. Add a pinch of cumin for some Mars fire.

Black—Burn a black candle on a Saturday (endings) to ward off a freeze response in stressful situations. Journal responses to threats so your brain knows what to do instead.

Be Prepared with Everyday Carry Gear

These are things we can have on our persons daily that can be useful in the event of an attack. (Check the local laws, and use the Title and Code for your state/jurisdiction; sadly just asking the police isn't worth your time. The police aren't infallible, nor are they under any obligation to be truthful with you. If they don't like the idea of someone carrying pepper spray, they may tell you that it's illegal. Look it up for yourself.)

THINGS THAT FIT IN A POCKET OR PURSE

- Pocket knife for cutting through materials, such as a seat belt in event of an accident.

- Cell phone

- Bobby pins (great escape tool!)

- Handcuff key on key chain or bracelet

- Tactical pen (aim for any soft areas on an attacker)

- Cash

- Flashlight

> Auf is an aspect of Ra, the god of the Sun in Ancient Egypt, so who better than the guiding light through the underworld to bless your flashlight in case of emergency? Draw a sun on your flashlight and anoint with diluted frankincense oil or pass through burning frankincense smoke, as frankincense was burned in the morning. Ask for the flashlight to help you find your way in your own personal underworld in case of emergency.

THINGS YOU MIGHT CARRY IN A LAPTOP BAG

- Smaller bag (like a reusable grocery bag). They have a million uses and fold up flat enough to not take up too much space.

- Bulletproof panels are a good idea, they can fit in the document compartment of a bag and can usually withstand pistol-caliber firearms, as well as rifles up to .308—I have tested these myself with varying rifles and calibers for a shooting magazine.

- Poncho in case of weather
- Knife
- QuickClot and first aid supplies
- Flashlight
- Multitool
- Lighter
- Paracord (works for tying, as well as escape)
- Duct Tape, small roll (this stuff solves a world of ills)

Binding with Duct Tape

This tape has a million uses and comes in every color in the rainbow, as well as many patterns, for myriad uses. In craft stores there are patterns for creating things like duct tape wallets, flowers, coasters, and belts. "To bind" means to tie two or more things together, and we can bind positive things to us as well as keeping someone from performing an undesirable action. Many witches think of binding someone from harming others, thanks to popular culture, but it can tie beneficial things to us as well. Because of the adhesive properties of duct tape, why not stick something like prosperity, protection, or positive outlook to ourselves? You can print positive affirmations, promises to stick to a budget, and more on an index card inside the duct tape that serves as the base for a wallet. The duct tape makes these projects incredibly durable and will protect your magical intention for years to come.

THINGS TO HAVE IN A VEHICLE
IN CASE OF EMERGENCY

- Toolbox

- A small axe in case of shrubbery or roadside hazard

- Tow rope

- Hand-crank radio in case of dangerous weather

- Matches or tea light candles for warmth and light

- Crowbar

- First aid kit

- Road map

- Fixed-blade knife (not folding) in case of entrapment

Blessing Knives

These tools are carried for many reasons, from self-defense to chores around the home, but they need care just like any other tool. A good all-around knife maintenance oil is Kurobara brand Tsubaki Camellia knife oil. It's a great rust proofer and it can help keep your knife from collecting dust and debris in your bag or pocket. Camellias are an evergreen shrub and they have an association with the moon.

Hold the bottle of oil under the full moon and ask the blessing of the moon to protect you. Visualize the oil in the bottle glowing with the power of the moon. Spray the oil on your pocket knife, fixed blade knives, athames, bolines, and more to cleanse, protect from rust, and empower. Carefully wipe off, keeping an eye out for any double-edged knives. Reapply as needed.

- A small shovel/e-tool in case you get stuck in the mud

- Seventy-two-hour food ration kit

- Extra food rations

- Emergency water pouches

- Paracord

- Bolt cutters in case of entrapment

THINGS TO HAVE WITH YOU FOR A HOTEL STAY

- **Flexible Adhesive Bandages**—You never know when you'll need a bandage, but even more important, it keeps someone with a reverse viewfinder from looking in on you through the built-in peephole. Just apply to the peephole on the inside of the door.

- **Doorstop alarm**—It looks like the traditional wedge-shaped door stop; however, this one is designed to let out a hundred-plus decibel shriek if someone manages to get your door open while you're asleep.

- **Portable door lock**—This handy device is comprised of two pieces: one goes between the door and the strike plate on your hotel door, and the second locks in place with a steel bar, so even if someone has a key to your room, they cannot physically open the door until you open it from the inside. The *security bar* on the hotel door makes us *feel* safe, but it can be defeated with an envelope.

Personal Security on the Go

- If you're carrying a bag, there are a few features that make an average-looking bag more secure. Features to look for:

☛ A strap long enough to be worn across the body—
Cross-body bags mean it can't just be slipped off of your
shoulder as someone runs by. And while we're thinking
about straps . . .

☛ A reinforced strap—Steel cable embedded in the straps
of bags is a more common safety feature than ever before.
This prevents the strap from being cut while a thief
attempts to take it from you.

☛ RFID blocking—With the advent of RFID (Radio
Frequency Identification) built into security access cards,
credit cards, and passports, it's important to protect your
information while it is still in your possession. Popular
places for people to convene mean there are people
walking around with scanners collecting all the personal
information that just happens to walk by. They can
steal your credit card numbers, name, birthdate, place
of employment, and the like just by standing in close
proximity to you. You won't know until there's a problem
at the bank, or something appears on your credit report.
(Also: Check your credit report regularly.) RFID blocking
bags, wallets, and passport holders are all great items to
have in your personal protection arsenal. It's like a small
Faraday cage for your pocket.

☛ Slash-proof fabric—Crowded areas like the subway/tube/
public transit are ripe for this type of crime, due to the
closeness of others and potential for innocuous jostling. A
thief gets close to you and cuts open (usually the bottom
of) your bag and takes what they want, while you are
carefully holding the straps and wondering when your
train arrives.

☛ Carabiner style zippers for clasp security—This means the bag can't be easily unzipped surreptitiously to take valuables from the bag.

■ **Tactical Pen**—I mentioned this in the previous section. These writing utensils are anything but ordinary. They come in many shapes and sizes, from a large permanent marker style, to something that looks like it was made from recycled tank parts. I've been carrying one for over a decade and they go everywhere. Pens are allowed in courthouses, police stations, and on airplanes; the most secure places most people visit allow pens. A good tactical pen is usually made from aircraft aluminum, so it's light and sturdy. My favorite version has a crenelated bezel on the top (think of it as a teeny crown for your pen), but it's sharp enough to get a DNA sample from your attacker. Other styles contain things like handcuff keys, glass breakers, and more. They're usually a common size so that any pen refill will fit your new best friend.

Scenarios

Now that you know how to spot trouble and have assembled some tools, it's time to take a look at a few scenarios.

"CAN YOU TELL ME WHAT TIME IT IS?"

This is a seemingly harmless question that people ask all the time. What it can be is a technique called "bitching up." It's an opening salvo in an attack, used to catch intended victims off guard.

In 2010, I had a part-time retail job while working security full-time. I was hitting the local grocery store after the store closed (around ten). I parked in front of the shop doors, under the parking lot lights. I was openly displaying a firearm (never leave a firearm unattended), a small pistol on my hip, because it was safer to have it on me, but I did not yet possess the Concealed Carry Deadly Weapons (CCDW) license required to conceal it under my clothing. (My state doesn't require a license to open carry. Every state is different.) I ran into the store for necessities to make dinner, and likely took a little longer than I should have. (See? Even I *should* myself sometimes; it's a hard habit to break.)

When exiting the store, I noticed a few things right away. There was a strange man standing at the rear of my SUV with a few cigarette butts littering the ground at his feet. This tells me that he's been standing there a while. I'm carrying two bags in my non-dominant hand, so my right hand is free. As I walk towards my vehicle, he starts walking directly toward me. He looks down at his bare wrist and asks, "Can you tell me what time it is?" He isn't waiting for a reply. He's reaching out to grab me. As I put my hand up to ward off an attack, he sees a firearm on my hip, and mumbles "my bad" and changes direction. I was able to make it safely to my car and escape.

I can hear some of you asking, "*Did you call the police?*" I didn't. I went home and told my husband what had happened, had an emotional moment, and promised myself I'd mention it to their staff the next time I was in. Two days later, my phone rang. It was my friend, Beth, calling to tell me the store gossip. "You'll never guess what happened last night!" She proceeded to tell me how a woman was leaving the store between ten and eleven at night, when a man walked up to her, asked her what time it was, and then grabbed her and demanded she give up her wallet. She handed it to him and even though he had what he wanted, he proceeded to punch her in the face until she lost consciousness.

Courage Medallion with Athena

This is an easy craft you can imbue with courage for you to carry with you, even make with children to carry with them. Grab a coin from the change tray with a high nickel content (in the United States, I use a quarter because it's a good size to hold). The metal nickel has the associations of problem solving. Athena's association with courage isn't the only reason she was chosen; she is a goddess of crafts and reason as well. One of the problems with security risks that happen in day-to-day life is the estimation of the threat level. If someone makes you uncomfortable, but hasn't done anything deliberately harmful, it can be difficult to reason out where the boundary is. Having the blessing of the goddess of war and reasoning is especially helpful as she inspires us to fight for what is right. Take your coin of choice and paint it with the symbol of your choice. If you're adept with art supplies, a helm is a great choice for one side of the coin, and an owl on the other. If (like me) your art lies elsewhere, a spear and a snake make a good pair for both sides of the coin. Once the coin is decorated to your liking, pass it through the four elements or ask that the coin be blessed with courage. Carry it with you. (If you have a relationship with another goddess aligned with courage, talk with Them instead.)

What We Can Learn

There are all sorts of "coulds" and "shoulds" but both myself and the other victim did what we thought was the smart thing to do. We are often told that merely complying with the demands of a would-be attacker negates the threat, and it might, but, then again, what the attacker might want could be your life. Or he could have merely been hungry. In this case, my advice would be to toss the wallet aside so that the thief goes after it, rather than the intended victim. There is also a tip where we construct a faux wallet or billfold to toss in case of a holdup. They are usually constructed with a copy of some dollar bills (in this country, photocopying one side of a bill isn't illegal; check your local laws) and a fake credit card from junk mail that can be paperclipped together and tossed to distract would-be thieves. *There is no foolproof method for staying safe, only working as best we can in the situations in which we find ourselves.* He could have been after a vehicle rather than money. **Carjacking tip:** You don't have to be James Bond to survive a carjacking. Just move! Movement saves lives because action is always faster than reaction. Move your position. Forward, backward, right, left, it *doesn't* matter, just *move.* If you're ever in a situation where someone is shooting at you, run in a zig-zag pattern. It's much harder to hit a target this way.

Self-Defense

If you are attacked from behind, take a step backwards toward the attacker to throw them off balance. Then repeatedly strike the ribs. If you have your back to them, use those elbows. If you manage to face the attacker, punching upward or at a downward angle is best. Ribs are wide and flat; they're made to withstand direct blows, not ones coming at an angle. Go for the sensitive areas of the body: the underside of the jaw, the sinuses and nose (especially the sensitive cartilage at the septum), groin, and tops of the feet. Remember what my mom told me: "As long as our mothers have been telling young girls, 'Go for the groin,' their fathers have been telling them not to let us."

Never go to a second location. **Fight!** If they want to take you to a second location, it is to do something worse than kill you. Fight, claw, scream. If you go to that second location you will die. Never give up.

If someone winds up on top of you, strike ribs and kidneys. Lock elbows down at your sides. Use elbows to keep them centered over your hips. If you can, trap your attacker's leg by hooking your leg on top of theirs, and then use your hips to drive them up and off of you. Now you are on top, and in control. If they attempt to grab you with their legs, lean back. You'll raise their pelvis, exposing their belly. Bring a tight fist down onto the neighborhood of the belt buckle (Carefully! Don't hurt yourself on the metal) and when you hit them there, their legs will spring open and you can escape. Just tell the police to look for the guy who looks like they peed themselves.

DO YOU HAVE A STALKER?

How do you know you have a possible stalker?

- The first time you run into someone is an accident.

- The second time you run into that person is coincidence.

- The third time they "just happen" to pop up is enemy action. Take care.

Stalking and Death Magic

The prospect of having someone acting in an obsessive way is incredibly scary. Let us ask deities of death to grant you a boon: the death of the stalker's obsession. Apollo is a good deity to petition because his arrows can bring healing or death, and he was even sacrificed to in order to avoid plague. Write a petition to the death deity of your choice, and fold it up. Grab a black candle, the banishing herb of your choice (I recommend asafetida because of its associations with banishing evil; warning, it's called Devil's Dung because it smells awful), a candleholder, and the oil of your choice (jojoba is a smart choice due to the magic of overcoming obstacles). Place a pinch of the plant chosen on top of the folded paper, and place the fireproof candleholder on top. Anoint the candle with your oil. Carve the name of the stalker (if you know it) into the candle surface, place into the holder, and light. Best performed on a Saturday or at the dark moon.

How to Spot Someone Following You

Walking:

- Try a pause and turn. Without warning or slowing, quickly peek over your shoulder. Don't linger; they can be gaining on you.

- Pretend to be lost, need to tie your shoe, anything. Step out of the flow of traffic discreetly and bend down to tie your shoes. In a large crowd, they are being swept forward in pursuit of you, while you are stationary. They'll keep looking ahead trying to keep pace with where you were last seen.

- People won't want to be spotted; amateurs will stumble or falter.

- Use reflective surfaces like mirrors, car windows, and storefront windows to watch behind you.

- Duck into a store, count to twenty, and leave again.

- Change your look as best you can. You can take off or add a hat, change the color of your top, remove or add a layer of clothing. If they're looking for someone with brightly colored hair and a green top, be someone in a cap with a white top on. If you have a noticeable logo or design on your shirt, consider turning it inside out. Umbrellas, backpacks, and newspapers are great props for diversion, too.

Driving:

- Try slowing down on the highway. If everyone is doing 65 mph and you slow down to 45, people will pass you. People who are following you will slow down so they don't lose you.

- Try stopping at a light and waiting. Other motorists will honk and eventually go around you at a light. Amateurs will slow down too so they don't lose you.

- Drive fast then slow, or walk fast then slow. Varied pace makes it harder to track you.

- Above all, avoid following patterns or sticking to routines, as much as possible. Change your route to and from work as often as possible. If possible, vary when you take lunch, as well as where. If you're known to be somewhere at a certain time, don't be there.

Remember:
- Keep your hands at nine o'clock and three o'clock on the steering wheel as best you can.

- Don't cross arms over the steering column (allowing your arm to cross over an airbag can lead to a broken arm if deployed).

- Keep your thumbs outside the steering wheel, never inside to avoid a broken wrist in the event of an accident.

- If an unmarked car attempts to pull you over with flashing lights, make sure they're the real police. Put on flashers and slow your speed while calling emergency services to verify that this is a real stop. Pull into a well-lit, well-populated area. If you feel safe pulling into a police station, do that. A fake cop stands no chance of passing for a real cop in a police station. Trust but verify.

If you spot someone following you, you have options:

- You can lose the tail.

- If you're driving, drive like you're lost. Turn on your left turn signal, and turn right. (Always use caution; don't get hurt trying to avoid getting hurt.) Go around the block a few times. If you're near a police station, consider driving through their lot to scare off a tail.

- If you're walking, have fun with them! (Hand notes to strangers, give strangers money, go to *lots* of random stores.)

- Confront them. Very visually write down license plate, call police, make them pick a different target. (This can be dangerous; only do this as a last resort.)

Security Precautions in the Event of a Stalker

- Do not have mail come to your house.

  1. Get a PO box, go to the UPS Store, or similar place.

  2. Forward all mail to your new box.

  3. Don't put your physical address on your driver's license or identification. We take for granted how many times a month someone asks for identification. If this has your home address on it, Biff the Bouncer can come by one night to see if you changed your mind about that drink. (Yes, this happened to one of my students.)

- Grab a new key chain for your keys—the kind that links two rings together with a small metal plunger. When you hand your key to a valet, or get your oil changed, you hand them only the single key they require. The rest of the keys you need—house, office, and so on—go on the other half of the key ring. I've seen incidents where the *Bad Guy* made a copy of the house key and address after the woman who owned the car turned them down for a date, and another one where they robbed the house while the car was being serviced.

- If you fear you have tracking software installed on your phone without your knowledge, buy a burner phone (with cash if possible), use call forwarding to send all calls to your temporary phone, then turn off, break, or destroy the bugged phone. You can buy a new phone—we can't buy a new you.

- Check the wheel well of your car, under the trunk, and any publicly accessible parts of your car for small GPS trackers.

- Many new cars come with a spare key already made for you. If you choose to keep a spare key *on* the vehicle in case you get locked out, have a new key made, not the spare. Automobile keys currently have small chips in them so that your vehicle recognizes your key and will allow it to start. Without that chip, it will unlock the door, but not start the car. This way if someone finds the hide-a-key they can't use a real key to steal your car. They would need to know how to hot-wire it. That type of theft your insurance will likely cover; if they drive away with your key, not likely.

- If you fear there is audio or video surveillance in your home, small, handheld bug sniffers are available cheaply from electronic shops and websites. If you want to check, but don't have the cash on hand, grab a small portable radio with an antenna or cheap headphones, and tune to static at the low end or higher end; lower frequencies are more commonly used. As you walk through the home, use the antenna to sweep the area most likely accessed. The antenna will alert you to a radio broadcast from inside the walls of your home. The pattern of static will shift slightly and the texture of the noise will change. Look in visually cluttered areas of the home, where knickknacks are gathered, on the face of a clock, or in or around air vents. Pay special attention to loose screws that may indicate a camera behind an air vent.

- If you have a landline, pick up the receiver. If you hear a few clicks before the dial tone, it's possible that your phone is bugged and isn't safe to discuss things like your security protocols or other sensitive information.

Blackthorn's Protection Magic

KIDNAPPING

What to Do if You Are Kidnapped

The first 24 hours are most critical. Do what you can to relate to your captor. Use your own name as often as possible, humanize yourself in the eyes of your abductors, tell them about your family, your pets, your friends. Hell, make up an imaginary family!

Avoid looking at captors; if you don't see their faces, you are less of a threat to their feeling of security. If they are easily showing their faces, it's bad news, and even more important that you *get out*.

Act weak or submissive so they don't raise their mental threat level. You want them to underestimate you so that you can escape.

Plan your escape.

How to Resist Kidnapping/Unlawful Capture

How to Escape Duct Tape—Hands Front

People assume that because duct tape is strong, escape is pointless, and this couldn't be further from the truth. Never give up.

- ☛ Place elbows as close together as possible while being taped.
- ☛ Raise hands over head.
- ☛ Pull down hard and *fast*.
- ☛ You create the same angle we use when tearing tape from the roll and the tape will tear.

How to Escape Duct Taped Legs—Hands Front

- ☛ Wedge your hands between your legs and wiggle under the duct tape.

- Keep those elbows farther apart to create a good triangle shape.

- Extend hands flat and shimmy against the duct tape. This will create the same shape for tearing tape, and you'll escape.

How to Escape Rope—Method 1 (crossed hands)

- Cross your hands if you can when you are being tied; it'll create more slack in the rope when you're in position.

- If you can't cross your hands, make two fists facing each other. This also creates enough of a gap so that when you move to escape, you have what you need.

- Keep those elbows farther apart to create slack.

- Extend hands flat and shimmy against each other and you'll slip out of the rope.

How to Escape Rope—Method 2 (paracord)

Paracord shoe laces, very handy. You can buy paracord very cheaply in craft stores or military surplus shops. Just replace your standard laces with whatever color you like. It has a high tensile strength, usually eight hundred to one thousand pounds. This technique may work with commercial laces; if you're in need, try it. Paracord is the better option—proper prior planning and all that.

- Untie your shoes.

- Thread the shoelaces between your hands, under the bindings, and tie them together.

- Sit down; recline back if possible. Tension helps increase friction.

- Lie back and bicycle feet in circular motion using the friction on rope to cut it. This can take 5–30 seconds depending on how thick the bindings are.

How to Escape Zip Ties—Hands Front

- Elbows together.
- Lock facing up between hands.

Method 1 (break)

- Raise hands over head.
- Pull down hard and fast to break the lock. It might scrape or pinch, but it's still safer than staying trapped.

Method 2 (paracord)

- Create two slip knots, one on each end.
- Thread the rope between your hands.
- Sit down.
- Slip both slip knots over your shoes.
- Recline back and bicycle. Friction on zip ties will cut it in 5–30 seconds.

Method 3

Use Kevlar thread in the same way as the paracord method.

How to Escape Zip Ties—Behind Your Back

- Make sure the lock on the zip tie is facing away from your body and between your palms. Tighten the tie if there is any slack to make it easier to break.
- Keep elbows loose and pointed towards your sides.

☞ Raise your hands away from your body, and bring the joined hands down onto your bottom as hard as you can, breaking the lock.

How to Escape Handcuffs

Method 1—The Bobby Pin

Premake this lock pick:

☞ Use pliers to straighten a bobby pin.

☞ Remove rubber nub on flat end.

☞ At ¼" from the end, bend up at 45° angle.

☞ Insert at top of key circle until you hit metal.

☞ Rotate down and tilt right. You should feel the metal catch to release.

Method 2—The Shim or Barrette Method

For this you'll need the metal triangle-shaped barrette that snaps into place.

■ Pull middle out of barrette and snip off end so you end up with a V.

■ This gets inserted between teeth of cuffs. While pressing the shim between the teeth of the cuffs, squeeze, and pull back on the teeth to release.

■ This method can be used with many items that would fit between the teeth of handcuffs, including a strip from a windshield wiper blade.

Method 3—The Wrist Flex

If you flex your wrists while making fists as they put on the handcuffs, it's likely you'll be able to work your way out of them without dislocating a thumb. (Trust me, that hurts.)

The most important thing to remember is that you *never give up*. I'm going to keep saying it—it's that important. Mindset is everything. If you even entertain the idea of failure, it's all over.

How to Escape Chained Hands

- Cross your hands if you can when you are being tied, it'll create more slack in the chain when you're in position.

- If you can't cross your hands, make two fists facing each other; this also creates enough of a gap so that when you move to escape, you have what you need.

- Keep those elbows farther apart to create slack.

- Extend hands flat and shimmy against each other and you'll slip out of the chain.

- Try to work up a sweat; it'll make the chains easier to slip off.

How to Escape Chained Legs

- Place the toes of the right foot on top of the left foot. It will look as though your legs are as close as they can get together, but you're creating a gap in the back side to give you slack when you're in position.

- Keep those knees farther apart to create slack.

- Extend legs flat and shimmy against each other in an up-and-down motion and you'll slip out of the chains.

- It's even easier if you're wearing pants or leggings; you can slip out of the pants and then pull them free of the chains.

Defense

Most of the Pagans I've talked about personal security with tell me they carry a knife. In the next breath they tell me they've never trained in knife fighting, self-defense, or any other combat art. They expect their instincts to take over. Sorry, it doesn't work that way. We don't rise to the challenge; we fall back to our lowest level of training. Every time. No matter what you choose to carry with you, train with it. These are perishable skills. We are able to pull off our lowest level of skill, because there is no perfect scenario. The bad guy isn't going to stand there politely while you fumble in the bottom of a purse for pepper spray or keys to stab him with.

Force-on-force scenarios are dirty, messy, and usually blessedly short. Don't get me wrong—it'll feel like an eternity spent wading though Jell-O. Either the threat is eliminated, or the fight ends because one or both parties lose all momentum. Fights are *exhausting*. Just remember the only rule: survive. There is no such thing as dirty fighting, this isn't a ring and there are no points for style. Biting, scratching, clawing, anything you can do to make them rethink their life choices. If that means bouncing your attacker off a car, or a fire hydrant, do it. You need to escape the threat. Your job is to make it home.

IMPROVISED WEAPONS

If you can pull a fire hydrant out of your back pocket, great, but the rest of the time, you may need to improvise a weapon to defend yourself. When I teach this class in person, it's easy to grab a bag and improvise, so do me a favor and grab your bag, a briefcase, a purse, whatever you might carry on a regular basis. I want you to dump it on the floor (gently!) and look at what you've got. As always, your objective is to escape to safety.

- **Pens or pencils**—As I mentioned above, pens are great defensive tools. Aim for any soft spots on the human body. There are plenty of spots ripe for poking, scraping, pinching, or gouging.

- **Paper clips**—These have thousands of uses; you can pick handcuffs or simple door locks, complete a circuit, jab, gouge, and more.

- **Magazine**—Jab a tightly rolled magazine and it can break the skin, or be used as a small defensive baton or offensive bat.

- **Laptop power pack**—It's already a dense object on a rope of sorts. You can use it as a flail and hit someone from a distance, or as rope or cording to defend against punches and kicks, or even tie up the bad guy until the police arrive.

- **Tape**—If you have electrical tape or duct tape, you can tape the magazine around the power pack and add more mass to your tools.

- **Legal pad or notebook**—See magazine.

- **Phone**—It can be used as a diversion so you can run away!

MARTIAL ARTS VS. COMBAT ARTS

I get a lot of questions from people looking to invest in themselves through martial arts. That's great. We need all the tools we can get. When it comes to which martial art is best, you'll get as many opinions as you do when you ask for definitions of magic. The simple truth is, any training is better than none. Here are a few hints: *black belt factories* exist, so don't walk into just any place with toddlers in pajamas. These martial arts franchises are best suited to helping children develop a sense of self, discipline, and friends. They aren't bad places, but they might not be what you want. If you want a gym that'll help you lose some weight or keep you active, they're great. For learning more defense-oriented materials, as with most things, my philosophy is the smaller the better.

Small businesses, small farms, small dojos. If it looks like a handful of people working out of a hole in the wall, I'm there. That's just me. Staying alive isn't about points, or referees, or belts. It's about the ability to "stay in the fight" so to speak.

If you want to spar against opponents for points, you'd be happier in a martial arts franchise advertising karate or Tae Kwon Do. If you want to survive a knife attack, you want combat arts, such as Krav Maga, Kali, Sanda, or the like. They're all great. They all have something to teach. You just need to understand the context of what is being shown. Kata (form) without context is just art. If you decide to hit up a dojo, just be really honest about what you want, and why you want it. I walked into my first dojo at sixteen and told the very forthright woman in the office that I wanted to learn self-defense against rape. I spent the first three months learning the mount escape I describe above. Variations on that theme were all I did for the first three months, and the entire first year was just self-defense. They didn't know if I'd like to stick around until black belt, and neither did I. It taught me a lot, and no matter what style is available to you, it has something to teach you, too.

> **Quick Note:** Suffixes in some martial arts end in -do or -jitsu: Tae Kwon Do, Judo, Jujitsu, Aikido, Aikijitsu. These are very telling about the practice you'll find inside. The suffix -do means "the way of" and is more philosophical, can be meditative, stresses de-escalation, and may provoke great discussions about the way the art is applied. The suffix -jitsu is about the more fight-oriented, martial applications of that art. Nothing is wrong with either choice, or choosing no art at all.

PEPPER SPRAY

When the world is uncertain (when isn't it?) I get a lot of messages asking about the ins and outs of buying and using pepper spray. The first thing I always say is to check your local laws, because it could be illegal to carry. If it is legal to carry, the code may specify what strength is legal for citizens to use. Remember, there is no such thing as nonlethal self-defense technology. There is only *less lethal*. There is no way for us to know who has a heart defect, who has asthma, and who might be at risk for a traumatic brain injury. Defending yourself with pepper spray could cause a fatal asthma attack. When we defend ourselves with the self-defense technology available to us within the law, we lessen our risk for criminal prosecution, but we cannot make ourselves immune from civil litigation. Even beanbag rounds, pepper balls, and rubber bullets can be fatal if deployed incorrectly.

When people ask about self-defense for a myriad of situations, the most common response is to "carry pepper spray" but that leaves out a host of issues. Those with asthma are discouraged from carrying pepper spray, in case they inhale the overspray and incapacitate themselves or wind up in a medical emergency.

Things to Consider When Purchasing Pepper Spray

Does this brand have an expiration date on the canister?

After two years the propellant contained in the canister disperses and the can is now dead and will be of zero use to you in the event of an emergency. Brands with lesser safety protocols won't bother to print an expiration date on the can. If it doesn't have an expiration date already printed on it, use a permanent marker to write one on yourself. Keep in mind, without an expiration date, it's hard to know how long that pepper spray has been hanging out on the shelf.

Is it Mace or pepper spray?

Mace is a chemical agent more in line with military tear gas. Pepper spray gets its name from the capsaicin extracted from peppers to be the irritant. The chemical in Mace is a nerve agent and likely not effective on anyone under the influence of drugs (like PCP) or alcohol. Capsaicin-based products are more effective against a wide array of attackers and those effects can last from fifteen minutes to an hour. Mace has largely been removed from the civilian market due to injuries to civilians during its use.

When you find a brand that appeals to you, buy **two**. I know they can be expensive, but it is important.

What You Need to Know

- ☛ How far this can will spray

- ☛ How long it will spray for

- ☛ What the spray pattern looks like (a cone, a fogger, or a stream)

Never use fogger types inside; you're as likely to walk into the cloud of pepper gas as the intended target is. A cone spray pattern can hit innocent bystanders, whether you're inside or out. I highly suggest a stream pattern, and if at all possible, a foaming gel. It can get behind glasses and it often contains a UV dye that lasts up to a week, so even if the attacker washes off the burning, foaming mess, they'll still wear the UV proof of their crimes for several days.

If you deploy the pepper spray, empty the canister until the threat goes away. Just like fire extinguishers, the particulates in the canister will clog the nozzle and allow propellant to leak out, rendering it useless. If you spray it, even if it's an accident, that can is now trash. Buy another one; your life is worth it. We can replace the can—we can't make another you.

STUN GUNS VS. TASER

With the availability of portable electronics for safety, the recommendation for stun guns and tasers has become more common. First things first: what is the difference between the two? A taser (Thomas A. Swift's Electric Rifle) is (usually) a pistol-looking device with a detachable cartridge that shoots two fishhook–looking projectiles into a target. When the trigger is pulled after hooks have been deployed, they deliver an electric shock intended to incapacitate an attacker.

The problems with tasers are many. They make a *lot* of waste. There is the plastic of the cartridge housing: many companies fill this cartridge with confetti containing a serial number intended to allow police to track and trace the use of the item in case of misuse. There is the issue of the metal barbs themselves: (a) they are dangerous to the environment, people, and pets, and (b) if both barbs don't land properly, the cartridge is useless and must be reloaded in an attempt to fire again. (Say one barb lands in skin and the second lands on a thick leather jacket, or doesn't land at all. I can guarantee you that your attacker isn't going to wait around for you to reload, they will either be lining up their next attack (yikes) or running away (great!). The only real plus compared to stun guns is that tasers cycle the electricity in pulses. This

means if you are shocking the attacker and they grab you, you'll be able to let go of the *zap* button before both of you are seriously injured.

As for stun guns, you may have already seen one of these in your life and not known it. They have become so popular for the civilian market they can look like anything now. I've seen canes, flashlights, cell phones, even *shocking* brass knuckles. (Brass knuckles are largely illegal and frequently more dangerous to the user than the assailant. Used improperly they can break your fingers, quite easily.) What classifies something as a stun gun is the fact that the device delivers an electric shock via two *fixed* prongs. In deploying this handheld device, you have a very short range as you have to be within reaching distance of your attacker. Unlike the taser, if your assailant grabs you during the scuffle, you would also be zapping yourself. Like the taser, your muscles will seize until you let go, but unlike the taser, your letting go would be around the time you pass out from the shock, as these small appliances don't have the smarts to cycle the electricity and allow you a chance to let go of the charge button.

My Self-Defense Story

Content Warning: firsthand survivor account of stalking and attempted murder. Identifying details have been changed for the safety of the author.

A few years ago, I was starting a new assignment with a new (to me) security company. There was a lot of personal pride in this assignment, as I'd be the first woman to be assigned this post. The current security team had been in place for decades and worked as a well-oiled machine together. On my very first day of training, we had a bomb threat, a death threat, and a suspicious package. My first training session with an officer we'll call Will happened in the afternoon after a long day of greeting personnel and checking badges. Will stopped cold mid-sentence; it happened so suddenly, I worried he might sneeze. "Look," he said. "At the front door. The man, with that woman." I discreetly looked out my office door to the revolving doors beyond. I saw a man of a slight, athletic build, holding the exit door for a blonde woman.

"You stay away from him." His tone brooked no argument. It was as cold as ice, the sweet, jolly Santa-looking man replaced by a seriousness that I'll remember all my days. "The woman with him? There have been others before, but they always look like that by the time he's done with them. Defeated." I saw the slump of shoulders and the ducked head as she followed three steps behind him, postures I'm familiar with from an abusive childhood. I didn't know it then, but that was the day I caught the eye of a monster.

This particular monster didn't have fangs or claws; he didn't change his shape under the full moon. He wore the white jacket and baggy houndstooth pants of a chef. You see, this man, we'll call him Daniel, was in the employ of the restaurant in the building where I now worked. The café closed after the lunch rush, around one-thirty. They finished their closing and prep for the next day by two pm, and from the vantage point of my office off the lobby, I could see the kitchen staff leave every day. Since I was the first one in in the morning, I was the first to leave at two-thirty daily.

A few days later Daniel was found lurking near my car after work, "hoping to catch me" as I'd left for the day. He hoped I'd not noticed him lurking in the bushes near my SUV for half an hour. I've been in security long enough that I noticed it the first time, the week prior. It felt like he hoped he'd found a lost lamb as he approached me that June day. "I like your bumper stickers," he started. "I don't really understand them, but I like them." He was attempting to form a bond with me and, through flattery, hoping I'd open up about myself and engage in conversation with him. "Thanks," I said, just wanting to get home. I left him standing in the middle of the sidewalk, without a second glance. For months afterward, he was waiting for me every day, in the alcove behind my parking space. If I parked elsewhere, he'd wait there. I tried ignoring him, I tried insisting I wasn't interested, but nothing deterred him.

Sometime later (he stopped his daily lurking when it got too cold to wait outside for half an hour daily) he started making noises about my routines. He had talked to someone. When the fall arrived, I'd gone back to school on Tuesday and Thursday to finish my degree in Criminal Justice with a minor in psychology. In addition to working full-time and going to school full-time, I was also working another part-time job to pay for school. He started casually mentioning the mall where

I worked, and then less casually. He would mention in passing that he used to teach culinary studies at the college where I was taking classes and that he knew "all the secret ways" around my school.

Since his on-demand cook station was the one at the direct entrance to the restaurant, I had to walk past him twice a shift. Every day was a new quip and new ploy for attention. Until one day six months later, he mentioned that he wanted to bring me coffee at my second job. Oh, no. Uh-huh. I was nipping that in the bud immediately. "No. I don't want anything from you. I don't need anything from you. I don't drink coffee; if I did drink coffee, my husband would bring it to me." I wanted no ambiguity. It wasn't until later that I learned all he heard was, "I don't drink coffee."

A week later was the hustle and bustle of the holiday season in the United States. It was the Monday after Thanksgiving and everyone was in the holiday spirit, and wanted to be anywhere but at work. As I walked into the café there Daniel was, waiting for me again. "Hey!" he started, with a furrowed brow, "Where were you yesterday? I came to the mall looking for you." I wasn't going to give him the satisfaction of telling him I didn't work yesterday. He mimed holding two cups and said, "I came in the Disney Store entrance, but I couldn't find you."

My first thought was, "What adult man with no children calls it 'the Disney Store entrance'?"

"I brought you hot chocolate. I. Couldn't. Find. You." Still miming holding the hot chocolate, he started shaking angrily and turning red in the face. I fled past him, unsure what to say at this point. I grabbed my lunch from the sandwich cart and sat down. It wasn't until I had half finished my turkey wrap that I glanced up and saw him boldly staring at me. Laser focus, staring. I quickly finished my lunch and headed towards the doors.

"You know, you look tired," he said, as a way of getting my attention.

Now I was angry. "I'm working two jobs and going to school. Black Friday was a nightmare, of course I'm tired." I started to walk away.

"I see that. Since you're so tired, I thought maybe I'd help you out." He then told me that he'd been waiting outside of the mall where I worked, daily for some time, hoping to catch me coming out after the store closed, by myself. He stated in no uncertain terms that once he found me, he planned to kidnap me, throw me in a motorhome, and drive two hours south to a local beach, where he planned to rape me, strangle me to death, and leave my body on the beach for "some mom with a baby" to find. He had been lying in wait in an attempt to kidnap me from work, and it was just luck that he hadn't spotted me yet. "Are you working tonight?" he asked with a disturbing smile. Let me be clear. He never yelled; he had a perfectly flat affect and described my murder as though he were ordering a cup of coffee. In a crowded room. In broad daylight. All of the things I'd been told would *ward off* the monsters.

I can't tell you what I was thinking at the time, only that my brain had clicked off, and all I could hear was an internal dial tone, while my psyche attempted to wrap itself around this new information. I'm sure that I was in shock. I felt disconnected from my body, a robot going through the motions. I fled back to my office without a word. I called the office across the lobby. "Sandy" was the office building contact, and she had been in the management office of the building for twenty-seven years. She knew everything about everyone. "Sandy, can you come to my office please?" "I'll be right over."

As soon as she closed my office door, I shakily launched into my story. About a third of the way in she interrupted me to say, "Amy, you stay away from that man."

"That's literally what I've been trying to do for six months."

"Amy, he's dangerous." My brain went back to his Disney Store comment, and I decided to pull up the state sex offender registry. There he was. "Tier 3" it says, "high probability of violent behavior" reads the red warning label. The page detailed his past history—the crime that got him on the list? Aggravated sexual assault of a boy one to eleven years of age. In this state *aggravated* meant there was a weapon involved. He did twelve years, and it wasn't enough. Here he was again.

Somehow, by the grace of the gods, I got home that day, and the next hours passed in a blur. I remember going to school and meeting with my faculty advisor asking how to proceed. I knew I had to talk to my boss, and we'd figure out where to go from there. I came in at five-thirty the next day as always, and I admit I was a wreck. Going from the basement—where I checked in with the night shift, got my radio, and clocked in—to my office included a desolate corridor of back alley hallways inside this building that the kitchen staff also used. I was worried I'd run into him before I could get help.

Now, I got my black belt at twenty-one, had been a martial artist for fifteen years, I had been shooting since I was sixteen and had been shooting pistol competitively for five years and a firearms instructor for five. I knew how to defend myself. My first year of martial arts was modified from a self-defense for women curriculum, not the "black belt factory" ads I had seen on TV. The thought of having all of my training taken away to be at the mercy of this man left me cold and numb.

I waited until my boss came in at eight, and I called my partner to cover my office before heading to the basement. I explained I needed to talk to him and launched into my story. I got probably one-third of the way into the story when he asked if he could invite Daniel's boss into our discussion. Of course I said yes. I wanted this handled. When "Greg" came down, I started over for his benefit. I got to the part where Daniel admitted to an attempt on my life and a continued fetish revolving around my murder, and my boss sat with his mouth agape. "The first question is, do you want to involve the police?"

"Yes. I believe him. The thought of murdering me excites him."

Greg asked me if I'd like to make a formal complaint against Daniel for their company files. An emphatic yes. "Now that you've agreed, I can fire him. I can tell you that you're not the first woman to complain about him. You're not even the tenth. Every time I ask if they want to make a formal complaint they say the same thing, 'I don't want to get him in trouble, I just want him to leave me alone.' It starts the same way, he's leaving his phone number in women's lunches, and the harassment goes up from there. I just needed someone to put it in writing to fire him." He didn't blame these women for being frightened of this pattern of behavior, or for their apprehension around reporting him. I was thankful he didn't place blame, but also that he wouldn't hesitate in firing him now that we had it in writing.

An officer came to take my statement and said, "You have a case for terroristic threatening, and likely stalking," and he offered to come back at the end of my shift to walk me to my car in case Daniel came back to the property after being fired.

The really important question I was dying to ask blurted out. "Look, I've done all the things they tell people to do to be safe. I am a black belt, this guy knows I'm a competitive shooter, I teach this stuff, for goodness sakes. Why am I being targeted?"

He solemnly looked me in the eyes and said, "He gets off on the challenge. He's too cocky for *suicide by cop*. He wants to see who is better."

Because there were no witnesses who agreed to come forward, the officer who responded let me know I needed to come pick up a copy of the report so I could file the warrant needed to have him arrested for terroristic threatening. When I arrived at the police station to pick up the report the next day, the officer let me know some things he found out, but that weren't part of the report. Not only was Daniel a convicted rapist, but also his most recent victim of record filed a report and a restraining order against him, and when he was arrested, he had chloroform in his car. "Be careful," he warned. This woman got as far as having him arrested, but when Daniel immediately received bail, she fled the state and the charges were dropped.

I wrote out the warrant, attached the copy of the police report, and had to go in front of the judge, just as if I were a police officer hoping to get a warrant. I was incredibly lucky because the judge sitting on the bench that day is also a professor of criminal justice at a local university. He treated it as if it were a lesson and let me approach the bench and show him what I had. He praised the warrant as "better than the officers" he "sees most days" and granted it. I was told that because it was a Friday, they'd look for him until they found him, but he might not come home until Sunday night.

Monday morning bright and early, I got a phone call from the original officer. Daniel was arrested Sunday night; they found a kit containing very disturbing equipment and he was granted bail. "Let me know if he shows up." The trial was scheduled for April.

I can't really tell you how the months passed, but I can tell you they were scary. I couldn't stop living my life; I refused. I still had to go to work, and for my own sanity, I had to pretend that everything was okay. The morning of the trial there was snow (uncommon for this area) and I hoped and feared there would be a snow delay. I got to wait in a victim's services area where I could hear the proceedings, but I didn't have to see him any more than I did in the waiting area of the courtroom. (That was sickening, and I'm glad I didn't give him the satisfaction of seeing my anxiety.)

He admitted to the judge, in court and on the record, that he planned, intended, and attempted his plan. The lawyer for "our side" let me know that since his prior conviction happened in another state, it couldn't be brought into evidence for this case. If it had happened in state, yes, but I live in the conjunction of four states, and even though it was only ten miles away, it was on the other side of a state line. Daniel got one year probation. I was granted a protection order that expired one year from the sentencing.

I took my restraining order, along with multiple copies, to the courthouse to apply for my concealed carry deadly weapons license (CCDW). I'd been teaching the classes for the CCDW for years. I loved empowering people, but I kept telling myself I didn't need it. I did. I do. The receptionist at the Office of the Prothonotary where I turned in my application told me, "I'll see you in six months." I was bereft. The court system was supposed to make this situation better. They were supposed to help protect me from a deranged man who had followed me, threatened me, for months and months. Instead, I got a piece of paper. It wasn't magic. It wasn't going to (and sadly didn't) keep him away from me.

Thank the gods I live in a state that allows open carry, the ability to carry a firearm (in my state only pistols qualify) as long as it is holstered and visible on three sides. As long as I didn't need to go somewhere prohibited, like the post office, I was golden. I could continue to live and work while I waited for the in-depth background check, classes, and so on that were a part of my state's process. (The cost all totaled was around five hundred dollars, not including the cost of a firearm.) Sadly, the safety measures that we put in place to protect people from *bad people* can also hurt innocent people. In my state they require you to publish your name, home address, and phone number in the local paper with a CCDW notice. Theoretically it is so that if you're a bad person, your neighbors can call and tell them not to allow you to have a CCDW. The problem then is that the man I had spent the last year being afraid of, also has access to that information, because it's in the newspaper.

I get a lot of questions from people, especially Pagans, when they find out I carry a firearm. Very often the first question has to do with the Wiccan Rede. "What about *Harm None*?" To that I remind them that *rede* means advice or counsel. Rede doesn't mean law. It's saying, "If you go through life trying to hurt as few people as possible, great. You'll probably have a decent life." What it is not saying is "on pain of death, you cannot ever hurt anyone." It simply isn't possible. The road to hell being paved with good intentions, and all that. If you do a job spell to get the shiny new job you just applied for, that's great. But if you get it, everyone else who applied for that same position didn't get it. They also have bills to pay. That could cause harm. We have to really look at how we approach magic because of this. Some practitioners choose to never do magic for personal gain. That is a personal choice. It isn't mine, as you can see in this book, but it is still valid. I live my life as best I can, and I try every day to be a better person than I was yesterday. That doesn't mean someone gets to hurt me either.

I have had people assume that my carrying a firearm (especially when by law I had to open carry) was a political statement—it isn't. I've had people confront me as though I were doing something wrong—I wasn't. And that's okay. I understand the need for people to question their own beliefs and we do that through dialogue. I grew up anti-gun. I didn't understand why anyone would own them. Even once I discovered shooting was fun, I never saw myself carrying a firearm. It wasn't until someone said, "It's you or me." I've been dead, and I'm not ready to do it again.

I don't have all the answers. I know that there are people who know that firearms aren't for them. That is okay too; no matter what your reason, if your mind, body, or spirit says, "No guns," I respect it. Just know that I didn't make this choice lightly, or easily. I hope to the gods I never again need it, but I know that I have it.

One year and a day after the trial at the courthouse, I walked into my grocery store and literally bumped into a man walking out the door. It was Daniel. He'd gotten a job at my grocery store, just to prove he could. He shouldn't have been able to, because that would put him in the direct path of children. How did he do it? As soon as his probation was over, he moved states, so that his name wouldn't turn up in a state background check. That's how he got a job in my building to begin with. He said he knew how to get to me, and he proved it. For those of you asking if I renewed my now-expired protection order, I couldn't. The state allows you to renew the order only if you have three incidents within a six-month period. So, he timed it out very carefully. He would show up twice, then disappear for a while, show up once, disappear. He spaced out those encounters so that I couldn't meet the legal threshold for the protection order, but still often enough that I knew he was still thinking about me, still fantasizing about my abduction, rape, and murder.

Making the Choice

"Owning a handgun doesn't make you armed, any more than owning a guitar makes you a musician."—Col. Jeff Cooper, *Principles of Personal Defense,* 1978

Should you choose to carry a firearm—train. Train as though your life depends on it, because it can. Under stress we default to our lowest level of training, not the highest. Without consistent training, practice, and manufactured stress, we cannot hope to rise to the occasion. This means taking classes. Lots of them. The largest training organization in the United States offers classes from introduction to self-defense, to firearms in the home, and classes for carrying outside of the home. If you are uncomfortable with large classes, seek out individual training. There are firearms instruction groups for LGBTQIA+ individuals; there are groups for People of Color (POC) who are looking for an instructor. There are also groups for women, for the elderly, and the list goes on.

Also, consider *carry insurance.* There are organizations who offer insurance policies in case of a use-of-force lawsuit, that can cover you in the millions for a small monthly fee.

The Aftermath of a Self-Defense Scenario

In the even you are engaged in a self-defense scenario, once the physical fight is over, the mental fight begins. If you've read this much of the book, I'm guessing you're a magical person and likely have your own set of morals and ideals. That's good. It is important to review them from time to time, see where you stand on certain topics. Self-defense is one of those topics. Whether or not you choose to carry a defensive tool I've discussed above, or even one I haven't, it is important to think of the repercussions of those choices before making them.

When choosing whether or not to carry a defensive tool, consider that you could be in a situation where you have cause to use it. Sadly, whether or not a theoretical attack results in deadly force, there will be judgments, from friends, family, and community. Even if the attack is clearly not your fault (again, it is never the victim's fault) we can be the subject of scrutiny, derision, or even subsequent attacks.

If you choose to employ a firearm, each bullet has a lawyer attached. If you shoot an attacker in defense of your own life and it is considered a "legal shoot," you won't be arrested. That's great, but you are still vulnerable to civil lawsuits from the heirs of the person with whom you engaged. If you legally defend yourself from that bad person, but you injure someone else as well, can you live with that? Even if that shoot is considered legal, you may spend tens of thousands of dollars proving your innocence in court. If you are found innocent of criminal harm, your friends, neighbors, or family may have strong feelings about the incident.

If there is no weapon involved, and you merely survive an attack, there will be people who don't believe you, who question your motive or actions. "Why were you there?" "Why did you X?" "Why didn't you Z?" Let me be clear, it is not ever the victim's fault, and in the eyes of our friends and loved ones, they need to understand what happened, and why. Our culture teaches us that if you're a good person, bad things won't happen to you. It's toxic and ableist. They love you and fear for your safety. We may never know why this thing happened. Honestly, that isn't even the point. What these people are looking for is a way to make it not to have happened to you, and not to them either. If they go through their lives thinking, "Things like that only happen to *those people*" (meaning anyone other), then they can pretend that the world really is safe and warm. The best thing I can offer is: (a) Decide how much emotional labor this person is worth. If it is a random person that you have no emotional investment in, feel free to ignore their questions. (b) If your equation decided that this person is worth your time and effort, check in with yourself honestly and see if you have the emotional bandwidth to discuss this very upsetting time with them. It is perfectly reasonable to tell them, "I can talk with you about this, but not today." Also, "no" is a complete sentence. It is a valid choice, and one you are empowered to make for yourself. You may never feel that you can discuss certain things with certain people. They aren't entitled to your pain or emotional labor. They simply aren't. It can be a shame response on their part. They may feel they 'should' have protected you, or done something differently. That is their burden. You can let them know how you feel, but you can also guard your healing.

> *"Should is a false god."*
> —*Karen Marie Moning*

PART III

SPIRIT

(Emotional Security)

7

Essential Oils for Protection

Recommended Carrier Oils for Dilution

Jojoba—This is not a true oil; it is a vegetable wax that is liquid at room temperature, so it is great for keeping oxygen that will spoil your oil out as long as possible. It's got a long shelf life! I have jojoba-based blends that are over ten years old, and not rancid yet. Yes, they will go rancid at some point, because all things decompose (except that sweet, divine honey!). It has a higher price point than some of the oils available in the carrier oil market, but it is worth it for the shelf life that you get from the purchase. The magic of jojoba is that of courage and the ability to not let any obstacle stand in your way.

Fractionated Coconut Oil—Coconut oil is another wax; the expressed coconut *oil* is solid at room temperature. Fractionated is the liquid wax at room temperature. Again, this one has a longer shelf life than the oils listed below. Coconut carries the magic of a single focus, the drive to accomplish a goal.

Meadowfoam Seed Oil—This is a gloriously stable oil from the seed of the meadowfoam flower, native to California, Oregon, and Washington state. These flowers are prized for the marshmallow-flavored honey they produce, but this little known seed oil is over 98 percent long chain polymers, giving it a shelf life of up to three years when stored properly! That's a great return on investment. It carries the magic of sweetening someone's disposition toward you as well.

Cautions

- Do not ingest essential oils.

- Do not apply undiluted essential oils to the skin without the express direction from a clinical aromatherapist. (Lavender is the only exception to this rule.)

- Do not apply essential oils to anyone under twelve years old without the express direction of a clinical aromatherapist.

- Never apply essential oils to an infant for any reason. Their liver and kidneys cannot process them and the oils can damage internal organs and cause burns on delicate skin.

- There is no governing body grading essential oils. Terms like therapeutic grade, certified therapeutic grade, pure, and the like are not backed by science and are solely marketing terms used by selling companies. They are meaningless in regards to the purity of the product.

TEST THE CONTENTS OF YOUR
ESSENTIAL OILS AT HOME

Method 1: Watercolor Paper

At craft stores and paint supply shops, you can easily find notebooks with thick, watercolor paper. They are absorbent enough to make sure that the oils will not penetrate the subsequent pages below the one being tested upon.

1. Draw a square, circle, or other shape to mark where you'll be placing the oil.

2. Write down all the information from the label you can (brand, Latin and common names, method of distillation if provided, any lot numbers, batch codes, or anything else pertinent).

3. Place a drop where intended.

4. Let it air dry without fan or other mechanical help.

5. Check on the sheet in an hour, a few hours, and twenty-four hours.

6. The oil should be largely evaporated.

7. Note your observations. Are there water spots, oil slicks, or colors present?

After twenty-four hours there should be little scent remaining (the deeper the note, the longer it takes to evaporate—the scent of vetiver will linger longer than orange). There should be little to no color, depending on the oil source. For example, distilled orange will be colorless, but expressed orange will leave an orange stain inside the cap of the oil bottle. Vetiver is a grass, so when sourcing the oil (from the roots), it can be quite dark in color.

It should be quite apparent if the company has added colorants to the oil for aesthetic reasons. Example: One vendor I tested had essential oil of lemongrass dyed green. Though the leaf is green, the essential oil is colorless.

If the pages look like a tear-stained letter, the oil has been watered down. There's no ethical reason to do this.

If the paper looks like the bottom of a french-fry bag, the essential oil has been diluted with oil. An ethical company will let you know that the oil has been diluted, and with what (for allergy purposes, as well as to preserve your budget). Example: Frankincense is produced from the sap of the frankincense tree. It took twenty years for that tree to begin producing the sap that has to be processed to become frankincense essential oil. That's a lot of upfront cost before the process begins, so the oil can be quite expensive (hundreds of dollars per ml). So essential oil companies dilute the oil with carrier oils such as jojoba, coconut oil, or sunflower oil to reduce the overall cost for the end user.

Method 2: Water

This method works best with a clear container with a lid, ideally a plastic water bottle.

1. Add a small amount of water to the bottle (2 oz. is plenty).

2. Place one drop of the essential oil being tested in the bottle.

3. Put the lid on tightly and shake.

4. Observe the interior of the bottle. If the liquid is now cloudy the oil has been treated with an emulsifier so that water can be added. If the interior of the bottle is coated in oil, the essential oil has been diluted with oil, for cost reduction, increased profit, or other reasons.

The Magical Pen

For essential oils that have a high probability of sensitization on the skin (black pepper, rue, cinnamon, clove, and others), place one drop of the essential oil into a 10 ml roll-on bottle. Fill the bottle the rest of the way with a carrier oil (fractionated coconut or jojoba is preferred for longer shelf life), replace the roller top, and now you have your own magical pen. You can write on candles, magical contracts, copies of court documents, petitions, and so much more. This can be used for any essential oils or blends, but is really well suited to irritating magical materials, like Chinese hot pepper infused oil. Signs, sigils, names, and more can be written on magical candles before lighting, and as an anointing oil applicator for large groups. As an aside, companies are now offering semiprecious gemstone roller ball applicators (rhodonite, labradorite, rose quartz, and many others) to accompany glass in a number of colors (jade, brown, violet, cobalt, and more). Your magical pen can have the energy of magical stones without losing the volume of oil to chips of stone.

Essential Oils in Protection Magic

Creating protection perfumes, diffuser blends, and more from essential oils is a great way to utilize active protective qualities of plants and also reinforce the qualities of your own personal witchcraft aims. First, we need to break down what you want to protect, and why you want to protect it. Clarity in your purpose is also helpful. Protecting your income stream is going to look different from protecting your child as they go off to school. There are so many plants associated with general protection that it can be intimidating. That's okay, you don't need to use all of them, or even that many. One or two will give your working the flavor of protection that you need for it to be effective. To increase your efficacy, feel free to incorporate

other plants to fine-tune your protective endeavors. I talk about this idea frequently and call it *Magical Math.*

Some of the plants geared towards protection are galangal, birch, copal, and lilac (that's why they're such a popular landscaping plant). Plants can have more than one or two uses, such as rosemary, which has hundreds of magical uses. This is why rosemary is a great plant to have on hand to substitute for any missing magical herbs because it is so versatile. So, if you add plants with alternate uses you can create a very specific spell.

If you wanted to protect your income, you could use plants that are associated not only with protection, but also prosperity or money. For example, clove is associated with protection, bringing luck into the home, and also increasing financial freedom. Two different herbs could be utilized together, like cherry for financial gain + grapefruit for protection = safeguarding your finances. What might that look like? You could take cherry pits and grapefruit seeds and place them into a black pouch (protection) with shredded bills (the source of anxiety) on a Thursday (for luck, money, power, and protection).

Protection Herbs

Herbs associated with protection will be discussed below, then the subject will be broken down into smaller, more specific categories.

Acacia (*Acacia penninervis*)—This tree has been used in food, medicine, baking, making wooden tools, and furniture for centuries. The acacia blossom honey is soothing, and herbal companies often add acacia fiber to herbal supplements for soothing throat and stomach. Magically this protective herb can be placed into protective charm bags, to be carried by loved ones. Wands for protection magic would do well for witches, as this wood is very popular. And because it grows in the desert in abundance, acacia has also been a featured wood in the Bible as well as other magical histories. The Ark of the Covenant is said to have been carved from acacia wood, a singular feat because the wood is hard enough that if tools aren't kept razor sharp, the wood can shatter. Runes or magical symbols can be stained on the wood for further intentions. Acacia blossom honey is a potent protective substance you can add to your morning tea to create a protective aura that stays with you all day.

Angelica (*Angelica archangelica*)—This plant is so protective its Latin name reflects its celestial heritage, and it is the plant thought to have sprung up from the earth when the Archangel Michael stepped foot on the planet. In the 1300s during the height of the black plague, a monk dreamt about the flower itself. As he told it, an angel came to him in his dreams and told of its usefulness to protect people from the ravages of the plague. The essential oil has a warm, musky fragrance and is supremely useful as a magical fixative. The oil comes from the fibrous roots of this hearty plant, and as such its dark scent will help the other oils blended with it to maintain their scent for hours or days. As it is not only protective, but the scent of the oil also helps release negative thought patterns, it is especially suited to help protect the hearts of those embroiled in the grieving process. Be careful—using angelica on the skin can cause phototoxicity.

Angelica can:

- Be diffused in a (home) recovery room to help protect patients from the pain of medical recovery.

- Be placed on a cotton ball and carried in a pink (self-love) pouch for acceptance of circumstances to protect from further harm.

- Use its fiery energy to protect your finances. Just print a copy of your bank statement or other financial document, and anoint with angelica oil or place with a small piece of angelica root. Best practice is to place in a mirrored box also anointed with angelica. Do this on a Sunday for protection, or Thursday for stability.

- If your work/livelihood depends on being liked or popular, diffuse angelica oil in your workspace to help protect your popularity and success.

- Encourage the *balance* in *work/life balance.* Anoint a yellow candle (clarity of thought) with diluted angelica (one drop in a 10 ml roller filled with carrier is perfect) and burn on a Sunday (for success).

- If a self-defense situation has occurred, diffuse angelica oil to cleanse the space and ground frantic energy.

- Protect children. With bulky coats, you can snip a spot inside the pocket, insert a piece of angelica root into the lining of the coat, and restitch the pocket. The root will survive multiple washings. You can also anoint the coat in a small spot near the hem where it won't be noticed, but (a) it has a strong earthy smell, (b) it'll wash out so it would need to be repeated more often, and (c) the dark color of the oil will stain a lighter fabric. If your child's book bag looks anything like mine did as a kid, you can put a small piece of root inside the bag and they'll likely never notice.

- Defend against evil. Mix three drops of angelica essential oil into three teaspoons of table salt. Place a small pinch in the four corners of the home on the inside. This can be repeated on multiple levels of the home if they are present. Take that working up a notch by charging the mixture under the full moon before placement.

- Defend against negative spirits and hexes. Mix three drops of angelica essential oil into three teaspoons of table salt and stir counterclockwise. Add the salt to a warm running bath. Bathe and submerge yourself at least once. If you don't have a tub, you can stand in the shower and do this, just wash carefully after, so the sun doesn't burn you.

- Be useful for psychic protection. If you fear psychic attack, use your angelica magical pen to draw protective symbols on your person, in a place that won't be exposed to sunlight. (Phototoxicity warning for seventy-two hours after application.)

- Protect your current group harmony and number of friendships. Angelica is a perfect ally to work with. You can make lovely charms with angelica root or essential oil on cotton balls that are empowered with your love for the group. If your friend group isn't as magically inclined as you are, anoint a photo frame with diluted angelica and place a copy of a photo of your favorites. This also works nicely for poly groups.

- Be added to other herbs in your protection workings to increase the power of the spells as a whole, ensuring that they all work in concert toward your goal.

- Protect your connection to your higher self. Your being able to listen to your higher self in times of stress can be a benefit for all involved, but if you are unsure if the *voice* you are hearing is your own selfish desires, add one to three drops of angelica essential oil to a teaspoon of witch hazel in a two-ounce spray bottle. Give it a quick shake with the lid on, and then fill the rest of the way with water or an appropriate hydrosol. Mist over the head lightly and envision you are able to clearly hear your best self. (**Self-care note:** If you are hearing voices that urge you to hurt yourself or others, this is not a voice with your best interest at heart. Reach out to friends, doctors, or therapeutic intervention for help.)

- Guard your inspiration. Add a drop of angelica essential oil to a splash of witch hazel and then fill with water for a paintbrush rinse water that encourages your creativity.

 **Anise** (*Pimpinella anisum*)—This plant is brightly associated with the star shape of its scent twin's seedpod. This anise is the small seeds that lend their flavor to gum, cookies, and desserts, as well as savory dishes. That piney-sharp scent that we associate with jellybeans and alcohol tonics alike is a top note that brings to mind beneficial thoughts (thanks to the Mercurial rulership) and strong protective energies due to its Jupiter association. Getting people together in order to appreciate what each brings to the table is the perfect use of this essential oil. If you are working with the seed itself, consider placing an arrangement of candles on a bed of the seed for a decorative place setting that encourages cooperation in groups, board meetings, Pagan Pride Day committee meetings, and more. These seeds love to cling together so consider allowing it to help your protective endeavors keep from dissolving into a pile of backstabbing arguments.

Anise can:

- Protect babies from colic. (As noted in the caution section, never apply essential oils to babies; their liver and kidneys cannot tolerate them.) Place a piece of root (out of reach) near their crib or wherever they lie.

- Conserve our ability to eat in the face of anxiety. Diffuse anise essential oil in your space one hour to thirty minutes before mealtime to stimulate digestion and hunger.

- Protect intestinal health. Both teas and cookies (and digestive biscuits) have aniseed as a popular ingredient for promoting digestion. It also has been used for centuries as a vermifuge or antiparasitic.

- Guard our spirits during divination and astral travel. Simply add aniseed to a warm bath, or add five drops of aniseed essential oil to a tablespoon of salt (any kind) and mix well before casting it into a warm bath. Keep the lights low; candlelight is encouraged to settle you into a meditative state. Don't worry if you fall asleep after your bath, you're still doing the work needed.

- Defend those attempting to conceive. Place a drop of anise essential oil on a tissue and place it under the center of the lovemaking.

Basil *(Ocimum basilicum)*—This herb is associated with delicious foods from around the world. The plants have a wide variety of shapes and some different colors, like the Thai purple basil. The shiny, blousy green leaves are so voluminous that they look as though they are umbrellas for small sprites. This beauty is associated with protecting those in grief, and it even has its own divination methods to accompany it. Men wore sprigs of basil in their caps to signal marital intent in Italy, where basil was also used to determine marriage-
ability. A fresh leaf was placed into the hands of the intended and if the leaf wilted, it was thought that the match was ill-fated. Protecting hearts isn't the only thing this darling of the mint family has to offer witches. It is stimulating for the brain (so it is not recommended for those who suffer from seizures) and helps keep a clear head in times of emotional distress. If you picture your most clearheaded friend in an emergency, who knows what needs to be done and when, that's basil. It knows where the emergency blankets are, where to find the first-aid kit, and where the doctor's numbers are. The essential oil is a known antidepressant and helps banish insomnia. The protective qualities of this essential oil are for the mind, as well as the heart.

Basil blends well with:

- Roman chamomile (*Chamaemelum nobile*) for heart healing, after grief.

- Orange (*Citrus sinensis*) essential oil for protection and emotional clarity in confusing times.

- Grapefruit (*Citrus paradisi*) for a double dose of protection with a side of renewal.

- Frankincense (*Boswellia carteri*) for banishing emotional blockages while protecting the heart so it can love again.

- Lavender (*Lavandula angustifolia*) for releasing toxic shame and guilt—you are worthy of love.

- Marjoram (*Origanum majorana*) to protect the family against evil, including evil within a family; if you or a loved one is in danger, please consider contacting an organization dedicated to escaping domestic violence.

- Black pepper (*Piper nigrum*) for psychic protection, to protect courage, and drive away evil.

- Rosemary (*Rosmarinus officinalis*) to protect your name, character, or reputation.

Bay Laurel (*Laurus nobilis*)—This silvery green tree is native to the Mediterranean region and is associated with Apollo, largely credited as the god of the sun, but also governing prophecy and oracles. The Oracle at Delphi is dedicated to Apollo and was a popular site for pilgrimage far and wide; even kings would make the trek to visit the Pythia to discover their fate, seek advice, and ensure their legacies. Their admonition to "Know Thyself" has been debated since it was inscribed into the temple wall and, as such, can make a great meditation exercise while diffusing bay essential oil. The magic of fire is rife within this potent protector so picture it burning through any negativity before it can reach your space. My protective cloaks and jackets are anointed in a discrete place with oils like bay and their cohorts so I can carry my protection everywhere.

Bay can:

- Protect romantic feelings after an argument. Diffuse bay essential oil during the make-up discussion process with people you care about: friendships, romantic and platonic partners, webs, and polycules. It will ensure that peace rules, emotions are released as needed, and everyone can transform into the best versions of themselves.

- Protect self-love and positive self-image. Anoint a pink candle (self-love) with diluted bay essential oil and burn on a Friday while reciting things you like about yourself.

- Protect your finances. Place copies of bank statements, investments, or any financial documents in the center of your home with bay oil or bay leaves, in an envelope, a home mirror box (see the Protection in the Home section) if you keep one, or even hidden behind something on a fireplace mantel. If you save printed bank statements place a bay leaf inside the file folder as well. Burn a green candle (money) on a Thursday (protection) to renew the vigor of the spell. Consider using a bay essential oil magical pen (see the Cautions section on p. 128 for directions on making a magical pen) to draw protective runes, sigils, or symbols. (See Laura Tempest Zakroff's book *Sigil Witchery* (Llewellyn 2018) for a primer on creating your own magical symbols through art.)

- Preserve your luck. Good luck is hard to come by sometimes; preserve the luck for everyone in your home by cleansing your space regularly in the manner appropriate to you. If you burn plant materials (check out my book *Sacred Smoke* for creating your own practice from the ground up), seal your cleansing with protective herbs such as bay or clove (it brings luck into the home), and the ways listed here. Remember, nature abhors a vacuum. When cleansing a space, remember to fill it with an intention of your own, and good luck is a great one.

- Protect your mental health by combining bay and basil. One drop of each in a 10 ml roller ball makes a calming scent that protects your peace of mind; feel free to add a few drops of lavender to calm you and the strong scent of basil. Just fill the bottle with the carrier oil of your choice afterwards and cap. Remember, *avoid basil* if you have a history of seizure disorders.

8

Incense Recipes for Protection

Incense is a magical amalgamation of dried plant materials of differing shapes and sizes to create a mystical blend of ingredients to serve a specific purpose, even if that purpose is "it smells nice." Filling your home with pleasing aromas has been an important part of home-keeping since we settled as a people. Rushes (grasses) were brought into homes when dirt floors were still a part of the home experience. They kept feet warm when the natural floor was still too cold to be comfortable to walk on and or sleep on, and they kept the air fresh in a home. Herbs were strewn around the floors to freshen the scent of homes, tents, castles, and more. In Irish history, queens went barefoot whenever possible to show status—they were rich enough to afford fresh rushes daily to keep their feet warm and safe.

In medieval history, nosegays were small bundles of herbs and flowers that were given as gifts to perfume the air around someone, as both bathing regularly and indoor plumbing weren't yet *en vogue* and gutters were used for chamber pots, and a fresh scent might be readily welcome. Then came the perfume renaissance; creating perfumes to cover bodily odor with naturally available materials was an incredible scent revelation.

In magic, we look to herbs, oils, room sprays, essential oil diffusers, and more to change the way we feel through our sense of smell.

The practice of aromatherapy goes hand in hand with magic, because both are creating change in our environments in accordance with our will and intention. By creating your own magical incense blends you are taking a step into your own power to change aspects of your life. In this chapter we will talk about herbs as magical allies, working with the spirits of the plants as a whole and the guiding spirit for the genus and species of a plant. For example, peppermint will have a totally different personality from spearmint. By connecting our incense blends to the allies they represent in the plant world, we can have a total and complete view of our natural allyship. Some of these plants that have magical properties listed below won't have much of a scent, but the energies they lend in herb form are formidable.

Where do I find herbs for incense?

The first and easiest answer to this question is your kitchen's spice cabinet. Some of these plants aren't ones that we associate with incense as a general rule, but that doesn't negate the magical power that they might add to the blend. I'm looking at you, garlic.

Garlic (*Allium sativum*) has been known as a protective plant spirit for hundreds of years, and it has been known to protect us from everything from the common cold to the ever popular vampires. While it may have some people wondering about stinky breath, a pinch of dried garlic in an incense blend won't add much smell, but it will add a potent protective punch. If you're leery of the smell of this protection, try sprinkling a pinch of garlic salt from the pantry inside the four exterior corners of the home. If you live in a circular home (I'm jealous) just try for as close to the cardinal points as you can.

Psychic Protection

Burning any of the below plants will protect your mind and intuition, but for a really incredible scent, try mixing a few together.

Bay Laurel (*Laurus nobilis*) is associated with psychic protection. The correlation is easy to see when you find out that Apollo's love of Daphne led her to be turned into a laurel tree. (She asked, rather than marry him, to be turned into a tree.) He pledged his love to her would be reflected in his worship. His first temple was said to be grown out of bay trees, and the Oracle at Delphi, the Pythia (the oracle herself) was said to inhale the fumes of the burning bay leaves to impart her prophecy. We now know that most of those prophetic gifts came courtesy of the toxic fumes coming out of the ground, but the associations remain. You can find more about this gorgeous tree in the Essential Oils for Protection chapter, as well as an entire chapter in *Blackthorn's Botanical Magic*. This is also a potent ally to protect against abuse and to spiritually purify ourselves after abuse has happened.

Cloves (*Syzygium aromaticum*) may now be associated with fall pies in the United States, but these potent flowers (yes, that little bud is a flower!) are not only associated with fall gourds, but also useful for psychic protection. Clove is also beneficial for luck, as it is said to bring luck into the home. Another mind association, this potent, spicy scent is also connected to magic involving the memory and protecting you from malicious mouths and their gossip. Their magic of purification also lends itself to incenses for keeping a home energetically cleansed for our psychic safety.

Cumin (*Cuminum cyminum*) is associated with fire and Mars, as it burns away any connections that are stealing your thunder. This fiery member of the parsley family is commonly used in dishes needing a smoky heat. Add it to dishes from China, India, and Mexico (the three largest consumers of cumin) while envisioning fire burning any negative attachments away from you and family.

Marjoram (*Origanum majorana*) is within your spice cabinet's reach. It is a *first cousin* to oregano, and at a glance, the two look similar. This Mediterranean herb is not only great at letting us know who is attempting to poke at our psychic defenses, but also ideal for banishing toxic, abusive, or unwelcome family members from your home. It's a strong ally for any protection work, but this is an airy plant, so burning it as an incense while making plans for protective measures is a great use of your time. It creates a bubble that evil cannot penetrate.

Purification and Protection

Aniseed (*Pimpinella anisum*) is commonly used in protection magic for infants, which could be due to the ability of the seed to remedy colic. The internal protection also applies to adults for whom this seed has antiparasitic actions for killing off intestinal parasites.

Sage (*Salvia officinalis*), a.k.a. garden sage, may be related to the white sage grown in the desert, but this *grow-it-yourself* replacement doesn't take away from indigenous peoples' practice. The *Salvia* family has nearly a thousand genera, including *Salvia rosmarinus* (rosemary, formerly *Rosmarinus officinalis*). Over six hundred of these genera are

from Central and South America alone, so keep in mind calling something "salvia" as a common name, with over nine hundred species, is ambiguous at best.

Using Stick Incense

If you don't have access to incense-making materials, or you are leery of using the bounty found in most spice cabinets, never fear. Stick incense is still magical. Though it may look like a collection of dusty sticks, incense as we know it still contains elements of the natural world. The stick is usually bamboo, since it grows quickly, is easily dried, and is a plentiful resource. In our yearning to connect with our witchcraft we can overlook the gift of stick incense because blending our own herbs can feel incredibly magical. That being said, there are so many wonderful incense companies that create sticks that our ancestors would never have dreamed of. I hesitate to name them, since the memory of the written word extends beyond the lifetimes of the authors who create them, but I promise, if you have the time and ability to look, you will find brands that extend their hearts and gifts to making incredible products, some even handmade!

9

Tarot Spells for Protection

These cards can be used by themselves or in combination with other materials to achieve a personalized protection visualization. The images described are from the Rider-Waite-Smith, which is commonly used as *the* tarot deck in the majority of tarot learning books and websites. They will apply to traditionally styled tarot decks, but feel free to substitute your favorite tarot deck in your visualization. Any of the below spells can be done with or without your own tarot deck. You can print images from an internet search and use them as magical talismans, covering them in petitions, prayers, stickers, glitter, whatever says "magic" to you. If you don't have your own tarot deck or access to printing materials, it will work just as well to visualize the card in question. Remember, when you're using the imagery of the tarot in your magic, you are not just holding a card. You are holding the magical lineage of every person who has looked to these cards for answers, control of their lives, and a better circumstance.

Freeform Tarot Spells

When making magic with multiple cards, consider the shape they create.

Three Cards in a Triangle

The two foundational cards support the third card.

Main Focus

Supporting Card   **Supporting Card**

In this layout the Main Focus is The Hanged Man (trust); Supporting Cards are Temperance (purpose) and The Star (hope)

Three Cards in a Line

The two outside cards can protect the center card. Useful for personal protection.

Protective Magic   **Main Focus**   **Protective Magic**

In this layout, Protective Magic is The Magician (manifestation); the Main Focus is The High Priestess (clarity); Protective Magic is The Hierophant (learning higher truth)

They can also be arranged like a math problem:

Support Card

Support Card

Intended Outcome

(**The Hermit**, wisdom) + (**The Chariot**, perseverance)
= (**Justice**, fairness)

If you see cheap tarot cards at swap meets, flea markets, or resale shops, grab them up. They don't need to be complete decks to be useful in magical practice. You can do all sorts of crafts and projects with incomplete decks, from tea service trays protected with resin, to framed spells for long-term goals.

Major Arcana Spells

0 The Fool—The image of a figure with a small pack on a stick over one shoulder and a small dog joyfully barking at their feet, unaware they could step off the cliff waiting below if they aren't careful.

In protection magic: The Fool can be used as a meditation to keep you on the right path and well away from injury—useful for personal protection, not well-suited to home protection

1 The Magician—In this card we see a figure in red and white robes with a wand aloft, standing behind an altar complete with cup, wand, pentacle, and sword. This card is reminding us that we possess all the tools and potential to create anything we desire. This means we can also unmake something, not destroy, but make it so that it never existed in the first place.

In magic: It's a great card for reversing magical attack. Anoint a black candle (banishing) with diluted ginger essential oil (adds speed and power to a spell) and burn the candle in front of a mirror (return to sender) with a copy of The Magician card leaning against the mirror to add to the intention.

2 The High Priestess—A feminine figure enrobed in white and blue is seated between a black pillar (Boaz) and a white pillar (Jachin), harkening back to the pillars at the entrance to Solomon's temple that are often depicted in Freemasonry. On her lap is a scroll that appears to be titled *Torah*, and pomegranates and lilies rise from the background. She reminds us to listen to the inner voice within us all to find our own peace.

In protection magic: The High Priestess is great as an early warning system to keep you apprised of your situation and warn if there is anything threatening your peace. Add an image of The High Priestess card to the back of a line drawing of your home, or a photo of the exterior to alert you if someone attempts to harm anyone inside the home.

3 The Empress—A feminine figure is seated on a throne amid a field of growing things. Her gown is covered in pomegranates, she carries a scepter, and twelve stars adorn her crown (for the months in a year or the houses in astrology). In setting up your protections, the Empress is a fantastic card for guarding your fertility, prosperity, artistic endeavors, and loving relationships (note the astrological symbol for Venus in her card).

In magic: If your loving relationships (platonic or romantic, sexual and a-) need a little extra nurturing, make a copy of this card and tape it to the back of a photo, a note, or other token from partner or partners to strengthen that connection. Consider a regular practice of anointing yourself with rose water and reminding yourself that you are also worthy of love.

4 The Emperor—A bearded figure sits on a throne of stone, wearing armor and holding a scepter. This is the card of power, ambition, and authority. Use this card in magic to protect your social standing, or in achieving your goals (especially in career). If you have trouble seeing yourself as an authority in your field (imposter syndrome) turn to The Emperor for help.

In magic: Use this card as a focal point underneath a candleholder. Then anoint an orange candle (action plus thought) with diluted black pepper oil (eloquence in speech). See the chapter Essential Oils for Protection for making a magical pen for candle spells. Burn it on a Tuesday (victory) or during the waxing moon (increase). Consider framing and placing the card on your desk, even if it's behind a more innocuous photograph or motivational poster.

5 The Hierophant—Another seated figure, this time carrying an elaborate staff, hands aloft in front of two supplicants. A pair of crossed keys lie at their feet. Two elaborate stone pillars decorate the backdrop. This is the card of leadership, of "taking up the scepter" and leading people in a new direction. This is a card of teachers, thought leaders, and tradition.

In magic: If you would like to uphold or protect a currently standing tradition, use this card upright. If you would benefit from breaking down toxic traditions, use this card in reverse. If you would like to be granted a speedy divorce from your spouse, anoint a black (banishing) candle on a Saturday (endings) with diluted jasmine essential oil (justice). Burn the candle (safely) over an image of The Hierophant that speaks to you. Keep the card with you (perhaps in your shoe for domination) until your divorce is safely granted.

6 The Lovers—Two nude figures stand with mountains in the distance and an angel overhead crowned by the sun. One would assume the card was merely about romantic themes, but it largely has to do with choice and making good decisions. What is best for you?

In magic: If you need protection to get out of a bad situation, but you aren't sure which way is up, grab an image of The Lovers card that speaks to you, then light a white candle (all colors of light for best intentions) on a Sunday (protection and hope) anointed with diluted clary sage (for wisdom). Keep the image with you until you have safely escaped the threat.

7 The Chariot—A single figure stands aboard an ornate chariot, complete with a starry canopy. To the chariot, two sphinxes are hitched, each one pointing to their respective corners of the card. The feel of the card talks about the drive of the querent (in this case, you) and whether or not those sphinxes are leading you to your victory or defeat.

In magic: This is a useful card for protection during road trips, as well as all travel by car. Empower a printed image of The Chariot that speaks to you, perhaps framed with blue kyanite pieces (protection during travel) and keep it in your car as a protective token.

8 Strength—A delicate character in a white robe is crowned with flowers and an infinity symbol. She is engaging with a lion; whether that strength is seen as prying the mouth of the lion open, or petting it in order to open its mouth, is in the eye of the beholder.

In magic: If you need protection to overcome impossible odds, grab an image of the Strength card, a peach candle (strength), and diluted ginger oil (courage). Burn the candle on a Sunday (strength). Fold the image and place inside your wallet until adversity wanes.

9 The Hermit—A lone, bearded figure clad in gray holds a lantern aloft with one hand and a staff with the other. This card denotes the wisdom found in solitude as well as the benefit of being different. This card reminds us that it is okay to be yourself, and that just maybe, sometimes it is soothing to regain your independent identity.

In magic: To protect yourself from crimes against you, find a copy of The Hermit card that you enjoy, and with a bold permanent marker write, "(Your name) is protected from all theft, all crime, all harm," over the image of the Hermit. Empower it under the full moon and carry it in a wallet, purse, or other daily carry item.

10 Wheel of Fortune—This card features a brightly colored circle decorated with alchemical glyphs, and at each corner of the card is a different elemental. A sphinx rests upon the top of the wheel. This card embodies the cycle of life, the passage of time, and the luck that keeps it turning. Let's protect that luck.

In magic: This card is ruled by the planet Jupiter, so if your luck needs to turn, turn, turn for the better, grab a gold or green candle (luck) and anoint it with diluted grapefruit essential oil (for blessing, uplifting) on a Thursday (protected growth), and place it on top of an image of the Wheel of Fortune that appeals to you. Allow to burn completely; keep the image in your phone case, bag, wallet, purse, or anything carried on a daily basis.

11 Justice—A crowned figure is seated on a dais enrobed in red, holding a sword and scales. This is a card about honoring your commitments, for good or ill. Very useful for court cases, but beware, if you are in the wrong, you will find out pretty quickly.

In magic: To protect the equity during contract negotiations, court hearings, or mediations, anoint a copy of your favorite image of the Justice card with diluted frankincense oil (protection from abuse) and keep it on you during the proceedings.

12 The Hanged Man—A figure in a blue doublet and red leggings is hanging, suspended upside down by one foot, while their head is crowned by the light of knowledge. This card is commonly interpreted as the sacrifice of something small for the gain of something greater. A change in view results in a change in perspective.

In magic: To protect your spiritual growth and enlightenment during times of duress, find an image of The Hanged Man that appeals to you and a white, gold, or silver candle. On a Monday (emotions, enlightenment) or during the full moon (union of sun/success and moon/enlightenment), anoint your chosen candle and the copy of the Hanged Man card with diluted melissa (lemon balm) essential oil (compassion). Allow the candle to burn down completely, then carry the image of the Hanged Man with you until the threat has passed.

13 Death—A skeletal figure rides in shiny black armor on a white horse. They carry a black banner displaying a white Tudor rose. Popes, paupers, and peasants fall in the wake of the rider. This card carries the energies of endings, but they are for the best and, when faced head on, can be virtually painless. Think of that banner as a protector of hope and peace.

In magic: If things need to change before you, allow the Death card to protect a peaceful end to things that no longer serve you. This isn't a hex, it's *landscaping*, pruning away the dead limbs to allow for new life to grow. Find an image of the Death card that appeals to you. With a permanent marker either name the thing that no longer serves you, or write "That which no longer serves me" on the face of the image. On a Saturday or the dark moon (endings), if possible, anoint the image and a black candle (endings) with a diluted bay (laurel) essential oil (communicating release). Place the candle in a holder on top of the image, and burn completely. Keep the image in a safe place while your shifts are happening.

14 Temperance—The image of a red-winged angel stands with one foot in the water and one foot on land, pouring water between two goblets. Yellow iris flowers grace the foreground and the sun sets over the mountains in the distance. Temperance is the card of balance, especially in the home, and seeing the end of harmful things in your life.

In magic: To protect your happiness, sense of balance, and peace in your home, it's time to get crafty! Grab an image of Temperance that sings to you, an unfinished wooden frame, and paints in colors that make you feel peaceful and at ease. On a Friday (beauty, luxury) set a place for yourself; feel free to add some romantic lighting and burn your favorite incense. Waft your image, the frame, and your bottles of paint and brushes in the smoke of your favorite incense and take a wholesome, deep breath. Remind yourself that you are in charge of what you want to do with your happiness. Then paint the frame in whatever manner makes you happy. Feel free to anoint the finished work with incense smoke as well. Hang the portrait of Temperance over the main entrance to your home so that all who enter are granted the same peace you feel right now. Feel free to charge it occasionally under the light of the full moon.

15 The Devil—There are three figures present in a darkened cave-like room. The Devil sits on a stone throne with two human figures chained at his feet. The important thing to notice about this *scary* tarot card is that both of these figures are capable of simply taking the chain from around their necks and walking away. They choose to feel trapped, when they have the power to leave; they must simply make the choice and stick to it.

We can make the choice to protect ourselves, even in situations that feel inescapable.

In magic: If you have the drive to make your wishes, hopes, and dreams come true, the Devil card is for you. You could use this card to influence others, but instead we are going to work on our drive to succeed and make those dreams a reality. Take an image of the Devil card that speaks to you, a red candle (ambition), and diluted cinnamon leaf essential oil (be careful and take them to a sunny window if possible). You are making a reliable daily plan to achieve your goals. First make a list of every single thing needed to create the goal you seek. Once you have the list, anoint your red candle with the diluted cinnamon essential oil (wash your hands thoroughly after touching it, as it is a sensitizing oil), place the list along with the image of the Devil card on top, and place the candle in a candleholder. Light and allow the candle to burn down completely. Then get to work on that list!

THE TOWER.

16 The Tower—A striking sight, a stone tower in the midst of a terrible storm is hit by lighting with such force that the tower itself and the people formerly inside are falling toward the ground, with fearful expressions on their faces. This card denotes sudden, abrupt, or shocking change.

In magic: Use the shock factor inherent in The Tower card and disrupt any nasty spells aimed your way. Craft time! If you have a small box to use, great. If not, check out a local craft shop where there is usually a section of boxes and containers for painting. You can choose from wooden boxes with shiny brass hinges, or paperboard boxes that'll absorb the paint and look great. The size of the box isn't as important as making sure you can fit the *protectee* in the box via a photo or drawing. If you're doing this for a home, have a copy of a floor plan, a drawing (doesn't have to be Da Vinci, Picasso works, too), a photo, or other token.

Choose one or more images of The Tower card that appeal to you and print them out. (If you are a talented artist, you can draw or paint instead.) You will want enough small images of the Tower to cover the box at least twice. You will also need sponge brushes and gesso, glue or other sealing medium. On a Saturday (endings) sit where you can work undisturbed. With the sponge brush, cover the box (top and sides, not bottom, and skip the inside for now) with your choice of adhesive medium. Grab your favorite image of The Tower and save it for last. Start covering the box with collected images, sides and top, making it as layered and haphazard as you are comfortable doing, as it makes it harder to attack the *seams,* if someone's magic can't find them. You may need to keep scissors or a razor knife handy to cut the images, or even to cut the box open before the glue dries. Once the box is complete (we aren't doing the bottom because if it gets humid it will have a tendency to stick to the surface it is sitting on, and the same goes for the interior of the box; it would glue itself shut—ask me how I know), cover the top in your preferred medium and place your final image in the top center of the box, then cover it as well. (Don't worry, the glue will dry clear.) Once it is dry, paint the interior of the box a nice, dark black (protection). When the paint is dry, feel free to put photos of yourself, your home, and people living inside the home into the box for safekeeping. Close the box, and empower it for protection. If you don't already have a personal method for empowering objects, you can sing, visualize the box surrounded by the light of the sun for protection, pass the box through incense smoke, or whatever feels right to you. Place it in an out-of-the-way corner of the home, so it isn't disturbed. You can open the box and place tears of frankincense (blessing) or dragon's blood (protection) to empower it once or twice a year or if there is a focused, directed magical attack on the home or someone in it.

17 The Star—This serene card features a nude figure kneeling half on land and half in the water (reminding us of the Temperance card), pouring water both on to the land and back into the clear blue water they are kneeling in. A prominent star shines overhead in gold hues (Air element, Divine Male) with white stars (cleansing/rebirth) in the background.

In magic: When in the midst of a protection emergency, it can be so easy to feel hopeless and despondent, or that the threat will never end. It will. The good news about all situations in life is they end. The bad news about all situations in life, they end. To this end, The Star is here to help you maintain hope, faith in your goals, and wishes granted. Find an image of The Star that whispers hopeful words to your heart. Grab a gold or yellow candle (for thoughts and plans), a candleholder, and some diluted Sweet Orange essential oil. Its acidity and solar associations are brightening and will burn away any miasma that attempts to bring you, or your hopeful thoughts, down. Anoint the candle with the diluted orange oil, as well as your image of The Star. Feel free to write your hopes or fears on the copy of The Star. Place the candleholder on top of the image and burn on a Sunday (protection, hope). Allow to burn all the way down, and carry The Star image with you until the emergency has passed.

18 The Moon— In the foreground you see two canines barking at the large moon overhead. Between them, a lobster is crawling up onto land, bringing wisdom from our subconscious with it. In the distance we see two towers (duality) framing the moon. This card is associated with Cancer in astrology, and when it appears in a reading, it should remind the querent that things look differently in the moonlight; you might not have the whole picture. Enemies can look like friends, bad can look kind, and danger can appear safe.

In magic: Ask the moon to grant you clarity by granting you intuition (also ruled by the moon). If things aren't as bad as they appear, the moon will let you know. Grab an image of the Moon card, a notebook and pen, a dark-colored bowl, and water. Bonus points if you can do this under a full moon, but any Monday will suffice. Take three deep breaths in through your nose and out through your mouth while you ground any excess or nervous energy. Sit in a comfortable position, and ask the moon to shine well on your divination. Set up The Moon card where it can easily be seen from your vantage point over the bowl. What we will be doing is called scrying, a kind of divination that relies on elements of nature to send you messages. Stare into the water, looking at the reflected light, and allow your eyes to soften their focus until you can see the light but not the details of the surface, while you continue to breathe softly and let your mind wander. You may see images or have seemingly random thoughts pop into your head. If you might lose track of them, try to write them down without looking at the paper; the handwriting won't be great, but you don't want to lose your sense of trance. I notice that my trance handwriting is markedly different from my awake and aware handwriting. If you think you'll remember it, it can wait until you're back in your body, so to speak. Trance is a skill that can really improve with time and attention.

Keep the moon image under your pillow to allow the moon to bring you messages.

19 The Sun— In the warmth of The Sun card, we see an adolescent figure (youthful enthusiasm) riding a white horse (rebirth) in front of a low brick wall, backed by sunflowers. The light of the sun takes up a good 50 percent of the card's image. The card represents abundance (think of how many sunflower seeds are in the card, thousands), joy, and can denote a marriage in a reading.

In magic: Use it to protect a relationship. The Sun card is bright and happy, and it can help us to find things in our life to be grateful for. If you are worried that you might have challenging times ahead with partner(s) or a relationship in your life (romantic or platonic, sexual or a-), grab an image of The Sun card that is a breath of fresh air, an orange candle (mental fortitude and adaptability) on a Friday (love and romance), and diluted benzoin essential oil (calming, soothing, and purification). Anoint the candle as well as the image of The Sun with the diluted benzoin oil (harmony). Place the candle in a fire-safe candleholder and place the candleholder on top of the image of the Sun. If you feel empowered to, write the source of your anxiety on the copy of the card. Allow the candle to burn down all the way, and feel free to (safely) burn the image when you are done.

20 Judgement— The Judgement card shows crypts all standing open as nude figures of all ages stand up from their graves giving praise and joyful exclamations to the angelic herald trumpeting them from their eternal slumber. It can herald a change in status for the better, a promotion, a proposal, or other bump in status. It is a fresh start in a new life, but not the *from scratch* start The Fool signifies.

In magic: Use the Judgement card to protect your life-changing moment and to bring it about. If you have been stuck in a rut, unable to move forward or back, allow the herald of change to trumpet your accomplishments to the heavens. Grab whichever image of the Judgement card calls to you, a yellow candle (success), and some diluted aniseed essential oil (fulfillment). Anoint the candle and the copy of the tarot card with aniseed oil on a Tuesday (passion), while imaging the next big thing coming your way. If you don't know what it is, but you know it's time for bigger and better, you can write "bigger and better" on the printed copy of the card. Place the candleholder over the image to empower it as it burns. Allow the candle to burn down completely and carry the card with you until the next big thing hits.

21 The World— In the image of The World, we see a nude figure in the center of a laurel wreath (champion) holding two white wands (balance, rebirth). This is the successful completion of the cycle, but as life and death lead to rebirth, the learning cycle of the tarot continues.

In magic: To protect you during international travel, take a green candle for health and well-being on a Saturday (as The World is associated with Saturn) and a copy of The World card. Write "Infinite Possibilities" on the face of the card copy and anoint with diluted tangerine essential oil (defense). Anoint your candle with the diluted tangerine oil and place over the upturned World card. Burn until it is finished, and tuck the anointed World card into your passport wallet to protect you while you travel.

Oracle Decks

Just a word on oracle decks, those beautiful, free-form divination tools—because oracle decks vary so widely, there is something out there for everyone. Use the imagery that speaks to your soul, the style of magic you employ, and the type of magic needed for the end goal. With the advent of self-published tarot and oracle decks, it is possible to find decks for very small, niche communities and specialty interests. There are decks that I use for magic, ones that I use for divination, and in some cases, I have multiple copies of decks that I adore so that I have one for magic, one for client readings, and one for myself. Whether you store them in silk or keep them pristine in their original boxes, oracles are here to act as magical support for all of your needs—just reach out.

PART IV

Additional Information

10

Timing Your Protection with the Stars

Protection and Days of the Week

Sunday (Sun)—The success of protection done under the sign of the sun is practically guaranteed. The sun's protection magic is that of burning away anything that stands against you. Work your magic on a Sunday to bring warmth and hope, and it will make you realize that all your goals for yourself, your magic, and your success are within reach. The sun is associated with medicine, light, knowledge, music, poetry, and more, through Apollo. If you want your creative pursuits blessed by a solar deity, you can't find a better day of the week than Sunday.

Monday (Moon)—Protection magic involving the moon is the nurturing protection of a mother's love. It protects your inner self who is vulnerable to the slings and arrows of people who don't know the harm in their words. The moon can protect your psyche and your intuitive traits, so if you have been plagued by doubt regarding your intuitive abilities or feel that your psychic senses are vulnerable to attack, do a working on the moon's day, Monday. To protect your health, work preventative magic on a Monday, as healing is associated with Artemis/Diana.

Tuesday (Mars)—To protect yourself from the actions of others, a more active approach may be necessary. To ensure victory, work that magic on a Tuesday. Tuesday is the point of the spear, and all of your will and drive is the energy in your arm that throws it. Tuesdays are a great day for protecting your passion projects with magic. This day is also beneficial for putting rivalries to bed. Mars is also known as a god of agriculture, so if you are starting a garden (magical or non-), you can ask that it be blessed on a Tuesday.

Wednesday (Mercury)—Wednesday is ruled by Mercury, so working magic for protecting the ways and means of your communication, as well as the way your messages are received by others, is potent on this day. The idea of starting new things under the auspices of Mercury is a great one, as invitations are ruled by the fleet-footed god. Starting your home's protection plan on a Wednesday is likewise well aspected, as Mercury/Hermes isn't just a messenger, he is also the patron god of thieves, so he might be able to put in a good word for you. If you would like to turn your passion project into a full-fledged business, start the tough work on a Wednesday as Mercury/Hermes also rules trade.

Thursday (Jupiter)—The day of the week reserved for the kings of the gods—Jupiter, Zeus, Odin, and many more all have Jupiterian influences. Oak is another plant associated with these fathers of pantheons, as oak trees are more likely to be hit by lightning, so their association with Jupiter, Taranis, and Zeus makes sense. Jupiter's magic is inherently protective. It is good for protecting business ventures, as it offers protected growth, so you don't grow so big, so quickly that you go out of business. Zeus was also called the Lord of Justice so if you have court

case coming up and need the protection and blessings of justice, petition him on a Thursday.

Friday (Venus)—The goddess of love, luxury, beauty, and the arts—if you need the protection of the art you produce, the ability to enjoy luxuries responsibly, or want to protect loving relationships, Friday is your day. Because Friday is associated with luxury items, for magic protecting your finances, this is perfect timing. Who wouldn't want to spend a Friday night drawing up a budget and asking that it be blessed and protected by a goddess?

Saturday (Saturn)—Saturnian magic is that of endings, binding, and more that create stability in the realms. Use this day to banish people from your life that mean you harm (whether you know who they are, or not). This can include stalkers, two-faced or jealous friends, past relationships that still haunt us, as well as abusive people in our lives. Sometimes those people are people that we love, but if they aren't healthy for you, here's your permission slip to let them go from your life, even if they appear to mean well most of the time.

Moon Phases in Protection Magic

Waxing (Increasing)—The waxing moon is the time to increase protection in the home, and for yourself or your family: increase in personal security, protection from court cases, and protection of a growing business, or personal status.

Full—When the moon is at its zenith for the month, establish boundaries; do general protection work or protection from specific persons, powered by the union of lunar and solar.

Waning (Decreasing)—This is a good time to release anything that is harmful in your life and banish threats to your security like debt, housing inequality, food insecurity, and systemic societal issues. It also works well for purification and magic aiding in the recovery from abuse.

Dark—Bring an end to known threats, even if the target is unknown.

> If you know you have a stalker, but don't know their name, you can still banish them based on the way they make you feel. You can place wards specific to that issue under the dark moon. For example, you can sprinkle dried mugwort in a ring around your property to keep them at bay. If you don't have a large amount of mugwort, make a mugwort tisane and sprinkle it around the perimeter of your property. For more information, see Protection in the Home.

New—The moment there is the barest sliver of light in the lunar surface in the sky, you can work magic for psychic protection. It's increasing but will still carry the energy of the dark where our intuition flourishes without all the distractions of the daylight hours.

11

Other Correspondences
for Protection

Following is some additional information for protection magic.

Colors

For color magic (perfect for creating your own candle spells), feel free to go back to your color wheels. Magically blending the primary colors, you can create and fine-tune magic for your needs, wants, and desires. Orange carries the passion and vitality of red with the thought and planning of yellow. Blue is tranquil and yellow is thoughtful, so using green in your magic can be self-assured. The reverse is also true: if you need a green candle but have none, burning a blue and a yellow can lend an intention that might be lost if you'd rather not substitute a white candle.

White—White contains the magic of rebirth, clarity. Use the color white in your magic to cancel out magic aimed at you *before* it can get to you. If you fear the magic has already taken root, reach for a black candle instead.

Gray—This color is especially good for use in home warding setups. You can energetically fill your home wards with gray mist, so that any harm directed at you will get lost in the mist and burn off before it can find its mark. Great for magical self-defense.

Black—Black contains the magic of banishing, binding, and negating. Use it in your protection magic so that your enemy cannot find you, for you are invisible in the dark. Black is wonderful for hex breaking, as well as protecting yourself from falling into old patterns of behavior and bad habits.

Brown—Protect your personal and environmental stability, especially financial (relating to physical goods, like homes and transportation methods). Because of the stability of brown (think tree trunks) it's a great color for magic invoked to protect your work life and professional standing in your field.

Red—Protect your enthusiasm, your passion for life, the enthusiasm for your hobbies, or do a ritual to feel brave in the face of adversity.

Pink—Protect your friendships from outside attack; protect your family as a whole from harm.

Orange—Utilize orange for ensuring you stay adaptable to change, especially in the face of adversity.

Yellow—Manifest strength for the work ahead. Think of it as a call to action, to pay attention.

Green—Protect your finances! I'm serious when I remind you that people who don't have your best intentions in mind will absolutely attack your finances just to make you miserable. Protect them.

Blue—The color blue is ideal for protection of health (both physical and mental) and well-being. It restores your personal equilibrium just as the water that blue reminds us of.

Indigo—This denim-colored magic is ideal for a deep peace and tranquility that you can feel into your soul. Use this color in magic to protect your greater attitudes towards yourself and your personal practice of inner reflection.

Violet—Violet and lavender are both purples that are associated with spiritual protection, as they relate to the stone amethyst and the theoretical seat of psychic power, the pituitary gland. Use purple in magic for psychic protection, as well as to protect you during your dreams. Nightmares weren't originally just bad dreams, so much as evil spirits that watched us sleep and brought horrifying visions.

Silver—Protect yourself from a crisis of conscience, or protect yourself by refusing to give up on yourself. Petition for lunar protection.

Gold—Petition for solar protection. Protect a streak of good luck and repel bad luck.

Plants

GENERAL PROTECTION PLANTS

Benzoin	Bindweed	Birch
Cinnamon	Clover	Cloves
Copal	Cranberry	Cypress
Dragon's Blood	Eucalyptus	Frankincense
Galangal	Geranium	Grapefruit
Hazelwood	Heather	Helianthus (daisy, sunflower)
Heliotrope	Holly	Hyssop
Juniper	Lavender	Lilac
Marjoram	Motherwort	Mugwort
Mullein	Myrrh	Neroli
Orris root	Patchouli	Pennyroyal *Caution, abortifacient
Pine (needles, nuts, cones, other)	Raspberry	Rosemary
Rue *Caution, abortifacient	Sage	Sandalwood
Sweetgrass	Tangerine	Tansy
Verbena (lemon, etc.)	(Blue) Vervain	Vetiver
Willow	Wormwood	Yarrow

BANISHING MAGIC

Angelica	Cumin	Dragon's Blood
Eucalyptus	Frankincense	Lilac
Mistletoe	Peach	Peony
Peppermint	Pine (all parts)	Rue
Sunflower		

PSYCHIC PROTECTION

Angelica	Basil	Bay laurel
Benzoin	Cinquefoil	Clove
Galangal	High John the Conquerer	Hyssop
Lemon Verbena	Mandrake (not "American Mandrake" *Podophyllum peltatum*)	Marjoram
Mugwort	Myrrh	Patchouli
Peach	Rosewood	Rue *Caution, abortifacient
Spruce	Vetiver	

PURIFICATION PLANTS

Aniseed	Bay laurel	Benzoin
Bergamot	Chamomile (any)	Clove
Frankincense	Hyssop	Juniper
Lemon	Peppermint	Rosemary
Sage (garden is fine)	Star Anise	Thyme
Verbena (Vervain)		

RELEASE (SITUATIONS, EMOTIONS, PEOPLE)

Asafoetida *Warning, odor	Bay laurel	Camphor
Menthol	Pennyroyal *Caution, abortifacient	Peppermint
Rosemary		

RELATED ACTIONS

Plant	Action
Tangerine	Defense
Cinquefoil	Increase the power of a spell
Copal	Increase the power of a spell
Damiana	Increase the power of a spell
Lemon	Increase the power of a spell
Patchouli	Increase the power of a spell
Vetiver	Increase the power of a spell
Bay	Endings
Camphor	Endings
Menthol	Endings
Myrrh	Endings
Pennyroyal *Caution, abortifacient	Endings
Rosemary	Endings

Specific Protection Situations

ABUSE

To Avenge Abuse	Petition
God	Bran or Hephaestus
Goddess	Justia

To Recover from Abuse
Onion, cut in half and left for three days in recovery room

To Protect Against Abuse	
Color	Black
Stones	Jasper, Lapis Lazuli, Obsidian, Smoky Quartz, Black Tourmaline
Plants	Bay, Dragon's Blood, Frankincense, Saffron

COURT CASES (RULE IN YOUR FAVOR)

Color	Purple
Day	Thursday
Crystals	Adventurine, Bloodstone, Brown Chalcedony, Rose Quartz, Diamond
Herbs	Deertongue (*Dichanthelium clandestinum*) Galangal (*Alpinia officinarum*): carry in court, or chew and spit on the floor of courtroom for judge to rule in your favor. High John the Conquerer root Bay Marigold Pine (nuts, cones, needles) Tobacco

Acknowledgments

To the friends who knew the story and helped me live it. To the badass women in my life, Janna, Ashli, Jill, Mel, Jenni, Laura, Kristin, Judika, Caroline, and many more. To my lord Brian and all of my WM family. To all of the amazing humans at Red Wheel/Weiser Books, your friendship and care are more precious than jewels.

Further Reading

1. Practical Considerations (Before You Start)

Toxic Positivity

If You Had Controlling Parents: How to Make Peace with Your Past and Take Your Place in the World by Dan Neuharth, PhD, LMFT

It Didn't Start with You: How Inherited Family Trauma Shapes Who We Are and How to End the Cycle by Mark Wolynn

The Self-Confidence Workbook: A Guide to Overcoming Self-Doubt and Improving Self-Esteem by Barbara Markway, PhD

Toward a Psychology of Awakening by John Welwood

Post-Traumatic Stress/ Complex Post-Traumatic Stress

Complex PTSD: From Surviving to Thriving by Pete Walker

The Body Keeps the Score: Brain, Mind, and Body in the Healing of Trauma by Bessel van der Kolk

Waking the Tiger: Healing Trauma by Peter A. Levine

Women, Food, and God: An Unexpected Path to Almost Everything by Geneen Roth

2. Crystals for Protection

Protection Stones

The Crystal Bible by Judy Hall

The Crystal Bible 2 by Judy Hall

The Crystal Bible 3 by Judy Hall

Love Is in the Earth by Melody

The Book of Stones by Robert Simmons

Crystal Basics by Nicholas Pearson

3. Psychic Protection

Grounding during Protection Emergencies

Life Ritualized: A Witch's Guide to Honoring Life's Important Moments by Phoenix LaFae and Gwion Raven

6. Personal Security

FIREARMS

Making the Choice:

Armed America: Portraits of Gun Owners in their Homes by Kyle Cassidy ("Every picture in *Armed America* could be a pro-gun advertisement—or an anti-gun poster. That's what makes it so riveting." *Washington Post,* July 29, 2007.)

The Home Security Handbook: Expert Advice for Keeping Safe at Home (and Away) by Lynne Finch (If you are not sure you would carry a firearm outside the home, this is a great book to help examine safety plan inside the home.)

On Combat: The Psychology and Physiology of Deadly Conflict in War and in Peace by Lt. Col. Dave Grossman and Loren Christensen

Deadly Force—Understanding Your Right to Self Defense by Massad Ayoob and Jeff Weiner

Concealed carry information:

Taking Your First Shot: A Woman's Introduction to Defensive Shooting and Personal Safety by Lynne Finch

Female and Armed: A Woman's Guide to Advanced Situational Awareness, Concealed Carry, and Defensive Shooting Techniques by Lynne Finch (You'll see me in this one. Lynne needed instructors to model techniques.)

Living an Armed Life: A Woman's Guide to Adapting Her Carry to Her Changing Life by Lynne Finch (This has great information for concealed carry for those with movement challenges, while in a wheelchair, on crutches, and with a cane.)

7. Essential Oils for Protection

Blackthorn's Botanical Magic by Amy Blackthorn

Aromatherapy Anointing Oils by Joni Keim Loughran

Mixing Essential Oils for Magic by Sandra Kynes

8. Incense Recipes for Protection

Sacred Smoke by Amy Blackthorn (This guide helps you create your own cleansing smoke practice without the need to appropriate someone else's culture and beliefs.)

The Complete Incense Book by Susanne Fischer-Rizzi

Incense: Crafting and Use of Magical Scents by Carl F. Neal

9. Tarot Spells for Protection

365 Tarot Spells by Sasha Graham

Tarot Spells by Janina Renée

Madame Pamita's Magical Tarot by Madame Pamita

Additional Resources

Blackthorn's Botanical Brews by Amy Blackthorn

WitchCraft Cocktails by Julia Halina Hadas

Bibliography

Adams, Douglas. *The Hitchhiker's Guide to the Galaxy.* New York, NY: Del Rey, 2021.

Auryn, Mat. *Psychic Witch.* St. Paul, MN: Llewellyn, 2020.

Blackthorn, Amy. *Blackthorn's Botanical Brews: Herbal Potions, Magical Teas, and Spirited Libations.* Newburyport, MA: Weiser Books, 2020.

Blackthorn, Amy. *Blackthorn's Botanical Magic.* Newburyport, MA: Weiser Books, 2018.

Blackthorn, Amy. *Sacred Smoke: Clear Away Negative Energies and Purify Body, Mind, and Spirit.* Newburyport, MA: Weiser Books, 2019.

Cartwright, Mark. *World History Encyclopedia.* Accessed March 1, 2021. *ancient.eu*

Hall, Judy. *The Crystal Bible.* Cincinnati, OH: Walking Stick Press, 2003.

Cooper, Jeff. Quotes. BrainyQuote. BrainyMedia Inc. Accessed January 25, 2021. *www.brainyquote.com*

Melody. *Love Is in the Earth: A Kaleidoscope of Crystals: The Reference Book Describing the Metaphysical Properties of the Mineral Kingdom.* Earth-Love, 1995.

Moning, Karen Marie. *Shadowfever.* New York, NY: Delacorte Press, 2010.

Morrison, Dorothy. *Bud, Blossom, and Leaf: The Magical Herb Gardener's Handbook.* St. Paul, MN: Llewellyn Publications, 2004.

Neuharth, Dan. "15 Ways Being Raised by a Narcissist Can Affect You." *Psychology Today.* Sussex Publishers, March 23, 2020. *www.psychologytoday.com.*

Raab, D. "What Is Spiritual Bypassing?" *Psychology Today,* January 23, 2019. Retrieved January 15, 2021, from *www.psychologytoday.com.*

"Salvia Rosmarinus." Royal Botanic Gardens Kew: Plants of the World Online. Accessed March 25, 2021. *www.plantsoftheworldonline.org/.*

Walker, Pete. *Complex PTSD: from Surviving to Thriving: A Guide and Map for Recovering from Childhood Trauma.* Lafayette, CA: Azure Coyote, 2013.

Zimbardo, Philip G., Robert L. Johnson, and Vivian McCann. *Psychology: Core Concepts.* New York: Pearson, 2017.

About the Author

A professional intuitive, Amy Blackthorn is the author of *Blackthorn's Botanical Magic, Sacred Smoke,* and *Blackthorn's Botanical Brews.* She has taught self-defense classes since attaining the rank of black belt in 2002 and has been a certified firearms instructor since 2010. Her broad background in executive protection has allowed her to travel extensively and train with some of the best instructors and companies operating today. The founder of Blackthorn's Botanicals, Amy also has a certification in aromatherapy and was ordained by the Order of the Golden Gryphon. She lives in Delaware. Keep up with Amy's book news at *amyblackthorn.com,* view her tea shop at *BlackthornsBotanicals.com,* and follow her on Instagram @amyblackthornauthor.

To Our Readers

Weiser Books, an imprint of Red Wheel/Weiser, publishes books across the entire spectrum of occult, esoteric, speculative, and New Age subjects. Our mission is to publish quality books that will make a difference in people's lives without advocating any one particular path or field of study. We value the integrity, originality, and depth of knowledge of our authors.

Our readers are our most important resource, and we appreciate your input, suggestions, and ideas about what you would like to see published.

Visit our website at *www.redwheelweiser.com*, where you can learn about our upcoming books and free downloads, and also find links to sign up for our newsletter and exclusive offers.

You can also contact us at *info@rwwbooks.com* or at

Red Wheel/Weiser, LLC
65 Parker Street, Suite 7
Newburyport, MA 01950

CPSIA information can be obtained
at www.ICGtesting.com
Printed in the USA
JSHW012318011222
34212JS00002B/2

9 781628 974522

Praise for Harry Mathews

"A brilliant and unsettling book. . . . Mathews weaves into each of his several story-threads more unexpected twists than you'll find in the average multi-volume Victorian novel."

—Tom Clark, *LA Times Book Review*

"*Cigarettes* has the delicate yet rigorous architecture of latticework: if we concentrate on the light streaming through its apertures we are still attentive to its carpentry; if we focus on its geometry the light is, of needs, a constant presence. It is a triumph of the imagination."

—Gilbert Sorrentino

"In *Cigarettes*, Mathews takes us more interestingly than ever into that unfinished work of art, the self, exposing powerful dependencies and subtleties in a cast of characters distinct and poised yet half-goping toward others and themselves. The plot, the tale, the laying bare, are intriguingly staged and timed in a novel as imaginative as it is disturbing."

—Joseph McElroy

"Mathews has perfected a witty, supple, and aphoristic style, capable of many effects. . . . An odd and gratifying novel."

—*New York Review of Books*

"There is a relentless quality of incident, but Mathews runs the whole sequence without a hiccough of implausibility or forced conjunction."

—*Times Literary Supplement*

"A brainteasing game that is both absorbing and exhilarating. . . . As a stylist, Mathews manages to tinge familiar objects and places, such as New York, with a delectable strangeness."

—*Publishers Weekly*

"Like a clever gamester, Mathews teases the reader with plot twists and jokes as he subtly but seriously examines the nature of perception."

—*Booklist*

Other Books by Harry Mathews

FICTION

The Conversions
Tlooth
Country Cooking and Other Stories
The Sinking of the Odradek Stadium
The American Experience
Singular Pleasures
The Journalist

POETRY

The Ring
The Planisphere
Trial Impressions
Le Savior des rois
Armenian Papers: Poems 1954-1984
Out of Bounds
A Mid-Season Sky: Poems 1954-1991

MISCELLANIES

Selected Declarations of Dependence
The Way Home
Ecrits Français

NONFICTION AND CRITICISM

The Orchard
20 Lines a Day
Immeasurable Distances: The Collected Essays
Giandomenico Tiepolo

Harry Mathews

CIGARETTES

DALKEY ARCHIVE PRESS
Dallas / Dublin

Library of Congress Cataloging-in-Publication Data:

Mathews, Harry, 1930-
Cigarettes : a novel / by Harry Mathews. — 1st Dalkey Archive ed.
   p. cm.
   ISBN 1-56478-203-4 (pbk. : alk. paper)
   1. Interpersonal relations— New York (State)— New York— Fiction.
   2. City and town life— New York (State)— New York— Fiction.
   I. Title.
   P S3563.A8359C5   1998
   813'.54— dc21   98-23363
                                                                  CIP

Grateful acknowledgment is made for the following:

Excerpt from *Two Serious Ladies* by Jane Bowles. Copyright © 1966 by
Jane Bowles. Reprinted by permission of Farrar, Straus & Giroux, Inc.

Excerpt from *Parade's End* by Ford Madox Ford. Copyright © 1950
by Alfred A. Knopf, Inc. Copyright renewed 1978. Reprinted by
permission of the publisher.

Excerpt from *The Big Sleep* by Raymond Chandler. Copyright © 1939
by Raymond Chandler. Copyright renewed 1967 by Mrs. Helga Greene.
Reprinted by permission of Alfred A. Knopf, Inc.

I'VE NEVER BEEN IN LOVE BEFORE by Frank Loesser from
"Guys and Dolls." Copyright © 1950 by Frank Music Corp. Copyright
renewed 1978 by Frank Music Corp. International Copyright Secured.
All Rights Reserved. Used by permission.

TAKE HIM by Richard & Lorenz Hart. Copyright © 1951, 1952 by
Chappell & Co., Inc. Copyright renewed. International Copyright
Secured. All Rights Reserved. Used by Permission.

Dallas / Dublin
www.dalkeyarchive.com
Printed on durable/acid-free paper in the United States

In Memory of Georges Perec

Contents

"Let me tell you a story on the subject," said the Linnet.

"Is the story about me?" asked the Water-rat. "If so, I will listen to it, for I am extremely fond of fiction."

—Oscar Wilde, "The Devoted Friend"

Cigarettes

Allan and Elizabeth

JULY 1963

"WHAT'S HE MEAN, 'I suppose you want an explanation'? He doesn't explain anything."

The gabled house loomed over us like a buzzard stuffed in mid flight. People were still arriving. Through the lilac hedge came the rustle of gravel smoothly compressed, and swinging streaks of light that flashed beyond us along a pale bank of Japanese dogwood, where a man in a white dinner jacket stood inspecting Allan's letter with a penlight.

He passed the letter around. When it was my turn I read, in another revolution of headlights, ". . . the state I was in—barely seeing you when they were taking me away . . . Darkness, blinding light . . . I couldn't manage a squeak." I too was confused. Even dazzled by Elizabeth, could this be Allan?

I wanted to understand. I planned someday to write a book about these people. I wanted the whole story.

After an absence of many years Elizabeth that day had come back to town. A little after midnight she went to the "casino," as the last private gambling club was called. Allan was leaving. Having drunk too much and started a noisy argument, he was being politely bounced. He passed Elizabeth in the glare of the

lobby. At the door he was told, "Next time, Mr. Ludlam, please keep it down. And watch yourself on the road."

"Thank you. Who *is* she?"

"Beats me."

Outside, the night was hot and starry. Allan started driving home, stopping on the way at the Spa City Diner. Maud would have long been asleep.

He had two cups of coffee, chatting with late-night customers. He wished he could visualize Elizabeth exactly. (He remembered the sparse whiteness of her clothes, the flurry of her red-gold hair.) He knew she had seen him; her ready acceptance of him in those circumstances made him wince.

Allan had cleverness, if not wisdom, and he prized it. He held the world and himself in contempt. Recently he had shown kindness to me when few others had. My best friend had died, and gossips had cruelly blamed me for it. "You're lucky," Allan told me, "learning young what bastards people are. 'People,'" he added, "includes me." He meant that befriending me made him no better than the others, only smarter. He mistrusted his own decency.

On his way home, passing the Adelphi, he saw a red-haired figure in white crossing the faintly lighted porch. He braked. Perhaps a minute passed while he recollected that he was a local worthy, that he had already demeaned himself, that he was still drunk. He parked his car and went into the hotel. On night duty he found Wally, who had known him for thirty years. Allan asked if it was too late for a nightcap. Wally said, hold the fort, he wouldn't be a minute.

The lobby looked empty. Allan stepped behind the front desk to examine in the open register the arrivals on this first day of July. He stopped at a familiar name: Elizabeth H., the woman in the portrait Maud had just bought. He had met her once or twice, long ago. She might have been the one at the casino. Perhaps he had unconsciously recognized her—that

would explain her effect on him. Hearing Wally returning, he noted her room number.

After a minute spent sipping his highball, Allan said he was going to the john. Out of sight, he entered the honeyed glow of the carpeted stair. On the third floor he turned right. He had no plans.

Behind one wall a pipe produced a spasmodic whine. Unless, Allan thought, a chipmunk was trapped in the old timbers; the sound struck him as animal. He counted door numbers until he reached Elizabeth's.

The whine was coming through that door. He pressed his ear to the wood. The voice was not a chipmunk's. Allan dropped to one knee and set his eye to the keyhole: Yale. The edges of the door lay snug in their jambs.

The high voice sang waveringly on, needling Allan like a stuck car horn. He tried the doors of the adjacent rooms. The one on the right opened, and he entered a dark bedroom where light from the street revealed an empty bed. Crossing the room, Allan raised the window and leaned out. A ledge a foot wide ran across the building at floor level. From the window at his left faint light was shining. Gripping the window frame, Allan lowered both feet onto the ledge and slid along it. Reaching the light, he was confronted by backlighted blue shepherdesses strutting in a monotony of willows. The curtains allowed his sight no chink. Again he heard the voice sustaining its reedy cantillation. In the lobby, when the woman had looked at him and then looked away, from the unbuttoned top of her dress one unhaltered breast had slipped and been tucked back smoothly into place. He had conceived her nakedness under the white cotton and the cinched broad belt buckled with golden snakes.

He looked down at the street—anyone there could see him—and began retracing his path. Downstairs, Wally waved him out into the fervent night. Allan was so astonished that

if Maud had woken up when he came home, he might have told her everything that he had done.

In his letter, Allan wrote Elizabeth, "I kept wondering, was it really your room? Your voice? Who was with you? What exactly was he or she or they doing to you? I didn't want answers—I wanted *you*. I felt *deprived*."

Finding Elizabeth took him a week. He had many friends in that little town: some of them said they knew her; one of them had been asked to a party where she was expected. Allan went too.

The party was being given at a large house on Clinton Street, near the edge of town. Allan pointed out the woman from the casino across the lawn, and his friend confirmed his hunch: she was Elizabeth. Allan peremptorily declined to be introduced to her. Twenty minutes later he regretted his refusal. He had hoped to catch Elizabeth's attention; she had not even looked at him. He derided himself as foolish and incompetent. Two waterless drinks aggravated his helplessness.

Turning away from the crowded bar, where he had gone for a third helping, Allan found Elizabeth waiting behind him. He looked into her eyes as hard as he could. She did not recognize him. He was comforted that she hadn't remembered his disgrace, discouraged at having made no impression on her. He hoped, absurdly, that she would see at once that she already obsessed him. She smiled: "You look lost."

"I was. You're the reason I'm here." He had lost all assurance, so that what might have sounded impudent rang true.

Elizabeth slipped her arm into his. "Tell me what's up."

They moved out of the crowd. Hardly knowing what to say, he confessed his expulsion from the casino and his having seen her there, in some disarray. Elizabeth laughed: "At least *you* noticed." Allan's embarrassment attracted her more than the usual urbanities. "And now?"

Allan thought of the voice in the hotel and blushed again.

"How about dinner? At the casino? You'll put me back in good standing."

"OK. But if we play, you'll have to stake me. I've got barely enough for bed and breakfast."

At the casino, after reserving a table, Allan bought five hundred dollars' worth of chips and gave half to Elizabeth, for which she kissed him on the cheek. They agreed on roulette.

Leaning over the seated players, Elizabeth bet all her chips on the first turn: a hundred and fifty dollars on black, the rest on 17. "Pure superstition," she told Allan. "It *never* comes up."

Quinze, impair, noir, et manque were announced. ("Close, at least," remarked Elizabeth.) A man yielded his seat. The croupier slid a hundred and fifty dollars towards her, neatly stacked.

Allan sat down across the table. He felt mildly irritated. He decided to ignore Elizabeth's play and concentrate on his own. Before betting, he kibbitzed a list of recent turns from a neighbor and watched six more himself. Allan liked roulette. It tested his self-control: he made himself bet at foreordained intervals and on numbers he had chosen statistically. He scored early that evening with a 6 *en plein* that put him ahead two hundred dollars. (He glanced at Elizabeth's chips: worth a thousand at least.)

He won another two hundred during the next half hour. He had more than doubled his stake, and their table was waiting: time to quit. An old man was sitting in Elizabeth's seat.

"Nice going."

As he turned, his nose grazed her breasts. "And you?"

"It was extremely exciting—close to two thou at one point. Shit!" She pointed to the wheel, where the white pellet was cruising in 17.

Allan's irritation returned. He was irritated with himself. He knew that Elizabeth would have played no differently with her own money; and she had cost him nothing, since he had

made good her loss with his winnings. She was looking at him without remorse, almost with contentment. She did not care whether she lost or won, and that made him jealous. He hated losing. He could not help thinking of Maud. Elizabeth was beginning to frighten him.

She told him later, after slapping him hard in the face, "You bastard, stop holding back!" One of her legs was hooked behind his knees, the other encircled his hips.

In love, too, Allan exercised self-control. He took care to please first. Elizabeth preferred abandon—no "mine" or "yours," certainly no yours and then mine. For Allan, a woman's pleasure guaranteed his own. It was money in the bank.

Elizabeth nailed him: "I love the things you do to me, but let's not spend all night paying our dues. It's *you* I want." He started to explain. She laughed: "Look, I like being irresistible, too. Stop running things."

He agreed to try. Trying only discouraged him more and shriveled his purpose. Elizabeth understood how he felt. She began playing with him as with a child. In a while he somewhat forgot his predicament; and then when he too was playing she slapped him again, just hard enough to toughen his desire with sportive vindictiveness. He let go, and kept letting go, and as he did so, a high, eerie, familiar wail filled his head. He forgot himself, he forgot everything, except for one off-stage, insidious question: Who's listening tonight?

The next day he wrote her a letter: "I suppose you want an explanation. . . ." He must by then have known that Elizabeth wasn't interested in explanations; he must have known that he had nothing to explain. He had urgently wanted to write her, and he had yielded to his impulse without realizing that it sprang from something he hadn't told her and wished he had—that he was married to Maud. He still did not mention Maud in his letter. He told himself that a woman like Elizabeth wouldn't care.

Elizabeth had learned about Maud with no help from Allan. When he next saw her, she had changed. She had become more interested in him, less so in "them." She had accepted her role as a married man's lover.

They met late in the afternoon, two days after their first encounter. When Allan acknowledged Maud's existence, Elizabeth insisted he talk about her. Once again he found himself baffled. He berated himself for not admitting his marriage at once. At their first meeting he had immediately suppressed the urge—what was he to say, "You're the reason I'm here, and I'm happily married"? At supper he had been afraid of displaying his desire. He felt that warning Elizabeth about Maud would seem as obvious as taking off his pants; and after that it was too late.

In twenty-six years of marriage Allan had sometimes been drawn to other women. He had never before loved two women at the same time. He now felt compelled to keep them separate. Telling Elizabeth about Maud, like the thought of telling Maud about Elizabeth, made him afraid of losing one or even both of them. Even in his private thoughts, pretending he had two unconnected lives felt safer. (He was unexpectedly troubled by the portrait Maud had bought: a painted "Elizabeth," chosen and paid for by his wife, was waiting to be hung on a wall in his house. Although Allan earned, as they say, "real money," he had always respected Maud's, augustly self-replenishing, as the guarantor of their position. He did not love Maud for her money; he had also never known her without it.)

He struggled with his novel passion. He could not understand Elizabeth's many kindnesses at their second meeting. She struck him as all too obliging—eager for details about Maud, fussing over a present ("My favorite demisemiprecious stone!"), agreeing to meet him whenever he could get free. Her docility suggested, illogically and inescapably, that he no longer mattered to her. If he had, she would have made more

of a fuss. Had his silence concerning Maud brought this about?
He must have disappointed her in other ways, too. When he
asked her, she swore he hadn't.

They met several times during the rest of that week. To
Allan's amazement, Maud made it easy for them. His stay-at-
home wife started partying every day. Once he knew Maud's
exact plans, he would notify Elizabeth and, later, drive to her
hotel.

Sexual vacations begun in dalliance may become exhausting
exercises in self-discovery or evasion. Allan had fallen in love,
and hardly knew it, and labored vehemently to control what
he refused to admit. Elizabeth did her best. Touched by his
confusion, she wished he could like himself a little better, and
she let her own liking for him express itself openly and attentively. Her compassion only put her further out of reach. Allan
felt she was turning him into a fool. He had lost his script.

He had hoped that Elizabeth would fall desperately in love
with him. That might restore his worth. He could then anticipate the pain of letting her go.

Allan consoled himself with their pleasure—hers, his—and
resorted to it with growing fury. He grew pale beneath his tan.
Elizabeth began to look at him with maternal concern.

A week passed. Their fifth meeting left him more disheartened than ever. He had gone to Elizabeth in unusually good
humor. He had pleased himself by writing an effusive letter
of thanks to a man who had helped him. He had reassured
himself with propitiatory acts—changing into a striped mauve
shirt she admired, going to the barber's, drinking only water
at lunchtime.

He had hoped that when he entered her room she would
fall into his arms. Instead, she gave him the quickest of kisses
and a glance, not unkind, implying that men never looked
more ridiculous than fresh from a barbershop. She sat him
down on the couch to watch television: the sixth at Belmont.

She followed the race like a child at a circus, with the kind of look he yearned to kindle in her eyes. At the finish she shrieked.

"You see," she explained, "he's a friend."

"The owner?"

"The horse." His name was Capital something. "I'm thirsty for gin-and-tonics."

They drank awhile, until Elizabeth at last embraced him. They undressed, bit by bit, caressingly; finally Allan went into her like a fist. She shrieked again, she started laughing, wrestling him like a happy ten-year-old grappling with a roommate. She pulled his hair and called him Capital something. She did nothing to conceal her happiness. He watched himself giving in, and gave in. Once again she was proving too good for him. More than good: the thing itself. Stratagem and skill would never get the better of her. She had nothing to lose. He lay under her feeling plundered.

She coddled him and kissed his mouth. He turned his head aside: "You don't know what I've been going through."

"I guess not. I've been having too much fun."

"You don't really care who I am . . ."

"Let me think. This is Sunday, you must be—"

"You never even call me by my own name." The words shamed him. A nervous weariness was seeping through his body. Elizabeth looked down at him, perplexed. She felt motherly again—a step away from passion, as he might have noticed if he'd stayed awake.

They decided to take the next day off. Allan pleaded business; Elizabeth accepted his suggestion with an inward smile. She told him she would go riding at ten. He could reach her later if he wanted. She hugged him goodbye: "Goodbye, Allan—sweet Allan."

Allan hadn't lied. He had an appointment the following morning, with a man whose trade was horses. They had a

tricky deal to conclude, one that Allan expected would keep him late; but he was driving home before noon. Approaching his driveway, he stopped at the sight of a horse on the lawn, tethered to a birch tree and cropping the grass. He parked on the road and skirted the grounds to the back door of his house.

He let himself quietly into the pantry. From the front rooms came familiar voices: Maud's and Elizabeth's. Allan took off his shoes and tiptoed up the back stairs to his bedroom, where the voices did not carry. He thought: I'd better get this job finished. He picked up the phone to call the city. Through the dial tone he heard Maud speaking, her voice far away, then abruptly stilled. Someone else was using that particular downstairs extension.

He heard no click of a handset being replaced. Dialing his number, Allan said "I love you" into the speaker. His call was promptly answered.

Knowing that Elizabeth was listening, he felt a sickening need for her as he began stating his business. He wanted to be sick in her lap and be forgiven for it. After telling himself, hang up, go downstairs, talk to her, Maud or no Maud, he went on giving instructions.

He carefully repeated his words so that Elizabeth would remember them. He was making an arrangement that would reveal him as unscrupulous, even criminal. He wanted Elizabeth to understand that she did not know him at all, that he was more than the man she thought she knew. She would junk him for good, but with a certain astonishment, a certain respect.

He crept downstairs. The women's voices sounded louder. He listened from the hall:

". . . you still want that milktoast?"

"That's for me to decide!"

"It's him or the portrait. You can't have both!"

Each vehement declaration was followed by a silence as of

mythical personages raising high the boulders with which they would assail one another.

"You're disgusting!"

"It's my portrait, isn't it?"

"*Of* you—hardly yours!"

"Cut the crap, Mrs. Miniver. I need something to show for my week."

Allan gazed across the living hall to the front parlor. He stepped forward, then turned away, realizing how foolish he would look without his shoes. Elizabeth's words made him want to disembowel her, and at the same time want to cry. Through the library door he saw the still-unframed portrait resting against a wall. He remembered how light the painting had seemed for its size. Taking it from the library, he carried it out the back door.

Allan brought the portrait to the city that afternoon and stored it, wrapped in a sheet, in the back of his commuter's apartment. Leaving the house, he had planned to burn the painting; now he was unsure what to do with it. He did not know what to do with himself, either. He could not imagine speaking to Maud. The next morning, however, he felt a new concern for his wife, or at least for her opinion of him.

Allan's deal of the previous day required him to find supplementary insurance for a racehorse. The horse, a competent, veteran gelding, had come up lame after his last race. Because only one stablehand knew of this, the owner planned to subject the horse to a hard workout during which he would almost certainly break down. This would supply the pretext for destroying him. The owner aimed to collect all he could in insurance claims. He had been told that Allan might help.

As a partner in an established firm of insurance brokers, one that dealt chiefly with large businesses, Allan could not be expected to insure one horse. It might seem even less likely that he would help out a fraudulent small-town client. However,

Allan had already involved himself in much greater frauds than this. For years he had periodically swindled the insurance companies he usually represented so well.

He would have found it hard to provide a sensible explanation for this clandestine activity. It had begun in the late summer of 1938, when the hurricane that ravaged the northeastern United States swept through the site of an unfinished, undercapitalized housing project in Rhode Island. Allan was approached by its developers and their contractors with a discreet plea to rescue them from imminent bankruptcy. They suggested that he arrange to have them reimbursed for the damages they would have suffered if they had completed the project, as would have been the case if the construction schedule had been met. Allan realized that proving their claims unfounded would be a hard task for the best of inspectors, given the devastation wreaked by the hurricane in that part of the state. He found himself tempted hardly at all by the ten-percent commission, tempted considerably by outrageous wrongdoing: no one he knew or worked with would dare contemplate such a risk. He accepted it, got away with it, and became—like someone who audaciously tries a cocktail for breakfast and soon finds himself a chronic morning drinker—addicted to professional deceit.

Allan was now being asked to persuade a small insurance company to offer preferential terms to the owner of the doomed racehorse. This was why he had put through his call to the city. He made it clear on the phone that his own commission had been attended to.

The gelding was to be killed that week. Allan knew that in such a small town, with her love of racing and horses, Elizabeth was sure to hear of the event. She would then understand what his phone call had signified. However, he had forgotten about Maud. At the time it had not crossed his mind that in their screaming match Elizabeth might tell Maud what she had

heard. Allan felt confident that after twenty-seven years Maud would not abandon him because of a week's infidelity; but she had no inkling of his other, devious business career, and this sordid affair might disgust her. He couldn't blame her if it did.

Allan also craved to be forgiven. That next morning, he called Maud a little before noon.

"A horse? Just a moment." Maud's voice faded: "Do you know about Allan's insuring a horse?" She spoke again into the phone: "We don't know a thing about it."

"We?"

"Elizabeth and I."

"Elizabeth . . . ?"

"Your Elizabeth."

"She's there?"

"I've invited her to stay." Allan kept silent. Maud added, "Keep in touch. Someday I might invite you to stay, too."

Oliver and Elizabeth

SUMMER 1936

THE TOWN LIES on a low plateau of scarcely relieved flatness; its humid climate swings from fierce cold in winter to fierce heat in summer; yet visitors have been coming here for generations, to "take the waters" of its saline springs, to attend the fashionable August meet, and to observe each other. Though remote, the town has seen even its year-round population grow as its safety and amenity make it more and more attractive to prosperous big-city families. A thriving black community, established years ago by seasonal waiters and stable grooms who decided to settle here, has helped give this small and sheltered place a cosmopolitan air.

Twenty-seven years before Elizabeth's return, the town had been chosen as the seat of a July political convention. One evening early in the month a garden party was given on the grounds of one of the twenty-room "cottages" on North Broadway. More than two hundred guests attended, dressed in pale summer colors, all too much alike for anyone's comfort but their own, clustering in groups as irresistibly as starlings. Among them, one young man stood conspicuously apart and alone. He hadn't come back to the town in twelve summers, since he was ten.

He had enjoyed watching the noisy throng (whom would he meet? like? love?); nevertheless he decided, after a second glass of champagne, that he should either mix or leave. He saw a face he knew—a young woman he had once been introduced to. He went up to her. She looked blank.

"You don't remember me? Sorry—I don't know a single soul . . ."

"Not even me!" she exclaimed. He named their mutual friend. "You're Oliver! I'm Elizabeth Hea—"

"I recognized *you*."

"Terrific. Say, I don't know anybody either, at least that I'd want to. Let's team up and take our pick." Before Oliver could state his doubts, Elizabeth had imprisoned his left arm. "You go first. How about the lady in blue—pretty nifty, wouldn't you say? Not too old for you?"

"Not at all. I like older women." He was a year or two younger than Elizabeth—an abyss to one fresh out of college.

"I *see*—and she's so spry for twenty-six! Excuse me," Elizabeth said to their prey, "this delightful young man whom I've known for ages and can vouch for his adorably low intentions is nuts about you, and shy, so I thought I'd do you both a favor. This"—her hand clenched Oliver's shrinking elbow— "this is Oliver Pruell."

The name briefly drew Maud's gaze: "I thought I remembered all the Pruells . . ." Because Oliver did not seize the opening, Maud turned back to Elizabeth. She made a distracting go-between.

Elizabeth kept Oliver continually off balance, introducing him with statements like "I can't imagine what he sees in you, but he's dying to meet you." He was soon relishing the game: he met two post-debs, the governor's wife, and a hooker of terrifying beauty, while introducing Elizabeth to the judge, author, and athletes of her choice.

He became rapidly obsessed by Elizabeth herself. Meeting

the hooker may have predisposed him. Even then, he continued to think of Elizabeth as "older" and so "too old for him,"
until, as he was leading her towards some outlandish hunk of
a halfback, she nudged him, with complicity more than intimacy: he was standing right behind her, and he felt her but-
tocks press against his thighs, soft and muscular as a tongue.
Caught in midsentence, he could barely play out his part.

Near the end of the evening, Elizabeth was accosted by
a pawy young man impervious to her evasive chatter. Allan,
a little drunk, would forget the incident. Oliver stuck to
Elizabeth's side, not letting the other man's back or elbow evict
him, until he went away. A grateful Elizabeth asked Oliver to
take her home.

She was staying with friends nearby. She didn't suggest
going someplace else, or ask him in, or sit with him on the
veranda. She only kissed him on the cheek, as if to say, I like
you, I trust you. This was not what he was looking for, but he
dreaded being clumsy. She *was* older. He needed an invitation.

On her way in she said, "I'm going to the Meville Baths
tomorrow. Join me? I'll be at the pavilion at a quarter of ten.
Ask for cell number eighteen. It's supposed to be the nicest on
your side." Oliver went home content.

Next morning at Meville Baths, a private venture specializ-
ing in mud (it was dignified as *fango*, in a bow to Battaglia in
the Euganean Hills), guided by a debonair Negro in seersucker
uniform, Oliver found awaiting him in Room 18 a tub of what
looked like steaming shit. He was issued a hooded terry-cloth
robe and a pile of towels, given instruction in mud use, and
left alone. He gazed dubiously into the tub. What good to him
was this last resort of gnarled rheumatics? Having undressed
and draped a towel around his hips, he slumped onto a stool,
raising his eyes longingly to the frosted bluish skylight.

He heard a scrape of metal and, looking around, saw a door
by the bathtub open slightly. A coral-nailed foot slid through

the interstice. The door swung open to reveal Elizabeth. She kept one hand behind her back and with the other held to her throat an unvoluminous towel which, dangling as she stepped into the room, uncovered symmetrical fragments of still-un-muddied, clothesless skin. Because a lady was entering the room, Oliver of course stood up. Elizabeth asked, "Care to tango in the fango?"

Oliver felt his own towel slipping. As he grasped it with both hands, Elizabeth smoothly sidearmed from behind her back a mudball the size of a Hand melon. It caught him fair between the eyes.

He stood there blinded, suffocating, naked. Elizabeth's snicker reached him from a distance. She had withdrawn to her own room. She hadn't closed the door between. Oliver gouged the gunk from his eyes and mouth, scooped copious handfuls from the tub, and strode after her, set on revenge.

Now wrapped in a bathrobe, Elizabeth was standing in her room by the far door. As he advanced, she told him, "Wait," and he obeyed. She then emitted a shriek of heartrending terror. Another shriek followed; he still didn't understand. Someone was running down the corridor. Oliver raised one mud-filled hand. Elizabeth, still wailing, stepped away from the door, which opened to admit a sturdy matron whose apprehensive expression changed rapidly to one of bewilderment and then outrage. Oliver hurriedly turned back towards his own room, only to find that Elizabeth had slipped behind him. Whimpering disconsolately, she now barred his way.

The matron was moving towards the tub. Oliver saw the alarm button dimpling the wall above it. With the cunning of a beast at bay, he kept his mouth shut, slapped a fistful of mud over the button, and bolted out the door and down the corridor of the ladies' section.

Chronometrically his flight lasted twenty seconds. He passed one customer with her attendant; another,

unaccompanied, who did not notice him; and a cleaning woman trundling a cart full of woolly sticks. In imagined time his course approached infinity, and during it he met other figures less palpable and far more real: his father jubilant at having his worst fears justified, his mother chalk-white on the sickbed to which his disgrace had brought her, the foul-mouthed trusty on his chain gang. He experienced terminal revelations about man's fate and the nature of reality. He recognized truth as both absolute and incommunicable, time itself as irreversible and irrelevant. He verged on a mystical understanding of *caritas*.

A racket of flapping feet—his own—recalled his circumstances. He then entertained the clever thought that the women's rooms might all have rooms for men next to them. Doors between bolted only on women's side? Why not? Women, women never molest men, ha ha, only men women. Togetherness possible if OK with girls? Baths big lovenest? He tried the next door: open, room empty. Unbolted party door: open, room empty. Opened door to far corridor—nobody there, all chasing maniac on other side! Lucky Oliver! He cantered back to Room 18, where, shutting himself in, he squatted breathless on his heels.

He'd better keep moving. Wash first. He stepped up to the basin. More luck: from the mirror glared a mud-masked face that might have belonged to Al Jolson, or anyone. He had remained anonymous. His still-gasping mouth was opening in a grin of chiaroscuro dazzle when, from under his raised arms, two sharp-fingered hands began curving around his chest to tweak his nipples. He started to giggle. She made him fuck her in the tub.

Over lunch he asked her: Why not last night?

"Where? Front porch? Back seat? No-luggage hotel? We still," she added, "need a place to go. I think I know where. Doesn't your skin feel *mad?*"

They drove out to the village called Lake George. At first Mrs. Quilty acted hostile. She had long ago worked for Oliver's mother, and she told him, "You're no Mr. Ratchett, you're Oliver Pruell. Master Oliver, what a thing to ask!" Oliver prepared to flee.

Elizabeth said, "All the more reason to help us, Mrs. Quilty. I've never talked about you with Mrs. Pruell, but I'm sure she has nothing but praise, and Frederick Stockton recommended you in glowing terms—"

"It's a difficult time we're living in, that's what I say," Mrs. Quilty interrupted. "Hard saving money, what with the government takes it all in taxes, even keeping the house in repair, you have to start paying city prices to people, and when all is said and done, there's no respect anymore, no respect from the young anymore, no respect at all—someone my age, used to be young men would tip their hats, now you're lucky if they nod." Mrs. Quilty barely paused. "It's eighteen-fifty a week, in advance, if you please."

Elizabeth made Oliver try out the room at once. His qualms were forgotten.

He asked her, "Who's Frederick Stockton?"

"Your father must know him. He had an arrangement with Mrs. Quilty. He also introduced her to other gentlemen. Hence the righteous indignation. She was quite an artist, it seems. That's how she paid for the house. You shouldn't have let her put you down."

"If she ever told my mother—"

"She doesn't give a hoot about your mother. She just knows you do."

"So why did she bother?"

"To show who's on top. You're too vulnerable, sweetie. Listen: you can be the way people want you, or they can be the way you want *them*."

"OK." Oliver pondered: "Even my mother?"

Elizabeth smiled: "I see what you mean. . . . Does she still keep a time clock on you?"

"No. But she thinks a lot about me."

"Sure. She's a mother."

"I never know *what* she's thinking about me anymore. I'd rather have you to come home to."

"You'd like me for a mother?"

"You bet I would."

"Not a chance, baby." She sank three nails into his perineum. "Love you like a mother? Even Mrs. Quilty knows better than that."

Oliver reddened. "Love?" Elizabeth gave him a noisy kiss. She trapped him with her knees and elbows. "Hey!" he complained. "Am I supposed to love you?"

"What do you think's going on?"

"I don't think anything. I don't know. I've been having a terrific time. I love this . . .

Elizabeth let him creep his way to the next question, which he voiced a little high:

"Do you love me?"

Arching her brows preposterously, Elizabeth replied, "Dunno. Been having such a terrific time. . . . Dumbbell." She licked his lips.

Oliver felt towards Elizabeth an enthusiastic curiosity as to what she might do next, and not just in bed.

He had "written" in college; now he wrote her poems. They fell sneakily between the erotic and the obscene. She read each one slowly back to him, making him squirm, asking for more.

At the end of the third week in July, Oliver received a letter from Louisa, the friend who had originally introduced them. She quoted what Elizabeth had written about him: "My Oliver! So elegant, so smart, and what of it? That's what trust funds are for. He has something else that may redeem the greed of his forebears and the repulsive expense of his education: enough

talent to scram. He's just written a sonnet about my derriere that's so good that I swear to (a) get it published and (b) go riding every day to make sure it still means what it says. . . . Reading this, Oliver told himself something like: She thinks, therefore I am.

Elizabeth's comments also dismayed him. Had he no worth except as a writer-to-be? Would he have to scram? Oliver liked his comforts. More immediately, he felt sick at the thought that, if his poems were published, his mother and father might read them—a ridiculous fear, and a real one.

On an afternoon in mid-August Elizabeth suggested they go fishing on Lake Luzerne.

"I hate fishing."

"At least you'll find out what might have been." He had an inkling of what she meant: his father cajoling a trout fly through forbidding foliage.

"What are we fishing for?" he asked as he pushed off their skiff.

"Who knows. Middlemouth bass?"

They took turns rowing. Twice Oliver pulled up a round-eyed, rough-scaled perch, which smacked the metal bucket for a while. In the middle of the lake Elizabeth racked the oars.

The afternoon was gray and placid. They lay in the bottom of the boat. Oliver rested his head against the cushioned plank at the stern, Elizabeth tucked herself against his side, a cheek in the crook of his shoulder, one hand inside his open shirt. The water slapped the slowly turning boat with varying briskness.

He watched the boat's slow gyrations, the little waves accumulating to slap it gently. Over the lake from reed-lined shores came a mulchy scent. Water and hills wavered in diffuse gray light. It was as if life had ended and he were dreaming a recollection. He could not tell what he was feeling. His feelings had turned into repetitions of waves and of the grayness that almost did not change, under the bright low sky.

He let the boat drift. He had no place to go. He did not think, except as part of the dreaming. Everything that had ever happened was only seeming, a seeming of having been dreamed, not mattering, without matter. The boat rocked sleepily, turning this way and that, providing his feelings, his thoughts, their objects. For one moment quickly gone he tried to say what was happening to him (maybe Hegel, maybe Heine; they didn't matter either). He had nothing to grasp. He was surrounded entirely by the dream of his being. He was surrounded by nothing. He did not need anything outside himself, outside this dream.

An hour passed. He gazed into the sky. The darkening grayness altered in the west. Above the silhouette of hills glowed low, scalloped reefs of emberish red. "Nothing outside us stays." Thought again subsided into the murk of woods and water, the clouds in their moment of fire and extinction looked to him like his own life being given shape, a hymn of pleasure and melancholy.

To the east the sky had assumed a darker and more soothing complexion: a slope of cool blue, or coal blue, the color that as a child he used to call policeman blue. He thought of the uncle the mention of whose name turned grown-ups silent, in disgrace, having squandered his money and his good marriage with other women. He was living in a suburb of Cleveland with a Mrs. Quilty. Blue, blue, policeman's blue. Oliver looked into the darkness and felt a shudder of power, realizing that his life belonged to him entirely, that there was no one else. He would never know such happiness again. When Elizabeth woke up, night had fallen.

Oliver's parents came back from Europe. He divided his time agreeably between Elizabeth and the family house.

On the morning of the last Wednesday in August, Elizabeth took Oliver to the track, leading him through the stable area to a particular stall, where a handsome bay stallion glared out at them.

"Assured, by Sure Thing out of Little Acorn. And look." Elizabeth pointed to the local listings in the *Morning Telegraph:* Assured had been entered in a thousand-dollar claiming race that afternoon. "They must be nuts. We can't not buy him. It's the best bargain since Louisiana." She wasn't kidding.

Oliver began arguing with her: something was wrong with the animal, where would they find a thousand dollars, what would they do with a racehorse? Elizabeth: she'd seen Assured work two days earlier, they'd raid his piggy bank, they'd buy another horse so it wouldn't be lonely. "You're right about one thing, though. It is fishy. Let's ask your father."

Mr. Pruell was a member of the Association, which at that time ran the track. Since Oliver's adolescence he had become a mystery to his son, who hoped he would remain one as long as possible. Oliver had a plan, kept secret even from himself: he would become so triumphantly successful that Mr. Pruell's dragonlike nature would be disarmed before he could unleash it. The summer had fostered Oliver's confidence. Elizabeth had authenticated him. She now threatened to mix up parts of his life that had remained comfortably distinct.

He implored her not to consult his father. Elizabeth knew he had no reason to worry and told him so. He refused to accompany her. This childish stubbornness offended her.

Elizabeth saw, perhaps too easily, that Mr. Pruell liked her and loved his son. She phoned him, he invited her for noon-time cocktails and listened to her story.

"He can't really be claimed, you see—it's just a race to keep him fit. All the same, I'll check." He called up the owner, then told her, "Yup. The genteel fix is in. You understand—we all know each other here, and in cases like this, it's hands off. You'll have to look for another horse."

"Another dream gone! Mr. Pruell, this morning in the cafeteria, over at the track, I heard a man talking about Assured—that's how I knew he was running. I don't think he's heard about your arrangement."

Mr. Pruell made several more calls, the last one advising Assured's owner to scratch him. "Good girl. There's some fellow from out of town—Jersey, I hear—"

"Me too."

"Not Jersey *City*, surely? I should have been told. You deserve the Juliette Low medal," Mr. Pruell fondly added. "Now, you stay for lunch, and I'll take you to the track—the owner wants to thank you in person. Where's my little boy?"

Oliver went to bars. "How's Elizabeth?" he was asked. No one in town had ever seen him without her. He skipped lunch. He arrived at the track before two and stood in the infield with rented binoculars. He soon spotted her in the clubhouse with his father and some other men. One of them, lanky and young, stuck close to Elizabeth, staring at her, talking to her whenever he could. Elizabeth did not notice Oliver. Assured did not run. He went to Mrs. Quilty's: no message.

That evening Oliver drove out to Riley's Lake House, where a good band was playing. He stopped at the bar. A group of young people came in, some of whom he knew. He took a seat at their table, next to the lanky man he had seen at the track. Oliver began talking to him. His name was Walter Trale. How did he like it here? He had come here to work. To work—at his age? Yes, he was already earning his living, as an animal painter. Oliver said he liked the way animals looked unpainted. Walter laughed and explained that he did portraits of favorite animals. He had just painted Assured. He had made thousands of dollars since he was fifteen. He would go to college anyway, starting next month—gee, next week. "Unless I drop everything."

At this, Oliver felt delectable foreboding. He leaned invitingly towards his companion. Walter confided, "There are moments, you know, when the doors fly open—no, you see there aren't any doors at all."

"Holy smoke, Walter. Tell me more."

"Once I fell in love with a circus elephant."

"Walter, you can't expect me to believe that."

"You know how kids get crushes, don't you? I was eight. I wanted a picture of him, so my mother took some snapshots. He came out looking like a bag of fog."

"Mmm."

"One night I had a dream about my elephant. It was as if he was on a screen, but he didn't look like a bag of fog, he was all there. So next morning I drew him the way he looked in my dream. I had my love souvenir, and in one night I'd learned how to draw animals. They say it's natural talent, but the only natural thing is I was crazy about that elephant."

"You know, I wouldn't tell that story to everybody you happen to meet."

"I just love animals—I've loved all kinds of animals since then. The funny part is that I could never draw people."

"Why? Don't you love people?"

"I never felt as though I didn't. Still, you can imagine, getting so much attention and money, spending all this time with these rich old guys and their wives—I wondered, am I some kind of fruitcake? So today I met this person."

"You mean, a *woman?*"

"It wasn't so much that she was beautiful, it was the way she moved. Her fingers and knees moved the same way her face did, or maybe it's the other way around. You understand what I mean?"

"Boy, do I!"

"I couldn't take my eyes off her. She could see I was going crazy looking at her—" Walter broke off. Oliver asked him what had happened next. "She was really nice. She's coming to pose for me tomorrow. I can't believe it."

Oliver could. He was starting to say, "Well, I have to take a shit something awful," when the band boomed into "Stompin' at the Savoy." They gestured goodbye in the din.

Oliver went back to Mrs. Quilty's. No messages. He sat in their room. He hadn't called either; but he was the one who had been left out. Events had taken place where his presence

had not been missed. Elizabeth and his father, Elizabeth and
Walter (her business, of course)—Elizabeth had revealed herself as a kind of person he hadn't suspected: a right bitch.

Unfair? Had she treated *him* fairly? His weeks with her had
exhausted him. She had demanded so much. She kept wanting
him to change. Like buying a horse. She was insane to think
he could write.

She had given him a wonderful vacation. Now vacation
time was ending. Next week came Labor Day, when he must
go back to the city and find a job. But why not get the jump
on everybody and do it now?

He was discouraged at the prospect of staying alone in the
city, until he realized he could call his friend Louisa. He could
then be the first to explain what had happened. She must
know other girls.

Oliver left a letter for Elizabeth with Mrs. Quilty. In it he
blamed himself for the day's events, although he did mention
"others you have met." He said he was not surprised that she
was leaving him. "While I benefited from being your lover, I
don't think I benefited you, because my character is entirely
inadequate. I'd never be able to keep up with you . . ." He
should have written "down with you"—Elizabeth had pulled
him earthwards. Oliver resembled a balloonist, unable to steer,
able only to rise or sink, and now he went up, up—firing the
air in his mind until he floated once again among comforting
coal-blue pinnacles.

He left the next day. Elizabeth never answered his letter. In
December he received the latest issue of *The Presidio Papers*, a
little review published in San Francisco, containing three of his
poems. Such a magazine, he told himself, would never come
into his parents' hands. He was wrong. When his father died,
years later, Oliver discovered that throughout his life he had
collected erotica old and new. He found *The Presidio Papers*
in his collection.

Oliver and Pauline

SUMMER 1938

TWO YEARS LATER, after graduating from college, Pauline Dunlap came to stay with Maud Ludlam, her sister, and Allan, the husband Maud had taken the summer before. Maud, who was six years older than Pauline, had acted as a kind of foster mother to her ever since their father had become a widower.

Their father had died that March, leaving his entire estate to his daughters. The orphaned sisters learned, in the weeks following his death, that the conditions of their inheritance were known only to themselves and their father's lawyers. No one else seemed aware that Mr. Dunlap had amassed a great deal less than the many millions attributed to him, or that, as a believer in primogeniture, he had bequeathed nine-tenths of his fortune to his elder daughter. Since Maud was now married, the sisters decided to keep these facts to themselves: Pauline might benefit from appearing as a conspicuous heiress.

Oliver, who had known Pauline in boyhood, rediscovered her early that summer. He had come up on vacation from the city, where he now worked in his father's office. Both he and Pauline knew at once who the other "was" (a Pruell, a Dunlap), they enjoyed meeting once again, and when, later, during the party that had reunited them, a thunderstorm caught them

29

out of doors together, a complicity emerged. They had taken
refuge under an immense copper beech when lightning trans-
sected the night and revealed Pauline picking her nose. Oliver
couldn't pretend he hadn't noticed: "So that's how you spend
your free time."

Pauline waited for the thunder to rumble away. "I couldn't
wait. It *is* a basic pleasure."

The shower ended. They walked back to the lighted house.
Merely sprinkled, Pauline's elegance had not been impaired.
Had Mainbocher or perhaps Rochas, Oliver wondered, clothed
that well-turned young body? She wore a dime-size yellow diamond on one hand, chunky green stones around a wrist; and
at her throat, hung from a velvet band, a sumptuous tear of
a pearl lay pink against her skin. Even after the rain, her hair
kept the neatness of its image in rotogravure, combed sleekly
back from her rounded forehead, the snug curls behind her
ears starred with real, unwilted cornflowers. Eyes pure white
and blue looked at Oliver with moist glitter as she implored,
"You won't tell?"

"Never—provided you have supper with me tomorrow.
Otherwise . . ." Oh, tomorrow was impossible. But not the
evening after.

They dined. He liked her enough to take her out again.
He liked her because she trusted him so readily. She liked
him because he was easy to trust. He had a hold on himself,
the know-how of someone who has not just been to schools.

She less liked his stopping at the politer kind of caress.
Oliver could not have said what inspired his punctilious reticence. He simply felt that he could not take advantage of such
candor. His decorum may have expressed a fear of seducing
someone rich: among other things, "trust" meant taking good
care of people's money.

At one roadhouse supper he watched her nimbly shatter-
ing a lamb chop with the stainless-steel chopsticks she always
carried. Her one-handed performance undermined the known

laws of physics. Oliver asked, "How do you manage? You're better than any Chink."

"Oh, don't use that word! Did you see the newsreels? Families bombed out of house and home! I *long* to go there, to do *something*. They need help so badly."

"Are you being serious?"

"As far as I can tell."

"Then go. Join the Red Cross. Volunteer with the Quakers."

"Oh, no. I have to see for myself. *I* want to be the one who decides what to do."

"You can still go there—"

"I can't afford it."

"You're *not* serious, you see? You could hock half your jewels and rebuild Nanking."

"They're not mine. Not yet," she quickly added. Leaning forward, she momentously confided, "Not only do I pick my nose, I'm on an allowance till I'm twenty-five."

"And by then your charge accounts will be surging through five figures. . . ."

"Oh, Maud buys me my clothes. But not China." She ate some more chop. In a most endearing way, she looked through his eyes, right into him: "Why won't you sleep with me? Is it me or is it you? Should I try Tabu? Lifebuoy?"

He hesitated: "It will be your first time out, won't it?"

"I'd start with the second if I could."

"You're as svelte as the *V* in Veedol, but—"

"Don't tell me! Just, please, give it sometime your most earnest consideration." He promised to do that. Pauline continued, "Maud's a dream, but of course I'd love a little independence—you know, my own dough?" She added, "What's the fun of owning a horse if you can't pay for its oats?"

He explored legal possibilities with her, none of them very promising. "Try Lady Luck."

"Oh, I love to gamble. But how? The market's dead as a doormouse. Anyway, you still need capital to get started."

"You like horses—"

"Don't tempt me! My roommate did work out a terrific technique for betting."

"See? Your worries are over."

Oliver was joking; not Pauline. For the next week she was inaccessible before sundown. She spent her days in the Association library, which kept a complete set of the *Morning Telegraph*. She used the paper's charts to verify and improve her roommate's system.

The system decreed that, to be playable, a horse must have won its last start over a distance no shorter than that of its forthcoming race. To this requirement Pauline added certain strict indicators of the jockey's form. According to her research, when jockey and horse satisfied her conditions, which she cleverly reduced to three algebraic equations, she could pick a winner every third race.

Her method had one disadvantage. It eliminated so many entries that she could only bet on one race in twenty, and when she turned from theory to practice, a week at the local track gave her two chances at best to venture her five dollars. She lost once, and won once, at nine to two. While strengthening her confidence, the results also made clear that earning seventeen-fifty a week would not transform her life.

"I think I'll peddle my charms instead," she told Oliver, "something I may do anyway if you don't get off your fanny and into mine."

"Chopsticks, that's *not* your way to talk."

"Wrong nickname, toots. The point is, so far my system's no answer to a virgin's prayer. I suppose I could raise the ante."

"May I point out that Ma Bell and a good book can put every track in the land within your greedy reach? You'd have eighty races a day to pick from instead of eight."

"Terrific, but where does one find a bookmaker?"

"Just ask me."

"You do get around."

"In this town? There's one under every rainspout."

Oliver began taking her bets. Play increased dramatically. Pauline became even more infatuated with the lure of mastering risk, and her system at first worked better than Oliver had expected. But soon she grew impatient again. Her hopes had risen higher, and her rewards had remained slim: hours of calculation and a dozen bets for a profit of seventy dollars. She wanted China.

One day Oliver brought her bad news: their bookmaker had not appeared, and they had missed a winner. As he anticipated, Pauline responded with more fright than anger: "If I can't stick to the rules, I'll be wiped out for certain."

Oliver by now had become irrevocably involved. He did not know why—certainly not to help. (Scarcely a hundred dollars were at stake.) It felt to him more like a kind of seduction, one in which he was playing a spidery, rather feminine role. When he took her money, his skin would prickle electrically, as though he were masterminding a conspiracy.

"You're right," he replied. "You have no reserves, and at this rate you never will. I've got an idea."

"Oh, hurry."

"There's something called a martingale. When you lose, you double your bet, and you go on doubling till you win. Then you recoup all your losses *and* you get paid off on a bigger stake."

"OK. So I bet five dollars and lose, and next time I rebet that five plus another five makes ten"—she had her pad and pencil out—"and I lose and bet five plus the fifteen is twenty—right, doubles every time—and twenty at three to one is sixty instead of fifteen, so: I'm ahead forty-five dollars instead of . . . five? Why have you been hoarding this wisdom?" Before he could answer: "Wait! What if I lose? I'd be out, um, thirty-five instead of fifteen—couldn't that get expensive?"

"You bet the thirty-five with your next five and get it back—eventually you're bound to win. You say you never have runs of more than three or four losses."

"I showed you my tables. I ran into some bad streaks, but they were few and far between."

Oliver knew better. No matter what the game, losing streaks come as surely as nightfall; and sooner or later every gambler discovers the martingale. Oliver watched her charm herself with its promise.

He himself found charm in her growing dependence. He thought of repeating the drama of the unplaced bet in order to replenish her confusion but, instead, simply warned her once or twice that his bookmaker was out of town. "The powers that be always seem to do their being elsewhere," she cried. Her impatience made her the liveliest company. She almost succeeded in unbuttoning his deliberate propriety.

After a week, events of themselves produced a crisis: Pauline had seven straight losses. The last one cost her three hundred and twenty dollars. She dreaded putting up twice that amount, dreaded not betting. Oliver offered to stake her. She refused as vehemently as she could—not vehemently enough, she knew, although not insincerely. Oliver remarked, "You sound as though you'd be doing *me* a favor."

To Pauline, this suggested a way out: "I'll make a deal with you. If I can't pay you back, I'll bequeath you my maidenhead. And you *have* to accept it."

"Pauline, you're a babe in the wood."

"To hell with it. I'll ask Maud."

The prospect of having her in his debt excited Oliver. "I consent. But I insist on choosing the place and time."

"Maybe. I'll give you a week's leeway. While 'cherry-ripe themselves do cry. . . .' The horse is Disrespect. And he's going to win. Then I'll rent a real man, you churl."

This cunning insurance contented Pauline. She found fresh

hope in her future. Disrespect finished out of the money, however, and with the loss her confidence shriveled.

Pauline was overcome with unexpected, unappeasable
shame. Oliver's reassurances left her cold: "Even *if* the money
didn't matter, *I* do. I won't let you let me off. I'm not a silly
little girl."

"I know. We should have opened a joint account, then it
wouldn't have mattered." Oliver did not know what he meant
by this badinage.

In spite of their agreement, Pauline's remorse quenched
any thought of not paying the debt in cash. She decided to
earn the money. Oliver was surprised and not very concerned.
Whether Pauline paid him back or not, he was becoming the
center of her life. Never before had he so dominated anyone.

As for the money, Oliver had little faith in any gambling
system, certainly not in Pauline's. He had laid off none of her
bets; she had had no bookmaker except himself. She owed him
nothing—he was holding six hundred and thirty-five dollars
that belonged to her.

Pauline asked Maud to help her find a job. Maud, unaware
of Oliver's importance in her life, suggested his father, a
good friend who, at this time, was busily reorganizing the
Association, of which he had been elected president. He might
well think of something for her to do.

Disconcerted at first, Pauline quickly convinced herself that
Oliver presented no obstacle to her approaching Mr. Pruell.
She called on him the next day. They did not talk about jobs.
He had noticed more than Maud, and he knew how his son
spent his evenings. He liked Pauline. When he took her into
his study, it was he who made an appeal: "Are you in love with
Oliver? I hope so. I need help."

"Help with *Oliver?*"

"It seems to me he's turned into another person. Until a
year or so ago, he used to treat me like an old fart. He knew

what life was all about, and I was the slave to business. Now he not only respects and trusts me, he's actually gone to work for me. I'm worried."

"Don't you think he's happy the way he is?"

"How can he be? When I was twenty, I wanted to be a writer too. But I had no gift for it, so I went to work and made money instead. Listen, my dear, from the start I had a notion that if I made a fortune it would be so a child of mine could lead any kind of life he wanted. Why should Oliver do what I've done all over again? If he wants to write, he should write."

"Are you sure that's what he wants? He's never breathed a word—"

"He has real talent. You look skeptical. Well, I haven't much to show you since he left college, only some poetry, and that"—he took *The Presidio Papers* from a locked drawer—"extremely off-color. Still, you're a big girl." He handed Pauline the review.

She read about ten lines, after which, despite her host's warning, the volume tumbled to the floor. Pauline turned very pink, from more than embarrassment.

"I'm an idiot, forgive me." Tactfully, Mr. Pruell did not even smile at her predicament. "You'll have to take my word for it. You know, fathers usually discourage this sort of thing."

"Who was she?"

"And before it slips my mind, don't tell Oliver about the poems. I'm supposed not to know."

Pauline promised. She would have promised Oliver's father anything.

"Cherry-ripe, remember?" she chided Oliver that evening.

"How could I forget? *You* seemed to have." He kissed her in the mouth. "Let's meet at Meville Baths at eleven."

"In the *baths?* In the *morning?*"

"Ask for Room Thirty-two."

Oliver knew the time had come. Pauline's fresh fervor

hardly surprised him; it confirmed his belief that power sticks
to those who disdain it.

Oliver made exuberant love to Pauline—his poetry come
to life. After the baths, he enjoyed her in other unlikely and
even more public places: a treehouse, a moonlit green on the
golf course in Geyser Park, the bottom of a rowboat on Lake
Luzerne. They also used his room at Mrs. Quilty's, spending
long afternoons there. He did things with his mouth she had
never dared imagine. He invented the ways she felt.

His exuberance was not feigned. In reenacting the things
that Elizabeth had taught him, he made them his own: they
became proofs of his mastery. He watched Pauline fall in love
with him with heartfelt joy.

He knew she would want to marry him. He let her broach
the subject and told her, "You live in a style I won't afford for
years."

"I'll eat cereal three times a day. I'll save the box tops."

"That's just what I mean."

"I only want to live with you forever. It can't cost that
much." Oliver shrugged. "I'll get a job."

"My beloved, qualified *men* are unemployed these days."

"I tell you, I know people."

"You're a swell girl, Pauline, but you've been schooled for a
life of idleness. What would our friends say if I let you work?
I'd hold down two jobs myself if I could, but there aren't
enough hours in the day."

"Oh, I don't want you to work *more*, I don't want you to
have to work at all—not in an office."

"What do you suggest I do—make book?"

Pauline took this for a possible pun: "Ask your father to
help. He thinks I'm good for you."

"He *is* helping. I'm on the payroll."

"I bet he'd set you up."

"If I were on my own, I'd like to show what I can do by

myself, not with *his* money." Pauline smiled. Where Oliver meant starting his own business, she envisioned late nights over a typewriter.

"There must be something we can do—*I* can do. Oh, why am I such a twerp?" Oliver kept very still: as if, holding a sure hand in a game of chance, he were waiting for his adversary to plunge. "If only . . . ," Pauline was saying, and Oliver did not budge; did not light his next cigarette.

Pauline had decided not to tell Oliver about her true expectations. She honestly believed the matter irrelevant: she'd always had enough money, and they would have enough. She saw nevertheless that, to be convinced, Oliver needed tangible prospects.

Maud wanted her to marry well. Maud had money to spare. Would she spare it? Why not? Oliver never knew what bitterness then came between the two sisters. Pauline had only told him that she would ask Maud to advance the date of her inheritance. Oliver accepted the lie and discounted it—wills could not so easily be changed. He did not care. In his own way, he was as indifferent to money as she was. He was getting what he most wanted: Pauline was committing to him everything she had.

Two days later, Pauline told him what she had obtained from Maud: her spending money would be doubled, their father's house in the city would be put in her name. Oliver was impressed. He maintained a show of reluctance for a day, then yielded, all too content to declare to the world that this lively, beautiful, sought-after young woman had preferred him to all others.

Mr. Pruell gave a party to announce their engagement. Maud did not attend; she was traveling in Europe. She did not even get back in time for the October wedding. Because of a war scare, her train out of Vienna had been canceled, and she missed her sailing. Oliver might have guessed at other

reasons; he felt too happy to look for them. Like a driver who has found a shortcut on his daily route, like a soldier who has won an objective without bloodshed, like a writer who has made his point thriftily, he drew happiness from his own efficacy. At the engagement party he realized that the money he had kept from Pauline's seven bad bets covered the expenses of his courtship down to the last dinner and drink. He indulged himself by confessing this deceit to her.

"You're a cad and a bounder," she said, "putting me through that torture for nothing."

"But we still have the money!"

"And what if I'd won, huh?"

"You're delightful and adorable, but when it comes to practical matters, leave them to me."

A note of seriousness in his words affected Pauline: "I want to leave everything to you! A propos—how about a date in your treehouse?"

Oliver took her in his arms and nibbled her eyebrows. "Why don't we wait? Let's make our wedding night a second first time."

"You're kidding—no? OK, if you say so." For a moment she felt stifled by the dog-day weight of his benevolence. She wanted to put her hand on his cock, in front of his parents, in front of their friends. She only asked, "No more treehouse? No more Mrs. Quilty?"

Oliver smilingly shook his head. He would never make the mistake of confusing Pauline with Elizabeth, or her demands with his own needs. She belonged to his life to come, the life that now stretched ahead of him like a succession of well-ordered, discreetly lighted rooms: the marble-flagged entrance where Pauline in long gold dress stood waiting by the door; the upstairs drawing room furnished in Louis XV, with a few cushioned couches and armchairs covered in softest gray and beige, their ease set off against the evening-dress formality of

a grand piano; a dining room whose mahogany table, almost black in candlelight, was surrounded by tuxedoed cronies smoking cigars and drinking port; the ground-floor den with its chesterfield sofa and chair, its desk full of secrets, its private telephone, a refuge in which to explore the solitude that gave a man of the world his most substantial pleasure. She belonged to a perspective that he could enter without the slightest qualm or effort. If he could claim little originality for this perspective, he nonetheless took pride in it as in a personal creation, perhaps because he felt so entirely its possessor.

Oliver's self-esteem did not lessen when he learned, much later, the facts of Pauline's inheritance. He never overtly reproached her, and in truth the revelation left him almost grateful. After all, it confirmed that he had the right to manage things, the right to show condescension and pity, the right to control.

Owen and Phoebe: I

SUMMER 1961- SUMMER 1963

YEARS LATER, ON the very July first that Allan Ludlam discovered Elizabeth, and in the same town, Owen Lewison instructed his bank in the city to settle a large sum of money on his daughter, Phoebe, then on the eve of her twenty-first birthday.

This was not the first time Owen had decided to endow his daughter: two years earlier, he had told her that he was establishing a trust fund to provide her with an income of her own.

He had spoken to her on a day in mid-August, while they were sitting outdoors in a shade of maples. Beyond the blurred distances of steamy fields and hills squatted blue-tinged Adirondacks. Phoebe blushed through her damp tan.

"Poppa! What have I done—"

"Go on—you do everything wonderfully."

"You don't mean school? That doesn't even—"

"Oh, yes, it does. But this isn't a reward. I want you to learn how to run your own life."

"Poppa, I plan to go to work—"

"Well, I *want* you to work."

"Then—"

"But with room to maneuver. So you can be choosy. So you won't be tempted straight off by some well-heeled john. Two hundred a month ought to help."

"That's fabulous, Poppa—"

"And with luck it'll grow."

"Poppa, what if—" She hesitated. "What if something special comes up—like buying a car? Not that I want to, but—"

"Ask me. It'll be a pleasure."

Owen explained that he would keep control of the capital: "That's what needs to do the growing. You do agree I can manage that best? You can see, too, that it would be a mistake to deplete it for something like a car."

Of course Phoebe agreed. She had already begun making a plan. Knowing that she would have money of her own was reviving a particular desire.

That spring she had attended an extracurricular lecture at her college. The students had invited as speaker the first long-haired young grown-up male she had ever seen. He wore boots and jeans with his suede jacket and string tie. He lived in the Rockies, and he spoke of their areas of unsullied wilderness. He spoke of the inroads being made in the wilderness by urban man. He spoke of the corruption in capitalist society, how it degraded whatever it touched, individuals included, out of its need to turn a profit. The wilderness, he said, encouraged individuals to remain simply themselves: it forced them to acquire a knowledge that proved incomparably useful for leading happy, self-sustaining lives. He had long held revolution as his political ideal, but he now saw that the time for revolution had not yet come. Until that time came, he recommended renouncing society. No one asked the speaker what, in the wilderness, people did with their evenings. Phoebe and her peers, usually so skeptical, accepted his precepts raptly.

Soon afterwards, in the city, she met a young man who fleshed out the lecturer's vision. He was to spend the coming

year in New Mexico as a forest ranger. She had gasped her
admiration, which had led him to suggest: Come along.
Although he loomed golden and vast, Phoebe could not then
even dream of such a prospect. Now she wrote to him: had he
meant it? He phoned back to say he had.

When Phoebe announced that she was leaving college to
help guard the timberlands of the southwest, Owen, who
hadn't smoked in a decade, compulsively clutched an empty
breast pocket. He considered himself swindled.

He knew enough to hide his feelings and dicker. He at first
expressed only surprise, commenting that it seemed a foolish
life for her to lead—she couldn't even do the work. Phoebe
claimed she could; she'd been a star on pack trips, better than
most men. (His own fault, he reflected—he'd raised her like a
boy. Her brother had been the indoor child.) Perhaps. But why
stop two years short of her B.A.? She replied that a diploma
in art from a progressive college didn't have much pull these
days—it could even be held against you. Owen asked: And
the art itself? For ten years she had wanted to become a professional painter. (Owen could accept that possibility. He didn't
expect his girl to go to law school, and everyone had pronounced her talent genuine. She should go on studying art.
Afterwards she might grow out of it, or she might succeed. He
imagined visits to her then, in the city. . . .) Art, said Phoebe,
what's so great about art? "I'll be doing something real."

"Even Marx knew better than that—remember 'productive
work'? Nothing very productive about staring at trees."

"Poppa, *you* said room to maneuver—"

"I meant, to get someplace in the world—the 'real' world.
Not run away from it."

"You're taking the money back?"

Owen wanted to know more. "These 'friends' in New
Mexico—do they include a boyfriend?"

"What are you so afraid of? I'm not spending my life there.

He's not a boy, he's a man," Phoebe couldn't help adding.

Owen was afraid—-not of what Phoebe imagined, but of being excluded. He sincerely wanted Phoebe's freedom and saw himself as part of it.

"You'll be junking the benefits of nineteen years. You're too bright for the forest primeval—"

"But it's what I *haven't* learned—"

"—and if you want to go off with a 'man,' say so, for Christ's sake."

Of course there was a man—someone to provide the excuse for change. Phoebe got herself stuck defending this man she hardly knew. She embarrassed herself; she made herself angry; she grubbed for justifications.

"As soon as I want something, you welch."

"Phoebe, I'd be irresponsible—"

"Bullshit, you want to run my—"

"—what's best for you. Please watch your language when you're talking to me."

"The best is what *you* . . . That's what the money's for—to depend even more—"

"Forget about New Mexico."

"Goodbye, Poppa." She left before she started crying. (How could this clever man act so dumb?)

Phoebe went walking for two hours. Back home, she made some long-distance calls, packed two bags, and caught an evening bus to the city.

She left before her mother came home: Phoebe called Louisa the next day to explain her decision. Later, she kept in touch with her, so that both her parents would always know that "she was all right." Eight months passed before Owen saw her again.

Phoebe never left the city: the prospect of life in the wilderness with a golden youth had quickly lost its allure. She stayed for a while with the family of a college friend. She realized that

her first task was to earn a living. Her old painting teacher helped her find jobs as an artist's model; daring to pose in the nude gave her confidence. She proposed herself to several photographers, some of whom did fashion work, one of whom shrewdly distinguished, among her many attractions, her slim feet and ankles. He specialized in shoes. Four months after leaving home, Phoebe became a professional model from the knees down. A few well-paid hours a week supplied her needs.

While Phoebe was learning how to support herself, her teacher introduced her to several artists. Phoebe went to their shows, visited their studios, met them after work. Their lives appealed to her. They had not yet been uprooted by a booming market; the Cedar Bar was still a flourishing club. Their work filled her with a passion of emulation, not of any one manner, but rather of the zany dedication the various manners expressed. She began coveting a style of her own.

She did not imagine she knew anything. She was preparing herself for art school, hoping Hofmann would accept her, when she saw a show by a painter called Trale, someone her teacher had often mentioned. This small retrospective, his first in many years, was hung in a gallery on East Tenth Street. Phoebe spent an hour there on her first visit and went back the day after, and the day after that, to make sure that in Walter Trale she had "met her master." She decided to make him exactly that.

Owen would have admired her efficiency. She persuaded friends of friends to introduce her to Walter, and later to recommend her. She let him often be reminded of her, strolling past him at the Cedar, for instance, on de Kooning's obliging arm. When at last she called on him, with six drawings, decorously smudged into a semblance of originality, he found himself on her side from the start. He looked at the drawings, and at her, and accepted her request to become his apprentice. She would do his chores, model for him occasionally, and work under his guidance.

Walter lived in a loft building on Broadway and the corner of Ninth Street; he found Phoebe a kitchenette studio on the floor below him. She settled into a new life. Walter took his role seriously. Between what he made her do for him and what he made her do for herself, she scarcely had time to display her feet.

On a warm, drizzling mid-April morning, two months after Phoebe moved in, Owen paid her a visit. She had told him to meet her at Walter's, where the door was never locked and he could just barge in; which is what he did, a little early, having made the unfamiliar trip to the lower East Side in less time than expected. He did not see Phoebe at first. Near the far end of the vast room, Walter Trale was sketching a nude model, and the sight of her compelled Owen's attention. The model was not sitting still: she was slowly turning under the painter's gaze, as though performing a slithery dance, lying, crouching, kneeling in turn, shifting from one position to the next with a slow-motion regularity that struck Owen as both impersonal and hypnotic. The woman was young: her skin glowed, her nipples showed a uniform pink. He caught a glimpse of pink lips amid the slidings of her thighs before the long hair fell away from her face, which revealed itself as Phoebe's.

Owen told himself, it's a setup. Seeing him, Phoebe said, "Oh, shit!" Walter put down his stick of charcoal, wiped blackened fingers on a white cloth, and held out a hand to his dazed visitor.

"Oh—Mr. Lewison! I guess this isn't what either of us planned. Sorry—just trying to get in one last drawing." Owen watched Phoebe's bottom disappear into the bedroom. Walter said, "She's a great model. She knows how to move."

"Is that so?"

Walter forged on: "She *really* knows how to move. Not just lying there, like a still life. You know, the French call a still life a *nature morte*—who wants a model to be a cadaver?

Like they're supposed to play dead, and we pretend they're 'problems in form.' Talk about treating a woman like a thing! I mean, why leave out the desire, the liveliness, if you're painting a nude, you *can't* leave it out, it's probably the most real thing there is—you remember Renoir, 'I paint with my penis'? So when Phoebe"—Owen's upturned eyes reminded Walter of Perugino's saints—"said, Let me try moving all the time, then I could keep seeing the life in her, I said, OK, and it works. You know, in a way it's not her I paint, it's her—"

"That's extremely interesting," Owen said as his daughter, dressed, came back into the studio.

"She's a remarkable girl, in more ways than one," Walter concluded. Owen took Phoebe out to lunch.

With her clothes on, Phoebe looked as radiant and unfamiliar to Owen as she had naked.

"Poppa," she told him when they were seated, "I want to say something right away." Owen thought: bad news. "Your giving me a hard time last summer was the best thing that ever happened to me. It made me learn what to do with my life."

"Hardly to my credit."

"Yes, it is. Taking the money back was great. I'm managing to pay my own way. When you came into Walter's studio (isn't he fab?) I realized that one good thing poppas can do is be mean, sometimes. I love you for it. I do love you, Poppa. I hope you approve of me a little."

"You're looking well." Owen made insinuations about her private life. Phoebe said she was too busy for men (she meant, one man).

"And your 'fab' friend?"

"He's *your* age, Poppa. Almost."

"Exactly."

A visit to Phoebe's studio nearly convinced him. The not-so-big room, bright even on a wet day, reflected a committed life: a thin couch, a chair, an armchair buried in laundry, in

the kitchen a table strewn with the debris of breakfast assuredly for one. The walls were papered with drawings, gouaches, and unstretched oils; the floor, stacked along its edges with stretchers and rolled canvas and paper, was a labyrinth of paint cans open and shut. There were two easels, a large and a small, and by the window, with a swivel stool at either side, a ten-by-four expanse of thick plywood set on sawhorses, without a squinch free of professional clutter.

"Hey," Owen asked, wrinkling his nose at the turps, "you *live* here?"

Phoebe opened the window. Turning back, she found Owen examining the canvas on the larger easel. "Don't ask me, I'll tell you! It's been driving me bats. Ever since I got hooked on Walter, at that show in January, I've wanted to copy one of his paintings, except he wouldn't hear of it. I kept coming back at him, and one day he said, OK, you asked for it. What he's making me do isn't copying exactly. I have to get the same results the same *way* he did. He can tell—you know, if the stippling is done with a soft brush or a stiff brush, or the paint is laid down with a spoon handle instead of a spatula. Which direction his hand was going. What he drank the night before. . . . This was my favorite of all he'd ever done. An old thing—'A Portrait of Elizabeth.'"

"Elizabeth seems to have led a hard life."

"I've scraped it down four times already. I don't think I'll ever get it right. Each time I try, though, I get five hundred and fifty-three new ideas. If you see anything you like, Poppa, just ask for it."

From a pile on the table he picked a soft-pencil self-portrait. Phoebe's eyes looked bemusedly out of it into his, and, during the ensuing weeks, he looked back at them often, with a fascination made up of resentment, yearning, and uncertainty. He realized that he admired his daughter. The thought of seeing her again made him timid.

In those days Owen often came to the city without Louisa. Calling Phoebe before one such visit, he offhandedly said, "I don't want to be bothering you. . . ." She answered, "You'd better had!" He offered to take her out for an evening. Where should he reserve a table? Would she like to see a play?

"Not much. Let's see how we feel. Whatever we do, I'll enjoy it. Come for a drink at my place. Maybe we'll just stay in and watch *Bonanza.*"

Owen had wanted to do as well by Phoebe as his own father had by him. His father, a hardworking small businessman, had had his career cut short by a fatal car accident during Owen's last year at Ann Arbor. Owen at twenty-one had found himself owner of a factory in Queens that supplied processed graphite to pencil manufacturers. Knowing little about the business, he agreed to run it: it was well organized, he knew he could learn quickly. A few months later a fire broke out in his stockroom, destroying the entire inventory and half the plant. Accountants urged him to collect the insurance and write off what was left of the factory. Doing so, he made a significant discovery.

Two companies of firemen had appeared during the fire. They had declined to do their job until Owen had the wit to offer them twenty-five dollars each (a week's wage at the time). A more experienced businessman might have known that this practice was common, but Owen was outraged; enough so to list this graft in his claims to the insurance company and thus symbolically denounce it. He expected no compensation. The claim was nevertheless paid.

From this windfall Owen drew a conclusion that eventually turned into a plan; this he submitted to an old friend about to graduate from Columbia Law School. The friend reacted favorably. Owen suggested they go into business together, using as their working capital the money he had collected from the fire.

Owen had realized that small businesses like his father's,

low in reserves of capital and dependent on high productivity, were at the mercy of a single disaster. A delay in reimbursement by their insurers—his own had taken almost a year—could wipe them out. Such companies would hesitate to press ancillary claims that might postpone settlement. Owen proposed creating a service that would take over cases in which a natural disaster had crippled a business, reimbursing basic claims immediately, making its own profit by exploiting secondary liabilities covered by the insurance. The outcome of Owen's dealings with the fire department had suggested that such profits might be large.

Owen and his partner founded a company to supply such a service. They took great care in the choice of their first clients. They proved themselves industrious, clever, capable of rock-ribbed persistence, even lucky. Their venture was so successful that after five years their presence in a case often persuaded insurance companies to settle quickly rather than risk uncertain legal battles.

Owen prospered. His career brought him not only wealth but satisfaction: his initiative and ingenuity were constantly challenged; he felt that he was usefully serving small businesses and, later, businesses not so small. His success introduced him to the society of the traditionally well-to-do—bankers and professional men who set themselves higher than unassuming entrepreneurs like his father. Owen envied the confidence such people showed in their own distinction. Because he was both prosperous and amenable, they accepted him readily enough. Eventually he married a young lady who, although poorer than he, belonged to a venerable Philadelphia family.

Throughout their marriage Owen remained devoted to Louisa. She had soon given him what he most wanted of her: a child, and particularly a daughter. During her two pregnancies he looked forward so intensely to their outcome that by the time Phoebe was born she was already the focus of his desires.

Owen was relieved to have a girl. He could cultivate her happiness—his own happiness—without concern for the combative and methodical virtues required of males. He watched over her education in and out of school. He made sure she learned early how to swim and ride, and later how to ski and play tennis. He took her to the ballet to kindle wonder in her and then sent her to ballet school. At her first sign of interest, he exposed her to books, plays, and music; and to sustain her precocious artistic bent he kept her supplied with everything she might need, from clay and crayons at three to oils and acrylics at thirteen. He remained a consistently fond, demanding parent. Good-natured and smart, Phoebe thrived under his supervision. By the age of seventeen, the contentment she felt in herself shone out of her like whiteness out of snow. Owen rejoiced in his parental success. By then his work had lost much of its challenge—it had become a means less to achieve than to conserve. He began looking to Phoebe for surprising triumphs.

Ten months before, their quarrel and Phoebe's departure had bred furious disappointment in him. Now that they had made peace, he still did not understand her. She had thanked him with convincing sincerity for "being mean"—a strange conclusion to draw from his nineteen years' munificence.

He came to her studio at seven, a benign hour on this late June evening, when the hot, clear air was suffused with cinnamon incandescence. Phoebe had prepared chilled unshaken gimlets for him. What should they do? They drifted out into the never-ending dusk. She led him across town to a steak house off Greenwich Avenue, modish but not deafeningly so. From their table, Owen looked about warily. Here, at least, bohemia seemed ready to spare him.

A wine from the shores of Lake Trasimene, which he never had seen, nor would see, opened in his mind vistas of remembrance and expectancy. He had begun speaking to Phoebe about some incident in his past when a sturdy swaggering

youth approached their table and cocked a hand in greeting:
"Hi, Phoeb."

"My father, Owen. Harry."

"No shit!" Harry observed. "Listen, doll, Bob is blowin' at
El Pueblo at ten. Thought you'd want to know." (Owen asked,
"Blowing what?" Phoebe answered, "Horn.")

After dinner, with conscious benevolence, Owen said,
"Why not?" They wandered around six corners to Sheridan
Square. The near-dark sky flared with the refractions of fire-
works upriver.

"It's a French horn," Owen disappointedly remarked, having savvily looked forward to trumpet or sax.

"That's life," Phoebe chuckled.

"Who's Bob?"

"Scott," Phoebe whispered. "And that's Woody Woodward
on alto, Doc Irons on vibes, Poppa Jenks on drums"—three
blacks and one white, all young, who at the stroke of ten filled
the gloom of the Pueblo with a clangor so intricately sweet that
Owen felt bewitched. A green smell spiced the air.

"They're very fine," he exclaimed.

Phoebe looked gratified. "They may join us after this set."

Owen felt a pang. He'd only conversed with Negroes who
worked for him. How well did Phoebe know them?

She was explaining: "Walter's sort of their sponsor—at
least, he got them this gig."

When, white-shirted and cool, the musicians sat down at
their table, they paid no attention to Owen. A few customers,
including Harry, came over to pay court. Otherwise they all sat
together quietly and contentedly, as if after a long day they had
settled on a veranda to watch the moon rise over cornfields,
or Lake Trasimene.

At eleven-thirty Poppa Jenks drained his glass: "Owen!"
Owen sat up like a schoolboy caught dozing. "Anything you'd
like to hear?"

"Uh—'All the Things You Are'?" Owen hazarded.

"Right. Right?" he asked the others.

"What's that shift—"

"Down a major third. G to E flat, same as 'Long Ago.'" To Owen he added, "Mr. Kern was an attentive student of Schubert, and a thrifty one."

They returned to their instruments. A young man in tailored denims bent abruptly over Phoebe: "Fourteen West Eleventh. Domerich. *Vaut le détour.*" The musicians broke once more into their wry jubilation. The Kern ballad was disseminated in a bustle of counterpoint.

Afterwards, Owen again said, "Why not?" and they made their way eastward, in night now, deep but not dark: through ginkgo leaf, window-light stippled the sidewalks with pale orange. The air had scarcely cooled—only, by alleyways, mild gusts on face or nape suggested swipes of a celestial fan.

After half an hour at the party, Owen asked himself what, if anything, was happening. Something must be happening, because he wasn't bored. Phoebe had soon abandoned him— for his own sake, he knew: he would do better on his own. He stood near the bar and watched the other guests, many of whom were also watching. For a while a pickup combo—bass, piano, sax—played in a far room. What talk he heard sounded mostly small, a counterpart of the nudging and touching, friendly, not particularly sexual, that brought groups together and dispersed them. A California breeze was fluttering the Thai silk curtains. In this mildness a few isles of agitation survived: "Then he asked me, 'If I go to bed with you here, do I have to go to bed with you in New York?' and I told him, 'Sweetie pie, of course not!'" Owen failed to match a face to the melodious voice. He did not understand why he felt so much at ease among people whom he didn't know, who seemed no more concerned with one another than with him, who nevertheless acted neither hostile nor indifferent.

His impressions made more sense when the dancing started. The stereo came on like the summons to a Last Judgment where all would be saved. No one asked anybody to dance because nobody could hear. People danced or didn't. The notion of "couple" was dissipated in a free-for-all that spread across three rooms.

Owen loved dancing of every sort. Earlier that year, when the Twist had first appeared, he single-handedly imposed it on upstate gatherings still attuned to Xavier Cougat. Here the Twist had followed the Conga into oblivion; a new, less definable order reigned. Owen began reducing the apparently chaotic movements of those around him to a pattern he could imitate.

When he entered the arena, he found himself facing a woman, scarcely younger than he, who bore a compelling resemblance to Angela Lansbury and comported herself with stylish abandon. He tried to follow her lead and couldn't. She drew suddenly close to him—he thought she was going to kiss him—to shriekingly murmur in his ear, "Don't do *steps*." He failed to grasp. . . . "No steps!" she insisted, leading him to the sidelines. "There aren't any rules. Just anchor one hip in space—make that your center, OK?—and let the rest go. Do what the music does—anything." She demonstrated. He tried, "*Any*thing!" she urged. "Shut your eyes and listen."

From time to time he stopped at an open window to cool off. He would then attempt, by smiles and gesticulations, to express to other bystanders his approval of the new culture. Once a young woman, as if to fortify his conversion, led him straight back into the action; once a young man. Owen's fear at the touch of that firm hand dissolved among the dancers.

He was progressing from exuberance towards fluency when Phoebe stopped him. In a quieter room she introduced him to Joey, a painter in his twenties with a problem she wanted Owen to consider: a fire in his studio, a landlord refusing to

pay for repairs. Insurance? Not the right kind, according to the owner, who Joey thought was stalling in order to evict him. Owen told him to call his office the next morning and ask for Margy; he would phone her instructions. It occurred to him how easily he might extend his services to individuals so plainly in need of them.

The party was subsiding. Owen and Phoebe followed a gang of celebrants down the walnut banister, out onto Manhattan's stony pave. Arm in arm they headed west in search of a White Tower. Owen said, "Then I'll drop you home. I wish I felt sleepier."

"I see!" Phoebe turned them back towards Fifth Avenue. "You trust me?"

"With a vengeance."

She was hailing a cab. "Belmont, please. Service entrance."

"You want the hotel, lady, or the track?"

"The track. Take the bridge, please," she added. So they could see the dawn.

The not-quite dawn: the cab glided smoothly towards chalk dust cascading out of stars into eastern cloud-of-light. When they set down at the stables, Phoebe led the way to the cafeteria, which was half full and wide awake. They took coffee and Danish to a table at which five males were sitting, the youngest a diminutive adolescent black, the oldest a sixtyish Chicano. The group affably made room for Owen and Phoebe and went on with an earnest discussion of a horse called Capital Gain. ("By Venture Capital out of No Risk," Phoebe explained. "These people work for the McEwans.")

Walter Trale had kept friends from the days when he painted horses. He liked going to the track, and sometimes brought Phoebe along. She had met several owners, and because she knew horses, she had talked her way into the stable area and made friends there as well.

Pushing away his tray, one man said, "Let's try him out."

All proceeded to the stables. Capital Gain was saddled and led forth. At the training track the young black was told, "Six furlongs, remember, and keep it tight. He may still hurt."

Dawn turned into day. When the horse pulled up at the end of the workout, the Chicano declared, "He's all right."

"He'll be up in six weeks," someone added. "Hey, Phoebe, want to walk a hot?"

The horse was huffing as it pranced sideways up to them. While a tall black held the bit, the exercise boy dismounted and handed Phoebe the reins. The horse turned a bulging eye on her, shaking his head like a wet-eared swimmer. Phoebe stood looking up at the head and spoke to it for a while before leading the animal towards the stables.

"Half an hour should do it," the man told her.

To Owen, his bare-legged and tight-skirted daughter looked alarmingly frail alongside the silver-gray stallion, three years old and foaming with power. Where had the others gone? He didn't say a word to her, he kept at a cautious distance; but when Capital Gain reappeared around a corner of the stable, Owen saw him jerk his head back without warning, pulling Phoebe off balance. As the reins went slack, the horse reared, wagging wicked forefeet above her head and whinnying huskily. Turning around, Phoebe held the bridle loose until the horse came down to earth and lowered his head. She stepped up to him and grabbed the reins closer to the bit, yanking them almost to the ground, holding them there with all her weight. The horse kicked and swerved and could not raise his head. A moment later, to Owen's horror, Phoebe with a stern cry of "You motherfucking" something-or-other began driving her small fist into the animal's neck. Soon after, she resumed her stroll, with the stallion again obediently in tow.

Near the end of Phoebe's stint, Capital Gain's owner arrived. Mr. McEwan had come to look at his horse. He was pleased to find him sound; pleased to see Phoebe, too. He

invited her and Owen to the clubhouse for a second breakfast.

They ate a much bigger, better, and longer meal than their first: fruit, eggs, bacon, toast, buckwheat cakes, tall shining pots of coffee. They sat at their table for an hour and a half, in low eastern sunlight, in early-morning shade. At last Mr. McEwan left for work. He had behaved with perfunctoriness towards Owen, who realized that here he was no more and no less than his daughter's father, until Phoebe injected some helpful information into their talk. By the end of breakfast the men were chummily discussing business. Owen looked on Phoebe with freshened eyes.

The day had started hot and dry. The pair wandered across the track, where groundsmen readied the terrain for the afternoon and sparrows hopped about rare droppings. They bowed through a fence into the empty infield. They sat down on shaded grass. Fat robins policed the grounds; yarmulkaed chickadees pecked their way up thickset branches; beyond the linked pools, black cutouts of crows were pasted against yellow-green baize. A breeze carried vibrations of urban traffic and an occasional drone from the sky. Owen leaned his head on his knees.

Phoebe was poking him. "Poppa, stick around. It's nice out here." Owen grunted assent. His eyes would not stay open. "Don't forget Joey." He nodded, sighed, and sat up. Phoebe held out her hand: "Try some of this, Poppa."

"What is it?"

"Medical snuff. Poppa Jenks gave it to me—he endorses it one hundred per, and so does Freud."

"You're sure?"

"Just don't sneeze."

"Sort of like nasal Alka-Seltzer."

He sat in a phone booth with a diminishing column of dimes, chattering to his secretary like a telex as he transmitted, as fast as he could master it, the clear stream of ideas flowing through his consciousness. He solved the case of the thieving

computer. He mitigated the death of the essential engineer. For Joey, he told Margy to check the insurance on the building, accuse Joey's landlord of being criminally negligent, and point out that with Owen's help he could become an honest profiteer. "What do you mean, am I all right? On a day like this, who could *not* be all right?"

Phoebe had disappeared. He looked through the club rooms. On the terrace, Owen thought he might soon float away. The infield remained almost empty—one idle groundskeeper, another man standing immobile in the shadow of his Stetson.

"He should sell that hat to a developer." Phoebe was behind him, carrying a big paper bag.

In a clump of copper beeches by the stables, on a table-cloth spread on the ground, Phoebe set out lunch: two club sandwiches, four pears, a slab of rat cheese, a frosty thermos of martinis. They ate and drank.

From the stables came the bustle of nervous men and the stomping of hooves. The time for the first race was approaching. Owen felt pleasantly restless: "Let's go take a look."

"This is no time for camp followers," Phoebe told him. "We'd be in the way."

"Well, I feel like joining the party."

"They thought of that. You get to bet."

As they strolled back to the clubhouse, Phoebe said, "I'll go scout the field and meet you at the paddock." At her return she announced, "My Portrait in the sixth."

"My Portrait is a horse?"

"By Spitting Image out of My Business."

Preferring to "check the form," Owen bought a *Morning Telegraph* and through the afternoon studied it with the reverence of a Talmudic scholar. When they left, after six races, he had lost less than he might have. He had also paid Phoebe back for their lunch, and she had bet the money on My Portrait,

who paid off at nine to two. She forced the winnings on him:
"I did it for you. I never bet."

"You—Miss Spunk?"

Phoebe persuaded Owen to take the train back—the fastest
way home, even if he dreaded an "awful crowd." Other early
leavers entered their car. They seemed quiet—no beer-heads,
no "youngsters." The last ones in had to stand, filling the aisle.
The train started up with a jolt and a clang.

Owen soon regretted his forsaken taxi. He found himself hemmed in by bodies bulbous or emaciated, all clothed
according to some perverse notion of unfunny clownishness,
each swaying face stamped with metropolitan distrust. His gaze
at last came to rest on a couple sitting across the car: neatly
dressed, not bad looking, in their Latin way—he had caught
a few words of Spanish. The man, who wore an open white
shirt and beige slacks, had a slender body, dark, thin features,
pepper-and-salt hair, and a black mustache. The woman, in a
cotton print dress and white shoes, looked younger—pretty, a
little coarse, perhaps, yet so amiable, her fine teeth flashingly
set off by her black, brushed-out hair. The man's merry eyes
caught Owen's at the moment Phoebe nudged him: "Just like
us."

The man's eyes looked into his with cheerful indifference.
Of course, a father and daughter. Like us: the man, therefore,
"like me." Owen searched for feelings like his own in the alert
face, whose nostrils flared ever so slightly as he stared. He
thought: What signs do my feelings leave in my face?

He turned away to consider someone nearer: a man with
florid swollen features, short strawy hair above a shaved pink
nape, a heavy belly that bulged through a half-untucked
Hawaiian shirt over low-belted pants of shiny plaid synthetic
gabardine—And so on, thought Owen, ad nauseam. Why
did he mind? His own body felt warm and stupefied. He
noticed that the light outside the train windows had become

detached from his perception of it; and he saw that a similar hallucinatory change was occurring in his neighbor. He was separating into disjunct entities—still a looming, monstrous straphanger, while his eyes belonged to another body, another space: through them shined light from afar. A disjunct light existed behind the appearance the man turned to the world. That slob body had become an empty vessel with autono- mous light inside it—a Halloween pumpkin. The pumpkin grinned at him, as pumpkins should. Why? It was answering his own smile. All right. Owen extended his smile into a little nod, as if to say, Win some, lose some; or, Been quite a day. He lowered his gaze. The awful crowd—should he care? He shyly glanced at others near him: veterans of one summer afternoon, each encased in his rind, each accumulating incon- gruities, pains, shames, even signs of happiness, to conceal that uncanny light—their masks, their lives. Phoebe was snoozing on his shoulder.

From Penn Station she took Owen straight to Walter's. Walter was giving a dinner, to which she was inviting him: she was cook.

For a while they remained alone in his studio. Phoebe hus- tled in the kitchen. Owen stood in front of the northwest win- dow, looking into a cherry-blossom sky festooned with jetliner trails. A molelike question was rummaging inside him: What is wrong with this? He ignored it and abandoned himself to the view of Jersey.

Walter arrived, then his guests—two women, two men. Each acted as lively and curious as a dog off its leash. Apparently they all led busy lives, in activities Owen could not recognize. What was, or were, sociolinguistics? Where was Essalen? Was a concrete poet a writer or a sculptor? Who was Theodore Huff? He was pleased to have discarded jacket and tie.

Phoebe made them all drinks (chilled gimlets for Owen).

He did not know what to say to these people. They didn't mind. While he sensed that they were funny, the context of their wit and gossip escaped him. At last he mentally put his tie back on and asked them questions. They asked him questions in turn, and he told a little about himself. The others listened attentively. He succeeded in getting credit for helping Joey the painter.

Towards the end of the meal, after Walter had urged him to talk about his work, Owen revealed something Phoebe had never known:

". . . Neither of us had capital—just the insurance from the fire. But you're right: we needed more than that to expand. We might have raised enough money from the banks, but it would have been just enough—it would have meant being dependent on them for maybe ten or fifteen years. We talked about the problem for weeks, and gradually we agreed on a solution—actually, we backed into it, because it wasn't only risky, it was illegal. That was twenty-five years ago, and I haven't even *parked* illegally since then. This is what we did. There'd been an accident on the waterfront in New London. A tug banged up a wharf, pretty much wrecking it, and on top of that some gasoline drums spilled and set the whole thing on fire. The wharf belonged to a ferry company. It was a company with high operating costs and a low profit margin, so the owners were happy for us to take over their claims. We paid them right off what it was going to cost to rebuild the wharf. Normally we would have gone on and made our profit on secondary claims like losses due to interruption of service, damage to reputation, stuff like that. But we found out that the ferry people had taken out a policy for fire with one company and a policy for maritime damage with another company, and furthermore, even though the business was chartered in New London, because its services involved other places such as Long Island they'd used one insurance company in Connecticut and

one in New York. So, since the wharf for all practical purposes had been wrecked twice over, once by the collision and once when it burned, what we did was press all the claims against *both* companies. I can tell you, we went through two very scary months. Once, inspectors from the two companies missed each other by minutes; and of course if they'd found us out, we'd have been through. But we got away with it. We cleared about a hundred thousand dollars—not enough to retire on, but that was still a lot of money in nineteen thirty-seven, and we felt a lot better set to take on the big boys. And that's what we did. We really buckled down. I don't know if I could work that hard anymore," Owen concluded. "Nowadays I do ninety percent of my business by phone."

A few seconds later he fell asleep. "Rack time, Poppa!" Phoebe shouted in his ear. Eventually she got him up and put him to bed in her studio. Their long day had ended.

When Owen woke up the next morning, he found a note from his daughter: she had "slept elsewhere"; he would find coffee, bread, butter, and eggs in the larder. She apologized for the evaporated milk: "I couldn't face shopping after the dishes." So she had gone back to Trale's place. Owen did not want breakfast. He missed his *Trib*.

Phoebe came in at ten. He warmed to her hug. She said to him, "Poppa, I've got to kick you out. This looks like a heavy day."

"A whole day without you? I don't think I can manage."

"It was fun, wasn't it? You keep right on playing without me."

"All right." He added morosely, "I really shot my mouth off last night."

Phoebe looked bewildered. "You were a smash."

"No kidding."

"Poppa, I just want to work. Why the soap opera?" Owen said nothing. "Want to meet for dinner?"

Owen said he'd see and put on his jacket. He felt hung over. Stepping out on peculiar lower Broadway, he looked forward to his office.

All day long, Owen talked to himself about Phoebe. She had downtown elegance, talent, and a passion for her work. She had friends low and high. She was attractive and smart. She had devoted herself to him without reserve. What more could a father want?

He wished she would demand the money he had promised her. Perhaps she could give him drawing lessons that he could pay her for. His irritation grew. He gave Joey's landlord a piece of his mind.

He imagined being old and widowed: Phoebe would take care of him. He would quietly watch her life out of the corner of his eye.

He wasn't old, he didn't need Phoebe looking after him. She had been cruel turning her back on him—you spend a hundred bucks, and next morning, see you later.

Remembering the bet on My Portrait, he silently begged her forgiveness. He called Phoebe to say he'd love to have dinner.

Phoebe that evening looked tired and worried. Some days, she told Owen, she felt she'd never make it. Her fingernails were caked, her hair bunchy, she wasn't wearing lipstick. Owen saw in these signs of trust a refusal to make an effort for his sake. She failed to suggest a next meeting.

He went on brooding about her. Something was wrong. Owen had become confused and didn't like it. Away from Phoebe, he thought wistfully of the night and day she'd given him. Why hadn't there been more? This first "why" soon led to others. Beyond all of them, "something must be wrong" lurked in a beckoning shade. If there was to be no more, why had Phoebe bothered with him? She had not merely been dutiful. Why had she led him on and then let him down? Allowing

these questions to seem real planted a crystal of suspicion in Owen's mind, which crusted with cold like a pond in plunging frost.

He reviewed once again the time spent with Phoebe. He told himself that she had not chosen their activities accidentally. She had given him new experiences of new kinds of people: artists, jazzmen, stable hands, a "beautiful crowd." What did they all have in common? The answer came to Owen on a hot, windy afternoon at the corner of Madison Avenue and Forty-eighth Street. When the light turned green, he stepped back onto the curb to stare into a wickerwork-iron trash can. Phoebe had been making a fool of him.

She had been teaching him a lesson: these new people had nothing to do with him. Phoebe had lured him into enjoying activities and attitudes that belonged to her, not to him. She was telling him, If you like my life so much, what can yours be worth? The year before he had opposed her; she was taking her revenge. She was showing him who had been right and was still right.

Owen had found something clear and nasty to batten on. He disregarded the noticeable thrill of suspecting that his daughter had betrayed him; he only relished his relief at having an explanation. He enjoyed his discovery so much that his sentiments towards Phoebe brightened perceptibly.

Owen saw Phoebe twice in August and once in September. He tried to make their meetings altogether casual. To Phoebe he seemed determined to undo what they had shared, pointedly refusing a stroll down Third Avenue one hot night because of "all the people," not going to a party because dancing was "no fun anymore." Owen would have denied such intentions. He had so thoroughly become the mistreated father that he forgot all his once-happiest expectations. He was defending this identity "innocently."

Phoebe occasionally prodded him. When Owen declined

having drinks at Walter's, saying, "Walter's OK, but you know I can't stand his friends," Phoebe asked, "Like Jack McEwan?" With whom Owen had recently dined.

Usually she accepted his comments docilely. Owen was therefore surprised to notice, after a time, an undisguised aloofness on her part. He had sometimes spoken frankly to her, he knew; didn't she pride herself on her broad-mindedness? Her coolness did not discourage him, but rather confirmed him in his role of responsible, misunderstood parent.

Something more preoccupying had strengthened his commitment to that role. In the course of the summer Phoebe gradually succumbed to what was first considered a mood, then a psychological state, and at last—much later—a disease. The condition revealed itself, slowly and relentlessly, in symptoms of fatigue, morbid emotionalism, and depression. During the following autumn and winter, two good doctors assured Owen that Phoebe was suffering from a type of neurasthenia. Influenced by his own passionate conviction, they attributed the source of her trouble to the irregular life she had been leading.

Whatever a child's age, her health remains a parent's prime concern. Owen found Phoebe the best doctors he could trust. Otherwise he kept to the background, reserving for himself the right to protect his daughter from the prime cause of her disorder—her wayward life. Wary of Phoebe's stubborn independence, he waited for an opportunity to intervene. One came late in December. Chronic insomnia had left Phoebe exhausted. Her resistance to infection had been sapped. When she caught the flu it turned into bronchitis, then pleurisy. She had to stop modeling; her money ran out. Having learned as much from her psychiatrist, Owen called up Phoebe and went to see her.

Her studio looked a mess; so did she—a frail, livid derelict. Owen made her some tea, chatted a while, then offered

to resume the payments from the trust fund he had set up the previous year. It "was still there, waiting for her."

Phoebe began to cry. She cried like a six-year-old, with long, violent sobs. "I *am* tapped out. I thought you'd given up on me.

"That's nonsense."

"You've been very hard. I felt so close to you last spring, last June—it seems ages."

"I've been worried about you, that's all."

"I feel so awful. Sometimes I feel like I'm dying."

"You don't take care of yourself."

"I do. I go to the doctors and take all the pills, and it doesn't ever help, not for long."

"Tell me one thing. Are you still taking drugs?" Phoebe looked at him incredulously. "Can you honestly promise me you'll stop taking drugs?"

"You should ask Dr. Straub. He tries out a new one on me every week."

"Not that kind of drug—marijuana, amphetamines, cocaine . . ."

"Do you think I'm crazy? I mean I'd *have* to be nuts to, the way I feel."

"It's not you—it's your friends I worry about. Can't you just promise?"

"No sweat."

"Good. With your money you could take a good long rest and get really well again. How would you like a week in the Bahamas? Be my guest. If it's good enough for Jack and Mac, why not us? One other thing—" Owen neither paused nor altered his tone of voice, warm and urgent. Why should he hesitate? The sight of Phoebe had not only appalled him, it had mightily reinforced his disposition: he knew what was holding her here, what had to be given up. "I want you to go to a real art school. You haven't been making the kind of

progress you should. I know Walter's a nice man, and I know how fond of him you are—I'm fond of him too. But he's not a good teacher." Owen thought that through her sunken cheeks he could see Phoebe's teeth. She said nothing. He concluded: "That's something I consider essential to your well-being. That's the first thing you have to do before we get you organized."

Phoebe glanced around the studio, its walls crowded with work that Owen had ignored. Copious tears again flowed over her face and dripped off her chin. In a voice steady enough, only a little hoarse, she told him to get out.

"I know it's difficult," he replied, "and I know you're upset—"

"You are a bleeding asshole."

"—but sooner or later you've got to face the fact that you're unwell *and* unhappy. Think it over. Ask yourself why."

As he left, Owen thought: She's a very sick girl. He had done what he could. He was glad she was in good hands. Calling on her had depressed and somehow elated him. Phoebe's insults had provoked a warm rush of what he did not dare recognize as relief.

He phoned Dr. Straub to say how concerned he was. He would appreciate being kept informed.

During the ensuing months, Phoebe kept getting worse: depression, insomnia, feverishness. In late spring she was taken to a hospital with pneumonia. Her doctors refused to release her unless she allowed them to perform certain tests. These enabled her disorder to be identified as acute hyperthyroidism, also known as Graves's disease. Phoebe began a treatment with a drug called methyl thiouracil. Its initial effect proved slight. At the beginning of June she agreed to return to her family's house upstate, not because she wanted to, but because her mother's insistence and her own helplessness left her no choice. Ten weeks afterwards, her treatment, no doubt begun

too late, was abandoned, and she consented to undergo a sub-total thyroidectomy at a nearby hospital, which she entered on the fifteenth of August.

At the time of Phoebe's earlier hospitalization, Owen's attitude towards her changed. He had plainly done her an injustice, and he knew better than to claim good intentions as an excuse. He had blamed Phoebe's condition on her behavior—a judgment that, as well as wronging her, encouraged the doctors he had chosen to persevere in their mistaken diagnosis. He told himself that she could never be expected to forgive or understand him. He must simply make what amends he could and pray that she would find a way to leave him in peace.

When she came home, he committed himself to a program of discreet and fervent atonement. He did whatever Phoebe asked of him without the least complaint. Owen's contrition was matched by Phoebe's contempt. As a condition of her return, she insisted that he move to the guest annex at the far end of the house. When she heard his voice, she often asked her mother to shut him up. Sometimes she summoned him to her bedside to supply new fuel for her scorn. ("What rich creeps did you insure this week?") Or she would demand things of him (such as reading *Two Serious Ladies* out loud to her; she wept at its beauties and raged at his boredom) as if he were a lackey whose career of swindle and rape had just been disclosed. Whenever he appeared she stared at him out of bulging, hateful eyes. When Owen came into possession of Walter's portrait of Elizabeth, he let her ridicule his motives for acquiring it and did not try to explain them. She was so outraged that the picture belonged to him that he had it sent up from the city to be hung in her room.

Phoebe's treatment of him comforted Owen. It allowed him to go on playing the dutiful, now penitent father. The role, hard and forthright, continued to reassure him. Owen dreaded above all the agitating uncertainty into which Phoebe

had twice led him. Of course she still loomed dangerously in his future. How would she behave once she was cured? Most likely she would want to be reconciled with him. Her harshness towards him could become the pretext for excusing his own unfair behavior. Owen abhorred this possibility and preferred being punished. He longed for Phoebe to live her life and leave him out of it.

On July first, Owen settled a large amount of money on his daughter. Unlike the trust fund, this arrangement made Phoebe truly independent. She would have no further need of him. To outsiders, his gesture seemed generous; intimates saw in it an expression of remorse and hope. Owen claimed he was fulfilling a father's obligations. He could scarcely acknowledge his eagerness to escape from fatherhood altogether.

In late August, after her operation, Phoebe asked Owen to visit her in the hospital. He went to her late in the afternoon. In her room, the dark glow from the lowered blinds and drawn purple curtains revealed an emaciated shape.

Owen had not seen her awake since the operation. Phoebe's hair, cut short and flattened with sweat, looked like a skullcap on a skull. Her skin lay waxily over the bones of her face. Owen experienced fright, revulsion, a spasm of pity.

At first she said nothing as she gazed at him out of huge inexpressive eyes. She held out her hand. The thin hot hand gripped him hard. He didn't know what to do or say; he began sweating himself. She finally spoke, in high, almost whimpering tones: "You're my father. I feel awful. I don't know what's happening to me. I feel so awful I don't feel anything else. I can't talk much. You mustn't stay long. I do want you to know"—from a box at her side Phoebe pulled a Kleenex and spat into it—"I wanted you to know . . . something. It was when my feelings got wiped out I understood, I understood something about you and me. We've been playing a dumb game, both of us. We've been turning you into a shit. You can

keep playing, that's all right, but not me. I plan to love you whatever you do."

Owen felt himself being gathered up into a wet, smothering shroud. He longed to scramble away from that room and his bony daughter. Her grip tightened. He cleared his throat: "Phoebe, you have to believe me, I've done everything I could to you."

He did not realize what he had said until she grinned: "Maybe, but I gave you a lot of help." She let his hand go. She shut her eyes, spreading wrinkles across her face. She looked like a crone. "I love you—ring that buzzer, will you? Please do it fast. Bye bye. Come back soon."

Owen hurried through the cooled corridors and lobby, out into the dank brightness that smelled of wet grass and decay. Tears simmered in his eyes. He had behaved so cruelly to Phoebe, so many times: how dare she love him? She had trapped him. She had had the last word.

Owen would have liked to cough up his feelings, as though he had breathed a beetle into his lungs. He could not identify his feelings. He got drunk. He woke up at three in the morning and wove fantasies of living under another name in a country he had never seen. He thought that he, or at least his life, had gone insane. He wished that Phoebe had never been born.

The Labor Day weekend passed. One afternoon Owen went into Phoebe's empty bedroom, where the portrait of Elizabeth, brought back from the hospital, had been set against a wall. Owen stared at it malevolently. He knew the woman in the painting all too well. Her masklike abstractness had made of her an unrelenting, unresponsive witness of his past mistakes and present helplessness.

He said aloud, "Up yours." He wished he had the nerve to piss on her. He spat on her instead and with his fingertips rubbed the spittle over her face. The paint felt slick and tough. Owen became deliciously aware of being alone in the house,

as if the house belonged to someone else and he'd sneaked into it like a marauding boy.

By the window stood a table littered with Phoebe's makeup. Owen took an eyeliner pencil and with a grunt of satisfaction drew blue whiskers across Elizabeth's ivory-gold cheeks. Under the soft point the surface held firm. Encouraged, he picked up tubes of scarlet, purple, and orange-red lipstick. He bedizened the mouth and eyes with spots, stripes, and flourishes. Holding the three tubes in a cluster, he enclosed the entire head in a whorl of grease.

He felt better. He even laughed at himself. Through the window he looked across his lawn and the lawns of his neighbors into the dark woods nearby, warped here and there by clear vapor rising in hot, late-summer sun. He found a box of Kleenex and began erasing the mess he had made. Tissue after tissue fell to the floor blotted with the colors of Phoebe's mouth. He used a soapy washrag to remove the remaining traces.

Soap and water proved less than sufficient. The paler areas were still misted with purple or pink. To complete the task, he fetched a can of turpentine from the cellar, tore a clean shirt into rags, and began lightly rubbing away the last stains. He had finished cleaning one cheek and was proceeding to the eye above it when his rag caught on a crust of paint running along the rim of the eyeball. Burnt sienna surged into the eye's light ocher. He wiped it off as gently as he could; the ocher in turn spread into the nose. Owen swore. He went into the bathroom and came back with a toothbrush. Having dipped it in turpentine, he shook it out and rubbed it half dry on his sleeve. Leaning his elbow against the canvas, he started to slowly and scrupulously brush away the misplaced paint. His diligence was succeeding when a brown speck sprang from the elastic bristles and slid down the upright surface. Instinctively Owen jabbed at it with the cloth in his left hand, spreading a fresh blotch of softened paint beneath the injured eye.

Stepping back, Owen saw that he had inflicted serious damage. He wondered how to repair it. Half irritably, half jokingly, he told himself: I own the goddamn thing, I might as well enjoy it. With a turps-soaked rag in either hand, he vengefully attacked the painting. Soaking the pigments of the right eye, he smeared its colors across the fiery hair into the pale landscape above Elizabeth's head. The smear looked like a horn. Who ever saw a cow with one horn? He drew a second streak from the other eye. He drenched the mouth and blurred it into a haze of mauve. The rest of the face he obliterated with the orange of her hair.

Owen carried the painting, toothbrush, and turpentine down to the cellar. He used a chisel to loosen the tacks on the back of the stretcher before stripping away the canvas. He pulled the stretcher apart and sheared the canvas into ribbons, packing them into a burlap sack along with the rags and toothbrush. Outside the back door, he stuffed the sack into a garbage can underneath other refuse. He took the disassembled stretcher to the garage and with a hatchet split and chopped the wood into insignificant slivers, which he dumped on a pile of unstacked kindling behind the neighboring shed. He then retreated to his room to wash his face and hands.

Owen and Phoebe: II

1962-1963

WHEN OWEN TURNED away from her the summer before, Phoebe could see what was happening; not why. Owen had begun treating her as an enemy. What had she done to antagonize someone she so loved? She kept her patience, hoping that if he did not end his hostility he would at least explain it. Later, she turned cautious and, sometimes, hostile herself. Owen then stared at her without surprise, as though looking at a curious old photograph.

Phoebe had begun suffering from two misfortunes. First, for several months she lost Louisa and Walter, either of whom might have helped her. Second, her insidious disease contaminated both her life and her perception of it.

When the thyroid gland misfunctions, the effects are not felt as symptoms. Depression and excitement, even indigestion, are interpreted as private, "natural" experiences. Not until September did Phoebe consult a doctor—a general practitioner who identified her trouble at once. She should, he said, be given the customary basal metabolism test; for that, he advised her to see a specialist in endocrine pathology. Owen recommended someone; she made an appointment; and her misfortune was then compounded by misdiagnosis.

Dr. Sevareid had an expert's insight: he had treated thousands of glandular disorders and could spot them at first glance. As soon as Phoebe walked into his office, he saw that she did not have thyroid disease. He told her so. Of course she should take the basal metabolism test—it could only prove him right. He forthwith introduced her to the nurse who administered it.

The test measured metabolic activity by recording the units of oxygen a patient consumed in a given time. In an adjoining room the nurse blocked Phoebe's ears and nose with rubber plugs and fitted a mask over her mouth. Through the mask she would breathe oxygen from a nearby cylinder; the plugs would restrict her oxygen intake to what the cylinder supplied.

After Phoebe had started breathing through the mask, the nurse went out of the room for about a minute and a half. When she returned, she checked the results on the monitor and was dismayed to find them abnormal—dismayed because she believed in her employer's flair as much as he did. During her absence, she said, one of the plugs must have worked loose and let in air. Since she could be fired for such negligence, she begged Phoebe not to tell the doctor she had left her alone.

She had no need to worry. Dr. Sevareid glanced at the results and remarked, "A little high, but nothing to write home about. You must have leaky ears."

Phoebe was pleased not to have to lie about the nurse and pleased not to have thyroid trouble. She was surprised to learn that she suffered from cardiac neurosis.

"Don't worry, your heart's OK—it's only a minor disorder of the nervous system."

Dr. Sevareid gave Phoebe what she craved: an authoritative explanation of her unusual feelings. She never doubted his judgment. He could describe symptoms she had never even mentioned—her breathlessness, her blushes. When he asked her to hold out her hands, they trembled helplessly.

"You can see the condition is physically real, even if it has

a psychogenic origin. It's what people used to call 'nerves.'" Phoebe blushed on cue. "You've probably been upset for a while about something or other, natural enough at your age— or any age." He smiled warmly and prescribed Miltown in moderate doses. If she didn't feel better within a month, she could always try psychotherapy.

The tranquilizer took the edge off Phoebe's anguish. But her spells of depression grew worse, with each passing day and night her angry heart beat faster, and she spent nights no less wakeful than before. She was perhaps most discouraged by the voice in her head. Originally no more than a murmur, it now grew into a merciless yammer, berating her with things she could hardly bear hearing—her own voice turned mean.

Phoebe named this voice her squawk box. She blamed it for making her heart pound, for keeping her awake at three in the morning, for rousing her every two hours when she slept. When, one day, she realized that she had begun talking back to the voice, she asked Dr. Sevareid for the name of a therapist. He advised her to speak to Owen. To Owen he confidentially recommended his colleague Dr. Straub.

Like Dr. Sevareid, Dr. Straub was experienced and honest. Phoebe could not know that to both doctors Owen had described her at length and in terms confirming his own prejudices. To Owen, that Phoebe was neurotic proved her way of life wrong and justified his mistrust of her. She had been mistaken from the start. He should have forced her to listen to him, forced her to stay home. Owen wanted her doctors to support these views, and he drew them a portrait of Phoebe that approached caricature: her life had lost all regularity, her friends belonged to the fringes of society, she took drugs, she indulged in sexual promiscuity.

Phoebe knew what Owen thought of her. Whenever she discussed her life with him, he remained earnestly uncomprehending. When she told him she had a hard time getting to

sleep, he suggested she stop staying up so late. She disliked being given advice fit for children and detested his conviction that he understood her. She decided to keep silent in his presence. She said to her squawk box that explaining things to him was like trying to change a political party by joining it. Her squawk box scolded, *Baby, is that how you talk to the doctor? He'll tell you who wears the nuts in the family.* Phoebe: "You're so *cheap.*"

Phoebe inspired kindness in Dr. Straub, and she welcomed this kindness. She could not guess how pathetic Owen's description had made her appear. Dr. Straub had readily accepted the description because she came to him tagged with Dr. Sevareid's unimpeachable opinion, and he needed evidence that her neurosis had substance.

Phoebe herself supplied further evidence. Her feverish excitement provoked a sexual itch, and she masturbated frequently. She had no male friends that especially attracted her, and she was misguided in her choice of strangers, even at social gatherings (the only occasions where she dared approach them). She had three one-night stands that left her feeling degraded. When Dr. Straub learned of them, Owen's account of her seemed even more plausible.

Unaware of her disease, beset with disagreeable sensations, Phoebe concluded that she must simply be strange—perhaps truly neurotic. A sense of solitude invaded her, whether she was alone or not. She decided that the world was leaving her to herself; and because she did not make the easiest company, she wondered what else might comfort her. Since even the most ordinary experiences now took on unusual intensity, she began speculating that the world around her represented more than what she had heretofore seen in it; that life, and her life in particular, depended on a less visible, more abstract, more significant reality. Looking for manifestations of this idea, she found them in abundance: in the unwittingly expressive

gestures of others, in the penetrating glances they gave her, in words that leapt at her from the humdrum contexts of what she heard and read.

Louisa, who saw Phoebe several times in November, was disheartened by her appearance, and even more by her obscure new way of speaking. Once, discussing Owen over the phone, Phoebe breathily said to her, "Darling Momma, how is it he can't understand? The bads, OK, but even when I'm ecstatic? I know that it's always just Nature working on my mind. So I feel it working on my mind—"

"Everyone has their ups and downs—"

"No. It's why can't *I* be a little voice in the big chorus? I'd settle for being a pocket thermometer."

"A thermometer?"

"You know, when the sun moved to the heart of the earth (it's still there, actually), anyone could feel it—even the Presidential Mediators."

"The who?"

"There's only one planet, Momma, whatever the astronomers say. You know what I call it?"

"No."

"An apple of love divine! By 'divine' I just mean a coherence of *apparently* contradictory vectors. That's what gives us a glimpse of the holy spirit. You know, the spirit of the hole? That's where the thermometer goes in. A joke, Momma."

"Oh—I see."

"Anyway, it's all the same, and it's *me*."

Louisa apologized for not understanding her and asked for time to think about it. Soon, however, all Louisa's time would be devoted to her son, Lewis, and she would leave Phoebe to Owen—he had always "adored" her and had her best interests at heart.

The words *hole* and *Presidential Mediators* had drifted into Phoebe's speech from conversations with her squawk box. She

had told it, "I'm just a worm in the Big Apple. . . ." *So, what did you see, huh?* "Cuter girls than me, I can tell you." *Cute boys, by the Lord. I know you—every boy's a cute one.* "No, they make me sad. They find a girl and lead her straight to the ice-house, to see what she'll be like when she's old. It's crazy." *You walk down the street and all you think about is love. You better keep your girlie hands to yourself, you little bitch.* "I do that all the time." *I don't mean that. It's the far slope I'm talking about.* "You mean the hill, with the convent of the Sacred Heart?" *Oh, you're the heart—the artichoke heart! Not the holy heart, because that wouldn't be a hill but a hole.* . . . Phoebe was stuck with this pun on *holy*. She pierced, she was pierced with the holes of her body. Through them she thought she might penetrate to the exalting light coursing through her.

In October, at the climax of the missiles crisis, the general fear affected Phoebe violently. With the danger gone, the abstract meaning she looked for in the world was briefly embodied in a heroic image of the President. She wrote him a letter:

> If we admit that Nature works upon the mind, war is then a question of mind. I know that you know this. While the sun was floating up over Brooklyn this morning, I saw that you had mastered the coherence of contradictory vectors that alone gives us a glimpse of light, which some call love divine, since it harmoniously fuses races, nations, and religions in a peace that passes understanding. Because you have mastered this conflict, I feel as if stunned with love, like a bell in a wedding of angels. You have (not on purpose) decked out each corner of my heart with exquisite fiercely scented flowers. Nor, walking beside you, would I forget her, still and ever an adorable feminine apparition pursuing me and encouraging me like the spring breeze in her smile. That's how I've been cured of my regrets, in fact.

Squawk box said: *Don't bother him when he's so busy.* "OK, I'll send it to the Presidential Mediators. They'll know what's best."

Phoebe showed Walter her letter; he suggested she sleep on it. If she liked writing, he asked her, why not keep a working journal? A great idea, Phoebe replied. The letter read like gibberish when she next looked at it, and she put it away in a drawer, while her squawk box sniggered, *You still adore Him. . . .*

Phoebe saw Walter less and less. Priscilla had come into his life, looking after him, taking up his time. Phoebe inwardly relied on Owen, because she still loved him and because he dominated her visions when, for instance, she woke up to challenge another long day in late-night blackness, alone, in a sweat, with her heart clobbering her from within. Owen did not call often.

At the end of November her brother, Lewis, was arrested in scandalous circumstances. Phoebe refused to believe what was publicly said about him. Dr. Straub saw in this sympathy a confirmation of her tendency to dissoluteness. He became more confidently paternal than ever.

Phoebe began her journal:

> In art we must start by eliminating all historical classi-fications, which only produce stifled characters. We want beauty novelty style for all ages and lands. It's Christmas, isn't it—"No Hell"? . . .

As if to acknowledge the season, her squawk box soft-ened its tone, doubling her own voice in dreamier obsessions: "Gounod's 'Ave Maria' . . ." *Vacation's starting—but not for Mary Stuart. Ave Maria Stuart! It's like Christmas in wartime. Oh, you remember! The dead on a picket fence at Gettysburg, and: 'Hordes across the Yalu.'* "Fronds and spines on those corteges. Wouldn't it be kindly to be reborn into happy

Old nights of Holy Mystery
Hearing Noel sung in Your honor
To the ends of the earth."

You've lost your French, Maria Stuart says. "I remember beautiful
Christmases. Reproductions in gifted books—Christmas was
a Prussian-blue sky with Wise Men and star. Also organ and
bells. Sometimes they boom death Mass—fears and pains."
We do have peace, sort of. "Only divine hands can stanch tears.
Away on country hillsides steeples are counting out solemn
carols. In small-town streets they sing in a smell of snow and
ozone. Here shadows are all over the snow, with shouts not
hymns." *You don't dare step into a church. You'd want to kiss
people, and they'd only let you sing and cry.* "Fervent wishes in
the wind! Deliver our hearts and eyes from irritation. Let's
raise one Christmas tree in the Morosco Theater, and another
in the Beekman meat market."

She spent most of Christmastime in bed, feverish, besnot-
ted with her entrenched bronchitis. The infection aggravated
her usual symptoms. She got up for Owen, who came with an
offer of help in exchange for her giving up Walter. Breaking
with him left her in a morbid state, even though he sent her
money afterwards. She celebrated Christmas day in bed alone.

Walter went away for a few days with Priscilla. Phoebe
agreed to look after a friend's cat. She soon began thinking that
it was all the society she would ever have. And nobody's fault
but her own. She didn't blame anyone for neglecting her, not
even Owen. Not even Louisa, who was hiding behind him.
"Look at me, twenty years old, with breasts as wrinkly as the
skin on hot milk."

Phoebe gave up all thought of modeling. She painted less
and less. (Her hand shook, exhaustion led to distraction and
excused it.) One morning her jeans fell down, slipping off her
unfleshed hips. She hugged the mess of her body. She hurt.

Sometimes the ache of her thrumming heart soared into a dazzling pain that sent her back to bed curled up and enduring.
Because her sensations, feelings, and thoughts never abated,
she came to the conclusion that she didn't stand a chance
against them. What was she proving by lasting as long as she
could? Survival meant only unremitting punishment. She
didn't deserve it; she didn't deserve herself.

One evening in early February, she got out of bed and on
the way to the bathroom picked up an X-Acto knife from
her worktable. She ran a warm bath and sat in the tub with
the knife in her right hand. After a few minutes she traced a
tentative incision across her left wrist, perpendicular to the
veins that ran blue and swollen underneath the transparent
skin. A rosary of red droplets sprang up under the point. Her
friend's cat had followed her into the bathroom and was sitting
on the toilet, perched on its hindquarters, staring at her. Its
gaze, one of perfect attention and indifference, was suddenly
interrupted by a pink-and-white yawn, during which the cat's
head disappeared behind its mouth. The animal then settled
on its belly, crossing its forepaws. Phoebe shifted the knife
to her left hand. Leaning her neck on the rim of the tub, she
began masturbating underwater. Her pleasure—faint, short,
unsettling—kept her alive.

Phoebe flipped the drain open and stepped out of the tub.
She put on a can of consommé to heat while she dressed. She
took a long time dressing. Later she went outside and started
walking, working her way east, through the clear and wind-
less night, cold but not frozen. She felt both numb and alert
crossing the city, numb to cold and filth, alert to a thrashing
rhythm within her. As she passed from one streaming avenue
to the next, each dark block between became a bridge that
lifted her into another half-abandoned hive where beings from
uncreated dreams slept and drifted, giddy from the shock of
their birth. They did not sadden her, she felt no sorrow for

them, and a glance from any one of them could only mean that someone wished her well; she went on. A half hour later she crossed under an elevated highway and found herself at the "river." She wiped her eyes stung wet by cold and airy dirt. Above the city glow, scattered stars glistened in a moonless sky, drooping close, teetering not unkindly over the convulsions of her thought.

She had grown cold. She hurried up to Fourteenth Street and found a coffee shop. She was wearing Russian boots, men's corduroy trousers, a Navy pea jacket with two sweaters underneath, ski mittens, and a plaid wool cap with its earflaps down. After ordering her tea, she took off the cap, the mittens, the pea jacket, and one of her sweaters. The other customers relaxed. Someone from space had become a nice girl with rather large eyes. Three young men at the counter began teasing her, betting how long it took her to get into all those clothes. And how about getting *out* of them? Phoebe hardly minded. She had attracted no attention in a week, or since wanting to die. One of the men said it was a crime to bundle herself out of sight like that—a pretty girl was what life was all about. His words gave the world back to Phoebe. She wanted to cry. When he asked if he could take her home, she said yes.

Back in her studio, he treated her gently and a little impatiently. Because of her skinniness she turned out the lights and got under the covers first. He started rubbing his hands over her. She cried out. He took this for a sign of pleasure; she meant something else. She was experiencing a visitation, or at least an unusual visit. It had begun snowing inside her room. Out of the fathomless dark ceiling, snow was falling and soundlessly pelting her. The flakes felt light and warm as they cascaded onto her and through her. "Wait," she pleaded, "it's beautiful—" The boy grunted knowingly. She let him be, surrendering to the soft tumult. She rose to meet and savor it, gliding through rings of splintery light, up, up. Where was she

going? Higher, she found or mentally assembled webs of incandescence out of which the flakes came sprinkling. She guessed, she *knew* what they were: stars. The teetering stars had spilled into the gloom of her mind. She had no strength to resist that shower or the spidery filaments above it that sucked her in. She recognized where she had come: into the abstraction called love. She was being pelted with love and sucked into it—and this poor boy was still bumping against her. Sure he was. Love had been broken into bits among us, the way light was pieced out around the sky: here and there, the same thing. A showering, never fixed, except in a fixity of change, in the motion of its fragments. Each star moved in its ring, each man in his life each woman in her life, longing to touch and never able to, and still one life, one us. That's why I love cloudless nights, Phoebe thought. Truth was shining around her. She drifted into the welter of light. She laughed incredulously, "It's us!" Her body shook with glee as he lost himself inside her. For a few days she had a hard time keeping him away.

Phoebe had to talk to someone about this joy. She approached Walter as soon as he came back. When she confessed that a stranger had restored her faith in life by telling her she was pretty, Walter scolded her. She was peddling herself to bums. They didn't care a damn about love and truth: "Their guiding light is getting into your pants."

She was disgusted with herself when she left him; and the disgust permanently cured her of suicide. Her piddling life did not deserve dramatic remedies. No sooner had she thought, When I got to the river I should have jumped right in, than her squawk box barked sympathetically, *The East River? Honey, you wouldn't have drowned, you'd have choked to death.* Phoebe wrote in her journal:

A leap into the unknown is a leap back into childishness—another dream that doesn't work, and pretentious, too.

She resigned herself to living as a sick, childish adult, as a succession of hopeful and shameful incarnations. She remembered her father, with whom she had shared years of love and to whom she had spoken viciously. She wanted to speak to him again, in some other manner.

Phoebe had not seen Dr. Straub for a month. At her next visit, in mid-February, he remarked that she had behaved irresponsibly by not keeping her appointments. Not only had she harmed herself, she had prevented him from reporting on her condition to Owen, who was greatly upset. Phoebe thus learned of the therapist's complicity with her father. She saw an opportunity to wipe the slate clean, since both she and Owen had now put themselves in the wrong: she had yelled at him, he had acted behind her back. She wrote him a letter:

> . . . I was painfully surprised that you could talk about me to someone, even a doctor, so confidentially. It's too bad you haven't observed the results. At least I now understand why he stares at me so hard without ever seeing me. (It's true I always wear the magic ring you once gave me!) Since I can appreciate your desire to talk to someone about me, perhaps you can appreciate that to me it seems fairly disgusting? I know you meant well—that's the way "your kind" behaves, you're all so *good* at that: summing up a life in a few words. Has anyone ever looked right through you and out the other side? . . .

Owen did not respond. Phoebe was afraid of saying what she didn't mean if she used the telephone; so she wrote another letter, this time to Louisa. Discussing Owen, she asked for help:

> . . . A question becomes evident: is it possible to communicate with a human being? To communicate what my life is—

Life goes on and keeps becoming what it already was. There are differences of form, that's all. Or I may feel that I'm still a lot of different people, but it's still one person struggling like mad—madly degrading myself—. . . .

There were moments when you smiled—you were irresistibly yourself, even if you checked the smile a second after it showed. I know all about that. . . .

I'm getting weaker and weaker, I let things happen abjectly. My room is a dream. So are the things in it, including my feet. Sometimes I scream dream screams. What I've lost is my confidence—my "insolence." I need tenderness, too—the infinite tenderness that goes with beginnings. So I scream like a little child who's been left out. Not just left out by people, by *things*. However, this does not make me feel inhuman, I feel *very* human. . . .

Louisa, when she came to see her, found Phoebe more than she could face. She did not know where to begin. She encouraged Phoebe to trust the medical help she was getting and withdrew—into Owen's shadow, as Phoebe saw it. Phoebe still refused to condemn Owen, reminding herself that he was paying for her doctors and sending her money. She reduced him for the time being to someone who wrote necessary checks.

With no one else to rely on, she clung earnestly to herself. That self had become more and more fugitive: she kept losing hold of her pain, her tremors, and her explosive feelings. One afternoon she went to a movie, *The Diary of a Country Priest*. In one scene, an older clergyman tells the young protagonist that anyone called to holy orders will find in the history of Christianity a precedent for his vocation. Walking home between ridges of grizzled snow, Phoebe asked herself if hers might not be Saint Lawrence on his griddle. At home she wrote in her journal:

If the old ways had not been hidden, we could deliver ourselves from death by death. The divine directive points toward voluntary consumption—best by fire, "to cleanse the errant soul."

Reflections such as this reconciled Phoebe to the "fire" cauterizing her from within.

Occasionally she would return to places and people she had enjoyed. Her volatile temperament prevented these outings from soothing her as she hoped they might. In the Cedar one February evening, a writer told a group at the bar a supposedly true story that amused everyone except her. The previous summer, two of his friends had traveled through New England by car. Late one afternoon, on a back road in the White Mountains, they had overtaken a line of forty-odd girls returning to camp at the end of a hike. The girls, who were ten to thirteen years old, looked tired out. The procession was led by a group of four counselors, young women in their late teens. The writer's friends pulled up near the end of the straggling group. They asked how far the girls still had to go. About three miles, they answered. Any of them like a lift? You bet! Four of them got into the back seat. The men explained that in exchange they would have to "give head." The girls didn't know what that meant; as soon as they were told, they scrambled out of the car. The men stopped to renew their invitation farther up the line. Other girls climbed into the car and climbed out. At last the men, drawing level with the counselors, asked, "A lift, anybody?" "OK." "Hop in." Two of the counselors settled in the back seat, nothing else was said, and the car drove off under the gaze of forty-six freshly enlightened little girls.

Phoebe at first missed the point of the story. When she understood the trick the men had played, she began to cry. Her friends looked at her incredulously. She smashed her beer on the floor and ran outside.

She felt angry less at her friends than at humanity at large.

Men and women looked at one another and saw only the stuff of contemptuous jokes. Tag thy neighbor, and any tag would do—Pole, Jew, cocksucker. She shuddered remembering the women who had been stuck with this ingenious disgrace. In spite of herself she laughed at the ingenuity and thought of the disgrace as something less than disastrous, an impulse that made her break out in fresh tears. She was no different. Even she could forget "love divine." She told herself after a moment, "Of course I'm no different. And *that's* part of love." Nevertheless she had begun excluding herself from the world that her love embraced.

A few nights later Phoebe had a dream. She called it her "dream of dissolution." She is attending a group event in a sort of sunken theater inside a big, old-fashioned hotel in the city. A froglike man is directing the group. Again and again he tells them, "Accept things as they happen." Long sessions of explanation and mental exercise are separated by five-minute breaks. After the first break, she notices that the cat sitting near her is missing. After the second, the woman on her left disappears. No one can leave the theater unobserved.

Phoebe now realizes what she has been warned to accept: creatures are disintegrating. They are vanishing definitively, without cause, without justification. Phoebe feels a fresh confidence. Although she knows that sadness awaits her, she no longer worries about what will happen. During another break, chatting with a short, lively woman in her sixties, she senses that this woman will go next.

When only five participants are left, Phoebe is possessed with a desire for a "saving egg." She does not understand what this means. During the next break, in a hotel shop full of exotic bric-a-brac, she finds a cream-colored porcelain egg and buys it. Rolling it in one hand, she experiences an elation both austere and sensual. Nearby, the froglike leader is talking to a dark intellectual boy whom Phoebe had known at college. The

three go back together and sit on the floor of the pit. Phoebe squeezes the egg, filling up with power. The frog man, who has begun a long speech, turns to her and softly tells her, "All right, lay off. I get it. You have the power."

A consoling warmth was stealing over Phoebe. She looked forward to waking up. She could not wake up because she had not fallen asleep. The dream, vivid as a movie, had come to her as she sat on the edge of her bed—the first of many such hallucinations. She clenched her left hand around the absent egg and hummed an old refrain:

> Earth is mother to all kinds,
> Crazy men and women.
> Earth is mother to all kinds,
> Crazy women and men.

Phoebe became chronically frightened. Her tenacious depression had convinced her that "she had failed." What had she failed at? Who was the "she" that had done the failing? She was frightened by the loss of anything she might call herself. Whatever she now was eluded her; "she" had dissolved into pure confusion. When she told Walter this, he replied, "Why the hell do you think I paint?" She noted:

So there you are with two fingers up your nose. Remove them. No problem.

She made herself go back to work. She decided literally to see who she was: she would paint nothing else.

. . . First, drawings of myself, in the old manner. Divide the surface into squares. Draw fainter lines through the center of the squares to form a secondary griddle. Insert my parts one by one:
P. Lewison, of medium height from head to toe. The

length of her head equals the distance between her chin and her nipples, the distance between her chin and nipples equals that between nipples and bellybutton, the distance between nipples and bellybutton equals that between bellybutton and crotch. Shoulders are two head-heights broad. Bones: through the skin you can identify ribs, also knobs of femurs, humerus, radius. Elsewhere: frontal bone, parietal bone, temples, brows. Features: eyeballs, hair, thin nose, middling mouth, rounded chin, scarlet cheekbones. Legend: draw two horizontal lines, letters between them in large and small caps: PH. LEWISON. Inscribed above: ST. LAWRENCE IN DRAG. Or BLEEDING HEART OF JESUS. Or SACRED CUNT OF JESUS.

Phoebe gave one such sketch to Dr. Straub, the person she most talked to, someone she wanted to thank. At their next meeting he analyzed the drawing for her. In it, he pointed out, he noticed blank eyes, hands hidden behind the back, genitals more detailed than the face. His comments made her cry. Because she rarely cried in his presence, he imagined that she had come to the verge of a useful discovery. She was crying for him. That night she wrote him a farewell letter:

> . . . O my psychiatrist! The human being has turned into a farm animal. The hands that handle her take all they find and give nothing back to what *must* be the source of life. You yourself pay taxes to the animal farm—you know we all end up in the stewpot. People love to eat out of it, and orders have been issued to the young to multiply and then suck each other's juices right down to the marrow. First we're pigs and donkeys, then animal suckers. . . .

This letter at last elicited a phone call from Owen: "You can't do this to yourself. You're in bad enough shape as it is, and now what's to keep you from going to pieces completely?"

Her squawk box had already been telling her this, in these

words. Phoebe wondered in terror if she had not already gone to pieces. No—she still had her feelings. They rampaged through her every hour of the day. Whatever being endured them could lay claim to a real existence. Only her body, the ground of that existence, kept letting her down. Each day she tried to will it back into wholeness if not wholesomeness: "Two feet, like everybody else. Left big toe, right big toe, left ankle, right ankle. . . . Stomach with diaphragm attached, ribs enclosing me like two hands. Lungs . . ." Her lungs remained sopped; when she ate, her stomach burned; a skinned rabbit's head stared back from her mirror.

Asking the head in the mirror if she was insane comforted her, because as long as she accepted insanity as a possibility, she knew she had some sanity left. "How can the possibility of insanity be cured?" she wrote. "By food, work, and faith."

She forced soup through her teeth. No matter how exhausted, she stuck to a daily schedule of sketching, writing, and reading. Faith proved harder. A relentless awareness of loss stuffed her thin chest with dated movies of lovers, parents, and friends.

Consolation began in a book. She had become the kind of reader authors dream of, for whom each sentence revises the universe. She could have sworn Sir Thomas Browne knew her plight when he wrote that

> Thy soul is eclipsed for a time, I yield, as the sun is shadowed by a cloud; no doubt but there gracious beams of God's mercy will shine upon thee again. . . . We must live by faith, not by feeling; 'tis like the beginning of grace to wish for grace; we must expect and tarry.

A passing cloud had come over her. This did not mean that her sun was dead.

Life is a pure flame, and we must live by our invisible sun within us.

She remembered her autumn ecstasies—"light and love divine." Others had looked at her strangely. In Sir Thomas's company she felt less strange, less alone: I don't know what it is, but I know I'm something, and it's all I've got.

The sudden spring fostered her confidence. After five months she at last stopped coughing. She imagined that soon her hands might no longer tremble. Lewis and his friend Morris took her into the Hudson River valley for a weekend, among reservoirs and rolling orchards. Sunday night she wrote:

Grapevines budding. I'm still only twenty. Yesterday apple trees opened petals of primal cream and pink. In a few months, Rubens's wreaths of fruit—vines ripening, apples on boughs. Tonight, light dripping with shadow, hill moon rising, sun withdrawing, forest shivering in the breath of summer to be. Someone told the hawthorn, Blossom!— Ph. unfolded. Someone told the whippoorwill, Sing!—Ph. sang. Brother and friend spoke hymns of farewell to this natural day. A beloved woman must speak with the breath of corollas brushed by a shuttling bird.

She went back to work in a loving frenzy. She started calling her friends again and went out to meet them. She wanted to wrap them all into her billowing cloak of love. They were busy, they were worried, they had to leave. Her work happened in visionary outbursts. Walter came to see it. He told her, "You're crapping all over the canvas. You *know* better." Even though she had met her only ten minutes earlier, Phoebe implored Elizabeth, who heard this judgment, to wait in her studio after Walter left. While Elizabeth watched, Phoebe destroyed her new work.

She then planned another self-portrait in the manner of

the old masters. But she didn't have the patience for such things. Her hand lusted after scrawls and tangles, "dirty combinations," dull orange smeared with dull green. Her brush scampered away from her.

In mid-May she gave up. She stopped seeing her friends. She stopped painting, although she still wrote a little. Increasingly she spent her days and mostly sleepless nights trying to guess the cause of her disintegration. What had she or anybody done that must be so painfully atoned for? Something—something obvious and stupidly hidden from her: "a secret lesson any old ocarina can repeat." She was condemned to learn this lesson the hard way.

In late May, her brother, Lewis, again became the object of public scandal. Louisa, who had spent months watching over her son, collapsed and was committed to a hospital. Phoebe went to see her. In Louisa's hospital room, mother and daughter broke each other's heart.

Phoebe stopped at a bar on her way home. She stepped from the sweltering day into air-conditioned chill. She sneezed into her whiskey sour. Her nose started to dribble. By evening she was coughing violently; before morning she was burning with fever. She phoned Walter, who took her straight to Saint Vincent's, where she was admitted with double pneumonia.

The two doctors in charge of Phoebe were appalled by her condition. They disregarded her psychosomatic explanation and quickly guessed at the truth. Phoebe did her best to frustrate them. She regarded them as mortal enemies. Whenever they approached her, her eyes glittered with wary loathing, and her squawk box, in a harsh mood, speaking on her behalf, pestered them with resentful insults.

As Phoebe saw it, two strangers had decided to meddle with her secret life. Under the pretence of caring for her, they were hunting down the scurrying, tiny identity to which she was now reduced. Her mistrust of them survived their successful

treatment of her pneumonia and the prodigies of tact the doctors exercised in discussing her chronic disorder. Their suggestion that this disorder might have a physiological origin infuriated her. The ecstatic pain that had grown in her over the past year had by now become the center of her reality. She could not bear having it made medically predictable. She refused to be helped. Only when Louisa arrived, four days after Phoebe's admission, was she lured out of her corner.

Louisa promised Phoebe that she would never abandon her again; she promised never to let Owen, or anyone else, interfere with her. Phoebe let herself be convinced, after exacting one more promise: she must never be left alone with her doctors. She then agreed to do what was asked of her, giving up responsibility for her nightmare illness with a relief that surprised her. For the first time since December, she menstruated.

Phoebe was given a second basal metabolism test, this time correctly administered. It recorded her metabolic rate at an abnormal +35. Methyl thiouracil was prescribed for her, one hundred milligrams to be taken daily. Louisa was told that Phoebe could leave the hospital as soon as she recovered from her pneumonia, probably in three or four days. She would need several weeks to become healthy again. During that time she should lead a restful life, she should be taken care of—in other words, she should go home.

After her first wild resentment, Phoebe endured her stay in the hospital with petulant resignation. Her fever came down, her lungs cleared; nothing else changed. Her heart still banged, she trembled and sweated, and the best pills brought her only brief sleep. When Louisa said she was taking her to their home upstate, Phoebe did not protest. She nonetheless took the decision as a defeat—the two years she had lived on her own were being written off. Her squawk box, meshed for a while with her own passionate voice, reasserted itself to denounce her surrender. It suggested that Owen had instigated what was

happening. Louisa was doing the dirty work while he rubbed his hands in the wings.

Phoebe's own voice fell to a whisper. It whispered more sound than sense, as though the squawk box had requisitioned the attributes of reason. One day it started saying, over and over, without apparent cause, "I quest, request, bequest . . ." (By now she could control her own voice no better than the box's.) At another time it repeated an inexplicable succession of letters inside her docile ears: b.s.t.q.l.d.s.t., b.s.t.q.l.d.s.t. . . . . Phoebe could not decipher the series. After making it yield "Beasts stalk the question lest demons sever trust" and "But soon the quest lured drab saints thither," she rejected the possibility that the letters were initials. She found it even harder to make words out of them, especially without a u for the q. No matter what she did, they refused to be dispelled. No matter what she did. Without meaning, unthreatening, merely insistent, the letters turned into a regular refrain inside her head. Phoebe had to insert her voice's other whisperings between them: "I b.s.t.q.l.d. quest s.t. I b.s.t.q.l. request d.s.t., I b.s.t.q. bequest l.d.s.t. . . ."

Phoebe quickly lost interest in the new diagnosis of her condition, which might have pleased anyone—anyone else.

Before she left, Louisa repeated to her again and again that she would take care of her until she was completely cured. She would not be sent to a "clinic." She would be protected from Owen as long as she wanted. For the eighteenth time Phoebe consented to go home. She set a condition, however: she would go alone, and by train—the way they had always come back from the city when she first traveled with her parents as a little girl. Phoebe's doctors urged Louisa to indulge her.

During her trip, Phoebe learned something about the series of letters. B.s.t.q.l.d.s.t. signified an old train careening down an old track. At slower speeds the train said,

Cigarettes, tch tch
Cigarettes, tch tch.

She found nothing to eat or drink during the four-hour ride. The carriage shook so hard she could not read. Before Poughkeepsie, under a three-o'clock sun, the air-conditioning broke down. People sitting near her kept moving away. When she saw Louisa, the pang of joy made Phoebe yell. Afterwards, in her unaltered room, she yanked off her clothes to slide between the sheets of her blond-pine bed. She slept.

Owen arrived the next Friday. When she saw him, pain came back—an unfamiliar pain, which Phoebe lived with for several days before she could name it.

At two in the morning, awake in her room, Phoebe sat by her window, staring out through hot moonlight at the trees, lawn, and houses that beleaguered her. She listened to the voices inside her. With obscure insistence her box kept reminding her of a photograph in her father's room. Thanks to her, that room was now unoccupied. Phoebe got up and found the photograph, a sepia portrait framed in engraved silver of her paternal grandmother, who had died of a stroke when Phoebe was two. She was dressed in black, with a wide-brimmed hat pinned to the back of her head, a jacket with enormous lapels, a tapering ankle-length skirt, and long silk gloves held loosely in her hands. Her features expressed gravity and alertness. Averted from the camera, her gaze seemed fixed on some disaster that confirmed all she had ever suspected. Phoebe put the photograph on her bedside table.

The novelty of Phoebe's pain lay less in its symptoms—the familiar ones of her disease—than in its source, which she imagined as outside herself. She could not at first identify that source, and only did so after Louisa revealed to her the settlement Owen had made on her behalf on the occasion of her twenty-first birthday.

What she then discovered would not have surprised anyone who had observed her in Owen's presence. Her every gesture and word expressed resentment and disgust. Whenever
he appeared, she would draw up her knees and grit her teeth,
reminding herself of demands to be made, reconnoiter-
ing opportunities for attack. Unable to see herself, Phoebe
remained unaware of the obsessiveness of her feelings. She
almost realized the "truth" while Owen was reading to her
late one afternoon:

> Mr. Copperfield chuckled. "You're so crazy," he said to
> her with indulgence. He was delighted to be in the trop-
> ics at last and he was more than pleased with himself that
> he had managed to dissuade his wife from stopping at a
> ridiculously expensive hotel where they would have been
> surrounded by tourists. He realized that this hotel was
> sinister, but that was what he loved.

Phoebe would have shouted "Just like you!" if at this moment
her father had not dozed off. Her rage diverted, she only
growled him awake.

A few days before Phoebe's birthday, Owen deposited
several hundred shares of high-priced securities in a custody
account opened in her name, and ordered the monthly transfer
of five hundred dollars from his checking account into hers.
The news of these arrangements brought Phoebe's emotions
into perfect order.

"He hates you," a woman said. In astonishment Phoebe
looked at the photograph by her bed. Two ravens rose out of
a summery field and winged their slow way out of sight above
the house. "He'll do anything to stop you."

"Why, you fifty-pint-old drunkess," Phoebe replied.

"I know him better'n anybody," the woman cawed.
"Remember the first time he stuck you with money? He'll
never change."

Owen congealed for Phoebe into a repellent image of self-ishness. She saw that he had pretended to encourage her freedom only to attack it better. He no longer even pretended an interest in her painting. Of course he must hate her. Perhaps he had always hated her, and he had lavished care on her as a child only to control her, to make sure she complied with his desires. To think how she'd loved him!

"Don't expect me to thank you," Phoebe told him after learning of his extraordinary gift.

"I don't," Owen answered, with a meekness that made her yearn to draw blood.

"I'm only accepting to make you pay something." Her grandmother coaxed her, "Tell him he's a fox and a pig!" Phoebe's throat choked with sobs of fury.

She sometimes spied on her parents, hiding inside the door of the terrace where they had drinks before dinner. One evening she heard Owen suggest to Louisa that Phoebe have a thyroidectomy. She thus made a second discovery. Her father would not content himself with dominating her life; he wanted that life itself. She thought of the ways he had intervened since last September: choosing her thyroid specialist, choosing her psychotherapist, insisting that her troubles were psychological, belittling her flagrant symptoms. He had pushed her to the limit of her disease; now he wanted to finish her off.

Mrs. Lewison Senior's black silks flapped around her fussily: "He may think he doesn't know what he's doing, but he sure is doing it." Phoebe, who had wet her pants downstairs, was sitting on the toilet in her bathroom. She had become fiercely determined. She would survive and win. Her father would die first. Or she would teach him pain. That would be even better.

Louisa never failed her. When Phoebe called, she came.

Phoebe called her more and more often. Louisa had become company, and also childhood love, belated and never too late. Phoebe wished she did not hang on to her mother so greedily.

For Louisa, apparently inexhaustible, this dependence was in itself sufficient reward. That Louisa never mentioned the operation did not disturb Phoebe: it meant that her mother had turned Owen's proposition down. After all, she herself did not speak about certain matters, such as her grandmother's eerie voice.

That voice was raised urgently when, on August first, Phoebe learned that Owen had acquired the "Portrait of Elizabeth": "He's at it again. Why, he never cared about painting. And you know how he feels about Walter." (Lewis had told her that Owen referred to Walter as "the man who ruined my daughter.") "But then, maybe he's speculating. To people like him, you know, art's just a commodity. No, that's not it. He knows how you feel about that picture, doesn't he? Take it from me, *you're* why he bought it. He doesn't want to leave you one single thing. He wants you to see he's running the whole show. . . ."

Phoebe rasped, "Shut up, you old bitch!" She'd been stung. Although she was willing to see vengefulness in anything Owen did, his simply owning the portrait hurt her most. When could he have bought it? Suspicious, she telephoned Walter's gallery. The painting had been sold—to Maud Ludlam. They were sure: it had been shipped to her in late June.

"What did I tell you?" the old woman sighed. "He's a dark one—dark as the ground owl of childhood fame."

Phoebe confronted Owen with what she'd learned. Since he now approached her like a sinner at confession, she could not tell whether her words truly upset him.

"Of course," he said. "I bought it from the Ludlams."

"Maud got rid of it after a month?"

"Why not? What difference does it make?"

"What the hell are you doing with that painting?"

"If you really want to know, I got it for you."

Phoebe sensed he was lying. She would pin him to the floor. "So why haven't you given it to me?"

"It'll be arriving any day."

"Is it mine or isn't it?"

Owen hesitated. He *had* thought of reselling the painting. "Would that make you happy?"

"Nothing you do could make me happy. Your owning that painting makes me puke."

"It's yours."

"I want papers to prove it."

"There's no need for that, darling."

"Yes, there is, *darling*. I want to make sure it's out of your fucking hands."

"When I promise you something—"

"Uh-uh. I want a legal document of ownership. Otherwise the world is going to learn about your hanky-panky with that wharf in New London. Remember, when you got two companies to pay off one claim?"

Owen laughed. "Phoebe, stop it. That's ancient history. Nobody gives a damn. I even told complete strangers about it—you were there."

"Not Louisa."

Watching him, Phoebe could not stifle a grin. She had guessed right. He walked out of her room. She would have her way.

Louisa took advantage of Phoebe's good spirits to broach unpleasant business. She told her that her treatment had conspicuously failed and that she should consider a thyroidectomy—the sooner the better. "You haven't gained five pounds since you came up here, and you're jumpy as ever. In your shoes I'd go crazy in a week."

"I went crazy months ago. If I could know—if I could be sure I'd get better someday, I wouldn't mind waiting. I suppose Owen thinks I should get my throat cut."

"He's got nothing to do with it. *You* think about it, and *you* decide. I don't want to keep secrets from you. I did find out

there's a good surgeon at Albany. He does four or five thyroids a week, there and in Boston. I told him about you, and he's available."

Phoebe said nothing. After a while Louisa again spoke: "I've told you *my* secret."

"I'm scared. It's mainly the anesthetic. I don't want to face that. It's like death."

"Not anymore, not with Pentothal. It's not like going under. You just disappear in a second, and then you're back. No anxiety, no memories—"

"I believe you, but that's *not* my secret."

"I don't follow."

"Momma, if I'm going to live, I have to agree to die first. Can I be alone for a while?"

Phoebe wrote her brother, Lewis:

> . . . Louisa is all kindness—real kindness—but I feel I'm losing her too. The sympathetic string of motherhood vibrates with hypocrisy. It has to—she has to disconnect from me if she's going to help. Is life always going to be like this? Yes, at least until death. That will do for an answer.
>
> Can you understand? I need someone to understand, and you can—you've survived worse than I. Will you come here to be with me? With you at my side, I might let them cut my throat.

Phoebe's grandmother attended her constantly—a presence not disturbing, not reassuring. She had been permanently transformed into a bird. Although large and black, the bird brought to Phoebe's room a sense not of ominousness but of placid, continuous movement, like the sound of planes regularly landing and taking off at a distant airport. The bird spoke less and less.

The portrait of Elizabeth arrived. Lewis brought it to her room as soon as it had been uncrated. When she saw it, Phoebe

was overcome by giggles. "It was mine all along! Hang it on the wall, over there. Lewis, please let me love you."

Her twenty-first birthday passed discreetly, marked only by a cake for three. The day before, Louisa had driven Phoebe to the Medical Center in Albany, where a surgeon examined her. Phoebe had taken to him at once, something that so astonished Louisa, after her lengthy precautions, that it made her almost cross. During the days that followed Phoebe thought only of her next encounter with the doctor, ruddy, plump, irresistibly confident. When she first looked into his eyes, calm as a cow's, life became manageable. Later, she experienced fright, and a familiar hatred of created things, especially herself. In her bedroom she rediscovered an owlish raven circling the ceiling, and Elizabeth in paints, whom she did not hate.

Following Phoebe's instructions, Owen brought the portrait to the hospital during the operation and hung it in her room opposite her bed. On the bedside table Lewis installed a record player that she could reach lying down.

Louisa and Lewis were waiting for her on her return from the recovery room. Whenever Phoebe opened her eyes—for a long while they merely rolled absently under half-closed lids— her mother said to her that she was doing fine, and Lewis grimly echoed her. They were not saying what they thought, only what they had been told. Phoebe's face looked bloodless and shrunken above her bandaged neck, to which two drains were taped.

Phoebe at first did not hear them and later did not believe them. She was emerging into a welter of drowsiness and terror. In spite of the tranquilizers she had been given, she had never felt sicker. The consequences of surgery did not frighten her: she simply knew that her symptoms had grown worse. Her heart bedeviled her ribs like a spike; sweat filmed on her arms and legs; her body had disintegrated into pockets of anguish.

The operation had succeeded, and Phoebe's reaction

corresponded to a new condition. Four-fifths of her thyroid gland had been removed. Left unchecked, the gland could only respond to the body's demand for the excess thyroxine, to which it had grown accustomed, by starting to grow back. To prevent this, Phoebe was given thyroxine in amounts greater than any she had secreted during her disease. In the course of her operation her pulse had not gone below 160; it now rose to 180. No one could have persuaded her that she was being cured.

For seven days she endured in virtual immobility because of the drains in her neck and the intravenous drip in each arm. She again lost all control of her thoughts and feelings.

The feeling of fear never left her, oppressive with someone at her side, unbearable whenever she found herself alone. Without either Lewis or Louisa, Phoebe would ring for a nurse every two minutes, although she soon learned that others provided only an illusory relief. Others could distract her, not calm what she most dreaded: that the next moment would prove as intolerable as the last, as it always did.

Lewis sometimes read out loud to her. Phoebe did her best to listen; in less than a minute her attention would unravel. Music worked better. She had brought her favorite records, among them some Haydn quartets. Halfway through one of them, at the end of the "Emperor" theme and variations, Phoebe grabbed Lewis's wrist: "Leave that." She played the movement over and over, at least four hundred times. She said afterwards that without it she would have tried to kill herself. Often her head filled with words that Haydn's familiar tune trailed after it, words she thought she had forgotten, a hymn from school days: "Glorious things of thee are spoken, Sion . . ."

Her bird still attended her, voiceless and mechanical, speeding incessantly from one corner of her ceiling to the next as if hung on an elliptical track. It made a whirring, whispering noise: *essesso, essesso . . .*

These things constituted her days and nights: the whispered *essesso* of the bird, the fourth variation coming to an end, grappling with the pillow to find the bell, reaching for Lewis's or Louisa's hand.

Before she left home, the portrait of Elizabeth had entertained if not consoled her; here it gave no comfort. Phoebe had her room kept dark. In the meager daylight from the blinded windows or by the light of the night lamp, the painting was blurred and distorted. The yellow blank eyes floated above the head; the folded hands, whose nails suggested a silver smile, shrank to dull stumps; the fiery red of the hair streamed down the canvas in muddy pulsations. Phoebe would look at Elizabeth, shut her eyes, and sing in time with the record,

> See the streams of living water
> Springing from eternal love

wishing for one thing: make it end.

She never cried. She never had time to collect her tears: too busy getting the Haydn restarted, clutching the bell, watching the door for the tortoise-footed nurse, waiting for the next moment to be less painful, and the one after that. If she had been able to cry, she would have cried for her poor body, regularly devoured by an insatiable, rubber-toothed monster.

After a week, her dose of thyroxine was reduced. Although Phoebe did not know she felt better, her sensations gradually came off the boil, and the terror that had swamped her subsided into a calmer sadness. The sadness filled her whole body, as the terror had, coldly now. The whir of the bird, the inexhaustible sweetness of the quartet, the portrait of Elizabeth assumed new functions as emblems of this sadness to which, without realizing it, Phoebe turned as to the purest hope. She had nothing to look forward to; she had simply rediscovered something that she could call "herself." For the first time, she

accepted her disease as a reality, as her reality. If her sickness meant sadness, she would become that sadness, keeping it all for herself, in the remnants of her body. "My body lies over the ocean," she sang. She also sang,

'Tis His love His people raises
Over self to reign as kings.

She smiled at the thought of loving her sadness—surely better than not loving at all, than not loving herself at all? Self-pity provided a first step towards sanity. Only a step—what next? Elizabeth's ivory cheeks and smiling hands had fallen into place. Phoebe sighed wistfully, "My Elizabeth, I'd like to set lighted candles at your feet. I'm better now." *Essesso*, went the bird.

Louisa and Lewis knew Phoebe was recovering when she made a small joke in a mode of that time: "If Stella Dallas married Roger Maris, she'd be known as Stella Maris." In their perpetual shadow, Elizabeth's unpupilled eyes became her stars.

Phoebe's convalescence remained slow. In the course of a year her disorder had disrupted the normal functioning of her lungs, her heart, and her digestive system. She had no physical reserves to draw on. Her doctors spoke about her condition with optimism and advised that she spend another week in the hospital.

Hallucinations still afflicted her. Voices neither hers nor the bird's rumbled through her darkened room: ". . . Who is she who on earth brings forth the sea? Who is he who on earth brings forth the sea? Who is she who lights up great days?" *Essesso, essesso.* "Who is he who devours? Where is the shoemaker the blue one?" *Essesso.* "Where is the red-white-and-blue shoemaker? . . . Phoebe did not take these voices seriously. Even the bird could now have left without being missed, although she thanked it frequently for its attentiveness.

Phoebe reminded herself never to use her sadness as a pretext for not acting. Acting meant getting what she wanted,
and she knew what she wanted: happiness. Happiness required
a world with no monsters in it. She had said to Lewis,
"Something's out there in the dark prowling around. You can't
see it, but you keep getting these horrible reports," and even
as she spoke she knew that she was only telling a convenient
story—an excuse for giving up. She had nobody to blame. She
asked Owen to visit her. She would not let him prowl outside
in the dark any longer. When he had left, she thought, "So
that's what heaven is: the living around us, no one left out."
This recognition brought her only a distant joy, because she
had become feverish again. In dog-day heat, she had managed
to catch cold.

Several nights later she had another visitor. Her fever had
gone and returned. She was lying in the dark, licking her dry
mouth and smiling at the viola's turn:

> Who can faint when such a river
> Ever will their thirst assuage?

She became aware of a glow to one side and a sound like a
voice speaking. She turned off the record player. The glow
was emanating from the only blank wall of her room, to her
left, beyond the window. At its center a circle of crystal had
formed. Superposed rings of crystalline rock began appearing within the circle, tinged with blue light from behind.
These blue rings opened inwards, brightening as they receded
through a self-creating distance that narrowed into a radiance
deep within the rock—an endpoint that Phoebe perceived as
pure white, dazzling and warm. As she lay there smiling into
that charming light, her bird flew noiselessly out of the hole.
"Is my bird going to speak to me again?" The owlish raven
had itself turned white. It vanished among the shadows of

the room, only to reappear inside the blue-white tunnel, once more flying towards her. Phoebe again heard the voice. It was calling her by name.

"Who is it?" she asked.

"It's your old pal," the voice answered. "You know who."

"Walter?" Staring into the shining circles of stone, she glimpsed what looked like a man in profile. She could not recognize him, although he reminded her of a stranger on the train home from Belmont. "I can't see you."

"No need," came the answer. "I'm waiting for you."

"Thank you, but I'm picky about my friends."

"Come *on*, Phoebe. It's great in here." The hovering bird turned back into the tunnel, showing her the way. Phoebe's body tingled with sprightliness.

"Thanks. It's not bad out here, either."

The apparition slowly dimmed. A minute later no light showed in her room except for the glint of her water glass, the faint blue aura of the night lamp, the red dot on the panel of her record player. Phoebe lay in bed wishing for someone to laugh with.

She felt buoyant when she woke up. The tunnel's glow still warmed her, and she remembered the profiled man with intense affection. He's my mentor, she decided. He's the man I'll go looking for as soon as I leave this dump.

Her unusual cheerfulness made doctors and nurses beam. She promised herself to pay no more attention to her discomforts. Later in the day, as her temperature exhaustingly rose and fell, she realized that her body was once again in crisis. Like the medication given for it, its disorder now belonged to the world outside her. She hoped, as night approached, that her anonymous mentor would appear in his tunnel. Even though he did not, his memory continued to enchant her; and early the next morning, before dawn, she was granted some solace. Her bird, which she had not seen the day before,

came back to her room, its first blackness restored, describing once again its customary ellipse. Its wings, however, made no sound. It rapidly gathered speed and soon was flying so fast that Phoebe could not follow it. She did not mind, she was elated. Out loud she said, "Look at that birdie go! Granny, you're wearing me out. I thought you were on my side."

The bird spun like the knot of a twirled lasso. Phoebe's heart raced as she watched.

"I wouldn't mind if you could just unlock the kettledrum in my chest of drawers and slow it down a notch. Granny, talk to me at least."

Phoebe sat up.

"Where is my chevalier, pray tell? Catalepsy got your tongue? OK, but someday I want to go riding again. Think of it, I can buy myself a chestnut now. Horseflesh will be mine. I'll go out riding in pursuit of my faithful bird's-eye, hear that? Meanwhile, the birthday girl is full of thirst."

She cleared her throat and coughed.

"My throat is full of thistledown. There are so many thirsts I want to do. First it will soon be time for love. I haven't had an orgy in thirteen weekends. It's a boycott, no less. And that's exactly who I want to start with—boysenberries and their big banjos."

Phoebe no longer cared if the bird was listening.

"Then a nice older piece of lettuce for salad days, full of suggestions and spinal trappings. And finally I want the man of my dreamy legs from somewhere in betweentimes. When I love that personality he'd better watch his outlooks! As former corpus delicti (almost) one will have knucklebones and depravities comparable to those of the avidest Elizabethan desperadoes, and you know how swank and murderous they can be! . . . Oh . . . Elizabeth—"

She tried to make out the portrait in the gloom.

"I haven't forgotten you, not for one secret. And what if

you were the one? I can see us in our warm and lovable drawing room, two wombs as one, wife to wife. I could fancy that.
Witnesses of each other's dreams. . . . But then who could I be
butterfly to (and housefly to, too)? Who could I waffle, who
could I babushka? I need real babes to sillytalk, and I can't
help thinking of all those malcontents with their malarkey
and solo prongs strewn around like landmarks, like pieces of
forgotten furniture."

Phoebe started laughing.

"Now there's a dimpled prognostic for a life! A dimity
landlady turning sprung floperoo easterners into pidgin pies
and daffodils of her cosmology! Because for me myself and
I, what will they add? Noteworthy nothingness. I'm my own
cosmonaut, thanks just the same, and my private universe
spreads from world-eaten rosaries to the swivels of skyrider
Galahads—and whatever that may mean," she added, "I swear
it's true." She looked around her. "My birds are spreading—hi
there, Granny!—or maybe it's my bod."

A shower of sparks burst along the path of the bird.

"I haven't forgotten you, either. You ever were and shall be
my ethereal booms. Zowie! You came out of my cecum, the
heaven-mapped loins, you and your flaky rinds, and it was
then I knew. What else can I ever know? East River to Long
Island Sound and out to sea, over which you so cunningly
twinkle. Winter, summer, winter again, going places we never
left, and all we have to do is sit through the movie and we're
there! Christmas! Why isn't it motherland? Granny, tell me
you're a nighthawk. I want to go outside and look, all that fun
and nonsense I'm missing—rockets zooming through bones.
Granny, where's my skylight? What's wrong?" Phoebe loudly
asked this of the circling bird, which was wearying, and she
could sympathize with that, since her enthusiasm had left her
breathless. She watched the bird slow down as it descended,

blindingly white now, settling gradually until it came to rest on the floor next to her bed—except that, to Phoebe's surprise, that part of the room had no floor: the bird plummeted abruptly out of sight and hearing.

Allan and Owen

JUNE-JULY 1963

As a rule, those who die young leave their personal affairs in a mess. Perhaps because chronic illness had long made his life seem precarious, the rule did not apply to Lewis Lewison's friend Morris Romsen. Long before he died at the end of his thirtieth year, he had drawn up a satisfactory will; and he had recently supplemented it with a generous life-insurance policy whose beneficiary was his associate, Priscilla Ludlam.

The provision for Priscilla came as a surprise to Lewis, and even more to Morris's sister, Irene Kramer. Particularly devoted to Morris, Irene was startled to learn that Priscilla had known her brother so intimately, amazed that Morris had never mentioned making her his beneficiary; and her amazement turned to mild suspicion when she found out that the policy had been written shortly before Morris's death by Allan Ludlam, Priscilla's father. While realizing that coincidence, or friendship itself, might explain the fact, Irene still wondered if some professional ethic did not forbid a father's writing such a policy on his daughter's behalf. She decided to consult Owen Lewison, since he had every aspect of the insurance business at his fingertips and she knew him well enough to trust his discretion.

110

Owen told her, "I'll be happy to check things for you." He had time on his hands, and worries to forget: Phoebe, about to emerge from Saint Vincent's, had refused to let him see her. "I'm sure Ludlam's clean, though. I've worked with his office a lot, I even know him slightly. There's no chance he'd try any monkey business."

"I know him too, and I know how well off they are, or Maud is. It just seems strange."

From an old acquaintance in Allan's company, Owen discovered that Allan had been recommended to Morris by none other than Phoebe; that on learning that Priscilla would be named beneficiary, he had at first declined to write the policy; that he had later agreed to do so only after Morris assured him that Priscilla knew nothing about it.

Irene ran the Kramer Gallery, which had opened on the West Side several years earlier and recently moved uptown. During a subsequent meeting with the Ludlams at her gallery, Irene confessed to Allan her "curiosity" about Morris's life insurance: "I didn't know it could be so all-in-the-family."

Allan blushed. "It usually isn't. It bothered me too, you know—"

"I do know. You're scrupulousness itself."

At his office the next day, Allan asked if Morris's policy had raised any problems. He learned of Owen's inquiry. He called Irene: had Owen acted at her request?

"Yes, he did. It was dumb of me, but Morris had just died, and, for reasons I still don't understand, he'd never spoken about Priscilla to me. Mr. Lewison said your conduct was exemplary."

"Irene, it was standard procedure."

Allan was relieved by Irene's reassurances. If Morris's policy gave him no cause for worry, he dreaded the possibility of having other cases come accidentally to Owen's attention— cases that might reveal his secret career of repeated fraud. This

career had always exposed him to high risks; to have an expert like Owen investigating him entailed a risk he couldn't afford to run.

Owen had suspected nothing. Allan had escaped danger unawares, as if he had casually brushed a spider from his neck and then recognized a black widow. He relished his luck. It enhanced and was enhanced by the euphoria of finding Elizabeth. For a while he abounded in a sense of the excellence of his life. He felt an immense gratitude towards Owen for having left that intact. One morning he wrote him a letter:

> . . . how really heartwarming it was to be vindicated by such a man as yourself. 1 want you to know that I value it highly and appreciate it deeply. . . .

It never occurred to Allan that he might more reasonably have asked Owen for an apology. Owen himself was dumbfounded. Fulsome praise was being heaped on him by a man whose probity he had implicitly questioned. Owen could hardly have guessed that Allan was lovestruck when he wrote the letter. He did check Allan's dates in *Who's Who* to make sure he wasn't getting senile.

Owen left the letter on his office desk. When he next picked it up, he again found himself wondering why Allan had written it. He was not about to borrow money. He needed no social favors. He was not going into politics. He must have had another reason, an unusual one, one that Owen could not suspect; one perhaps that he should not suspect. Was he hiding something—could Allan Ludlam have something to hide?

As the thought came to him, Owen was cheered: an entertaining possibility was brightening his bleak world. Sicker than ever, Phoebe had been treating him contemptuously; his son, Lewis, had sunk beneath consideration; having dedicated herself to Phoebe, Louisa had no time to spare; his work bored him. Now he had turned up a minor mystery that did not bore

him at all. Owen was delighted by the prospect that someone from his milieu had guilty secrets. Would Allan's resemble his own New London ferry caper? Or would it prove a more intimate peccadillo?

Intrigued though he was, Owen would probably have forgotten Allan altogether if he hadn't mentioned him to Irene at the end of the following week. She had heard from him too: "Walter's portrait of Elizabeth was stolen. Allan called to ask if our insurance still covered it. They hadn't had time to take out their own."

"I didn't know they owned it," Owen said.

"They bought it last month." Irene explained that she had recently offered a selection of Walter Trale's best work for sale. "We sent it up to them early in July."

"When was it stolen?"

"I don't know exactly. Allan phoned me yesterday."

Owen said nothing. He knew that Allan had told Irene at least one lie. No insurance broker would leave anything so valuable unprotected for two minutes, certainly not two weeks; and from Allan, a phone call would have sufficed.

What was Allan up to now? If he *had* insured the Trale painting, why lie to Irene about it? When Allan spoke to her, why did he only ask about insurance when he might have requested information about art thefts, and even counsel? Owen tried to imagine some undeclared motive behind Allan's call. He could think of none until an unlikely hypothesis crossed his mind: could Allan possibly want to make money out of the theft? Was he trying to collect all the insurance he could, the gallery's as well as his own?

Owen liked this eventuality. It struck him as crass and faintly lunatic; it reminded him of New London. His curiosity about Allan's secret was rekindled. He began asking himself, why not take a look? To Owen, as a professional, Allan's call to Irene and his claim to have left the painting uninsured made

the existence of some kind of secret probable to the point of certainty. On the other hand, why should Owen waste time solving an enigma that did not concern him? He found no reasonable answer to this question, rather a satisfyingly unreasonable one: he would enjoy solving this riddle far more than submitting to the rituals of penitence decreed by Phoebe. Even if in the end he found nothing, where was the harm in that? Surrounded as he was by domestic disappointment, wasting time appealed to him.

He decided to begin by approaching Allan himself. He had a number of social and professional excuses for doing so, of which Allan's letter was the most obvious. On the same afternoon he spoke to Irene, Owen started calling him. Allan had left his office; his home phone did not answer, then or later in the evening. Owen repeated his calls the next morning with no more success. He rang Allan's house upstate. A delicately mocking voice—Elizabeth's—announced that Allan was not expected back "for the foreseeable summer."

Owen was annoyed. The man might as well be deliberately evading him. He changed his plans. Before pursuing Allan further, he would learn everything he could about him. He wrote Allan to acknowledge his letter of thanks and express the hope that they would soon meet. Owen resumed his research, focusing it this time not on the minor question of Morris's insurance policy but on more consequent activities in Allan's past. If he had something to hide, it would very likely concern sums of money greater than those of personal accounts; it would have to do with the commercial insurance in which Allan specialized.

Allan's respect for Owen was soon justified: Owen needed only one coincidence to uncover his trail. He had begun by looking at cases in which his office had worked with Allan's, and as he was probing these records, the *Vico Hazzard* file, which he had had no intention of consulting, fell into his

hands. He then remembered that Allan had been involved in
that affair.

Vico Hazzard was the name of a medium-sized oil tanker
that during a storm in March 1958 had sunk fully loaded in
the Bay of Biscay, a hundred miles off the French coast. Or so
its owners claimed. The insurers discovered that on the day of
the ship's sinking the weather had been generally clement, that
only ten minutes had been needed to rescue the entire crew,
and that no oil slick had ever been observed at the site of the
accident. They rejected the claims, which were only settled
after a long judicial fight. (The owners had arguments of their
own: the ship's loading papers had been correctly drawn up; no
member of the crew would testify to sabotage or negligence;
storms come and go swiftly in the Bay of Biscay; oil sometimes
stays trapped in sunken tankers.)

Owen reviewed the file. Allan was not listed among the
brokers. His firm was nowhere mentioned. Owen asked colleagues who had worked on the case if any remembered Allan's
connection with it. Fortunately, one did, although she could
not precisely define it—nothing important. Pleased that his
memory had not misled him, Owen called a friend at the
company that had insured the ship. Could he find the time to
track down Allan Ludlam's role in the *Vico Hazzard* case? The
man answered, "I can tell you right now. He recommended
those sons of bitches to us."

"You're sure?"

"Positive."

"Why didn't Ludlam's office write the policy?"

"He was all for it, or at least he said he was, but his partners
decided they'd covered enough tankers."

"How come he was so sure about the owners?"

"They fooled a lot of people, including the judge. Well,
maybe they fixed the judge. The case was tried in Panama,
naturally."

Had they fixed Allan too? With Maud's small fortune, and the excellent living he made? Perhaps he had an expensive weakness, or a private one—gambling, another woman. Most people exhibited a much more obvious weakness: never having enough. Why not Allan? After all, Owen had postulated such a motive in his phone call to Irene and made it a premise of his inquiry. Owen accepted the implication of the *Vico Hazzard* fraud: Allan had been paid off to recommend dishonest clients to reputable insurers.

Notwithstanding a seemingly permanent hot spell, Owen spent more and more time in the city. His investigation absorbed him, and it soothed the sting of Phoebe's spiteful demands. He went to work early and finished his business by noon. The rest of his days, and soon his evenings as well, were devoted to the pursuit of Allan Ludlam's secret.

In his office Owen examined the files of many cases in which Allan had acted as broker. His conduct appeared consistently irreproachable—hardly a surprise, rather a confirmation that, as with the *Vico Hazzard*, Allan's improprieties took place behind the scenes. Then how could his influence be detected? Owen's enthusiasm briefly faltered as he realized that he was condemned to look for evidence only among frauds that had—at least initially—failed: those that had succeeded had vanished into the history of undisputed claims. Where should he continue his research? He knew enough to eliminate instances where the attempted fraud was too crude or too petty. Even so, assuming that Allan had stayed in the background, Owen still had to choose among the hundreds of cases of industrial fraud perpetrated by brokers other than Allan and his associates. Owen's hope revived when he saw that he could eliminate most cases by applying one criterion: with which brokers would Allan's recommendation count decisively? Here Owen's expertise served him well—he knew who knew whom.

Eventually Owen reduced his cases to the manageable

number of twenty-three. These he examined painstakingly. He exhausted the records in his office and those that had been made available to the public. In his search for information, he frequently found himself obliged to visit other insurance offices, where he claimed to be writing a historical article on reinsurance in modern times.

Three cases yielded the evidence Owen needed: the *Vico Hazzard* itself; the Watling Mining Corporation, whose coal mine near Etkins, West Virginia, collapsed from an unexplained blast in 1957; and Kayser Wineries, Inc., whose vineyards in the mountains behind Soledad were destroyed by late-spring frost in the early fifties. In each case the insurers had disallowed the claims advanced by their client because of probable fraud. Although fraud was proved only against Kayser Wineries, all three companies stood to benefit conspicuously from the disasters. Smaller tankers like the *Vico Hazzard* had become unprofitable soon after the closing of the Suez Canal in 1956. Before its destruction, the Watling mine, a marginal one, had been beset by labor troubles. When it filed its claim, Kayser Wineries had fallen critically low in cash reserves. The insurance company's investigation of the Watling claim determined that the explosion had occurred on a Sunday when the mine was empty, the electricity switched off, and no unusual accumulation of coal gas had been reported. The "frost" in the Kayser vineyards was shown to be hardly more severe than average seasonal temperatures: it might have damaged the wood of the vines, not killed them (two years later, production had returned to normal). The owners of the *Vico Hazzard*, the Watling Mining Corporation, and Kayser Wineries had all been recommended to their insurers by Allan Ludlam.

Owen had no material proof that Allan had known of the frauds or profited from them. If questioned, Allan could rightly insist on his negligible legal responsibility in the three cases. Doubtless he could justify his recommendations. Some

unexplored clues momentarily tempted Owen. A year after the explosion, the union official who had represented the Watling miners was summoned by a state committee to explain fifty thousand dollars of exceptional expenditures revealed by an audit of his personal account. Owen wondered if Allan's accounts might not disclose similar anomalies. Owen was gratified to have uncovered Allan's secret. He wasted no time speculating as to why someone so well off would risk his reputation in these illegal undertakings.

In his answer to Allan's letter, Owen had invited him for dinner and proposed as a tentative date the last Thursday in July. Two days before Owen completed his research, Allan called to accept his invitation. Owen suggested that they meet for drinks at his apartment and told him that, knowing their wives were in the country, he had also asked a woman they both knew to share their evening. He hoped Allan didn't mind: "She'll keep us on our toes. Nothing's duller than an all-male club. Sorry I only found one. Right now, ladies are in short supply."

The woman Owen had invited was universally known by her childhood nickname of High Heels. Forty-six and very pretty, she had been married twenty-four years to an uninterested husband for whom she had consoled herself with many lovers, Owen among them. He had not invited her innocently. His affair with her, begun the preceding winter shortly after his Christmas wrangle with Phoebe, had soon ended, not from disaffection but because the lovers decided that they preferred the reliabilities of friendship to the uncertainties of passion. They trusted each other intimately.

At first Owen had not known exactly how High Heels would benefit him. He assumed that the presence of an attractive woman would put Allan a little off his guard, especially since he knew her so well (he was related to her by marriage). Not until his investigation was complete did Owen find a specific job for her.

When Owen learned that Allan had successfully pursued a career of preposterous frauds, he began asking himself what light this might shed on his behavior in regard to the stolen portrait of Elizabeth. Owen was tempted to see in it the sign of yet another fraud, albeit a smaller, private one. Why else should Allan lie to Irene? Owen could not at first see what form such a fraud might take. Recollecting his own "crime," he had imagined Allan trying to collect insurance from more than one company. This interpretation presented difficulties. When a work of art is stolen, it rarely disappears; usually it resurfaces promptly, to be offered for sale if the thieves lack competence, more often to become the object of negotiations between them and the insurers. Allan of course knew this. He would not expect to be reimbursed if a work as valuable as the portrait were stolen from him; he would expect to get it back.

This suggested to Owen that the portrait had not been stolen at all. If Allan wanted insurance money, he must make sure that the painting never reappeared. What could give him such certainty? The work could be destroyed. Then why disguise the fact as theft, unless Allan himself had done the destroying? But Owen could not imagine anyone so money-smart demolishing a possession whose value would certainly grow. More plausibly, the portrait had been hidden. The possibility impressed Owen as perfectly compatible with Allan's behavior: secrecy, after all, had been a condition of his business frauds from beginning to end.

Owen knew now what he wanted High Heels to do. While Allan might, of course, have used any number of hiding places, Owen suspected that he would prefer one where he could keep his eye on the portrait. The house upstate could certainly be excluded: Maud would not be privy to her husband's illegal activities. The city apartment seemed much likelier, since it was primarily used by Allan as a place to stay during his working weeks, and during the summer he had it to himself. High

Heels must persuade Allan to take her home with him so that
she could learn if the portrait was hidden there.

Owen gave her a partial account of the facts, not mentioning his research or Allan's phone call to Irene, telling her only
that the Ludlams claimed that the portrait of Elizabeth had
been stolen and that he suspected them of having hidden the
painting instead, perhaps in Allan's apartment. He had, he
said, become intrigued by their strange behavior. No more
than intrigued: he had nothing to gain in the matter.

Owen was not surprised that High Heels unhesitatingly
accepted his request; and as Owen had correctly foreseen,
Allan was immediately drawn to her. Owen's good judgment,
however, was favored far more by what he did not know than
by what he knew. When he gave High Heels his account of
the missing portrait, he acted with unwitting shrewdness in
lumping Maud with Allan. He did not know that High Heels
was nursing a years-old grudge against Maud Ludlam and was
delighted to catch her out in a suspicious scheme; delighted,
as well, to date her husband. Nor could Owen possibly know
how sentimentally vulnerable recent events had made Allan.
His affair with Elizabeth had humiliated him, Maud had
forced him from his own house—he was ripe for consolation.
His long acquaintance with High Heels only heightened her
attractiveness by removing the barrier of unfamiliarity that
had, before Elizabeth, made him shy away so often from sexual adventure.

The evening with Allan and High Heels thus took Owen
by surprise. He had planned to coddle his guests into mutual
sympathy; he found himself with nothing to do. From the
moment they met in his apartment, the two conversed in the
liveliest fashion. By the time they sat down in the restaurant,
their understanding had started growing into overt complicity.
Owen felt almost an outsider at his own dinner. He even wondered, knowing the man's deviousness, if Allan had somehow

enlisted High Heels in his cause. Were they now allied against him? What if they were? *He* had nothing to hide, nothing to lose. (The thought had no sooner come to him than he remembered Phoebe, aged eleven, running out of school to meet him.)

After dinner, Allan asked High Heels and Owen to join him for a nightcap. Owen declined and left. Allan timidly asked High Heels where she would like to go—a favorite bar? her place? his? His would do fine. In the taxi she took his hand; they kissed in the elevator; they had barely crossed his threshold when they began making love, the first of three leisurely times.

Their delight in each other had the intensity of ignorance, if not innocence. Allan knew nothing about High Heels's grudge against Maud, or she about his domestic troubles. They applied themselves to slaking a mutual thirst that had naturally and delectably inflamed them, not asking questions, not needing to know. Waking up the following morning, they spent themselves on one another before exchanging a word.

However, once they did start to speak, High Heels eventually said: "What I'd really love is a toasted bagel." She had hesitated to pronounce these words. She knew that when she did, Allan would go out to the nearest deli, and she would search his apartment. What Owen wanted her to do seemed now a little squalid: spying on her new lover might prove as great a betrayal as disappointing her old one. She stuck to her agreement. She had made Allan happy, he still exuded warmth and attentiveness, and she sensed that the attentiveness revealed something other than warmth—an awareness that, no matter how much he liked her, she would never find a place at the center of his life, not even for a season. He paid attention to her now because he might find few other chances to do so; later meetings would still remain exceptional events. Allan was assuming that she knew this as well as he did, and he was not

mistaken. She did not mind his so carefully sweetening her own return to "real life"; and she knew she must expect no more of him. She too liked him, and, among other reasons, she liked him because he *would* go away, go back to Maud. She liked him for a good husband, after years with her own bad one; and she couldn't help imagining how her life might have turned out with a man like the one now lying in her arms. The thought flushed her with yearning: a yearning she loathed, brimming with regret, one she had sooner or later to cut short. When Allan proposed English muffins, she preferred the bagel that would take him away from her.

She found the portrait wrapped in a clean sheet, leaning against a wall in a doorless storage space next to the kitchen. She checked the dimensions and appearance and, after restoring her wearied face and body, returned to bed, where Allan found her.

To attest his gratitude, Owen sent High Heels two best seats for *How to Succeed in Business Without Really Trying*, a musical sold out five weeks in advance. For years, Owen had scarcely stretched his wits in business; he had now proved them as sharp as ever. Through his own flair, he had from meager evidence calculated exactly what Allan had done. He did not think of Phoebe for a whole day, he forgot his routine call to Louisa, utterly pervaded by a reassuring glee.

Late in the afternoon, four days afterwards, he kept ringing Allan's home number until he answered. Owen said he was in the neighborhood, could he drop by for a drink? By all means, Allan replied. He'd advise the doorman immediately.

Entering the apartment, Owen savored the coolness— the temperature outside had reached the mid nineties. Allan greeted him jovially, holding a gin-and-tonic in one hand and, with a help-yourself wave of the other, motioning Owen towards the bar: "I've been meaning to call you, damn it. Tonight you be my guest."

"We'll see."

Allan stared at the other man as he mixed his drink. Owen looked serious and alert. "What's up?"

Owen turned to Allan: "I came up here on a false pretense. This is really a business visit. Here's mud." He raised a glass full of chiming cubes.

"Chin chin. Well, we've been doing business for years, in an impersonal way."

"You're telling me. This is between the two of us."

"*Servidor de usted.*"

"You own a painting I'd like to . . . acquire—a portrait by Walter Trale."

"My wife and I own it." Allan walked past Owen to the bar. "I can tell you right now: Maud would never agree to sell."

"I'm not surprised. I saw it only once at Trale's studio, but I could tell it was special. By the way, for openers, do you think I could take a look at it?"

"That might be a little hard to arrange."

"No time like the present."

"You mean here? We'd never keep anything like that in town. A couple of prints, to show where the walls are, and that's about it."

"What are they? I still can't tell China from Japan. Could I see the portrait when I go back upstate?"

"Owen," Allan said with gentle reproach, "did Irene tell you the painting was stolen?" He also asked, "You don't know Elizabeth, do you?"

Allan's voice indicated that the question mattered to him; Owen could not relate it to what he knew. He said, "So what happened?"

"What happened about what?"

"How did it get stolen?"

"*I* don't know what happened. . . ." Allan did not mind playing such games.

"Then what have you done about it? Police? Private detectives? Who's your underwriter?"

"What do you think I should do? Art thefts are tricky."

"Irene was surprised when you asked her about the gallery's insurance."

"Is that why you're here—Irene again? Why should she care?"

"Irene's got nothing to do with my being here."

"Then why do *you* care?"

"I told you. I hope to own the painting."

"But that's out of—" Allan stopped. What was Owen getting at? The other man's eyes looked steadily into his, neither friendly nor unfriendly. "You wouldn't like to talk over dinner? The gin's gone straight to my stomach."

"This shouldn't take long." Owen sat down, crossed his legs, and set his drink on the floor beside him. Allan leaned against the wall, facing him. Owen had vexed him. "Would you mind telling me why we're having this conversation?"

"Sure. I think you made a mistake. You gave yourself away. You want the gallery's insurance to pay for the painting."

Allan suddenly wanted to laugh; he only said, "Wow!"

"I'm serious."

"No." Allan couldn't suppress a grin. He paused. "I don't know where to begin."

"Anyplace. It won't matter."

"I don't even know who insures the gallery—you probably do. I just asked Irene one question. That doesn't mean I'm making plans. What tickles me," Allan went on, "is that what you're accusing me of is how you make your money. You push all your claims to the limit."

"That's right. But only against one insurer for each claim." Owen mentally crossed his fingers, remembering New London. He thought: I should have never told those people about New London.

"I haven't made any claim. The painting is bound to show up. If it's cheap enough, we'll buy it back ourselves, and it probably will be." Allan was looking down at his guest with growing confidence. "If the people who stole it want to haggle, it wouldn't hurt to get the gallery involved. That's why I called Irene."

Because he held the ace of trumps, Owen had not pushed Allan hard. He had nonetheless cornered him. Allan thought he had won: the rosy assurance of his face attested it. He had once felt fear of Owen; his fear had proved groundless. If this time Owen was attacking him openly, he remained as innocent as he had been in writing Morris's policy. Allan could not help showing a slight contempt for Owen for being so mistaken.

At this point, Owen's attitude changed. He had anticipated confronting a colleague with professional irregularities. The irregularities had excited his curiosity more than his disapproval, and he had only expected to show Allan that although he was smart, Owen was smarter. He had imagined wanting the portrait only as a ploy: as a "serious" pretext at first, then as a position from which to press his adversary. Owen now found himself thinking in earnest about getting the painting for himself.

He had begun feeling a need to do more than outwit Allan. He was facing a rich, reputable colleague who for years had defrauded the system he claimed to serve, who now stood beaming with confidence because he had once again gone uncaught. Owen angrily dismissed his first intention of merely showing Allan up: values were at stake. He entertained no doubt at all that he had the moral fitness to mete out the punishment Allan deserved.

"You thought that up just now. I don't believe you. You know why?"

"No, and I'd be very interested—"

"I've been studying your career," Owen interrupted, "I

don't mean your legitimate accomplishments, I'm not questioning them. What I mean—what I've learned—is that you're a chronic swindler"—Owen spoke fast enough to cut off any protest—"and you've been damned successful at it. As I see it, though, you have one problem. A swindler who's been born and raised poor knows that if he loses, he loses everything. But someone with your cushy background feels safe, and he starts thinking he really is safe. He forgets about the risks. He makes mistakes. Like calling Irene."

If Allan was surprised, he didn't show it: "Owen, tell me what's on your mind. Something you think I did has made for a misunderstanding. Or maybe your interpretation of something I actually did. What's the point?"

"Three names to show you I know. And don't kid yourself—I'll know *you* know I know. In chronological order: Kayser Wineries, Watling Mining, *Vico Hazzard*."

After a few seconds, not moving from where he stood, his hands behind his back, Allan replied, "Who's arguing? Of course those were mistakes. Why me, though? A lot of other people were involved."

"They were mistakes, and you didn't make them. You let those other people do that. You advised them to."

"I advise all the time. It's part of the business—you know that. Has all your advice been perfect? My own batting average is pretty good—about nine-fifty."

"You bet it is. Remember the Circle C Ranch? They wanted you to double the coverage on their herd. Before recommending them, you made sure there'd been no brucellosis in the county for thirty years. You did your job. How could somebody like you not know the *Vico Hazzard* was sailing empty? Why should you bother with punk outfits like Kayser and Watling unless it was—"

"Look," Allan broke in, "it was investigated."

"It didn't come up roses, either. I know you're covered—you

were only counsel. And we're all so busy we never bother much with the past. But I'm on to you, old buddy." Allan said nothing. Owen added: "I'm not interested in making trouble for you, truly. Why should I be? I just want that portrait of Elizabeth. And no, I don't think I know her. I may have met her before the war."

The mention of Elizabeth sickened Allan. Two weeks before, she had been his; at least, he had been hers. He had spat on her feelings by parading his dishonesty in front of her. Perhaps she had revenged herself by telling Owen rather than Maud what she had learned about him. He asked, "So you know about the horse?"

For the only time that evening Owen was baffled. "Does Elizabeth have a horse?"

"Not *that* horse," Allan answered irritably. "You'd better ask the thief about the portrait."

"That's what I'm doing."

Why did Owen care so much about this "theft"? Before tonight, Allan had almost forgotten the story he had made up for Irene. "You mean *I* stole the painting?"

"Listen, I'm getting hungry myself. I'll make you a proposition. I find the painting, I keep it. And I promise not to tell a soul."

Allan still did not understand. Owen emptied his iceless glass, got up, and walked into the kitchen. Allan heard the stretcher being dragged across the tile floor.

"Do I have to unwrap it, or will you take my word?"

Allan lost his temper. For twenty minutes Owen had been preparing to make a fool of him, holding, and withholding, his knowledge that the portrait was there. "You'd better get out."

"You're right. Leave the painting downstairs sometime tomorrow, OK? I'll send a man over. Unless you'd rather I took it now."

"Big joke. Get the hell out of here."

"Ludlam, I understand how you feel. You'd better start understanding how *I* feel. I'm not interested in shooting you down. It'd be messy, and some of your shit would stick to me. Anyway, I'm not a policeman. I don't give a tiddlywink how you behave. But I can get you, and I will if I have to, because I do mind one thing: every time we guys went to bat for one of your crummy clients we were putting our money and reputation on the line. I risked my ass on account of you. You may never have to pay your debt to society, as they say, but you sure as hell will pay it to me. I'm letting you off cheap—one painting."

At this moment Allan remembered the toasted bagel. He spoke quickly, before dismay seeped into his voice: "Owen, the story about the portrait being stolen—it was an elaborate family joke."

"So what?"

"That's what we're—"

"That was *my* joke. I'm talking about your reputation. As I trust you realize, I am not joking about that."

Allan gave up. He hated to lose; he would hate losing; he could see nothing he might do to avoid it. For once his cleverness had failed him: the roulette wheel had been fixed by a woman he had not doubted for a moment. What he now wanted most in the world was to get Owen out of his apartment. He agreed to the price: "I'll drop it off at the front door on my way to the office."

"Perfect." Owen smiled. "Now, how about dinner? No? I'll be going. Just one thing I'd like to ask you. It's something that's had me wondering ever since I got interested in you—it's probably *why* I got interested in you." Allan stared at the bar. Owen continued: "How come you did it?"

Owen waited patiently for a response. After a while Allan looked up: "Because they're jerks."

"Who is?"

"Everyone is. Not *you*, maybe," Allan hurriedly added. "But most of the others. They're so successful, they make so much money, they have Pucci wives, beach houses, and malt scotch, and they don't have a clue what it's all about. They don't even know there's anything to know. They're sheep."

"But not you."

"You seem to enjoy playing games. Do I have to explain?"

"I only wanted to know. It's an answer. Here's a suggestion: since we're not *all* sheep, you should be prepared to let others do unto you what you'd like them to let you do unto them—I think I got that right." Allan had again lapsed into silence. "Look, for the record, we'll need sale papers. Let's list a price two thousand under whatever it cost you. You'll get a capital deduction—not much, but every little bit helps."

At the door, Owen turned back; Allan was gazing out the window at a rug-sized plot of dirt fourteen stories below, where a forsythia and three evergreen shrubs withered in hot, eternal shade. "You know, Allan, you didn't need to prove anything. You're a better man than you think."

Outside, he entered the sweltering city night. A year ago Phoebe had reported the first signs of her disease, and at the time the news had actually brought him relief.

Allan did not see himself as a man at all, rather as a little boy dreaming his way through some stupid childhood misfortune. He loathed himself for having given up so abjectly. Why was he experiencing such humiliation on account of a painting and a glorified public adjuster? What had happened? He had barely looked inside a cookie jar, and the pantry cupboards had crashed down around him. He had phoned Irene and told her his fib because he expected her to repeat it to Maud; Maud would have been horrified, either because she believed the story or because she knew he was lying—in either case, she would have come after him, and he would have been able to resume his life with her. The stratagem recalled other, more

tractable childhood misadventures, the ones he would instigate in order to recapture his mother's attention. A new shoe "lost" would do the trick. He would be scolded and punished and no longer forgotten. This time, however, a detective from the shoe store had arrived unannounced and threatened him with dungeons. It made no sense.

The intensity of his unhappiness nevertheless had its explanation. What sickened him, what squeezed his testicles up into his bowels as though he were leaning over a penthouse ledge, was the memory of High Heels. He could excuse her deceit (she could hardly have foreseen its consequences); but he could not endure having Owen to thank for his night with her. The thought unnerved every part of him, even the anger in his chest. He wished he could call her. She could take pity on him. She had no reason to despise him, not as he despised himself. He felt himself incapable even of speaking to her.

Maud, Elizabeth, High Heels—lost in one July.

Allan expected his anger with Owen to return in force, flooding and ebbing for days, even weeks. He had been too openly disgraced not to resent his attacker. Nevertheless his anger lacked the clear fury of vengefulness or moral outrage, and Allan, without noticing it, soon reconciled himself to his antagonist. Owen had fallen on him without warning, like a natural disaster, impersonally and arbitrarily (Allan never saw his error in writing the letter of thanks); and little by little Owen began to assume the mask of a one-time avenging angel, a fairy-tale comeuppance, a bugaboo, a caricature that even Allan unconsciously recognized as his own invention. At the same time Owen, the real-life businessman, took on a very different, although complementary, role as the audience Allan's spectacular frauds had always lacked.

It was Owen, in this double guise of hobgoblin and witness, who at last allowed Allan to give up his criminal career. The hobgoblin reminded him of the risks he ran; the witness, that

he no longer needed recognition. The gelding destroyed on the eighteenth of the month marked the end of Allan's secret life. Later opportunities presented themselves—crop failures on unplanted land, bank-engineered computer "errors." On each occasion he was checked by an invisible figure in his apartment who sat facing him, a melting drink in his hand. An unprejudiced observer might have concluded that Allan had summoned Owen into his life for this very purpose.

That evening, however, Allan wanted only to drive Owen out of his thoughts, preferably by retroactive murder. He stayed home, convinced that elsewhere he would feel even worse. For supper he made himself his next day's breakfast: eggs, toast, tea. Neither scenes from an earthquake in Macedonia nor *The Jack Paar Show* could temper his despondency. He went to bed early, with some magazines, without even a nightcap.

Lewis and Morris

SEPTEMBER 1962-MAY 1963

MORRIS HAD MET Lewis at Walter Trale's, less than a year before his death.

Lewis had lived with his parents for a year and a half after his graduation from college; more accurately, he lived with Louisa, while Owen did his best to ignore him. Although Lewis hardly felt at ease with Louisa, she tended him and forgave his moody ways. Lewis felt at ease with almost no one. He had few friends of either sex and made no attempt to keep those he did have.

He loved and trusted Phoebe. Their father had always favored her, she excelled where he endured; her absolute loyalty to him forestalled all resentment. She was three years younger than Lewis, and his rock. During his tedious months at home, Phoebe never asked him, "What are you doing now? What are you planning to do?" Lewis had answers to these questions; he knew them to be no more than shaming lies. He was doing nothing, and he did not know what he would ever do.

Lewis, anything but dull, suffered from an excess of misguided cleverness: he could disparage himself brilliantly in a matter of seconds. He knew literature, art, the theater, history;

and his knowledge surpassed what a college normally provides. His knowledge led nowhere, certainly not into the world
where he was supposed to earn a living. Lewis had once gone
to work in the bookstore of his school because he loved handling books and looked forward to being immersed in them.
He was then instructed to keep careful accounts of merchan-
dise that might as well have been canned beans. He soon lost
interest in his simple task, failed to master it, and quit after
three days. Eight years later, he was still convinced of his practical incompetence. College friends familiar with his tastes
would suggest modest ways for him to get started: they knew
of jobs as readers in publishing houses, as gofers in theatri-
cal productions, as caretakers at galleries. Lewis rejected them
all. While he saw that they might lead to greater things, they
sounded both beneath and beyond him—the bookstore again.
Other chums who had gone on to graduate school urged their
choice on him. Lewis harbored an uneasy scorn for the corporation of scholars, who seemed as unfit for the world as he.
He remained desperate, lonely, and spoiled.

During his second autumn at home, he read, in an art
magazine called *New Worlds*, an article by Morris Romsen on
the painting of Walter Trale. Phoebe, who had been working
with Walter since February, had recommended it to him. Lewis
took it to heart for reasons that had nothing to do with Walter.

Morris began his article: "A fish begins to rot at the head;
the rot in painting begins at the idea of Art." Lewis did not
understand these words. They swept across his mind like an
arm angrily clearing a table of its clutter. Reading on, he could
not tell whether Morris's pronouncements illuminated his subject; he knew they illuminated *him*.

Lewis had had fugitive dreams of writing, soon discredited
and abandoned. Morris was showing him what writing could
do. He advanced the notion that creation begins by anni-
hilating typical forms and procedures, especially the illusory

"naturalness" of sequence and coherence. Morris did more than state this, he demonstrated it. He made of his essay a minefield that blew itself up as you crossed it. You found yourself again and again on ground not of your choosing, propelled from semantics into psychoanalysis into epistemology into politics. These displacements seemed, rather than willful, grounded in some hidden and persuasive law that had as its purpose to keep bringing the reader back fresh to the subject. Lewis could not explain this effect, or why the article so moved him. When he reread it, doing his best to find fault with it, like a shy and incredulous father poking his newborn child, his first reaction held true, and his reservations were dispelled. He had found something in the world worth doing, after all.

Lewis did not tell Phoebe of his decision to become a writer; he informed her by letter instead. When he had talked to his parents about his new commitment, he had as he spoke lost hold of what he was saying, and enthusiasm could not compensate for vagueness. Louisa had been confused, Owen disgusted (did he expect them to support him forever?). Lewis wanted to make sure Phoebe understood: Morris's article had given him nothing less than a hope of salvation.

My burdens are isolation and a haunted mind. Now I can put the first to work and exorcise the second. Solitude will be my shop. Others will use what I make there, in *their* solitudes—a long-distance community of minds. I'll take the words droning inside my head and make them real— make them into things that strike, or stroke, or puzzle, or disappear. This is something 1 can actually do. A little something—doctors are more useful, actors communicate better—but buggers can't be choosers. Before, reading was better than not getting out of bed, but how what I read got written was weirder than Linear A. Enter Morris Romsen, and shazam.

Phoebe asked, would he like to meet him? She could easily arrange it. (Already sick, for Lewis she would have rolled naked in snow.) At Walter's next party, knowing Morris was expected, she asked Walter if she might invite her older brother. Lewis rejoiced; refused to attend; attended.

The party, which took place on the night of November first, included almost fifty guests. Phoebe mentioned Lewis to Morris and quoted one or two passages from his letter. She warned Lewis when he arrived that Morris might act aloof; he must forgive him for that. She also told Lewis that Morris suffered from "a heart condition, as they now call imminent death."

"But he's so *young*. Is that why he looks so sad?"

"He's had it since he was twenty-three. And no, I don't think so."

Morris surprised Lewis, and not by his aloofness. Lewis's poor opinion of himself made him expect worse than that, now more than ever: if choosing to write had exalted him, writing itself had only made life worse. After an exciting glimpse of freedom, he found himself still trapped between a pitying mother and an irritable father. He had written a little poetry both mannered and crude and kept a self-sniffing diary that could hardly qualify as a "journal." From Morris he looked forward at best to an acceptance of the stammering praise that constituted his only offering.

Because he liked Phoebe, Morris was favorably disposed towards Lewis. Whatever aloofness he did show sprang entirely from sexual prudence. He mistrusted his own peculiar inclinations, especially with a younger man whose penchants he knew nothing about. He openly welcomed Lewis's admiration; and Lewis, with astonishment, found himself, instead of stammering, conversing almost spontaneously.

They were standing under Elizabeth's portrait. Lewis said, "From what you wrote I'd imagined it different. Maybe that's what you wanted?"

"Ah, so?"

"No? I got something like: one can't really describe *any-thing*. So you pretend to describe—you use words to make a false replica. Then we're absorbed by the words, not by the illusion of a description. You also defuse reactions that might get in our way. So when we look at the painting there's nothing we expected—none of your false words, none of our false reactions—we have to see it on its own terms?"

"Not *bad*. So what's the point?"

"The point, the point . . . is, what's actually there? You leave the thing intact by giving us what isn't there—?"

"Promise not to tell? They won't get it."

"I don't either—I'm only guessing. I mean, some of the things you say are *wild*. What about: 'Our original heaven is the tempestuous sky of the vagina'?"

"Just more of the same." Morris pointed to the portrait. "Imagine writing about that mouth. Even if you keep it abstract—like 'a mauve horizontal'—people will look and tell themselves, incredible mouth, so mauve, so horizontal. And horizontality means this, and mauve means something else. Goodbye, Miss Mouth. 'Tempestuous sky' gets rid of the vagina, and vice versa, even if the words are still there, doing whatever it is words do. Of course, most people can't even see the print."

"So what about them?"

"Who knows? It's a dull delirium of a world. Lewis, take care of *yourself*. That's plenty for a lifetime, no matter how short."

Morris had called him by name; Lewis did not even notice. Not since childhood, certainly not since Phoebe's birth, had he once forgotten his own feelings. He had never met anyone like Morris, whose self-assured talent was disguised by attentiveness, and his endangered heart by distractingly good looks. Lewis had not expected Morris to be beautiful. He had not expected to love him.

Later they talked again. Morris had made his rounds; Lewis had watched him. Not thinking about himself had lightened Lewis's demeanor and made him agreeable. Morris suggested they lunch the following week. Lewis silently postponed his return home and accepted.

"You probably won't approve," Morris told him in parting, "but I'm going into business with a friend. I'll be buying and selling paintings."

"A gallery?"

"Out of my apartment."

Lewis was surprised. He did not approve. At their lunch he said as much: "With your reputation? They'll say you're promoting. Think of your authority now. It's priceless."

"It could work the other way. I put money in something, my opinion's worth that much more."

"But what *about* your opinions? Isn't a work of art going to look different when you've invested in it? Even Berenson—"

"*Even?* Be my Duveen! He knew what he was doing—so do I. I'd like to do my shopping uptown for a change. And I wouldn't mind collecting a wee bit for myself."

"With your eye? It's a piece of cake."

"Lewis, you're sweet to care, but. Look: there's oceans of money sloshing around out there. All I want is a beach pail."

"I know. And you're right, I do care. There's a better way."

"You mean," said Morris, waving his glinting Muscadet through a long bar of smoky sunshine, "I can have caviar *and* a clean mind?"

"The trouble is the selling part. That's what's compromising. But if you buy—"

"And *not* sell? Like to pay for lunch?"

"My pleasure. What I'm suggesting is *advising* buyers. There are dozens of rich people around who want to own new art. It's the latest ticket to whatever. They also want to look original and do it on the cheap, but they only know what they read in

the magazines, and that's not news. So you find them artists on the way up. You help the buyers, you help the artists, you help yourself—you get a commission on each purchase. You don't have to deal. No speculating with your own money. No temptation to promote."

"People want work that other people want, and they don't need me to find it. Know any eager buyers for unknowns? One or two, I daresay—"

"I've got eight." Lewis unfolded a typewritten list and read it out loud. He had pestered the names out of Louisa. "I've talked to three of them—the Dowells, the Liebermans, and the Platts. The Platts were suspicious. The others sound interested."

"You bucking for Eagle Scout, little boy? *I* know you're just being nice, but with some you might pass for a closet schmuck."

"But *you* know I can trust you."

Morris picked up the list and left the check. He liked Lewis. He behaved condescendingly towards him because he was twenty-eight, Lewis twenty-three and young for his years. Morris felt an irresistible craving to curtail the younger man's enthusiasm and to do this by acting hard. Acting hard gave Morris pleasure. Lewis willingly submitted. Such treatment gave *him* pleasure. Morris failed to notice this. Experienced though he was, he still hesitated to believe that anyone sincerely relished punishment, still found his own yearning to inflict it perverse.

Lewis knew only that he would unquestioningly accept whatever Morris said or did. He enjoyed Morris's disdain. Watching his friend pocketing the list touched Lewis more than any thanks. He did not guess that Morris, while showing interest in his proposal, had no intention of giving up his original plan; had he known, he would have admired his duplicity.

Lewis had carefully garnered Morris's occasional remarks about writing, and on his return home he tried some of them

out. Morris recommended imitation as a practice as useful as it was unfashionable. Choose a model, he had said, and copy it. The model will have substance, form, and style. You can imitate all three; you can imitate one or the other; you will probably fail to reproduce any of them, and this inability will point to what you can do, to what usually you are already doing. You will begin discovering your own genius. As his models, Lewis chose a poem by Wallace Stevens, a story by Henry James, an essay by William Empson. He had a wickedly hard time and savored it: the work kept him busy, and full of thoughts of his new friend.

He saw Morris briefly three weeks later. They drank martinis in a bar off Fifth Avenue called Michael's Pub. Lewis reported his attempts to follow Morris's advice about writing. "Advice? I read that in *Mademoiselle*," the other exclaimed. The riposte, Lewis thought, revealed the essential Morris.

Lewis had to cut the meeting short. He was expected elsewhere. He took a taxi to Second Avenue and Thirty-second Street, walked south two blocks, crossed to the southeast corner, and went into a bar. Scarcely a dozen men sat in its booths—a late place. Lewis passed through a door in the back into a smaller room. Two men by the window nodded to him. Through another door, he reached the building's service elevator and rode three stories up. He entered a loft that occupied the entire floor, now divided crosswise by a black rayon curtain. Six or seven men standing in front of the curtain smiled when they saw him. As he approached, they turned their backs to him and continued their conversation.

"I thought your friend was the one who strangled the bath attendant?"

"Only gossip, I'm afraid. But it taught me wisdom all the same—*never* be jealous of the past."

One man turned to Lewis and said, "Break a leg, Minerva—or shall we do it for you?"

Lewis had visited the loft more than once. Tonight for the first time he would star here: they were going to crucify him.

The elevator regularly swelled the group of men, until the closed space seethed.

Except for some ambiguous episodes at summer camp, Lewis had tried to keep his sexual particularity a secret. He knew that others shared his taste. He had seen proof of it, and, like Morris, hardly believed it; and insofar as his family's world was concerned, he might have gleaned his knowledge from science fiction. If he had examined that world more cunningly, he would have found as many brothers there as elsewhere. Lewis preferred the conviction that giving or receiving pain for pleasure belonged to a furtive milieu. At twenty, on a visit to the city, he had been spotted in the street by an alert big boy and properly cruised and bruised. He had then discovered clandestine gatherings where his taste was the rule. He dreaded these meetings and longed for them. They filled him with implacable sensations and the intangibility of old dreams, and they succeeded in briefly satisfying him with a melancholy peace. He attended them at long, regular intervals. They provided one place where he belonged.

He himself had chosen his part for this warm, overcast late November evening. The announcement of the event had disgusted him, and he had guessed that his disgust only gauged his desire. At a subsequent meeting, the others had shared the disgust, no doubt to encourage him—to shame him. They told Lewis that while he had no right to participate at all, the leading role struck them as too degrading for anyone else to perform. It required the lowest of the low.

He was assured that the performance would be no sham. The crown of thorns had been woven out of rusted barbed wire. He would be whipped with willow fronds peeled and wetted. High above the grungy floor, he would be nailed to the pine-log cross with real nails (needle-thin and hammered

home by an expert—with luck he might escape crippling). A Gem blade set in a bamboo pole would slit his side. The same pole would prod a urine-soaked sponge into his face. The only departure from gospel tradition (aside from a foot-square platform under his feet) was intended to keep him from seeing his tormentors. Why give him that satisfaction? "Don't expect to get gone on those upturned faces, Lulu. A rock like you could pull a real Camille. We'd rather full-focus on your cakes." They would nail him face to the cross.

Like any fledgling performer, Lewis suffered intense stage fright. It proved superfluous: he had nothing to do. Whatever was required of him was done by others. He was stripped, crowned, scourged, and lifted up by gangs of adept males; he could only submit to them, like a swimmer rolled in an endless succession of toppling breakers, or like a little boy with his head held underwater in the vise of a bully's legs. He held his breath until it was punched out of him. He was allowed no respite in his humiliations. On the floor he was pissed on, on the cross screamed at and pelted with bolts, sneakers, stinking pellets. He never had time to think or feel anything except his sensations, to which he surrendered in the certainty that they belonged to him absolutely and lay beyond his choosing. He heard himself sobbing: nothing more than the dross of his consciousness as it soared like a rocket into clouds—clouds of tar steam that choked him and made him drunk. He felt blood run down one hip and leg, not the cutting spear. He wondered if he'd shit. Pine bark chafed his swollen cock.

The voices in the room lowered. Something else was happening. A familiar ladder jolted into place beside him. The twenty-year-old who had so deftly nailed him up was setting pliers to his feet.

"Already?" Lewis moaned.

"Velma's here."

"Huh?"

"The orgy patrol. The vice," hissed the other, addressing his left hand.

Can anyone keep a crucifixion secret? The police had doubted it. (Two of their members attended these meetings.) They decided not to risk indiscriminate revelation; they staged a raid and turned the scandal to their own advantage. The raid was efficiently executed. No one was hurt. Only six of the thirty-four men present escaped to the upper floors, where they were permitted to spend an anxious night before absconding.

The police had tipped off friendly newspapermen. Early editions of the *News* carried a photograph of a nameless young man lying on the loft floor, half naked, somewhat bloody. Louisa's sister and Morris, among others, recognized Lewis.

Lewis had been taken to the emergency ward at Bellevue Hospital. After tending his wounds, the doctors on duty sent him to the psychiatric ward, where he passed a scary night. Word that he had been admitted as a pervert spread quickly. The ward's drunks and psychotics expressed no less scorn for him than his crucifixion audience, and theirs was meant in earnest. The few tired and jaded orderlies promised feeble protection. Although the violence remained verbal, Lewis waited for the morning in terror and, even after he had washed and eaten breakfast, did not dare sleep, praying fervently and incessantly for the arrival of a doctor who might authorize his release. Shortly before noon, he saw Morris standing among a group of visitors at the end of the ward. Lewis crouched behind his bed.

When Morris found Lewis, he squatted down and tendered him a little plastic shopping bag. Lewis stood up. The bag contained toothbrush and toothpaste, shaving articles, hairbrush, cologne, and a box of Band-Aids.

"I couldn't remember if you smoked—not here, I guess. How's tricks?"

"How did you find me?"

"Your picture's in the paper. Don't worry, it's a terrible

likeness. And nobody who'd mind reads the *News* anyway. Phoebe wants to know when she can come and see you. She sends lots of love."

"Phoebe!"

Lewis began to realize that his secret life lay open to the world. Everybody knew, or would know. Morris kept speaking to him matter-of-factly, and in time Lewis noticed the silver lining: Morris cared about him. His coming to Bellevue proved that. Thanking him, Lewis almost cried.

"Any plans?" Morris asked. Lewis knew what he meant: he couldn't go home. "Let me help. Not today, I'm afraid, but come and see me tomorrow evening. We'll, as one says, discuss your future."

Lewis left the hospital two hours later. In the First Avenue lobby he met Louisa, who had just arrived. Her teary consternation made him cringe. He welcomed her first words, however: "I promise you Owen doesn't know. I'll make sure he never does. Please tell me, are you all right?" Lewis's bandaged hands and feet (he was shuffling in heel-less straw slippers) gave him the look of a battle casualty.

"Yes. I'm sorry. Mother, I'm really sorry, but I can't stand being with you right now."

Louisa said she understood, put him in a taxi, promised not to interfere. She made him take the hundred dollars in her handbag. "Promise to call me if you need anything?"

Lewis booked a room at the Chelsea. Next day, making sure his parents had gone out, he fetched his few belongings from their place. At ten that night he arrived at Morris's apartment, which occupied one high-ceilinged floor of a converted brownstone on Cornelia Street. Lewis blushed when Morris embraced him. They sat down in a corner between lofty, slovenly bookcases. A decanter and two glasses had been set out on a low table beside a platter of toast and Roquefort cheese. Morris poured out the wine, one Lewis had never heard

of—sweet, French, and with *Venice* in its name. With the wine a warmth of relief and contentment seeped from his throat and stomach to the tips of his toes, to the tip of his nose. He licked the rim of his glass, shutting his eyes. Opening them, he found himself sitting in the same place, naked, with his ankles and wrists bound to his chair. Morris stood in front of him, bare to the waist except for chromium-studded black leather wristbands and a set of brass knuckles on his right hand. When Lewis's eyes met his, Morris said with a grin, "Now, Louisa, I'm going to beat the pie out of you."

First visit: Morris drugs Lewis, strips him, ties him to a chair. He threatens him with brass knuckles (made of metal-painted rubber) and does not use them, finding better things to do. Lewis soon reveals certain weaknesses (others might call them preferences). Barely awake, he says, "Do anything you like, but let me loose. I go crazy if I can't move." Morris draws up an armchair. "Louisa, you're crazy anyway. But I'd love to see what you mean." Lewis begins to cry. Morris taunts him, in accidental slang: "Poor Ella, such a sad route to go! How did a swinging skinner like me pull a dorky trick like Miss Thing. . . ." Lewis interrupts, "Don't talk like that. I'm not a screaming faggot, and neither are you. It makes me puke." Morris: "Poor baby! Did you just step out of a time machine? You can suck my Jewish ass! I'll talk any way I want." Morris harangues him late into the night.

Morris had a surprise for Lewis. On the following day he took him to Thirteenth Street just west of First Avenue and there, three metaled flights up a tenement stairway, led him into a two-room apartment. Although its size forbade even one closet, it had been properly maintained, and its rent was eighty-five dollars.

"Which I'll pay till you find a job," Morris told Lewis, who moved in ten days before Christmas.

The two men saw each other for drinks, for dinner, for

openings, for double features; never privately. For nearly two months Morris refused to let Lewis come to his apartment. Lewis's pleadings did nothing to shorten the interval.

Second visit: January 27, 6:00 P.M. When Lewis has undressed, Morris fastens his wrists to his ankles with short-linked metal cuffs. Unable to walk, Lewis hops after Morris at his bidding. A nudge topples him. Morris passes a rope through his arms and legs. Drawn tight through an eye-knot at one of its ends, the rope bunches Lewis's hands and feet, pressing his head against his knees, reducing him to a sack-shaped bundle that Morris drags behind him. In the kitchen, while he readies his dinner, Morris resorts to the jargon Lewis abhors and vents his disillusionment with the practice of sado-masochism, which he is planning to give up: ". . . It may mean short roses for us, but that's show biz. I mean B and D is so gaggy. And where does it all end? In a bug wing, at fat best. Just think—a nice girl like you already getting taken home! *You'll* probably end up popped. I wouldn't actually mind, except playing god must be your dream. No, this one plans to rejoin the fluffs in the vanilla bars. You should, too. It's not so bad. You could always turn out spinach queen. Or why don't you just try going it alone? That's you! I'll give you a fifi-bag to remember me by. . . ." Morris continues his monologue while consuming shrimp, chops, salad, flan, Petit Chablis, and coffee. Afterwards he settles down in his study. Twenty minutes later, Lewis calls from the kitchen. Morris answers the summons with an irritated "Do you mind!" and tapes a wool sock inside Lewis's mouth. Lewis fears he will choke and starts writhing on the floor. "*Must* you be so pigeon-titted?" The cuffs keep clattering. Morris hauls Lewis across the living-room floor. Opening the window, he loops the drag-rope over the top of the railing outside and pulls Lewis upwards until his back barely touches the floor. When the rope is secured to the railing, Lewis is immobilized by his own weight. The window

now cannot shut; through it pass bitter gusts and occasional fine snow. Morris returns to his desk.

Lewis had taken a temporary job as night watchman at a factory building in Queens. Afternoons, he haunted off-off-Broadway theaters, where he tried to make himself useful in any capacity that might lead to being hired. Three days after Lewis's second visit, Morris introduced him to Tom, the head lighting man at the City Center Opera. He had agreed to have Lewis apprenticed to him. This meant low pay and invaluable experience. The sudden opportunity intimidated Lewis. Tom coached him patiently, and Morris reassured him during his fits of self-doubt. After such kindness, Lewis could not understand why Morris again barred him from his apartment. He offered to run the most humdrum household errands for his benefactor. Morris remained adamant. For three weeks, Lewis had to content himself with public meetings, knowing that all the while Priscilla frequently visited the lodgings on Cornelia Street.

Third visit: February 14. Books fill every room in Morris's apartment, including the kitchen. Even the back door is hidden by a bookcase. This door is not, however, completely blocked: the lower shelves of the bookcase can swing out to allow passage of upright dogs and crouching humans. Lewis is permitted to return only if he promises henceforth to use this entrance. He is given a key. On Saint Valentine's night he makes his first appearance on his hands and knees, to Morris's satisfaction: "That's fine. *Don't* stand up. Wriggle out of your Peck and Pecks right where you are. You'll have yourself when you see what I've brought you." He hands the naked Lewis a straitjacket. Lewis bursts into tears. Morris snaps, "The party's over," and picks up his overcoat. Lewis begins obediently working his way into the straitjacket; Morris knots the drawstrings. With a short length of nylon cord he attaches Lewis's left foot to a leg of the kitchen table. He also fits him with a studded leather cock ring, its points facing inwards. Morris

then pulls up a chair and begins his talk for the evening. He
has taken for his subject Lewis's sexual inadequacy. Morris
explains that he has tried to lessen its effect by keeping Lewis
away as long as possible. Now he must speak his mind. He
has never had so boring a lover. He describes the delights of
some earlier affairs, long and short: ". . . One piece of ivy
pie was so righteous! Never been tampered with, and he still
knew twice what you know, Zelda Gooch. . . ." However, he
will not linger over his past. After fifteen minutes, putting
on his coat, he tells Lewis, "I'm out for dinner tonight. You
won't be alone, though. Phoebe's coming to see you. She'll let
herself in." Lewis huddles under the kitchen table. He pisses
on himself.

After weeks of insistence, Morris pestered Lewis into showing him everything he had written—his poems, his journal, his
imitations. "You'll need one reader at least, and I *am* on your
side, you know." For the first and last time, Morris became a
teacher. He went through Lewis's work with him line by line.
He refused to correct; instead, he invented exercises for Lewis.
He made him rework passages in other styles. (Lewis's "break-
through" took the form of a political polemic rewritten as a
love poem.) Morris took care to do these exercises himself,
keeping no more than a step ahead of his pupil. Little by little he weaned Lewis from his limitations, his "individuality":
favorite words, repeated sentence rhythms, obsessive meta-
phors, whatever let him shy away from the entirety of language
(as a novice skier, preoccupied with his skis, shies from the
buoyant steeps that can give him wings).

Fourth visit: March 14. Lewis finds Morris with Tom from
the City Center. Morris tells him that Tom will spend the evening with them. Two long boards are leaning against the man-
telpiece. A small vise is screwed to both ends of each board.
After Lewis has stripped, the men spread-eagle him against the
boards and clamp his wrists and ankles in the four vises. Only
the loose boards hold him in place; Lewis does not dare stir.

Morris and Tom sit down to dinner. They discuss Lewis while they eat. Morris speaks of his hopelessness as a writer; he reads a few hilariously incompetent passages by him out loud. Tom describes him at the theater—slow to learn, manually clumsy, so socially clumsy the entire staff dislikes him (including Tom). After dinner the two men sit together on the sofa in front of Lewis. They start kissing. Lewis falls to the floor, gashing one knee bloodily on the glass coffee table. Morris replaces Lewis's left foot in the vise from which it has slipped. Talking campily and incessantly, he and Tom caress one another. At last they put on their coats and leave. Tom's place, they agree, will be cozier under the circumstances.

The following afternoon, Lewis met Morris at an opening at the Stable Gallery. Morris greeted him exuberantly. He had sent a selection of Lewis's work to one of the editors of *Locus Solus*, a little magazine whose reputation was unrivaled. Three poems had been accepted. "You tell people you're a writer, they say 'Wonderful,' and *always* they ask next, 'And have you published anything?' Now you say yes."

The two pursued their study of writing several hours each week.

Fifth visit: April 15. The worst for Lewis so far. He picks up the evening's "toys": a full-length inflatable rubber suit that constricts its wearer whenever he struggles against it. Lewis climbs three floors of a dilapidated building on lower Varick Street. A small nervous man dumps a bundle in his arms and slams the door in his face. When Lewis crawls through the back door into Morris's apartment, he finds Morris waiting for him, naked except for a gag, a note in his outstretched hand:

Dear Louisa,
My turn. Put the contraption on me, use the pump to blow it up, and get out. If you do anything else, or if you come back, I'll never forgive you.
M.

In tears, Lewis complies with his instructions. Afterwards he goes to a restaurant. He can't eat. He decides to see a movie, a revival of *Twenty Thousand Leagues Under the Sea*. James Mason doomed to submarine exile makes him cry so hard he has to leave. He walks down rainy streets for another hour. How can Morris's heart survive the constricting suit? He goes back, crawls once more through the bookcase, and releases his friend. Morris is panting fearfully. Lewis holds the sweating body in his arms, murmuring brotherly comfort. Both men speak words of endearment, and like all of Lewis's visits, the evening ends in a prolific tenderness that lasts into the next morning.

Morris had imagined a prodigious book: for that place and time, The Book. It was to include fiction as well as criticism, theory as well as poetry, using the most appropriate medium to explore each facet of its subject: the finiteness of intellect and language confronting the infinity of the intuited universe. During the spring weekend they spent with Phoebe in the Hudson River valley, Morris invited Lewis to collaborate on the project. They would begin work on May 24, Morris's thirtieth birthday. The task would take at least three years.

Sixth visit: May 23. Entering the kitchen on all fours, Lewis finds Morris busily stirring five plastic basins with a broom handle. The basins contain black matter, heavy and wet. Morris hands Lewis the stick. His efforts have left him rather pale. He now only adds water to the basins while Lewis churns them. The basins, he learns, are filled with quick-drying cement. At Morris's bidding, Lewis carries them into the living room and sets them around the edge of a small area covered with layers of newspaper. Lewis undresses and stands at the center of the area. Using a housepainter's brush, Morris daubs grease over Lewis's head and body. Kneeling down, he then starts covering him in cement, first heaping it generously around his feet and ankles to form a massive base, then

applying a half-inch thickness over his limbs, torso, and head.
Morris leaves an opening for nose and eyes and with his fore-
finger jabs a passage into each ear. When he finishes, sweating
and breathing hard, Morris is visibly pleased with his crude
statue, whose arms stretch out sideways like a scarecrow's, giving it an air both of solidity and of helplessness. While the
cement is hardening, Morris goes off to wash and eat dinner.
On his return, he tells Lewis to move his arms and legs. Tears
and sweat are already dripping from the end of Lewis's nose,
and his eyes now wince with effort: he cannot budge. Morris
walks back and forth in front of him while delivering his customary monologue of abuse. He has hesitated, he confesses,
to tell Lewis the most important thing he will ever say to him.
He has spoken already of the repulsion inspired by Lewis's
degeneracy, by his lack of sexual talent, by his lack of talent
tout court. Morris has since realized that everything he has said
falls short of the truth: what makes Lewis ultimately repulsive
is his intrinsic self. His specific shortcomings only manifest the
underlying ugliness, stupidity, and heartlessness that constitute
his very being. With growing passion Morris applies his new
insight in appalling descriptions of Lewis's physical, mental,
and social behavior. Wherever he looks, he can discover only
failure and disreputableness. Some might consider his nature
something he has no control over, but this makes it no less
unbearable: "Even if I don't like reading you the stations, I
won't spread jam. So please, Louisa, get it and go. You're a
mess, a reject, a patient—I could go on for days. And don't
tell me—I have your nose wide open. I'm sorry. Spare me the
wet lashes, it's all summer stock. Because the only one you've
ever been really strung out on is your own smart self, and you
always will be. Think I'm going to stick around and watch the
buns drop? And for what—to keep catching my rakes in your
zits? Forget it, Dorothy. This is goodbye. Remember one thing,
though. No matter what I've said to you, no matter how I've

turned you out, the truth is"—Morris's eyes become wet; he turns a surprising shade of red—"the truth is, and I'm singing it out: I lo— . . ." Morris is staring past Lewis as his voice breaks off. Has he stopped because the telephone is ringing? His color veers from red to gray. He turns to lean on the back of a chair, except that no chair is to be found where he leans: he sinks onto his knees before lying face down on the floor. He rolls himself slowly onto his back, looking up at Lewis, who watches his lips form a repeated word (*Nitro, nitro*), then remain open and still. Morris breathes rapidly, until a moment comes when he does not breathe at all. Lewis shouts into the cement plastered across his mouth. He only makes his own head hum. Panic has started to overcome him when he realizes what has happened: Morris is playing a joke on him. He is deliberately scaring him out of his wits. Lewis's panic turns to rage. Morris has gone too far, inhumanly far. Lewis will never forgive him. Remembering their previous meeting, he knows that Morris may very well lie there half the night. He can only wait, and he is steeling himself for his ordeal when he notices Morris's eyes. They are fixed in an impossible stare. They never blink. Lewis counts sixty seconds, the eyelids do not move. The fly of Morris's shirt lies motionless over his chest and belly. Lewis keeps looking down at his friend. A grieving numbness is expanding through his body. Another minute passes before he thinks: I may be wrong. Perhaps Morris is only stricken, or perhaps if he's dying there's time to save him. Lewis screams another muffled scream, tells himself: Emotion does no good. Figure out how to get free. Earlier, Lewis has noticed a croquet mallet leaning against one of the bookcases. Morris would have used it to crack his shell. The phone is ringing again. Question: what can he use for a mallet? Answer: a fall to the floor. How can I fall when I can't move? However, Lewis can move, if only inside his skin. He can squeeze himself left and right, or front and back. Will this let him shift his weight?

Seven feet away to the front and left, on the coffee table where he cut himself, sits the phone. Lewis begins pressing towards it and then away from it, right heel to left toe, left toe to right heel. He begins to sway, minimally. He senses a tapping of the cement base on the floor. His hunch is working. The statue has started to rock. He must not fall backwards, away from the table. He puts all his strength into pushing forwards. The base goes tap-thump, tap-thump. A momentum has been established. A point comes when the backwards swing does not occur. Before falling, Lewis and his carapace balance for three full seconds on the front edge of the base, precious seconds during which he twists hard clockwise, trying to swing his left arm in front of him, and the arm does strike the floor an instant before his head and chest. The cement shatters to the elbow. The phone lies too high to reach. He yanks it by its wire onto the floor and pulls the handset in front of his face. The cement around his head has cracked. With his free hand he loosens a piece over his mouth. Running his finger over the rotary dial to the last hole, he dials zero. He hears an answering voice, barely audible. He calls out Morris's address, begs for help, explains that he is immobilized. He repeats his appeal over and over, long after the operator has connected him with the police. Still speaking into the receiver, he hears someone at the front door. Who is it? Why are they ringing the bell? and knocking? "Break it down!" he starts shouting. The bell still rings. He hasn't noticed the sirens before, several of them. Ringing and knocking stop. The door is being forced, a heavy old oak door equipped with three locks. Lewis has nothing left to do. He begins sinking into a weary, gloomy dullness. With despondent irony he tells himself that Morris will never top this. He is mistaken, in the sense that worse is to come. He is not otherwise mistaken: Morris has bequeathed him a legacy that will perpetuate and compound the experience of his six visits. Their last evening has become a moment of pain that

will engender further moments of pain, and these will have to be endured without any hope of Morris's returning, as he had before, from dinner or from Tom's place. In his guise of tormentor Morris will enshroud Lewis's life. Lewis will never want to forget him, and he will have no choice in the matter. A rosary of mourning, shame, and isolation has begun entwining him more finally than thongs and chains. Morris might well in these consequences be completing his last aborted sentence, which Lewis had unhesitatingly grasped in its entirety: "The truth is, I loathe you."

Lewis and Walter

JUNE 1962-JUNE 1963

PRISCILLA LUDLAM ATTENDED the same progressive liberal-arts college as Phoebe, graduating from it, a year after Phoebe left, with a major in art history. For her degree she wrote a commendable bachelor thesis, entitled "The Female Figure in Recent American Art," having as its true subject the work of Walter Trale. (Priscilla's tutor, the same admirer of Walter's work who had taught Phoebe painting, suggested the nominally broader subject to mollify her colleagues in the Fine Arts Department.)

As soon as she had completed her paper, Priscilla wanted Walter to read it. She gave it to Phoebe and asked her to bring it to his attention. It soon occurred to Phoebe that the paper might also interest Lewis, who at the time knew nothing about Walter except what she herself had told him. She sent him a copy.

An account of Walter's early portrait of Elizabeth constituted the centerpiece of the thesis. As a teenager Priscilla had heard about the portrait, which Walter had painted in the upstate town where she still lived. Priscilla set out to gather information about its early history. In her thesis she

154

compensated for her limited critical skills with an abundance of anecdote.

Priscilla had sharp wits. At twenty-two, however, her curiosities drew her less to analysis than to the rehearsal of life—to people, to attainment, to the city. She had not majored in art history because she thought herself scholarly or even "artistic": she was interested not so much in art itself as in those who created it. Art came as close to magic as a possession-prone world allowed. What did it take to become a magician? Priscilla's interest was encouraged by the unprecedented glamor, fostered by critics and buyers alike, of new American painting. When her tutor proposed that she spend a year studying Walter Trale, she accepted enthusiastically, because she could at once imagine him as another Pollock or de Kooning. She devoted many hours to staring dutifully at slides of Walter's work. If she came to feel at home with it, she could not be said to have ever understood it. It never touched her, at least not on its own terms. It mattered to her because she saw in it an expression of the artist's life. Her interpretations of the work surreptitiously concealed an imaginary likeness of Walter himself. He was a subject that did touch her; and her delineation of him made Lewis respond to her thesis with idiosyncratic sympathy.

Priscilla described at length the background of the "Portrait of Elizabeth": how Walter, at eighteen a precociously successful painter of racehorses, prize dogs, and cherished pets, was transformed by his meeting with the woman he was soon to portray. Elizabeth had revealed to him the "animal grace and transcendent sexuality" of a woman's beauty. Merely seeing her had initiated the revelation; but according to Priscilla, Elizabeth also intervened actively in Walter's life. She had seen *him*—seen him for what he might become—and through her friendship she had inspired him to become it. By her visionary wisdom Elizabeth made a creator of him. In Priscilla's view, it was not only through her beauty and intelligence that Elizabeth exerted

her influence but by fully assuming the role of Woman as muse and genetrix. It was this experience of Elizabeth as absolute Woman that Walter had recorded in his portrait of her.

Priscilla supplied engaging anecdotes to support her claim. Defending her interpretation of the portrait proved harder. If the painting looked inspired, what else did it look like? Certainly not Elizabeth. All biographers explaining art take their wishes as facts. Priscilla made the painting conform to her need, which was to establish in it the presence of *das Ewig-Weibliche* (as, knowing no German, she insistently called it). To her, the gold and white of the face invoked a medieval Madonna. The ocher of the eyes belonged to Athena (or perhaps her owl). The mauve lips stood for mourning (notice that the bared teeth are not smiling)—a demonstrable recollection of the *Pietà*. A mouth-colored mouth with no teeth would probably have suggested to Priscilla the Cumaean Sibyl; plain brown eyes the mortality of autumn leaves; pink cheeks the sacred Rose.

Priscilla never realized that her analysis suffered from self-indulgence, and Lewis did not care. Morris would later teach him what art criticism might achieve. For the time being he was seduced by her account of Walter the man. Priscilla's absolute Woman crystalized Lewis's own feelings; women had always struck him as awesome and inexplicably different. At no age that he could remember had he been close to anyone of the opposite sex, except for Phoebe; and if other women acquired mystery by their remoteness, Phoebe had become no less mysterious through intimacy—her love for him left him perpetually incredulous. Mystery meant an aversion that differed from his hostility towards men. Lewis disliked men because, as one of them, he knew all too well how they functioned. He knew, among other things, how they experienced desire. He was attracted to men because he wanted to rediscover with them this familiar, recognizable desire. Women had unimaginable

desires, and one particularly unimaginable sexual desire. He remembered at four watching Phoebe while her diapers were changed and staring at her big button. It looked anything but girlish. Lewis was not bewildered by the vagina, but by the irrelevant and impudent clitoris. He did not want it there. It was the stopper. It meant that women had been fashioned as unpredictable beings, that he could never trust them to behave in an accountable way.

With men, he knew how to provoke the aggressiveness through which he could respond to them. Even here women eluded him. Once, when he was nine, at a family gathering, he called a pretty eleven-year-old cousin a bitch. He knew the insult to be reliably bad because his mother had slapped him when he tried it on her. The cousin laughed gleefully, said he was cute, and pampered him for the rest of the day before withdrawing to Connecticut. They were not to be trusted.

In spite of dating one girl in late adolescence, Lewis's aversion never wavered. Because he kept his true desires hidden, classmates at school and college thought him merely shy, and they frequently introduced him to young ladies both nice and not-nice. He wanted no part of them.

Walter's experience of women, as Priscilla described it, confirmed Lewis's. Walter displayed generosity and ebullience, Lewis pettiness and anxiety; both could agree that in Woman mystery and power abide.

Lewis found a second reason to like Priscilla's thesis: it showed precisely the extent of his difference from Walter. Walter had recognized the power in women and faced it. Through Elizabeth, he had let it into his life. Perhaps he had even mastered it in his art and turned it into a power of his own. Walter was thus an exemplar of all that Lewis could never aspire to.

Lewis often had crushes on the men he admired. A fund of natural affection underlay his habitual mistrust. Because

he was frightened by the give-and-take of friendship, Lewis expressed this warmth either by provoking those he liked or by adoring them from a distance. In Walter, Priscilla had supplied him with a new idol.

Lewis confided his admiration to Phoebe, who at once saw in it an opportunity to move him into the living world he was so determined to avoid. When, in early June, he exclaimed over the phone, "What an incredible man!" she replied, "So why don't you visit? See the work yourself."

"I don't mean the work. I mean *him*."

"So come and see *him*."

Lewis began commenting on the current heat wave. He heard Phoebe saying to someone at her end, "My big brother thinks you're the cat's pajamas, but he's scared to meet you."

When Walter took the phone, Lewis had fled.

Phoebe did not let him get away. She called back repeatedly to tease, berate, and beg. She even lured him with the unlikely possibility that Lewis might somehow work for Walter. The proposal flustered him at first; soon, however, he began working it into his fantasies, until his fantasies themselves changed. Instead of worship, Lewis began dreaming of servitude. He could put his own inadequacy to good use. He could free Walter from whatever distracted him from his art. He would clean his brushes, wash his skylight, scour his toilet bowl, run errands in Brownsville. He accepted Phoebe's invitation.

In the days preceding his visit, walking through the town under dying elms and heat-wilted maples, or sitting with a book on the porch of the house, or lying in bed late at night, he thought of what his meeting with Walter might bring. He did not want gratitude or recompense. He longed ultimately to become indispensable to Walter. He imagined a career starting as charman and ending as watchdog.

Walter in the flesh only strengthened Lewis's devotion. He looked his forty-three years and looked them well. A

nonchalant alertness pleasantly animated his sprawling features, his wrinkles tempered his obvious candor with an aura of lessons learned. Lewis felt a surge of tenderness when he saw him. This would normally have ensured his protracted silence, but Phoebe kept prodding him to speak.

"It's incredible," he finally told Walter over sizzling shrimp, "how you started your career with such a really profound work."

"Profound? 'Digger III' profound? Sure was a *gloomy* beagle."

"I mean—I *meant* Elizabeth. Your first woman—I mean, the first person you painted was a woman. That's probably significant."

"No shit." Walter had not yet read Priscilla's thesis; Lewis had not yet seen the portrait of Elizabeth.

Phoebe said, "Lewis thinks you're accomplices in misogyny."

"Not misogyny, not really—" ("No, not really!" Phoebe camped) "—but, you know, that power," Lewis hurried on. "It's not that it's bad, just big. You don't want to get in its way."

"That's in the portrait?" Walter asked.

"Why, sure." Lewis looked startled. "I don't have to tell *you*."

"Tell me anyway."

Lewis discoursed on female unpredictability. He related the incident with his eleven-year-old cousin: "It wasn't as though she was genuinely fond of me. I was used."

"The trouble is," Walter said ruefully, "*they* never seem to realize." He was suffering at the time from a woman's unresponsiveness.

Although Walter liked him, and Lewis was as willing as ever to serve, he was frustrated in his aims by a rudimentary fact: he was a man. At the studio the next morning, after Walter asked what kind of work he wanted to do for him, Lewis replied, chores—cleaning up, shopping, soaking the beans. "That's no

kind of work for you," Walter said. He meant, among other things, that it was woman's work. Walter, who enjoyed chores, might have accepted another woman as helper; when Phoebe cooked dinner for him, he felt that her presence made a difference. A man could only add more of what he knew all too well.

Walter said, not unkindly, that he found Lewis's offer to play housemaid silly. Lewis was scarcely disappointed—he had been schooled, after all, in Owen's harsher ways. He readily withdrew to his first, safe role as worshiper.

Lewis did not see Walter again until the November evening when he met Morris. In the meantime, both their lives had changed. Walter was living with Priscilla; Lewis had been overwhelmed by Morris's article.

Lewis and Priscilla had once known each other well. Six years before, they had had a serious falling out, and they had not seen each other since. Before the November party Priscilla decided to bury the past. She wanted to please Phoebe, and she assumed that in six years Lewis had grown up. When she saw him arrive, she greeted him with a hug. Lewis was surprised and pleased; however, preoccupied as he was with the prospect of meeting Morris, he responded distractedly to Priscilla's welcome. She mentioned hearing from Phoebe that he had liked her thesis. He replied, "Yes, it was really nice. As a matter of fact, for a while it kind of obsessed me. But you've read Morris's piece? *That* says it all, doesn't it?"

Priscilla had worked hard on her thesis. Walter himself had praised it. In those few seconds Lewis squandered his credit with her.

Late that month Lewis was arrested in the crucifixion raid. Although a reader of the *News*, Walter failed to spot the incriminating photograph. Priscilla noticed it and called up Phoebe to check. Phoebe went out for the paper and phoned back to thank Priscilla for letting her know. Interrupting Walter at work, Priscilla told him, "Look what's happened

to Phoebe's brother, the poor guy!" She wondered how he'd become involved with such freaks. "They must have given him drugs. Nobody's that screwy."

Lewis often saw Walter that winter in Morris's company. In his behavior towards him Walter showed an amiable lack of concern. He knew that Morris and Lewis had become lovers, a relationship that, according to Priscilla, was "doing wonders—just what Lewis needed to get it together." She sometimes reminded Walter that for Phoebe's sake they should be kind to him. By this time Priscilla had become Morris's business partner.

Walter came to think of Lewis as a "case"—someone not all that sick who you still wished would get better. Inevitably Lewis reminded Walter of Phoebe, whom he was losing to her own "neurosis," and of Morris, whom he respected and rather feared. Lewis was to be tolerated and encouraged and, perhaps, avoided.

Morris died. Public and private accounts of his death were gluttonously sucked up by downtown gossips. Walter knew Lewis too little to resist the vague story that many people eagerly accepted: Morris had not died accidentally, and Lewis had not merely witnessed his death.

Lewis had changed in the half year that followed his arrest. Phoebe's old hopes for him had been essentially fulfilled: if Walter had done nothing for Lewis, Morris had done every-thing. He had offered Lewis the chance to earn a living, to write professionally, to recognize and express the love he felt; and, overcoming his chronic fearfulness, Lewis had taken that chance. He learned, for a time at least, that fearfulness could not excuse running away. He was proud that he could now handle a lighting console, that he was going to be published, that Morris had adopted him; prouder still of being able to get a job done, of writing for his own increasingly stern taste, of having turned his sexual addiction into a means of loving

one man. When Morris died, Lewis clearly saw the fullness
his new life had taken on, and how fragile, without Morris, it
had now become.

Morris had incidentally altered Lewis's attitude towards
Walter. While Morris always praised Walter's painting, he
treated the artist himself almost patronizingly—an attitude
completely at odds with Lewis's obsequiousness. At one
December opening, after Morris had walked away from Walter
in mid sentence, Lewis asked him how he could act so cava-
lierly. "I adore Walter," Morris answered, "but he says absolutely
everything that comes into his head. He can be *brainless*." Lewis
said he always listened to Walter because he was so perceptive.
Morris interrupted him: "In so-called life he doesn't notice
anything, except the visuals." Lewis once again ventured to
cite Priscilla's theory of Walter and Woman. "Louisa!" Morris
exclaimed to Lewis, who shrank, "that's infantile caca! Even if
Miss Priss is right, it's still only Big Momma Rides Again. Most
boys feel that way sometime—like you, *n'est-ce pas*, am I not
insightful? Walter probably didn't notice—Wonder Woman's
name for him was Cadmium Rose. Doesn't mean anything,
only words. My words for it were 'tempestuous sky of the
vagina,' remember, and *they* don't mean anything either."

"I never asked you—why 'tempestuous'?"

"What's rumbling thunder remind you of? *Basta!*"

Lewis returned to Walter: "You mean good painters can be
mediocrities?"

"He's not a mediocrity. I love him—warm as a farmhouse
bath on a frosty night. It's only those surfeits of well-meaning-
ness. . . . Maybe it's just been too easy for him. A good shit-dip
would have tightened and brightened him. But there's nothing
wrong with him. He's just not special."

Lewis began listening to Walter more dispassionately and
decided Morris was right. Not knowing he painted, one might
have taken him for an affable wholesaler, a well-read truck

driver, a debonair postman. Lewis saw that adulating Walter
did him an injustice: an extraordinary man can be expected
to do extraordinary work; from an ordinary man, such work
means that he has transcended his nature. If this notion still
smacked of sentimentality, it at least allowed Lewis to transform his idol into someone for whom he felt affinity as well
as respect. His own exertions as a writer—small compared to
Walter's thirty years' diligence—gave him a sense of comrade-
ship with the older man.

Morris's death cost Lewis his lover, mentor, and closest
friend. Within days he learned how alone he had become.
Newspaper reports, private rumors even less well informed,
were making of him a macabre celebrity. No one seemed
sure who had buried whom in cement; either way, the act
sounded deranged, if not criminal. The tale of the crucifixion
was revived and given wide circulation. Lewis learned that few
people knew the truth about him—that he loved Morris, that
he wrote, that he worked at the City Center. Many of Phoebe's
friends did not know he was her brother. Tom, at least, did
not let him down; and the regularity of Lewis's daily stint
at the theater sustained him during the weeks that followed
Morris's death. However, he valued Tom as his boss. Outside
the classroom, he had never worked for anyone; he was now
doing a competent job for someone who had trained him well
without ever overtly favoring him. Lewis refused to jeopardize
their professional relationship by making Tom his confidant.

He knew he needed a confidant. A year before he would
have turned to Phoebe; she now lay in a hospital in critical
condition. He dreaded facing Morris's sister, Irene. Each time
he wondered, who am I going to talk to? he would think, in
spite of himself, I have to ask Morris. Grief would then penetrate him, the cold, fleshly grief he had felt when he gazed
down at his lover's breathless lips. Phoebe was lost for now,
Morris forever. Lewis turned to their common friend.

He had seen and not spoken to Walter at Morris's funeral. On Wednesday, a few days later, he called the studio. Priscilla answered: Walter was busy, was there anything she could do? How was he?

"Same as you. Except you have company."

"Big deal. It's *awful.* There's this hole in my life I keep falling into. . . ."

"I do reruns all the time—I saw it, but I still can't believe it. Listen, when is Walter free?"

"When would you like?"

"Right away! I really need to talk to him."

"Gotcha. I'll tell him."

He gave her the number of a delicatessen that took messages for him.

When Lewis returned late that night, Walter had not called. At the theater, he had heard one of his companions ask another, "Jesus, is he still at large?" The next morning he received a letter from Owen's lawyer. It assured him that his father would assume his legal expenses. Lewis again phoned Walter, and Priscilla said to him, "Lewis! I'm so glad to hear from you. Can you come over tomorrow afternoon?"

"Tomorrow?"

"Darling, it's the best he can do."

The "darling" angered him, more because of his own helplessness than the intimate concern it implied.

Priscilla *was* concerned: she was doing her best to keep Lewis at bay. Only six months had passed since she had skillfully won a place in Walter's life, and she still considered her position handicapped by youth, inexperience, and a lack of credentials.

Most of Walter's friends had known him for years. All displayed forcefulness or originality or both—even the bums had clownish charm. Priscilla could not pretend to be "interesting." Only Walter's attraction to her justified her presence at

his side. She needed to fortify this attachment. She needed to establish herself at the center of Walter's life, with the rest of the threatening world kept apart from their private sphere.

Lewis presented no threat. His disgrace served her plans, however, now that Phoebe and Morris could no longer protect him. Priscilla had already consigned Lewis in Walter's eyes to the role of psychic invalid. She now wanted to banish him conspicuously from their life so as to confirm certain benefits she would derive from Morris's death.

Walter was feeling intense remorse over Morris. He had neglected someone to whom he was uniquely indebted. He told Priscilla he wanted to atone for his neglect by befriending the dead man's lover. The impulse had so far remained only a wish, because Walter shrank from seeing Lewis, whom he wanted to like and didn't and whose strangeness in the wake of Morris's death had become forbidding. Priscilla knew, however, that Walter's generosity would win out. Mere aversion was no match for it.

Priscilla sensed she could turn Walter's remorse to her own advantage and so delayed Lewis's meeting with him. Lewis had called back on Friday morning. That afternoon she had been summoned to appear at the reading of Morris's will. She had been informed that no legacy in the will approached in value the life-insurance policy of which she had been named beneficiary. She planned to come home that evening with public proof that she, not Lewis, had been chosen by Morris as his heir.

Not knowing that the insurance policy proceeded from a business understanding, Walter reacted as Priscilla had foreseen. She had been consecrated as Morris's intimate. Unmentioned in the will, Lewis was relegated once again to the fringe of things, a pathetic, suspicious silhouette. That evening, alone with Priscilla, Walter for the first time found the ability to vent the grief he had been withholding. He cried in her arms. Morris became a precious bond between them.

Walter woke Lewis up Saturday morning to briskly excuse himself from their meeting that afternoon. He suggested that Lewis join them for drinks Sunday evening: "We're having a few friends over." Baffled with unfinished dreams, Lewis sleepily accepted. The phone rang again: Phoebe. She was leaving the hospital to catch a train upstate. He asked if he could take her to the station.

"Thanks, but no. I've made such a deal about doing this on my own. I do want to see you. How are you? Better not tell me! *I'm* awful, too. Come home, soon, and we'll hold each other's hands."

Lewis had intended to see Walter alone. He went to the studio that Sunday because he preferred seeing him with others to not seeing him at all. He regretted the visit. Those guests who knew who he was (the others were soon told) treated him with careful nonchalance, pointedly discussing their politics, their diets, their vacations, confronting him with the undisguised curiosity reserved for movie stars and youthful victims of terminal cancer, with one difference: they never touched him, not even an elbow, as though he were threatening them with terrifying contagion. A cheery Priscilla took him aside and earnestly questioned him first about Phoebe, then about his work, and last about his grief, which, she too emphatically insisted, she more than shared. Lewis sadly realized that they were engaged in the conversation he wanted to have with Walter.

Walter behaved like the others. In the features of the man he had chosen to trust, Lewis saw himself registered in terms all too familiar: as pervert and pariah. When he noticed Lewis's gaze, Walter's inane smile almost split his face. Lewis later detected something else. Walter averted his eyes from him as from the thought of Morris, of Morris-as-corpse. Lewis had become a carrier of mortality as well as disease. (That suspended look reminded him of someone else, someone he could not then recall.)

Lewis wondered what Priscilla had told Walter about him. Why was she so set on keeping them apart? He was about to ask her (what could he lose?) when a great weariness settled on him. It had arisen, as well as from disappointment, from the sorrow that for ten days had followed him like a childhood dog; he had spent all his courage tending it. He looked at Walter once more. The openness of the face contracted into studied blankness. Lewis left.

He met Walter and Priscilla by chance the next morning, on the corner of Carmine and Bleecker Streets—Priscilla still cheery, Walter silent, standing behind her, contemplating Lewis with the appalled eyes that identified him as doom made flesh. As he was replying to something Priscilla had said, Lewis recognized that familiar expression: it was the way Owen always looked at him. Lewis's understanding of the couple he faced began to change. He lost track of what he was saying to Priscilla. His scalp prickled with sweat.

"What's wrong?" Priscilla asked.

Lewis lied, "I just remembered talking to Morris once on this corner." He kept staring at Walter. "You know how his being dead—you forget it for five seconds, and something brings it back—don't you, Priss? *You* know what an incredible man he was."

Thirty-seven years before, Walter had sat down conclusively on his little sister's best celluloid doll. Since that time, no one had ever looked at him as she had then, as Lewis was looking at him now. The aversion drained out of him; he reverted to his considerate, vulnerable self. Lewis did not notice this because of the tears of rage in his eyes.

He walked away. He did not see them again until early September.

Every year during the hot midsummer drought, on the hills overlooking the French Riviera, hundreds of acres of pine and

cork oak are laid waste by fire. At the end of one arid July, a thirty-year-old schoolteacher, passing a spot where underbrush had begun burning, got out of his car to observe the spreading flames. Other drivers saw him, assumed that he had started the fire, and reported him to the police. He was arrested. Overnight he provided the outlet for a nation's frustrated anger. Although he was cleared of the charge against him, to him this hardly mattered. Six years later he declared that for the rest of his life, no matter what he did, he would be remembered as the "Arsonist of Provence."

From the behavior of Walter's guests, from the remark overheard at the theater, from the exaggerated discretion of the countermen at his delicatessen, from Owen's coldly dutiful letter, from Phoebe's pity, from the telephone calls of junk journalists, from the silence of acquaintances, Lewis knew that he was similarly condemned. For years the mention of his name, his appearance in a room, could only recall King Koncrete or whatever tag stuck to him best. How many books would he have to write to obliterate his scandalous fame? Would he have to write them under another name? (Morris had said that Lewis Lewison was so good it sounded made up.) To read in Walter's face this squalid verdict hurt more than he could endure. Why had he blamed Priscilla? She had her old reasons for mistrusting him. Walter should have known better.

Lewis's situation excruciated him because he could see no end to it. Phoebe might console him at home; elsewhere he had no prospect of support or even sufferance, not if someone like Walter repudiated him. Lewis's awareness that his pain would last, that its unfairness would not modify its persistence, urgently demanded comforting: he needed someone to blame. Throughout his life he had always blamed himself for the failures that, loving mortification as he did, he had in truth often provoked. Now he chose to blame someone else. He hated his pain, most of all when he recollected his

happiness with Morris. He turned this hatred against Walter. Kind and candid, Morris's friend and Phoebe's, Walter should have known better. His blindness excluded forgiveness, and Lewis did not forgive him. Three months later, after the portrait of Elizabeth was brought home from the hospital, Lewis immediately noticed its disappearance and discovered that his father had destroyed it. He spoke to no one of what he had learned. Walter must be the first to know; Lewis must tell him. He waited until they met at another funeral to enact this small revenge.

Louisa and Lewis

1938-1963

SEEING LEWIS IN trouble held no novelty for Louisa. Since infancy he had schooled her in disaster.

When the Lewisons decided to have a child, Owen, although claiming to want a boy, was disappointed by Lewis. Soon afterwards he began saying how sad it was to be an only child, as he had been. Three years later, at Phoebe's birth, Owen saw his true desire satisfied. He devoted himself to her thereafter. Lewis was left to Louisa.

Lewis had already made her suffer. During her second pregnancy he had been afflicted with intermittent fevers that came and went without reason. He might be playing in his room late in the afternoon; Louisa would hear him whimpering and find him flushed and breathless. By nightfall his temperature would reach a hundred, sometimes rising to a hundred and four during the night. Doctors offered baffled diagnoses and prescribed aspirin and orange juice. As long as the fever lasted his head and body ached, he slept fitfully, he threw up most of what he ate. Louisa stayed in his room night and day, cooling him with wet sponges, reading stories, singing songs, talking until she ran out of words.

After three days the fever would abate, leaving Lewis weak and testy. Louisa knew that, at two, he could not be expected to acknowledge her care of him; she was nevertheless pained to find herself blamed for his miseries: "I hurt when *you're* there." Sometimes he would cry when she appeared at his bedside.

Louisa expected to feel surpassing love for a firstborn son. What love she felt was regularly distracted by the conviction that Lewis had come into the world with a nature she would never understand. Louisa found males strange—she even liked their strangeness, at a distance. Owen had proved a special case. Before they married, he had clearly wanted her, and Louisa did not mind that he wanted her in part for her good name and connections: she accepted his suit wholeheartedly, and her commitment to his career after their marriage maintained their mutual trust. Other men bewildered her. She found them full of abstract generosity and practical unkindness, broad-minded towards the world (and their dogs), impatiently suspicious of individuals who disturbed their opinions. Louisa may have been blinkered by the memory of her father, a big, brusque man who had died when she was five, leaving her family poor and herself haunted by a strong, elusive presence.

Even tiny, Lewis looked to her like another mysterious male. Her sense of incomprehension, and its attendant fear of motherly incompetence, made her swear to keep doing her best by him. Failures only renewed her dedication. As a result, her life with him was punctuated with "I must" and "if only." Whatever happened, she must, she must sustain him; and if only, if only she hadn't behaved in this or that way, what had happened might not have; and if only it hadn't happened, Lewis might be different. She never thought, "If only *he* hadn't," no doubt suspecting that such thinking had as its logical *terminus a quo*: if only he hadn't been born.

Fearfulness made Louisa vulnerable. Lewis learned that by demanding and blaming he could get the better of her. He

learned, too, that if he could lure her into a shameful business with him, she would forgive him anything. He sensed that Louisa would always protect him from Owen.

At the age of three he discovered how to make a shameful business of his genitals. With tantrums threatened or indulged, he would force Louisa to stay with him when he was in bed or in the bathroom and squeeze his penis in a special, reassuring way. A year later, by then too "reasonable" for such games, he would harry her with questions about his member: "Will it snap off when it's stiff? Momma, promise to tell me if I'm supposed to snap it off?" Until he was almost ten, he would get up at night in tears if she had not come in to secure the bath mitt in which he lodged his penis while he slept.

These tactics reduced Louisa to impotence. She complied with them, concealed them from Owen, and at last found herself depending on them. They became her most reliable evidence that Lewis trusted her and that she could comfort him.

When Lewis was eleven, the Lewisons rented a summer house upstate, in the neighborhood where they would eventually settle. Friends with children of Lewis's age made a place for him on picnics and swimming parties, and after a few days Lewis began bicycling into the summer haze to join his new acquaintances. One day he stayed home. He sat until evening on the porch steps. After that, he never again left the house of his own accord. He spent his afternoons reading comics or hunting through the unfamiliar library for "grown-up" books. On weekends he kept to his room, out of Owen's sight. His gloominess troubled Louisa less than his utter loss of insolence. He offered to help her around the house. He behaved almost gently with her.

One morning, having dispatched him to riding school, Louisa searched Lewis's room. In the bottom drawer of his commode, twenty-two stacked issues of *Action Comics* concealed a sheet of blue-lined paper on which a doggerel poem

had been penciled. Three quatrains followed its title, printed in capital letters: TO LEWIS WHO WE LOVE TO HATE. The last quatrain read:

> We think you'd be better off dead, get it?
> Cause you're really sick in the head, get it?
> You think you're sharp as a tack, get it?
> But you're really crazy as a *bat*, get it?

Louisa restored the page to its cache. When Lewis came home, she asked if he had had any problems with his new friends; he fell bitterly silent. Louisa spoke to other parents, who made necessary inquiries. She soon found out what had happened.

A few days before he began his solitary life, Lewis had asked all the boys he knew to meet him at one of their houses. Early in the afternoon, carrying a wicker hamper, he had joined a dozen ten- to twelve-year-olds in the mortifying heat of a third-floor attic.

Lewis had tried to initiate the meeting with a speech about "friendship and courage." No one listened, and he quickly proceeded to the main event. Opening the hamper, he turned it upside down, shook it hard, and kept shaking it until, twenty seconds later, a small bat emerged, soon followed by another. The two bats spent some time fluttering among the tumbling, shouting boys before settling on the darker side of a corner rafter. By then the group had evacuated the attic. Only one ten-year-old remained. He had retreated sobbing to a spot behind a queen post where he still sat clutching his knees, watching incredulously as Lewis, his hands sheathed in electrician's gloves, calmly plucked the bats from their refuge and returned them to the hamper. (Two days before, Lewis, in his own attic, had devoted three turbulent hours to techniques of bat catching.)

When he came downstairs, grinning with pride, Lewis

found his group dispersing. Two or three boys whom he addressed replied with scant, nervous words before biking hurriedly away. He had plainly produced an effect; he did not worry what sort of effect until the poem was dropped anonymously into the Lewison mailbox. As far as Lewis was concerned, summer had ended. No boy would now dare to be known as his friend. Lewis felt that he had been cruelly mistreated. He had only wanted to impress the others. Having succeeded in that, he hoped (this he barely admitted to himself) that he might propose to his admiring friends that they all confirm their companionship by masturbating together. It was this half-secret, not-unsociable wish that had inspired him. It did not merit ostracism.

When she learned about the bats, Louisa told herself that the author of the poem was not far off the mark: if not insane, Lewis seemed certifiably strange. He frightened her by what he had done, and no less by his perfect secrecy. Except for borrowing the hamper, he had given her no clue about his undertaking. She could not console him—she was unsure of what he might do in return. Above all, she longed to recover his trust.

Lewis gave her the chance to do so before the summer was over. He went alone into town one morning (something he was forbidden to do) and came back with a foulard by Hermès as a present for her. Suspicious, Louisa asked where he had found the money to pay for it. Lewis told several lies, all of them transparent. He was almost relieved when he had to admit to stealing the scarf.

Louisa lost her temper. To one of her upbringing, shoplifting was the first slippery step to armed robbery and hatchet murders. She slapped Lewis hard—the last time she ever did so. He yelled, "I did it for *you!*" and ran away in tears. Louisa realized that he had in his devious way confided in her. She must not lose him.

She followed him outside, where he had hidden between

two lush snowball bushes. The slap had worked. He fell into her arms, sobbing, "I'm sorry, I'm sorry." If she had been less shocked by his thieving, Louisa would have cried too. She hugged him as long as he let her. They walked twice around the house together, her hands on his shoulders. She explained that she must take the scarf back. She would look at other scarves, slip it among them, pretend to choose his, and pay for it; she could then keep his present. She made Lewis promise never to steal again and, if he did, to tell her at once. She did not mention his father.

In this manner Lewis implicated his mother in the first of many thefts, making her his ally against Owen, against a world both respectable and hostile, against his own ordinary yearnings. Her involvement enabled him to steal with zest. He knew that if the worst happened, she would suffer the consequences. Sometimes the worst did happen; and whenever he was caught, Louisa duly appeared to soft-soap the store owner, or floor manager, or policeman. Neither mother nor son ever acknowledged that they felt happiest together after these dramas.

Thieving brought Lewis another advantage: possessions. He learned that by threatening to steal an expensive object he could, once he convinced her that he craved it, make Louisa give him enough money to buy it. (He sometimes stole it anyway.) Cultural items like books and classical records best suited this blackmail, and Lewis assembled a library and a record collection remarkable for one his age. On his own, he acquired, among other things, two hundred and ten packages of chewing gum, a hundred and sixty-nine Tootsie Rolls, ninety-eight bananas, oranges, and apples, seventy-six pens and pencils, eighteen neckties, seven bottles of French perfume (although three were open samples), and five six-packs. His grandest failures included a top hat at Tripler's and a multipurpose electric tool kit at Sears; his proudest triumphs, a small dress sword filched under the malevolent eyes of a Third

Avenue pawnbroker and a first edition of *Madame Bovary*, which he spent twenty harrowing minutes slowly shifting from the depths of Brentano's, rack by rack, until, reaching the sidewalk of Fifth Avenue, he made a four-block dash with it into obscurity.

He told Louisa about most of his thefts, only neglecting to mention those too trifling to outrage her. He ultimately sought outrage rather than complicity, and he discovered after two years that his achievements left him dissatisfied, because Louisa invariably proved kind. Lewis had a secret hope and fear: that Louisa, at last turning against him, would inflict the punishment he deserved—leave him to the police, send him to a military academy, tell Owen. Louisa's governing rule, however, was to keep her crazy boy within eyeshot. She did not really care what he did, as long as he stayed hers—hers to watch, to listen to, to mollify, to save from his craziness. She scolded, complained, threatened, and always bought him off. After weeks of argument, she let him keep *Madame Bovary*. (He had made a rare choice, and she hated Brentano's.) Where Lewis was concerned, the observant Owen noticed nothing.

In Lewis's eyes, each kindness of Louisa's reshaped her into a likeness of the Connecticut cousin who had loved him for his rudeness; each kindness made her less dependable. In this he judged her unfairly (Louisa was consistency itself) and resented her sincerely: she had abdicated her parental function of providing pain.

After four years, their complicity ended.

The Lewisons continued to vacation upstate in spite of Lewis's unhappy summer. In time his unhappiness waned. The bats passed into half-spooky, half-glamorous legend. One day in July, when he was fifteen, members of an unfamiliar gang noticed the solitary Lewison boy and decided to adopt him. Fearing trickery, Lewis acted petulant and unresponsive. The others laughed at him and said they needed a good sorehead.

Even when Lewis had come to enjoy these funny companions, he never left himself unprepared for some cruel joke they
might be playing on him.

One of the gang, a girl a year younger than Lewis, openly
pursued him. She persisted in spite of his overt mistrust of
her. She biked at his side, let him dunk her when they went
swimming, and retrieved his nasty comments good-naturedly
("Just because I like you, Groucho, doesn't make me all bad").
One evening, while they sat together at the movies, she rested
her head on his shoulder. An hour later Lewis kissed her. He
pressed his jaws against hers, not feeling much, excited by the
idea of kissing. He knew he should try for more.

Behind his parents' house lay a farm, whose barn he had
often explored. Lewis brought the girl there two days later.
Piled to the tie beams with new hay, the high building was
deserted, as he knew it would be at four o'clock on a steamy
August afternoon. They settled in a corner, night-black after
the summer sunlight, and embraced between a cliff of hay and
a tar-scented wall. Lewis kissed her harder and harder. After a
while she let him squeeze her small breasts, then asked to go
outside. Lewis held her. She complained. He did not know
what to do. She would not let him touch her elsewhere, she
wouldn't touch him. He wrestled her to the ground and lay on
top of her, rubbing against her, trying to pull down her shorts,
poking inside them. The girl tried to bite him. Both were
gasping and sweating in that close corner. Dust from ancient
harvests, roused from the barn floor, drifted into their nostrils
and eyes. Lewis went on thrashing against her, unwilling to
stop. The girl began sniveling. She was frightened: no light,
seemingly less and less air, Lewis hurting her with his elbows
and hips. She took a deep breath to scream and choked on dry
hay-dust, coughing wretchedly. She shit in her pants. Lewis
smelled it. The girl had begun to utter faint spasmodic cries
when he ran away.

Louisa was standing in front of the barn door. She had noticed the two bicycles while walking by. Lewis did not speak to her as he mounted his bicycle to sprint off through the cornfields. Louisa found the girl inside the barn and brought her to the house to bathe and change. She made tea and talked to her. Louisa had no problems with women, whatever their age. She soothed the girl. Learning what had happened, she spoke of her chronic difficulties with Lewis. The girl had grown calm, almost content with their secrets by the time Louisa drove her home.

Louisa found Lewis waiting for her when she returned. He was wet-eyed with impatience. Once he knew that she had talked with the girl, he would not let her speak, fitfully spluttering forth his resentment: his life was none of her business, she should stay out of it, for good. . . . He ran off the porch, slamming the screen door with a bouncy clatter.

Louisa understood that the violence choking him did not represent shame for his assault. The girl had told her, "He didn't really do anything, but he got so wild trying." She had felt in danger less of rape than of Lewis's incapacity for it. He was ashamed to have his mother know this. He wanted never to face her again.

He stuck to his aversion and kept beyond Louisa's reach. He stopped speaking to her about stealing (in truth, he stole no more). In the years that followed he clung fiercely to an absurd position: he was helpless to prevent his parents from conditioning his life, and at the same time they had nothing to do with him. Louisa supposed that he would have given up eating if he had thought it put him in her debt. Lewis claimed that he owed his parents nothing, and that they owed him everything in compensation for the circumstances to which they condemned him. Louisa's concern and affection demonstrated only minimal decency, nothing to her credit and no help to him. How could she help him in his pursuit of philosophical

consistency, political integrity, or whatever other distant goal he had most recently set himself?

For eight years, Louisa depended on Phoebe for information about her son. She respected her children's intimacy. Fearful of weakening it, she never pressed her daughter to tell more than she volunteered; so her knowledge remained limited while her anxiety grew large. She worried about Lewis's social life (he never brought a friend home); about his love life (she thought he was homosexual—was he at least homosexual?); about his future (bleak); about his relations with his father. His life offered her little not to worry about. He seemed locked inside himself—a place that he enjoyed no more than any other.

If, month after month, Louisa kept speculating about her son, she never guessed at his career as a practicing masochist. The crucifixion raid devastated what trust she still had in her own insight and gave her anxiety something real to gnaw on. After she rushed to Lewis's side and he fled from her, she began spending much of her time in the city. She was determined to stay near him, hovering just out of his sight, hoping that she could stave off the next catastrophe. She feared for his life.

Morris's friendship with Lewis dismayed her because the more Lewis saw Morris, the less he saw Phoebe, and the less Louisa knew about him. She wanted to believe Phoebe's assertion that Morris was working miracles on Lewis's behalf. To Louisa, however, the crucifixion had proved her son insane, and she did not see how anyone could change that. Morris might have reassured her if she had approached him; Lewis's unpredictable reactions made her afraid to risk that. She went on worrying about Lewis, rarely seeing him, pleased when she knew what he was doing, disheartened when she didn't, her imagination then inflating itself with volatile, inaccurate terrors.

One evening in late May, getting out of a taxi in front of the Washington Square apartment house where she was dining, Louisa saw Phoebe walking by. Heading for MacDougal

Street, Phoebe did not look at Louisa or turn at the sound of her name. Anyone except Louisa would have been concerned for Phoebe; Louisa thought, what has happened to Lewis? When she called her an hour later and Phoebe failed to answer, she knew that something awful had happened. Louisa bravely telephoned Morris. At first his number did not answer either; it then rang busy for a full ten minutes. Louisa left her dinner and hurried across Sixth Avenue to Cornelia Street. At the door of Morris's building she pushed intercom buzzers until she found a tenant willing to let her in. She climbed the two flights to the apartment and began ringing the bell. A voice resounded far inside—perhaps shouting, she thought; she couldn't make out the words. She kept ringing and knocking. The man who had let her in came down for a look, a woman in a gym suit appeared on the stairs below. They think I'm bonkers, Louisa thought, but I'm doing the right thing.

The voice inside kept calling out. No one came to open the door. Outside she heard a siren approaching, a second and a third, each swelling to soprano frenzy before declining in a long, laggard wail. Downstairs the building door opened to thudding feet. She was surrounded by cops and unhatted firemen. Exquisitely, they lifted her to one side, then attacked Morris's door with an ax, a sledgehammer, and two crowbars. When it sprang from its hinges, Louisa was trembling with dread and eagerness.

She quickly got inside. Two objects lay on the living-room floor in a litter of newspapers: Morris's body and a long shattered stone, which four firemen promptly surrounded, chipping carefully at its black fragments. Louisa bent over Morris. He looked distracted, did not answer her, seemed not to breathe. She knew what to do. She began blowing air through the parted lips.

A policeman pulled Louisa away, led her to the large, wide-open window, and held her there. She started to lose control

and swore loudly. She twisted her head around and saw Lewis
lying among chunks of black stone. She screamed. Two white-
suited males forced her onto a stretcher and strapped her to it;
another man adroitly needled a vein in her left forearm. Louisa
woke up in a hospital room on the East Side.

She was still drowsy when, late the following morning, a
visitor was announced. She was surprised to see Lewis: "You're
all right? It's darling of you to come here. Wherever here may
be."

"You need someone to sign you out—this is the nut ward.
Phoebe's on her way, but I thought I'd speed things up."

"*Thank* you. How is Morris?" Louisa asked—a lying question. She knew she'd breathed into a dead mouth.

"He had a heart attack. He died right in front of me."

"Lewis, I'm so . . ." Tears were rising fast.

"What the fuck were you doing there?"

"I didn't know . . . Phoebe wouldn't talk to me." She sniffled
into a bouquet of Kleenex. "I'm sorry. It was hard enough for
you without my . . . Thank you for coming, I don't deserve
it. I *am* sorry."

"You don't deserve it, and you're not why I'm here."

"You said, so I could get out?"

"I'm trying to contain the damage. I hope you leave the
hospital, go home, and shut up. Let's say you don't answer the
phone for a week."

She recognized Lewis's manner, not its present motive:
"Lewis, I just don't understand."

"Remember the policemen at Morris's last night? Policemen
like to file reports. Some hotshot young prosecutor with a flea
up his ass held a press conference this morning. He made, shall
we say, selective use of the reports. There was Morris, there
was me, somebody was buried in cement, but he didn't say
who, just 'one of the parties.' And, big surprise, a certain Mrs.
Lewison was there too. You know what she did? She started

kissing the corpse. She was the mother of one of the parties, *not* the one who was the corpse. Get it?"

"No, I don't 'get it.'"

"You can't see how a freaked-out queer who'd let himself be crucified might horribly murder his mother's lover? What was that croquet mallet doing in the living room?"

"But no one who knows you could dream—"

"But no one does know me. Not anymore. Just go home."

"It never occurred—"

"Of course it didn't. It never does. You barge in and wonder why everything gets so distressing." Louisa stared at him. "Does it ever occur to you that you get exactly what you ask for?"

"It's *you* I get distressed about."

"You hung around all winter for *me?* You should have gone to Tierra del Fuego."

Lewis spoke quietly. He was drifting through limbo. He still did not believe Morris had died. If he had been asked what he desired, he might have answered his own death, although he was too enthralled by his sensations to contemplate suicide deliberately.

His cold words released in Louisa a flash of warmth. When he left, she thought: Perhaps he's right. Perhaps she had never helped him. Perhaps, as he implied, she had always behaved selfishly. Could she do better leaving him alone? It was that possibility, so obvious and so new, that filled her with sudden joy. "And good riddance!" She spoke the words aloud.

She did not quite mean them. She nevertheless let herself, very briefly, imagine the life she might have had if Lewis had never been born: not having to wake up every day, and most nights, convinced that the essence of life was raw fear. Louisa realized that on the previous evening she had suppressed more than Morris's deadness: entering the apartment, she had known that Lewis lay under the cement, and she had wished him dead

too. As she acknowledged her wish, words again broke from her: "My poor boy!" She had been the crazy one, after all. She started laughing. She didn't want him dead, never, she didn't want him not to have been born, she didn't want anything of him. With a pang of tenderness, a silent blessing she could never speak, she let him go. Then she started singing, "This can't be love . . . ," and laughed as she sang. She would stay out of his life as long as he wished; not a second longer.

Louisa intertwined the fingers of her hands and stretched her arms over her head. Below her window the city rose pallidly in hot, dirty haze. A garbage scow spun down the East River on the ebb tide. What would she do with her life, now that she had dumped her dreary load?

She had no time to consider the question, because Phoebe arrived. She could then no longer doubt to which of the few creatures in her neglected life she might, at last, be of urgent and unquestionable use.

Irene and Walter

MAY-AUGUST 1962

BECAUSE HIS SHOWS at the Kramer Gallery made Walter Trale famous, many assumed that Irene Kramer had discovered him. In fact he came to her late, less than a year before Morris died, with almost thirty years of painting behind him.

Irene had heard of him long before and had seen his paintings in group shows and in private collections. She had never found an opportunity to assess his work as a whole.

Although Irene was only thirty-four when she opened her gallery uptown, she had been selling art for twelve years, ever since she had finished four terms of art history at the New School—all the formal training she was to have. She had paid her way doing part-time secretarial work. Her father, who had started as an usher and who owned six movie theaters when he retired, might have paid for studies in law or medicine or business; to him, art dealing meant high risks and uncertain returns. He underestimated his daughter: Irene could have succeeded in almost any career she chose. She had intelligence and ambition, and she usually knew what she wanted. (She had, as well, a diminutive, perfectly restrained hourglass figure and a pretty face to which wide brown eyes could sometimes lend a melting beauty.)

While at the New School Irene met Mark Kramer, ten years her senior, a prosperous public accountant with a weakness for high culture. He persuaded her to leave the Bronx. From their brief marriage she learned that the sexual sincerity of the male may have capture and imprisonment as its covert goal. Mark soon wanted her staying at home being her wonderful self, not caring if that self demanded more. After her second year of study, Irene went to work as an assistant at Martha Jackson's. This meant not going with Mark to Europe, to the Bahamas, to Sun Valley. She could see little point in this, he in that. When they were divorced, in 1952, she told him, "Don't pay me alimony, give me a lump sum. We'll both benefit." His calculations proved her right. He borrowed the money she wanted. He felt so grateful that for five years he paid her rent.

Irene began buying paintings, which she sold from her apartment. She chiefly handled Europeans—Americans then were still condemned to being either too famous (and too expensive) or unknown. Since she had to recoup her investments in the short term, she left discovering the undiscovered till later. She struck some profitable deals; notably, in her first year, the purchase for six thousand dollars of twenty-two Klee gouaches (a year later she sold two of them for the same amount). It took her five years to establish herself as a reliable dealer, with access to works she wanted to sell and customers on whom she could depend. She then opened a small gallery on Sixth Avenue south of Fifty-sixth Street, financing it with her personal collection as collateral. The gallery barely sustained itself commercially, but it brought her into the public eye, and she made an enviable reputation for herself through her farsighted choice of painters. (Irene claimed that a good dealer had to know how to "buy potential"—had to know how to see, in paintings actually looked at, work not yet imagined even by the artist himself.) In the fall of 1961, when she gathered twenty of her best clients and presented her plan for

a new and larger gallery, they backed her without hesitation.

Morris's essay on Walter appeared in *New Worlds* the following May. He had already urged Irene to sign on this painter
whose talent had been proved and who had not yet become
fashionable. Irene had taken her younger brother seriously
and also a little skeptically—she had seen his earlier enthusi-
asms wax and wane. When Morris's article was published and
acclaimed (it was chosen for that year's *Trends in American
Painting*), Irene decided to take a careful look at Walter's work.

What she had seen of it she admired, and if she had avoided
it professionally, that had to do with commerce, not art. Walter
wore his originality strangely; he was a master in disguise, even
if he wore the disguise of a master. He could not be classed as
an abstractionist, even when he most resembled one. His fig-
uration had a disturbing offhand look, with none of the stark-
ness of Hopper and Sheeler or the stylization of Lichtenstein.
Now that Irene had started her new gallery, Walter's eccentric-
ity ceased to be an obstacle. She had originally become a dealer
to encourage new art. She could now do so.

Because she liked Walter's work, Irene had imagined that she
already knew it, forgetting that an occasional painting provides
poor insight into an artist's universe. Irene spent a week assem-
bling in her mind a complete Trale retrospective and found
herself increasingly fascinated the more she saw. She started at
Walter's gallery, then visited collectors, including those with
work from his animal years, and concluded her tour at his studio. Walter had kept for himself over a hundred paintings and
at least a thousand drawings, many of them among his best.
Irene spent a long afternoon in their midst. When she was
done, she knew that she had discovered a world that revealed
more than talent and intelligence and imagination. Walter's
originality resembled that of original sin. He had reinvented
the act of painting itself.

Walter kept away during Irene's visit, letting Phoebe play

hostess. The two women spoke little. Irene was absorbed in her study; Phoebe knew better than to distract her. As she left, Irene said, "He's better than anything I can say about him. I'll be in touch soon."

Walter had never cared much for public success, which he'd already known as a boy. He had never lacked confidence in his abilities. For twenty-five years he had been satisfied with earning enough to pay for his big studio and the parties he liked to throw in it. Now his attitude was changing. Morris's article had affected him too. The art market was starting to boom. Painters half his worth were selling for twice his price. If his time was to come, he wanted it to be now. Irene had opportunely appeared. Phoebe's account of her visit exhilarated him.

He waited for news. None came. He phoned her gallery. She was busy. She did not return his call. Three days later, he called again. Irene was out. "Walter *who?*" her secretary inquired. Next morning Irene did phone and made matters worse. Her careful praise of his work sounded like a checklist of routine compliments. She mysteriously concluded that this was not the moment to talk business: "I can't explain why. You can probably guess."

Walter could not possibly guess. In her enthusiasm Irene had made the familiar mistake of assuming that the man was as clever as the artist. Her remarks aimed at efficacy and discretion; to Walter, after ten days of silence, they signified indifference. He reacted morosely. His thrill of expectation grew sour with disappointment. With resentment as well: he felt his good will had been abused.

Walter found an explanation for this injustice when he stopped at his gallery the following day. His dealer was out—not surprising at two o'clock in the afternoon. The surprise was that he was lunching with Irene. Walter was informed by the admiring young assistant that they were meeting for the third time. "It's all about you, isn't it?" She would not tell him more.

Walter jumped to a conclusion founded wholly on suspicion: the two dealers were conspiring against him. Irene knew that in her gallery his work would fetch higher prices. She had not signed him on because she was planning to buy his paintings from his present dealer and resell them. The two dealers would split her markup. Since Walter would be no better off than before, they were keeping him in the dark.

As he paced along dank, warm streets that afternoon, these thoughts kindled Walter's mind with ever-brightening hostility. At home, he called his dealer, who only said, "*You're* asking *me* what's happening?" Walter never considered that the other man's curtness might be justified. It simply confirmed his suspicions and enabled him to savor in earnest his role as intended victim.

He decided to let his enemies complacently elaborate their scheme. His pleasure in wrecking it would be all the greater. His patience proved short-lived. A few days later an elderly friend from his *animalier* days took him out to lunch uptown. As Walter sat down, he saw Irene and Morris at a table on the far side of the restaurant. Throughout the meal he observed them busily conversing, so engrossed with one another they did not notice him until they were leaving. Morris then waved connivingly; Irene blushed as she smiled at him. As well she might: Walter saw at once that the conspiracy to exploit him had broadened. The critic who had rediscovered his work would now promote it and so merit a wedge of pie. And they hadn't even bothered to shake hands with him! Their nonchalance made Walter especially bitter. He refrained from venting his outrage to his lunch companion only by silently deciding to intervene.

As he walked the fifty-two blocks to his studio, he realized that Morris's complicity aggrieved him most. He scarcely knew Irene; perhaps she had a tougher character than he'd imagined. He knew his dealer well enough. Walter liked in him above all his pleasant lack of ambition; if Irene had proposed an easy way

to make money, he might understandably be tempted. Walter felt passionate respect for Morris. He thought him bright, eloquent, fervently committed to a rare idea of art held by few artists and fewer critics. Because of this commitment, Morris's essay on his work had convinced Walter that they shared an intense if impersonal affinity. Walter had been understood; he had been assigned the place he deserved, at the dark, sharp point of invention. That Morris could exploit what he had so intimately perceived jarred Walter painfully.

He called Morris and suggested that he come to the studio at ten-thirty the next morning. The suggestion had the ring of a summons. Morris deferentially ignored the tone and accepted.

Having overheard the phone call, Phoebe asked Walter what was wrong. For the first time he related his fantasy to someone else. As he spoke, he reminded her of Lewis, at age eight, on the verge of a fit. Wondering how many cocktails had preceded lunch, she did not dare speak her mind.

In the morning, she found Walter still sheathed in glum determination. Letting Morris in, Phoebe gave him a trouble-in-paradise look that pinched the smooth space between his brows. Walter mutely motioned him to a chair by the dining table, which had been cleared of everything except the telephone. Facing Morris across the table, Walter solemnly lifted the handset and dialed.

"Gavin Breitbart, please, Walter Trale calling," he declared, adding in ominous sotto voce, "My lawyer." He cleared his throat: "Gavin?" Standing painfully straight, he began delivering into the mouthpiece a long statement obviously, if inadequately, rehearsed. His voice reminded Morris of someone from the past—Senator Claghorn?

". . . a very grave breach of professional ethics, which I want you to start proceedings in the matter. . . ."

Walter stared belligerently at Morris while he listed his grievances: Irene's duplicity, her conspiracy with his dealer,

her plan to include Morris as a highbrow publicity agent.

Listening to him, Phoebe wished she had gone to New Mexico. Morris was emerging from perplexity into half-credulous mirth. No one could have taken Walter seriously if self-righteousness were not so crassly distorting his benevolent mug. When Morris heard himself personally implicated, he bent over and cut the connection: "Stop. Stop before they come and cart you off. What have you been sniffing—Drāno?" Walter scowled. Phoebe stared at her toes. Morris went on: "Listen, maestro, Irene wants you in her shop. She didn't like cutting out your dealer, so she offered him a percentage for the next couple of years."

"Exactly."

"No, not exactly. It's out of her pocket."

"Says who?"

"She does." (The phone rang: "Oh, Gavin . . . Later, OK?") "Your dealer's a piggy. He keeps upping the ante. She even thought of making him a partner. But that's finished."

"How come?"

"No contract, I believe. Irene got fed up. *He* suggested cutting your share, you know. She says screw him."

"Yeah, and not just him."

"Walter, can't you grasp that she's mad for you? Look, I knew something was up, so I told her to drop in. You'll see."

"That's what *you* say. Why don't you admit you're in cahoots? I saw you the other day. What are you, lovers?"

"As I live and bleed! *A*, I'm queer. *B*, she's my sister."

"Kramer?" Walter leaned one thigh against the table.

"Her ex."

The doorbell rang. Phoebe admitted Irene. Morris said to Walter, "Don't forget Gavin. He may have an emergency patrol on the way."

"OK—hel*lo*," Walter said to Irene, "something I have to clear up." He was reddening. A moment later he was telling his

lawyer, "It was a mistake. Forget it. It doesn't matter—no, the name *doesn't* matter. Listen to me. Well . . . Kramer." Lowering his voice, he turned his back to the others. They stood there politely hushed, except for Phoebe, prey to the giggles. "Look, I'm not alone . . ." Walter's voice petered out. He glanced at the others—Irene patiently watching him, Morris shaking his head, Phoebe red with restraint. He hung up. "Coffee? Beer?" He ran both hands through his hair. Irene gazed at him in nascent consternation. Walter was breaking into a sweat. "Irene, there's something I think—"

"Not a word!" Morris interrupted. "We'll never tell, will we, Phoebe? Not for lox and bagels!" Phoebe nodded as she wiped her eyes.

Irene said, "Mr. Trale, Morris thought this might be a good time to see you. Phoebe's told you how extraordinary I think your work is? I apologize for having taken so long to find that out. I'd love to show you—I'd like to give you *two* shows, back to back. A retrospective first, then new work. I can do well by you, I promise. I don't have to be told that you'll do well by me. Just having you under my roof would be a blessing."

She had spoken plainly and earnestly. Her low voice soothed Walter. He gulped her words down like lemonade in a hot spell. He made a few appreciative noises until he was again overcome by an awareness of his folly and began shaking his head in retrospective consternation. When he next looked at Irene, he realized that she was still speaking to him:

" . . . No? *You'd* rather?"

"I'm sorry—"

Morris reminded him, "Walter, it's *over*."

Irene resumed: "What I was suggesting is, I've been having trouble with your curmudgeon of a dealer, but if *you* agree, I can certainly come to terms. I can take care of all that, if you like."

"Great!" Walter replied. He stared at her as though he had

rediscovered his beloved elephant. The bell again rang, and
Phoebe went to the door: Priscilla stood there, thesis in hand.

Walter never even saw her. He went on staring at Irene,
who was turning the faintest shade of pink. It occurred to him
that she might like to sit down. "Coffee? Beer? Please don't call
me Mr. Trale. It makes me feel older."

"You *are* older, Walter," Irene replied, with a most agreeable chuckle. She was pleased to have secured this fine painter,
pleased that he was so likable—a nice, big baby. "Thanks, I
can't stay—I don't *want* to stay, because I'm going to your
gallery right now and settle things. I'm making sure you don't
get away from me."

"Who'd ever think of doing that?"

Morris and Phoebe might have been in Manitoba. Walter
was immersed in his abrupt conviction that Irene should take
complete charge of him. "I'll come with you. The three of us
can work it out together."

Morris said, "Leave it to the pros. You'll just work up a
froth."

Irene remained silent. Her smile—warm, faintly conde-
scending—was filling Walter with concupiscent awe. "You're
right," he agreed, at once asking Irene: "So I'll see you later?"

"I'll phone you as quick as I can."

"No, I mean *see* you. How about dinner?"

Phoebe shook her head. Even Lewis at four had never
sounded so demanding. "Say please!" she whispered. Irene's
smile widened; Morris pursed his lips.

Walter refused to be distracted: "What *about* dinner?"

"Walter," Morris chided, "this isn't Schenectady."

"What? Well—tomorrow? How about—"

"All right," said Irene. "The day *after* tomorrow. Meet me
at the gallery at seven." Morris reflected that she had found a
humane way of liberating them all.

Two days later, Walter arrived at the Kramer Gallery early,

a bouquet of sweet william in one hand. Irene told him, "I'm pooped. Can we have a drink here and go straight to dinner? I reserved at the Polo Lounge, in the Westbury. Ever eat there? You'll love it, although not necessarily the food, but you'll need a tie. I bought you this"—a strip of raw blue silk.

Walter formed no opinion of the restaurant. When not perfunctorily swallowing food, he sat with one forearm thrust across the table and the other perched on the back of the banquette, staring at Irene. She herself sat upright and still, folding her hands between courses, glancing sideways at Walter with smiles of affectionate amusement. At first, for his sake, she had tried to smile less—she smiled as though watching a doddering colt. He didn't mind.

Walter was doing his best to be adorable. He hurriedly drank enough to break down his own reticence. He laughed often; tears sprang to his eyes readily when a thought moved him; he disparaged and praised himself without affectation; he listened to Irene's words with conspicuous attention. Walter wanted to know Irene almost as greedily as he wanted her to know him. He failed to see that she knew him already, that he could do nothing to make her like him more.

She did not mind his courting her, although his method seemed startlingly direct, like a puppy rolling over to have its belly scratched. Colts and puppies made for fondness, not desire. She decided that disappointing him no less directly would prove the greatest kindness. When he reached over to stroke her arm, she tartly exclaimed, "You're not going to make a pass at me!"

Walter's eyes shone with relief. She had been the one to broach the hot, imminent subject. "Baby, I've never wanted anyone so much!"

She saw that it would take more than hints to discourage him. "You'll get over it, Mr. Trale! I may not have many rules, but there's one that I swear by: never go to bed with an artist.

194 HARRY MATHEWS

Certainly not one of mine."

"And every rule has its exception, right?"

"Not after seven years. My God, if Norman Bluhm ever thought I was seeing you—" Walter laughed. Irene saw that she would have to speak more bluntly: "You don't interest me sexually. Not at all. And I like you. If you have enough sense to understand that, we can have a nice time."

"Maybe you'll change your mind. I can wait." He hardly seemed willing to wait. For the rest of dinner he refused to talk about anything else. Irene finally heaved a great sigh of exasperation (Walter thought: I'm getting to her) and said, "Let's move out of here."

"I'll ask for the check."

"It's been taken care of."

"I invited *you*—"

"In my league, the dealer does the inviting. Where would you like to go?"

"Wherever you say."

"Your place?"

"Yes," Walter gasped.

"It's on my way. I'll drop you." She did not forget the sweet william.

Irene refused to date Walter again. She soon learned that this decision was putting her freedom and perhaps her career in jeopardy. Walter visited the gallery once a day, sometimes twice. He phoned her morning, noon, night, and in between. He tirelessly restated his longing and shared all his thoughts and feelings, which new love was delivering daily by the gross.

Irene agreed to another dinner if Walter would leave her in peace. Their evening together turned out better than she dared hope, even though it took place in Walter's studio, even though they spent it alone. (The other hypothetical guests never appeared; Phoebe vamoosed between drinks and the cleaning woman's jambalaya.) It happened that when Walter

turned on the oven, the pilot light had gone out. Lowering a match towards the burner, he ignited a soft explosion that frizzled his forward scalp and reduced his eyebrows to stubble. He thereupon withdrew into a mortified sulk, as obstinate as his lustful state and far less obnoxious.

On another evening Irene even let him take her home. She first subjected him to a demanding social round: a gallery opening, two cocktail parties, a long, late supper together. Only then, after Walter had drunk more than any stag's fill, did Irene maliciously invite him to her apartment. Walter, beaming like a prize student, didn't know what he should do with his diploma and had two more double scotches to find out. He woke up the next morning on the sofa with a friendly note pinned to his shirt instructing him in the use of Irene's coffee maker.

Walter tricked the gallery receptionist into revealing that Irene was to spend the following weekend in a resort town upstate. He followed her there but could not track her down, and in consequence he found no pleasure in a place full of old friends and memories—he stayed with Mr. Pruell, one of his first patrons; here, twenty-six years before, Elizabeth had transformed his life. Monday, in the city once again, Irene refused to relinquish her secret: "We all need a place to hide. Except you, I suppose."

Irene told him she would be busy through the coming week. Walter took the news calmly. He had a plan. Irene loved classical music; a highly touted performance of the Verdi *Requiem* was to take place at Tanglewood the following Saturday; Walter would ask Irene to drive up for it. He first had to reserve accommodations. Pleasurably furnished adjoining rooms were not easily found in that season. Fortunately, a family canceled at an inn in West Stockbridge.

Irene accepted his proposal. "What a great idea! We'll stay at the Broffs' in Lenox." Walter mentioned the inn. "Save your

bread. No, wait: let me check if there's an extra bed. They'll always find a corner for me." The Broffs were full up.

They arrived in Lenox at noon. At the Broffs', Walter verified the presence of three houseguests. Lunch turned into a winy meal attended by four more guests, after which the entire party removed early to Tanglewood, where they claimed a swath of field directly in front of the shed and settled on rugs and blankets spread out in a profusion worthy of a Caucasian tribe. Walter sat down next to Irene.

A couple of his neighbors stretched out on their backs. Walter followed their example. It was a cool, sunny day. He listened languidly to the gossip around him. When the talk stopped, he sat up to join in the applause for the musicians and then once more lay down. Summer sun warmed him from his crown to his soles. Soon the sound of voices and instruments began surging over him gently, like banks of warm fog. He paid little attention to the music: he had come here for Irene. He took care nevertheless to prevent his vagrant mind from deluding him into sleep. Sleep felt as tempting as a mud-bed to a hippopotamus, and he would not disappoint her so childishly.

His thoughts pursued images of a landscape consisting entirely of her. Today she had seduced him once again. Behind saucer-large mauve lenses her eyes glinted like birds vanishing through a screen of leaves. Her small, ripe body chided his attention under billows of buff and beige. He ached to unwrap her. He began an enjoyable game: imagining her body, he let quiet passages of music suggest an unveiling of it, louder ones still closer involvements. The sun warmed his delectations.

He was swimming through warm and enchanted seas like a happy, solitary seal; and he hardly felt a quiver of surprise when he sensed something like a responsive caress, as though the point of his pleasure had been dreamily handled.

He recalled where he was and opened his eyes. A cashmere

shawl Irene had been carrying lay across his hips, in the shape of a fore-Alp. Irene herself sat gazing intently towards the performers as they stormed into the *Dies irae*. Her fingers were locked tightly together, she had decisively sucked her faintly trembling lower lip between her teeth.

Walter loudly groaned. Surely he had reached an age when he could keep his fly buttoned? He briefly longed for a dagger or an icepick to plunge into his chest. With death not readily available, he resorted to flight. Gathering as he rose the shawl around his impenitent erection, he started racing across the sunlit expanse, thick with human obstacles that he skirted with immediate expertise, like an ace slalomist or broken-field runner. He did not slow down until he had reached the city and his own studio.

For several mornings he woke up to spasms of shame, as though shame were a cat poised to leap onto his belly the moment he emerged from sleep. He did not leave his studio until Tuesday. When, early that afternoon, he appeared at the Kramer Gallery, Irene led him straight into her office. Closing the door behind her, she sat down on a leather couch and motioned Walter to sit next to her. As she observed his thunderhead countenance, she found herself smiling once again.

"I thought I'd better bring this back."

Irene accepted the shawl. "What happened to you?"

"Oh, nothing. I just wanted to die. I still do."

"Why did you run away? No one minded. *Au contraire*, we all found you very impressive."

Walter looked up at her. If it pained him to have his anguish made fun of, Irene's forgiving him offered delicious solace. He managed a small laugh. "It was all for you, you know." He looked helplessly into her brown eyes. She said nothing. He unzipped his jeans and pulled forth a now wizened penis. "It still is. It's all yours."

Irene blushed and went on smiling. "Oh, my dear!" She

shook her head. Walter took her right hand and laid his member in its palm, where it rested still as a mouse. "My dear!" she said again. "So small, so sweet!" Bending over, she brushed her lips across it, with the faint smack of a childhood kiss. Someone knocked at the door. Walter made way for business.

That evening Irene disappeared. For four weeks, almost until the end of August, she could be found neither at work nor at home. Walter pestered her friends, in vain; not even his own friends would help him, not even Phoebe.

In early August he learned that Irene was staying at a secret retreat upstate. He learned no more than that. Irene remained safe with Louisa, the old and still-dear friend who had promised to shelter her for as long as was necessary from her distracted suitor.

Priscilla and Walter

JUNE 1962-APRIL 1963

PRISCILLA WAS FIFTEEN when she first heard of Walter. Old Mr. Pruell was showing her portraits of horses he'd owned. He spoke of the man who painted them with a warmth that made Priscilla curious.

"He was about your age. A natural."

"Does he still paint horses?"

"He's still painting. He makes a living at it. A nice man."

"Does he still paint horses?"

"No, he doesn't. He'd have been a millionaire. But he wanted to be a success as a, well, regular painter. It wasn't easy for him. Funny: he could manage stallions or rabbits, but give him a plate of apples, or a human being, and he didn't know where to start. Elizabeth changed all that."

Of course Priscilla wanted to hear about Elizabeth.

"She was a few years older than Walter, and very sharp. Attractive, too—big and handsome and graceful as a cat. She loved horses. Walter met her at the track one day, and I think he thought she was part horse. By the second race they were thick as thieves. Just good friends, though, they never went— they never fell in love. She had exactly what he needed—she was a *human* animal. She posed for him every day for the

next week or two. He must have done dozens of sketches, and finally he painted her portrait in oils."

Priscilla found the anecdote irresistibly romantic, even if Elizabeth and Walter had remained just friends. During the years that followed, she often asked family friends about them; and she had accumulated considerable lore by the time her professor of art history in college told her that Walter was destined for fame. Priscilla's teacher, who had already nourished Phoebe's interest in Walter, differed radically in her attitudes from the well-to-do families among which Priscilla had grown up. That Walter should be admired both by her and, for instance, by Mr. Pruell lent weight to Priscilla's sentimental fascination with him. Walter migrated from a world of fantasy and elderly reminiscence into that of flesh-and-blood heroes, among basketball stars, actors, and presidential candidates. Priscilla agreed to make him the subject of her senior thesis.

Learning and thinking about Walter almost convinced Priscilla that she already knew him. (She would later enjoy claiming that her thesis had brought them together.) As her knowledge of his work increased, she consistently translated it into terms she could call her own. Priscilla treated paintings like doors: she wanted to know what lay behind them. She sensed the power in Walter's art, and she could not accept that its source might be evident in the paint itself. It was to be found, she thought, in some extraordinary experience that the painting expressed. Thus she developed her theory of Walter and Woman.

Priscilla expected her thesis to bring her access to Walter. Her expectation was strengthened when Phoebe became Walter's assistant. Even if she and Phoebe were not close friends, they had known each other since childhood, they had gone to the same college, and as young women starting out in the world they were disposed to helping one another. With Phoebe as go-between, Priscilla looked forward to meeting Walter without delay.

Priscilla called Phoebe up soon after her graduation. Phoebe said that she would gladly give Walter "The Female Figure in Recent American Art." Priscilla should drop it off at her studio the following Tuesday. Priscilla asked, couldn't she give it to Walter herself? When was he usually home? What was he like? Was Phoebe having an affair with him? Phoebe told her, "I can't invite you in right away. One of my jobs is keeping people out. Wait till he reads it, then I'll fix something up."

Priscilla did not want to wait. One morning she showed up with her thesis at Walter's studio, where Walter was busy falling in love with Irene.

Priscilla apologized to Phoebe later that day, deploring her own ruse so frankly that she made Phoebe laugh. Priscilla knew better than to try again. Soon afterwards a new way of approaching Walter presented itself.

Going back to her parents' home upstate, Priscilla learned that Walter was visiting nearby. He had come only for the weekend, and he left Mr. Pruell's before she could catch him. She felt certain, however, that if he came back, she could instigate a meeting.

In August Walter returned for two weeks. Priscilla told Maud and Allan that she wanted to meet him, and they agreed to get her invited to any social events Walter might attend. Three such events occurred. At the first, Walter failed to appear. At the second, she spotted him across a crowded expanse of lawn; he had gone before she could reach him. At the third, she accosted him promptly, with a mutual friend to introduce them. Priscilla was wearing a dress of clinging silk jersey, its pale ground stamped with bold geometrical figures that enhanced the gentler lines of her young body. Walter looked briefly at the dress. When he raised his eyes, they stared through hers as towards some distant thing—the ghost of Irene. He spoke to Priscilla distractedly.

She was more disillusioned than disappointed. Priscilla

knew she pleased men; Walter's lack of response made her doubt not herself but him. She had never imagined that the Genius might be a jerk. She dismissed her interest in him as adolescent day-dreaming.

Summer ended—Priscilla's last long student vacation. She looked back on it without regret. In early September she visited the city, staying at her parents' apartment. She declared that she had come to look for work, although privately she felt uncertain what kind of work she might profitably attempt.

One evening, after a day of listless job hunting, she stopped at the Westbury for a drink. In the Polo Lounge, settled in a raised enclosure some distance from the windows, she observed through their high panes the allegretto traffic of Madison Avenue. It was almost eight o'clock. First lights winked on in the slowly fading dusk. The men passing by still wore jackets of pale gabardine or seersucker, the women chemises of crisp linen, earth-brown or olive-green. Priscilla shivered with yearning for the city around her, a yearning to belong. What part could she ever hope to play in this alluring, forbidding world? From the table next to hers a male voice unexpectedly addressed her: "It's magic out there, isn't it?"

Priscilla had been enjoying her solitary gin-and-tonic. Pursing her lips, she turned a look of definitive contempt on her neighbor, who was Walter. No line of her expression wavered as she recognized him. He did not recognize her. He winced under the look and continued to smile and even speak. "It sort of makes the locals look good."

She stared at him disdainfully before returning her gaze to the street. "The 'locals' look great to me. You're not one of us, I presume?"

"Well, I've lived here forever. Originally, I'm from Schenectady."

"From Schenectady? How interesting! I've never met anyone from Schenectady. I imagined nobody in Schenectady ever got away—except maybe to Albany."

"It wasn't so bad. It was a long time ago."

"I can see that. Some things, though, you just never can grow out of."

Six weeks of frustration had started to blunt Walter's longing for Irene. On her return, she had called him to discuss his forthcoming shows and nothing else. She refused even to acknowledge that she had gone into hiding because of him. He could not so much as apologize. Irene had locked the door on their private past.

Tonight, coming back to the setting where he had declared his passion for her, he was commemorating something he knew had ended, indulging a melancholy that was not without self-disdain. Watching Priscilla, he became acutely aware that for almost three months he had slept alone.

"Care to freshen that?" he asked.

"Tanqueray and tonic. Schweppes, please." She sucked on gravelish ice. She had yet to smile.

He ordered their drinks—her second, his fourth. They drank. He offered her dinner. She accepted, on the condition that they stay at their separate tables: "It's cooler that way." When he started to introduce himself, she interrupted, "No names! No *last* names. What's the point, for one meal?" She refused to hear what kind of work he did: "Can't men understand? The pleasure with strangers is leaving that stuff out." She was holding names and "that stuff" as her trumps. She considered Walter as he leaned into that cool space between them, revving himself up.

By coffee she allowed herself a little gentleness. "Thanks for the treat. I'm not all barbs, you know. It's just that most men . . ." She then asked him his last name. The question thrilled Walter; it implied that she might see him again. At his answer, Priscilla released like a glittering fan the full smile she had withheld all evening. She reached towards Walter and grasped his left hand in both of hers. Even to her, the gesture seemed impulsive; she blushed appropriately.

When she in turn told him her name, his response surpassed her hopes. He had read her thesis twice. Priscilla's theory of Woman and the Artist may have made bad criticism, but it had allowed Walter to recognize himself—"discover himself," as he put it.

Some males claim to dislike women, others to like them, but all share an original, undying fear. Every man is irrationally and overwhelmingly convinced that woman, having created him, can destroy him as well. Men are all sexual bigots. The distinction between dislike and like only separates those who resist women's power by attacking them from those who try to exorcise it through adoration and submission. Walter belonged to the adoring class. Priscilla had inadvertently caught his feelings when she described Woman as a Muse who could transform him. Gratified already by Priscilla's insight, he would have been delighted to be speaking to her even if he had not been suffering from loneliness, even without her stimulating display of coldness.

Three minutes after Priscilla had spoken her name, Walter invited her to see his new work. She said she'd love to. A taxi took them to the studio, where she stayed the night.

Once again Priscilla judged Walter accurately. Knowing that with her almost-beginner's experience she could hardly surprise him sexually, she divined that the gratification Walter most wanted was the gratification he might give *her*. She let herself be gratified, let herself pass again and again, with outspoken delight, from readiness to passion to affectionate gratitude. Priscilla did not have to feign. She did not like boys her age, who always seemed intent on proving something. Even if Walter was older than any previous lover, she had no reluctance to overcome. She had only to confound her animal and her personal desires. She wanted Walter, and wanted him to want her. This need expressed itself in profusions of pleasure. The next morning, Walter shyly invited her to stay on.

Priscilla accepted, with some anxiety. She had idealized
Walter, schemed to meet him, given him up as a loss. Now she
had possessed him after a single encounter. She scarcely knew
what sort of prize she had won, and she moved in with little
idea of what to do next. When she told her parents, Maud
acted astounded and concerned, Allan astounded and hurt.
Priscilla listened to them patiently (she had already transferred
her clothes, books, and records to Walter's studio). Certain
words of her mother's concentrated her own preoccupation:
plainly an attachment so hurriedly formed could be no less
hurriedly ended. How, if she wanted to, could she make sure
her new life would last?

Priscilla had no doubt that for the present her strongest
asset was Walter's heaven-sent desire, his desire for *her* desire.
During that first night with him she had discovered, almost
accidentally, a powerful way to express her excitement. She had
begun talking out loud while he was caressing her and felt his
fingers and tongue quicken as she did so. Afterwards, remembering the effect, she spoke at greater length, as roughly as she
could: "My cunt never felt so hot, darling, I'm turning to jam
inside, put another finger in, yes, baby, and in my ass, too, how
did you know. . . ." Her talking turned into a fond harangue,
a running commentary suitable for some blind voyeur with an
insatiable craving for detail. To Walter, her words magnified
their acts with impersonal erotic grandeur, and he was never
less than shocked to hear them issue from this expensively
educated young mouth. They made the mouth and the body
breathing through it all the more desirable, and the voice itself
was an almost threatening sound, one that demanded stilling.
This became Walter's delectable task, at which he never failed.

Walter's first weeks with Priscilla followed one another in
a stagger of satisfaction. He made her his one and only drug.
Priscilla grew more confident. Years before, however, she had
noticed how different from their ecstatic beginnings marriages

became, after two years, or one year, or three months. She
knew that while the contractual solemnity of marriage (real
even when taken lightly) might dampen enthusiasm, it also
provided a barrier to ending a relationship casually. No such
barrier protected her. She would need more than passion to
keep him. Priscilla decided to go on playing the self-possessed
woman Walter had met in the Polo Lounge. She demanded,
she refused, she disagreed. She knew she was acting. Even if she
made her part convincing by insisting on it, she never forgot
how vulnerable she remained. Out of bed, she had nothing to
offer that Walter could use. She had brains and energy, in a city
stocked with efficient women. Her family's connections were
rapidly losing their allure now that Walter had reached the
verge of fame. She almost regretted having money of her own,
since Walter might have enjoyed supporting her. Undeniably,
she possessed youth and good looks; they were not enough.
(Sadly, perhaps inevitably, Priscilla in her accounting ignored
what to both Walter and herself mattered supremely: she liked
him better than anyone she had ever known.)

Her anxiety was sharpened by the success of Walter's first
show at the Kramer Gallery, a large, well-chosen retrospective. She gauged the extent of that success by the almost smug
contentment of the guests at the opening. They knew they
were witnessing a rare conjunction of history and current
taste. Women in shantung pantsuits, men in cashmere jackets and silver-buckled moccasins, after a minute or two spent
in rememberable conversation with Walter, descended avidly
on Irene, whom some of them actually knew. She could have
auctioned the show for three times its stated price. As she
had foreseen, she and Walter were doing well by one another;
and that day she perhaps deserved to outshine him. She had
hung on her walls paintings that had long been accessible,
making their private value public. Priscilla felt towards her an
admiration almost free of envy. Irene had achieved all that she

herself might aspire to. She was the masterly intermediary. At that moment Irene's power impressed Priscilla as even more compelling than Walter's genius.

That power frightened Priscilla. Walter had loved Irene (mightn't he still?), and she was making him famous. She treated Priscilla with a plain politeness suggesting that the young woman might someday soon be gone. After their first meeting Priscilla was convinced that Irene had penetrated all her ambitions and doubts. Priscilla asked her if she had read her thesis. Irene answered, "I read it, and I liked it—I love good gossip. I wouldn't push your line downtown, though. They're all into Schapiro and Greenberg." She added, not unkindly, "You might try reading them."

Priscilla's fear revealed what she needed. It led her to imagine a day when she might offend Irene, who would promptly destroy her in Walter's eyes. (In truth, the two women misjudged each other. Priscilla thought too much of Irene's influence, Irene too little of Priscilla's pluck.) Priscilla saw that she must find someone Walter trusted who would side with her in a crisis.

She had hoped to make Phoebe such an ally. Priscilla had taken pains to anticipate any resentment her intrusion might have provoked, consulting Phoebe systematically about household matters, staying out of sight when she was working with Walter, reiterating her admiration of Phoebe's painting. Phoebe may have been surprised to find Priscilla at the studio on that mid-September morning, but she accepted her at once; and her ready acceptance finally discouraged Priscilla from enlisting her. Phoebe manifested no disapproval of Priscilla, and no approval either. She responded to Priscilla's advances amiably and with indifference. Phoebe was preoccupied with her own life and her burgeoning disease. She did not care whether Priscilla stayed or left.

Morris visited Walter shortly before the retrospective

opened. Priscilla had read his article in the summer issue of
New Worlds; it had left her more bewildered than enlightened.
Walter reassured her: no one would ever understand him as she
had, "but this is about something different—where the work's
going, not where it's coming from." She kept a wary distance
from Morris when they met.

Morris was Irene's brother—a fact, ominous at first, that
eventually brought her Morris's friendship. At the opening,
she saw him standing alone in front of a Manet-inspired
"Canoeing Couple," staring disdainfully at the crowd around
Irene. She went up to him: "Looks like a smasheroo."

"Mmm."

"You must be pleased."

"I am. But what a roadhog!"

"You think so? I feel Walter's happy staying in the
background."

"I didn't mean *Walter*. Oh, why do I have such a wildly jealous nature? But you, little princess, have every right to kvell."

Priscilla clasped the revelation to her. Clever Morris had a
foible. He was not "wildly jealous," except of Irene.

A week later she had a chance to exploit this discovery.
Morris phoned: could he stop by and see them? Come right
over, Priscilla told him. Morris found her alone and untypically
morose. He asked what was wrong. Her first evasions stimu-
lated his curiosity. Apologetically, she admitted to being worried about his sister. She was a brilliant dealer, Walter was happy
with her, and there was something wrong. She wasn't sure what.
Perhaps Irene had only guessed that Walter was great, without
really understanding him. In a way, and not intentionally, she
was exploiting him. "You know she's selling 'Spruce Fox' to
Chase Manhattan? It ought to be in the Whitney."

In fact the building's architects had only made an offer for
the painting; it had not been sold. Her half-lie, however, only
sharpened her point, which had touched Morris. Even as he

disagreed, gently assuring her that Walter was in good hands, he told himself that she was right. He advised Priscilla to keep her doubts to herself. Walter entered, and the three of them talked of other things.

If Priscilla did not again mention Irene to Morris, she took care to cultivate the sympathy she knew he felt for her. He had been pleased to be confided in, pleased to give advice. She asked for more. She phoned him for critiques of Walter's friends. When they met at social gatherings, she begged a few minutes of him to be taught what Stella or Judd was trying to do. She consulted him about where to buy the best smoked salmon below Fourteenth Street. She paid extraordinary attention to everything he said. Irene aside, not since childhood had any woman so fussed over him; and Priscilla had wit and looks and youth. How could he resist?

Over a lunch Morris said to her, "You may be right about Irene." Priscilla bit her tongue to keep from grinning. She had been waiting in strenuous silence for these words.

"Do you think I'm good for Walter?"

"You're better than good." Morris was joking, Priscilla saw her goal within reach. She had her ally.

She still needed a treaty of alliance. Like Walter's loving her, Morris's liking her could be ended by a whim. She needed a partnership of acts and facts.

Soon after, she asked him why he had never made money from his expertise. "Do you really like doing the spadework and seeing people cash in on it?" He replied that he liked his freedom. He could work when he wanted and sleep till noon. The prospect of dealing with framers, shippers, and accountants hardly appealed to him. "I could do all that," Priscilla said. Why should she bother? "To know what you know. I've got to learn about *something*."

She lured him with young painters excited by the prospect of his sponsorship and with works that looked like sure

bargains. After a week he confessed to being interested. He consented to a trial run.

Priscilla then took a critical step. She suggested to Morris that, given his competence and his high commitment, he should consider handling some of Walter's work. "Irene would never agree," he objected; "*Walter* would never agree." Priscilla said, "Let me try."

Walter had become a minor celebrity. Three glossy monthlies were scheduling articles on him. Museums were showing interest. Phoebe half-seriously proposed that he hire a social secretary. Elated by the public attention, Walter knew how to protect himself in private. His success never impinged on his attachment to Priscilla, and he even associated it with her advent: the unexpected happiness she had given him seemed to have expanded into the excitements of fame. Whatever he was doing, he remained peripherally aware throughout each day of the unharvested vocalizing with which she would rapturously conclude it.

Artists and their dealers are sure to have occasional misunderstandings. For Walter, any disagreement with Irene tapped a reserve of passion that his affair with Priscilla had not quite emptied. In November Irene sold "The Prepared Piano," one of his favorite paintings, to a collector in Des Moines. Walter was appalled: "He'll stick it in his silo, and it'll never be seen again."

That evening Priscilla suggested to Walter that such trouble should be avoided. Did he have to entrust all his paintings to one person? Walter replied that as he kept so many for himself, he felt obliged to give Irene the rest. Still, he agreed with Priscilla "in theory."

This gave Priscilla an opening. She had not yet told Walter that Morris had become a dealer. She broke the news the next day. Morris was exactly what Walter needed: a friend who understood his work, and who would never be irresponsible about selling it.

Maybe, Walter said; but what about Irene? When Priscilla
again brought up the subject, he said Morris was a great idea,
except that Irene would be dead set against it. Priscilla asked,
What if she agreed? Why, said Walter, it's a great idea.

Priscilla made an appointment to see Irene. She knew what
she had to do. Irene had no reason to share Walter's success
with anyone, not even her brother. Priscilla would have to
disguise the nature of the understanding between Walter and
Morris—she would have to lie. If the truth came out later,
Irene would know who had misled her. Priscilla accepted the
risk because she had so far been winning. She had successfully
courted Morris, she had held on to Walter, both men had
accepted her plan. If carrying it out meant lying, she would
lie and cope with the consequences when they occurred. If
caught, she would claim that she had been misunderstood
by Irene, or by Walter, or both. She might have to fight. She
would have a position to fight for.

Priscilla reassured herself by declaring her problem to be
essentially semantic. If I can find the right terms, Walter will
think my proposal one thing, Irene something else. How will
they talk when they discuss it? What words will they use? What
questions will they ask? Certain words, like *sell*, could wreck
her plans. "Irene, Morris has just sold my 'Last Duchess.'"
The probability of such a statement made her shudder. She
experienced moments of extreme doubt. She drew up lists of
all the words that might serve in discussions of commercial
transactions. So many other words could replace the coarse-
ness of *buy* and *sell*: *manage, handle, look after, take care of*
. . . Weren't such words the very ones Walter and Irene would
use? The proposal had sprung from a tense situation; it was
bound to remain slightly embarrassing to them and so encourage euphemism. Priscilla chose to trust her luck and her lists.
She could monitor Walter's communications with Irene well
enough to anticipate danger.

She prepared a version of her proposal to accommodate, for Irene's hearing, whatever Morris and Walter might say. Arriving at the Kramer Gallery for her appointment, she felt a new confidence: she was representing Walter professionally.

Priscilla told Irene that Walter deeply regretted their disagreement over "The Prepared Piano." He felt that neither he nor Irene should be blamed for what had happened. Couldn't such misunderstandings be averted by asking a third party to act as arbiter in the case of special paintings? He was proposing her brother for this role. What did Irene think? Morris's discretionary power would affect them only rarely. . . .

"Morris would be perfect," Irene interrupted. "I'd been hoping he'd do the same for me."

Priscilla did not understand this remark. "Walter will be—"

"He didn't need my approval. I wish the darling would grasp that I'm working for *him*. " Irene paused. "Why didn't he talk to me himself?"

"Because," Priscilla promptly answered, "he was embarrassed about your fight. So I agreed to stand in." Feeling like a pro, she decided to gamble her stake forthwith: "If you called him now, he'd love it." She watched Irene dial their number.

". . . so I'm not good enough for you, Mr. Trale?" Irene said. "You need a *man* to look after you. . . ."

She was smiling when she hung up. So was Priscilla as she went out the gallery door.

"I made it sort of ambiguous," she ambiguously told Morris. "You'll be 'making decisions' about certain paintings. She got the message."

"Miss Priss, you're a star. May I wonder why?"

"I told you—to pick your elegant brains."

"Be my guest. Just one tiny *nasty* reason to console me?"

"I want Walter, you know that. It's tough out there for a brat like me."

"Sho 'nuff. And something to show Mummy and Daddy, too?"

"Oh, maybe. It should keep Maud out of my hair."

Priscilla was to receive more tangible rewards. Morris insisted she be paid money for work done; her willingness to help him for nothing merely reflected the condescension typical of her class. He offered her a percentage of the sales she prepared. She agreed to this. In time she pointed out how dependent this had made her. She had begun earning appreciable amounts of money, and he had recently been having some cardiac "discomfort": "Don't you go and die on me, I've still got lots more to learn! And you know I'm not employable, except by you. Without you, I'm nobody."

He said nothing at the time. A few days later he mentioned taking out a life-insurance policy that named her as his beneficiary. Priscilla burst into tears. Morris gave her one of his rare hugs. "Dear Priss, think how ecstatic I'd feel bankrolling you from the void!"

In her conquest of Morris, Priscilla perhaps achieved her most impressive exploit. Intelligent, cynical, mistrustful of women, he let a little shiksa win his confidence by sheer will. He had justified adopting her by her charm, her loyalty, her usefulness, hardly noticing her strangeness to him, and how strangely he himself had yielded to her bizarre determination.

Priscilla's dealings with Irene impressed Walter, reinforcing his attraction to her with an element of respect. When she asked for work to bring to Morris, he found it hard to say no to her. Although she did not ask often (in the end, Morris never sold any of his paintings), the works sometimes mattered greatly to him, if only because they were new. Priscilla fought him tenaciously on these occasions, making his consent both an instrument and measure of her strength. Hadn't he promised her? Couldn't he trust her? Didn't he love her? Each victory left her a little surer of her place in Walter's life; and as if to prove that place supreme, she challenged herself to convince him that he should give Morris the portrait of Elizabeth. It took all her prowess, and a little over a week, to wear down

his refusal, resistance, reluctance. One morning she got up to find the portrait gone from the studio wall and standing by the front door, wrapped in a plastic sheet. For the first time since her arrival in September, Priscilla felt that she could call the city in which she lived her own.

Walter undoubtedly loved Priscilla, and he may have even enjoyed giving in to her. If he was annoyed at having to relinquish certain paintings, he lived too actively, and such losses came too rarely, for him to worry for long; and he was, after all, helping Morris. He saw the portrait of Elizabeth, however, as his primordial, self-made totem; as Priscilla herself had once written, not only his but him. Early that morning, he had remembered Phoebe's brilliantly faithful copy. She had painted it as a labor of love, love for him and for his work. She would not mind if he used it for a while to defend himself. While Priscilla slept, Walter, having put the original out of sight, left the copy where she would surely find it. She jubilantly transported it to Morris's before the day was out.

Irene and Morris

1945-1963

EVEN BEFORE HIS lover's death, Priscilla had caused Lewis pain. He had become morbidly jealous of her for having persuaded Morris to sell paintings. When playing the tormentor, Morris never failed to describe Priscilla's long and frequent visits to his apartment, which Lewis was allowed to enter barely once a month. Lewis thus pieced together the story of their unlikely friendship. He incidentally learned about Morris's lifelong relationship with Irene.

A week before Morris and Lewis met, Irene asked her brother to become artistic adviser to the Kramer Gallery. She had considered her offer carefully. The possibility had first occurred to her when her study of Walter's work had allowed her to admire the range and depth of her brother's insights. If Irene hesitated to hire him, it was only because she mistrusted her prejudices in his favor, and not only as her brother: as the person she had always loved most.

Irene approached Morris tactfully. She made it clear that she was not acting out of sisterly kindness. She emphasized that he would receive a good salary as well as a commission on sales, and that he could set his own schedule. She explained

how deliberately she had made her choice. For months she had felt the need of bringing in an adviser. She had eliminated several eminent prospects—Rosenberg and Hess would have seen a threat to their independence in being associated with a gallery; Greenberg had tied himself up with the Rubin gang. She had concluded that Morris suited her perfectly, even if he was her brother. If the fact might harm him in the opinions of some, she had decided that such opinions belonged to fools. She would not settle for less than the best.

Irene's tact expressed both her esteem and her affection. For perhaps the first time, she was acting towards Morris without a trace of solicitude. She was recognizing him as her equal, not in intelligence (she had known that for years), but as an adult in charge of his own life. Irene had sometimes doubted that she would ever know this happiness. She had been watching over Morris since he was twelve.

Their parents were almost forty when Morris was born, six years after Irene; they were in their fifties when he reached adolescence. They had difficulty understanding their moody son, and he them. Irene became close to her brother when she began mediating the family stalemates that more and more frequently punctuated his teenage years. She had always liked Morris, and her liking developed into love as she came to recognize him as a gifted, erratic boy.

If Irene helped reconcile him to his life at home, she could do little for him in school, where in spite of her coaching his work remained mediocre. During Morris's freshman year of high school, she began to be seconded by a powerful confederate: a history teacher called Arnold Loewenberg. This scholarly Austrian, whose studies had been long interrupted by the Anschluss and the war and who was only now finishing his doctoral dissertation, perceived beneath Morris's indifference to study a passionate and talented mind, which he set out to raise to its proper level. He befriended the boy,

introducing him to the pleasures of painting and music, lend-
ing him records and books of reproductions, telling him stories
of life in Europe, where history lay all around you and works
of art were recognized as emblems of that history. Almost in
passing he showed Morris how to work—how to analyze what
he read, how to organize what he wrote. Mr. Loewenberg also
demanded exceptional results of his pupil: first that he become
the best in his class, afterwards that he meet the standards of
a *Gymnasium* or *lycée*. After a while Mr. Loewenberg began
giving Morris failing grades whenever his work fell short of
these standards, and Morris's other teachers followed his lead,
with varying and sufficient severity—a benevolent conspiracy
that turned Morris into a prizewinning student by the end of
the year.

Arnold Loewenberg and Irene became friends. He provided her with valuable advice during her days as a student of
art history and invaluable encouragement at the start of her
career; even so, she felt most indebted to him for adopting
Morris. "You must never forget," he once told her, "that he is
an intellectual"—he pronounced the word with lip-smacking
emphasis—"perhaps will he someday become an extraordinary
one, but in a land of greed and ball games he will of course
experience hardships." From him she drew confidence that she
was not tending a talented misfit.

Morris was strange, and enjoyed being strange. Unlike
Lewis, he never suffered from friendlessness and related
despairs. He judged his fellows shrewdly, knowing how to make
them admire or fear or befriend him. At heart he kept distant,
relishing distance as a privilege; and this, more than anything,
worried Irene. She foresaw him doomed to the bitterness of
the unloving.

The summer following Morris's first year with Mr. Loewenberg, his parents rented a cottage on Kiamesha Lake. Irene
sometimes came for a weekend. One Friday she was given an

unexpected ride and arrived in the country several hours early. It was mid afternoon. Her parents had gone out. Standing in the empty house, she heard Morris's voice. She looked for him outside, then in the garage, where she did not at first see him, because she found herself face to face with someone else: Morris's younger friend Irwin Hall, dressed in his undershorts. His hands had been tied behind his back with wire; he was standing on tiptoe, so as not to be choked by the noose of thin white rope strung from a joist above his head. As Irene, sustaining Irwin with one arm, began loosening the rope, she heard Morris laugh and saw him standing in the shadows by the wall.

"Don't worry, pardner," he said, "just my big sister."

The rope came free. Irene exclaimed, "You guys are wacko. Morris, get his hands untied."

Panting slightly, Irwin said, "We were playing." The noose had chafed a stripe under his chin. His cropped blond hair set off the liquid, greenish-brown eyes cheerfully turnecl towards his friend.

Irene blurted angrily at Morris, "You're a goddamned creep."

Normally fearful of her, he only grinned: "You don't know it, Irene, but this man's dangerous." He was rocking from side to side with excitement. Irene unfastened the wire.

Afterwards Morris explained to her that all his friends played "outlaw and sheriff." Several months later, in the attic of their house in the Bronx, she found a mail-order kit hidden under a jumble of old cartons. It included leather-and-chrome thongs, two whips, and a zipper gag. The implements looked new. They had never been used. Morris had ordered the kit, like the magazine in which it had been advertised, to nourish fantasies, not acts. Acts frightened him. Irene's reaction in the garage confirmed what he had already surmised: kit and magazine might belong to the public domain, his desires were still

abnormal. They shocked him as they might have his father. After Irwin, he kept them to himself for two years. He then occasionally picked up a boy downtown and let his fancies free.

Once he mistook his prey and was himself beaten up. The damage proved hard to conceal, especially from an affectionate sister. Irene was again dismayed, less because of his sexual bent (she knew that sadomasochism was hardly "abnormal") than by a fear that it would reinforce his essential remoteness. She decided to encourage him forcefully in the activity to which, having proved his merits, he might be best tempted to commit himself; and with Arnold Loewenberg still her willing abettor, she persuaded Morris during his last year in high school to start seriously preparing for a scholarly future. Luckily, such a future had a special attraction for him: it inspired consternation in his parents. They feared it would permanently estrange their son. They could not, however, deny him the higher education so often proclaimed as one of their goals; and they were comforted when, of the colleges that accepted him, Morris chose NYU in preference to Harvard and Chicago. The choice would keep him closer to home, they felt, foolishly estimating in miles the distance between the Bronx and Washington Square.

Two years later Morris began majoring in art history. Irene played no part in this decision, which was initiated by a reading of Hegel's *Aesthetics:* art appealed to Morris as a historical register of society's metaphysical struggles. Irene continued nonetheless to influence his development. She had by now completed her studies, completed her marriage, begun her professional career. She introduced Morris, full of old theory and practice, to art that was local and fresh and to a society of artists still poor and unpublicized, bustling with experiment, with debate, with a sense of urgency worthy of a futures market. Morris was forced to confront his studies with present realities. He thrived.

That Morris should go to graduate school seemed obvious to everyone except his father, who said he should come home and manage the movie theaters, and his mother, who said he should just come home. Irene helped Morris win a scholarship and find a part-time job. She counseled him in his dealings with their parents. He won their approval at last and began his graduate studies at Columbia in the fall of 1954. He would have earned his doctorate in three or four years if his progress had not been arrested by an unexpected and serious heart attack.

Morris spent much of the next two years in hospitals. Times between confinements came to seem like vacations: for him, the reality that mattered was engendered by medical routines, by administered survival procedures. Morris's parents paid whatever the best care cost. Irene made sure he did get the best, in moments of crisis calling on specialists from other hospitals, from other cities. Irene saw Morris through tests and through days of waiting for their results, and through weeks when he was instructed to "do nothing but rest." She made him keep studying. She arranged for him to take examinations and write papers months late. When he was tempted to use his illness as an excuse for giving up, she did not let him forget the joy he found in the exercise of his gifts. Thanks to her, over the course of four and a half difficult years, he did much more than survive.

During this time Morris learned to think for himself. Now that he repeatedly had to face the possibility of dying, his studies took on new relevance. Because he might never see this drawing again, he looked at it with uncompromising attention. Words he heard or read or wrote reverberated like final declarations. He did not give up his philosophical bias, but he began looking at works of art less as symptoms of cultural history and more as individual actions. This change in his attitude did not concern subject matter, or symbolic values,

or even form in any general sense. As far as he was concerned, the "individual actions" that interested him were always rendered in terms of appearance—touch, grain, and tone. Morris became uncannily sympathetic to contemporary art; as though the threat of death had cleansed his eyes of all that kept him from seeing it as its declared self: an enterprise dedicated to shifting the center of art to the surface of its medium, where it properly belonged. When he discovered Walter's painting, he knew how to do it justice.

The change in Morris was hidden from Irene by the unevenness of his life. She noticed the events of particular days: how he slept, what he ate and didn't eat, the strength of his voice, the hints for the future in his doctors' pronouncements. Like a mother with her child, she relegated questions other than those of health to some hypothetical future time. She wanted Morris to endure the least pain, his nights to pass restfully, his recovery to be assured. After relapses had brought her many moments of hopelessness, his seemingly unending convalescence ended at last, and he finally recovered. Her devotion had been rewarded. In the meantime she had lost touch with him. Her brilliant younger brother had turned into someone to be nursed. Having encouraged the development of his powers, she came to doubt their importance, thankful to have him alive.

His article on Walter astounded her. Morris had cultivated her surprise, telling her nothing about it, not even mentioning his study of Walter, whose work he had first seen while finishing his dissertation on Lewis Eilshemius. As soon as it appeared, Morris brought Irene his first copy of *New Worlds*—a gesture that made it clear whom his essay was intended to please. Not even he had foreseen the delight it gave her. It so absorbed her that she had to keep reminding herself who had written it. The later approval of Morris's fellow critics strengthened her conviction that even if one article did not make an oeuvre, Morris had fulfilled his promise. Irene continued to

wake up thinking about him, but with jubilation now, not dread.

In opening her uptown gallery, Irene knew that her career was at stake. Although she did not doubt her own capacities, she had often imagined during the first months of her venture having a counselor who could share the pressure of crises and in calmer times encourage her initiatives. She now asked herself, who could be fitter than Morris for such a role? He had endured crises of terrifying proportions. He had led her to Walter and to her success with him. She asked him to become her collaborator.

A month earlier Morris would probably have accepted her offer. He had loved Irene since childhood; he possibly owed her his life. Her response to his essay had satisfied him gloriously, and he recognized her subsequent adoption of Walter as an acknowledgment of his acumen. Against these bonds, however, were arrayed darker feelings no less tenacious. Irene was someone he had always been obliged to admire. She had been bigger, then older, always a model at home and at school. Even his debts to her confined him. As his protector, his mentor, and finally his guardian, she had proved herself strong and good; Morris had been condemned to strangeness, perversion, and sickness. The strong have the privilege of giving. The weak remain dependent and grateful. But was Irene really the stronger? Who had done the surviving?

When Priscilla insinuated that Irene was exploiting Walter, her words spread through Morris like a stain. Irene was exploiting him, too. He had discovered Walter, and she was turning the profit. When Irene made her proposal to him a few weeks later, it occurred to him that working for her would restore his old dependency in a new guise. Priscilla had shown him that he could make money on his own doing precisely what Irene wanted from him. Forgetting his success and his promise, playing the resentful orphan instead, he declined her offer.

Initially this refusal did not surprise Irene: she understood

the reticence a big sister might inspire. She did her best to mitigate it. She invited Morris to set his own terms. She enlisted outsiders to plead her cause. Her efforts only hardened his position. (Robert Rosenblum declared that trying to change Morris's mind was like pushing gin at an AA convention.) He avoided Irene and her emissaries. A week and a half later, when Priscilla announced that Walter wanted Morris as *his* adviser, Irene gave up.

Even then Morris kept his distance from her, although she never again referred to her offer. He sometimes did; once to remark, in the worst faith, that even Lewis condemned her idea. Irene came to think of Lewis as an enemy.

At Morris's death, Irene cried all the more bitterly for the estrangement that had preceded it. She blamed herself harshly for it.

One morning in early June, Lewis met Priscilla and Walter on Carmine Street, and his disappointment in the painter turned to disgust. He went to see Irene that afternoon. Hoping to get rid of him, she met him in the gallery lobby. Lewis told her he knew the truth about Walter's business understanding with Morris. So did she, she replied. You don't, Lewis insisted. Irene said that she was too busy to argue; if he didn't agree, that was his problem. (She could hardly bear looking at him. He might have killed her brother.) Lewis lost his temper: "It's *your* fucking problem."

Irene left him standing there. Later she began wondering what might lie behind his outburst. When he called to apologize, she agreed to meet him again the next day.

This time Lewis showed patience. He told her about his affair with Morris, saying in conclusion, "I loved him more than I'll ever love anybody, and I know you did too." She asked him how Morris had died. Lewis supplied every painful detail. He then returned to the subject he had broached the day before: "Priscilla set up this deal—"

"Not really. It was Walter's idea."

"It wasn't. I thought you knew *that*. Morris would anyway decide which paintings of Walter's to sell—"

"Which *not* to sell."

Lewis explained the arrangement. Still bewildered, Irene was reluctant to understand. Lewis suggested they visit Morris's apartment. She could see for herself.

"It's impounded. We have to get a permit."

"*I* don't. How about Sunday night?"

Lewis had the key to Morris's back door, concealed by its bookcases from the police. Irene and Lewis crept through it, each with a flashlight.

Morris had hung Walter's five paintings in his bedroom. The portrait of Elizabeth faced the bed. Lewis went off to look for a sales list. Returning, he found Irene exploring the portrait with her mobile beam. Darkness hid her face; her voice revealed a changed mood. Lewis thought of his mother when he'd given her the stolen scarf. He shivered.

"Morris would never have sold—" he began.

"Of course he wouldn't."

"Even Priscilla—"

"Oh, Priscilla!" She paused. "As they say, the course of true love is paved with good intentions. . . . Let's get these things out of here."

"The paintings? *Now?*"

"What else? When else?"

Later that night, Irene justified her preposterous, no doubt illegal, ploy: if Walter was selling these paintings, she was contractually bound to help him. She spoke with the resolution of solid outrage.

On Tuesday Irene began discreetly offering Walter's paintings to reliable customers from out of town. On Friday Maud bought the portrait of Elizabeth. Three other paintings were sold before the end of July, the last on August first. Irene then phoned Walter to tell him what she had done.

She did not blame him for his role, or excuse herself. She thought that probably he would angrily announce that he was leaving her gallery. He only sounded perplexed. Hadn't Priscilla told her about the deal with Morris? Hadn't Irene called him to say she approved? "Look," he said, "basically it was so Morris could make some money. Is that so terrible? He certainly deserved it."

"I agree. Now, tell me, *cher coeur*, how did Priscilla deserve it? Oh, no, spare me the sordid details. . . ." Irene was finally grasping the truth.

"Priscilla?"

"There's something I'd like to know: what did she say I'd agreed to?"

"Every so often Morris would sell a painting of mine."

"To me she *never* said anything about selling—just giving you advice. Of course I know he was selling other work and splitting the proceeds with her." Walter's silence filled up her pause. "You know he and Priscilla went halves?" Another pause. "Ask her."

"She's away for the day."

"I'm sure she can explain it all. Still, I'd listen to her very carefully. You don't happen to own a tape recorder?"

Walter asked who had bought the portrait of Elizabeth. Irene began feeling remorse. She had behaved unfairly to Walter, who had only acted foolishly, not betrayed her. However, she had not behaved unfairly to Priscilla.

Walter was not thinking of Priscilla, not yet. After Irene hung up, he at once called Maud and told her that the real "Portrait of Elizabeth" had remained in his hands.

Pauline and Maud

SUMMER 1938

MAUD LUDLAM ONCE told Elizabeth that she'd had two children: her daughter, Priscilla, and her sister, Pauline.

Their mother had died when Maud was eleven and Pauline five. Afterwards, their father retained the best governesses for their care. When governesses began losing authority, Maud gradually turned into a foster mother. By then she had emerged from the worst of adolescence. She liked her role.

She also liked Pauline, who was sweet-tempered and zany, with whims that she clung to indomitably. From the age of three until her first brush with a policeman she went swimming bottomless, clad only in a strikingly superfluous bra. At six she started taking riding lessons; for her first horse show, she was given English riding togs, which she wore happily enough, except for the boots: if she dressed up, she said, it was going to be heels or nothing. For years she startled judges by riding in black cap, black coat, white shirt and stock tie, jodhpurs, and high-heeled dress shoes (usually Maud's, padded with cotton). When Pauline was eleven, an elegant Chinese guest of her father's showed her how to handle chopsticks: thenceforth she refused to eat with anything else, carrying her

own stainless-steel pair wherever she went, using it, to the stu-
pefaction of one and all, to neatly dissect thick pies and steaks.

Pauline's quirks sometimes embarrassed others, never
Maud. She admired Pauline's spunk. Far less daring herself,
she aspired merely to pass unnoticed. Her mother's death had
bequeathed her a chronic doubt as to her own reality.

Like a coach training a natural athlete, Maud encouraged
Pauline through puberty into young womanhood. The sisters enjoyed themselves, Pauline dashing around, Maud feeling useful as her loyal supervisor. Close though they were,
they showed tolerance rather than understanding towards one
another. They often said they should do more together—go to
Europe, for instance.

Their father, Paul Dunlap, had had a long career as a sensible investment counselor. He had increased tenfold the small
capital inherited from their grandfather, a real-estate developer
in Buffalo. He had speculated on America's entry into the
Great War, foreseen the postwar boom, guessed at the crash.
He retired a millionaire.

After his wife's death, Paul Dunlap for several years gave up
family life. Later, impressed by Maud's grades and her seriousness, he began confiding in her. Pauline stood outside adult
concerns, with all the charm, and all the impertinence, of the
household cocker.

Paul Dunlap established his preference for Maud in practice
and in writ. He taught her what he had learned as an investor,
or tried to—Maud had earned her good marks in literature
and languages, not economics. When he gave her money so
she could learn about handling large sums, Maud only learned
that large sums made her long for professional advice. She
did not see that her father, muttering vague praises of primogeniture, intended to leave her nine-tenths of his estate. He
was making her the head of the family.

Pauline was not instructed in money matters. From Maud

she gradually found out that she would have little control of the family fortunes, while Maud would have a great deal. After their father's death, Maud and one professional trustee became responsible for Pauline's capital. Pauline told herself, better Maud than some fathead at the bank. The disproportion of their inheritance did not distress her. It did not affect her life: Maud gave her the money she so happily continued to spend, and she readily acquiesced to Maud's suggestion that, to enhance Pauline's "eligibility," they pretend that their father had left them equally rich.

Maud had qualms. She asked Allan if he couldn't devise a way of evening their fortunes; Allan told her that it was clearly impossible. For the time being, Maud knew, problems existed only in her conscience. She nevertheless could not forget that a wall of almost a million prewar dollars had been raised between them and that it might someday prove more rugged than sisterly scrupulousness and trust.

In the shadow of that wall, Pauline had already changed. She had stopped growing up. Now twenty-two, she once again began deferring to Maud as she had at fifteen. By the time summer came, Maud felt as though she had been depressingly consigned to an older generation. Pauline came to her for every kind of advice. She refused to buy clothes without her, refused to wear them without her blessing: whenever she left the house, she would exhibit herself to Maud with a cheery "How do I look?" that for all its apparent impulsiveness soon became an ineluctable rite. Like any dutiful young girl, Pauline provided Maud with unasked-for, meticulous accounts of all she did; and she flattered her (Maud could find no nicer word) with equally needless attentions, with notes and even little gifts of flowers or a book, on every faintly memorable occasion in Maud's life—the day their mother died, the day she first met Allan, the day her next period was due. Maud groaned inwardly at each of these tributes, never daring to tell

Pauline how much they saddened her. She had once courted their father in similar fashion, until one day he firmly stopped her: "It's love insurance. Save yourself the trouble. You've got mine."

Pauline had Maud's love and must have known it. What she wanted, what she feared losing, was permission to go on playing as she always had. She did not want to talk or think about money that Maud had and she hadn't, just as she averted her eyes whenever she drove past the treeless, set-back, economy-size supermarket that had wrecked the alignment of their town's main street. She was determined to pretend that nothing had changed.

Her attitude reinforced Maud's own reluctance to set matters straight, as Allan kept urging her to do: Pauline would not live with them much longer, she must start taking care of herself. Maud protested, "I'm part of the problem. How can I help her solve it?"—a good excuse for doing nothing.

Early in July, in this summer of her twenty-third year, a few weeks after graduating from Wellesley, Pauline met Oliver Pruell. He began taking her out. Ten days later Pauline rose early to catch her sister at breakfast:

"He's giving me a big rush. I guess he's serious. He's infuriatingly proper."

"That's not necessarily bad."

"Two years out of college, and risque means holding hands?"

"He's not a fairy?"

"No. Maybe. I have a feeling he 'knows' I'm rich."

"What's his name?"

"May I keep that one secret from you? He's from a good family. He works on Wall Street, too. If he's not after my charms, though, he must want . . . Maud, how can I tell?"

Maud considered herself a poor counselor concerning men; during her adult life she had known only one intimately. She had met Allan three years earlier. They had quickly fomented

a friendly complicity: her self-doubt found a perfect comple-
ment in his assurance. They had "had fun," going to the theater, dancing late. He had proposed to her as though he were
doing her a favor he enjoyed. Her friends warned her that he
was thinking of her wealth to come. Her father disagreed, and
she, knowing Allan, knew better. She was a little surprised
when, three weeks after they had moved into their well-ap-
pointed East Side apartment, she found the bill for the rent on
her desk. Allan took for granted that she would pay for that,
for their trips, for their box at the Met if she wanted it, while
he assumed the cost of their cars and his clubs. Maud hardly
minded, because Allan was otherwise proving the best of husbands. From their courtship Maud had expected that he would
last as a companion; and he had. She had not expected passion.
Months passed, and Allan came home to her every evening
like a sailor on liberty. Maud found herself in love with him.

(Later, when the war abducted Allan to the Pacific and she
turned a horrifying thirty, Maud took a lover. Or rather he
took her; or rather he did *not* take her. A slightly impoverished
Baltimorean, of exquisite extraction and no less exquisite sensi-
bilities, began pursuing her ardently. At last she yielded. Maud
wanted to be confirmed in her bodily beauty; she got homage
of a more speculative kind. Michael, capable of satisfying her,
explained that he treasured that consummation so highly that
only marriage could properly enshrine it. He knew her true
worth—he had a friend at her bank, as she learned before
showing him the door.)

Maud gave her sister evasive counsel.

A month later, Pauline was ensnared by the losing streak
into which Oliver and the martingale had lured her. She owed
her beau six hundred and thirty-five dollars, as well as her
virginity. She decided to earn the money and asked Maud to
help her find a job. She said she wanted to work: "Anything.
Selling Fuller Brushes. I'm a disgrace as it is."

Maud was pleased. She foresaw wonderful benefits in Pauline's decision. She might discover the value of money (by which Maud somehow meant its irrelevance). She might earn, if not her living, at least her rent. She might leave Maud and *her* money behind her.

Maud sent Pauline to one of her oldest friends, a man of wealth and local influence, the president of "The Association" (the Association for the Improvement of the Breed of Thoroughbred Horses). Maud had failed to observe that Pauline had taken his son as her constant companion. She could not guess that it was because of this young man that she wanted to earn money.

Mr. Pruell, however, had often noticed Oliver and Pauline together, most recently sharing a bag of chips as they sauntered under the high elms of Broadway. He agreed to see Pauline (who told herself that, after all, a job was a job), but he had no interest in finding her work. He wanted her to look after his son. He confided his concern for him; he showed her Oliver's erotic hymns to Elizabeth. She fell definitively in love.

She wanted to marry. Oliver said they couldn't afford it. Pauline decided to involve her sister. She intercepted her on her way out to dinner.

"Did you get your job?" Maud asked her cheerfully.

"I love Mr. Pruell—I never really knew him."

"He's a dream, isn't he?"

"I'm dating Oliver Pruell—the one I told you about a month ago? It's serious?" The questions in Pauline's voice invited Maud's approval.

"How wonderful!" Maud answered, in dismay. How could she not have known?

The next morning she learned that she had no companions in ignorance: her "discreet inquiries" about Oliver became comic as each of her friends volunteered straight-to-the-point evaluations at the mention of his name. According to most, he

was handsome, polished, very much a Pruell, less admired than liked, no rogue—not one to marry a girl for her money, not with his expectations. Not absolutely reliable: two years ago, after a summer-long affair with Elizabeth, he had ditched her.

Pauline again spoke to Maud. She wanted Oliver to marry her. ("Of course I'm not pregnant!" "But you're sleeping with him?" "It was like pulling hen's teeth, but yes.") Although "mad about her," Oliver thought it greater madness to live on his present salary.

"He says wait till I'm twenty-five—till I 'come into my own,' as he puts it."

"How patient of him!"

As Maud feared, the problem rapidly got worse. Allan went back to the city the next day. With no invitation to rescue her, Maud dined with Pauline, who promptly asked her: "Can I talk about Oliver?"

"Will it help?"

"Something wrong with him?"

"Don't be silly."

"He says it's no dice." Maud wondered why this could not reasonably end the matter; however, they would not then be having this conversation. Pauline went on, "It wouldn't take much to change his mind, I think. Or do I mean 'I don't think'?"

"Are you sure he wants to marry you?"

"Oh, yes. He swears he'd marry me if only—" Pauline stopped.

"So there's a bill of particulars?"

"Oh, Maud, *he* promised me and *I* looked for the answers. I thought that maybe—"

"Could you explain the appeal of someone who insists on more money?"

"I should never have put it that way. Anyway, we *have* the money, don't we?"

"That's hardly the point."

"What *is* the point of having money if you can't use it to get what you want? You always said I should be happy."

"*That's* the point. And after all," Maud continued, knowing she could not ward off Pauline indefinitely, "what could we do?"

"If I got my share now, that would help—even if it's not as much as he thinks."

"It's impossible. Legally, I mean. You must know that."

"Sure. So what if I took my share out of what you have, and I pay it back to you at nine-oh-five A.M. on my twenty-fifth birthday?"

"I can't."

"You say you never know what to do with it all. And think: from now on I wouldn't cost you another penny."

"It isn't up to me. It's Daddy's money—"

"Oh, come on!"

"He *cared* about what happened to it. I don't like what he decided, but I *promised* I'd respect it. Even if I didn't, you know most of my money is in trust, and I'm only one trustee. It wouldn't work. I can't go against his wishes. Not to mention his will."

"Darling, who knows what he'd think now? Why don't you stop using a dead man to hide behind? If you disapprove of Oliver, just say so."

"It's not hiding. I'm responsible—that's the way the money was left to us. I wish *you* had it. My disapproving of Oliver has nothing to do with it."

"You see? That's why you're talking this junk. You wish I had the money! Do you think you'd have gotten Allan without it, with your big feet?"

Pauline left the table. The front door presently slammed. In the living room Maud refilled her glass with the dregs of shaken martinis. Sitting down, she told herself: I mustn't let her think such things about me. The glass sloshed in her hand. She had been blindsided by Pauline's attack.

She came down early in the morning to wait for her sister. Maud said to her that she had forgotten something they could do. The house in the city had been left to Maud outright. It was now rented. If Pauline wanted it, the tenants could be moved out by the spring.

Since the night before, she added, she had realized that she could ask to have the allowance from Pauline's trust fund increased, even doubled.

Pauline accepted. While she was pleased to have more income of her own, she reckoned it was the handsome corner house on Sutton Square that would appease Oliver.

During the night her feelings towards Maud had undergone considerable change. After rushing outside, she had promptly divested herself of her years of submissiveness; and like a snake in springtime, resentment had at once raised its sullen head. Again and again she angrily reminded herself of the unfairness of her position. She was as clever as Maud, she was prettier, and she was so much poorer! She would never have let *her* sister suffer from an old man's whim.

By morning, practice had hardened her indignation. When Maud made her offer, Pauline found it less than her due. Maud's concessions chiefly gratified her by putting Maud permanently in the wrong.

Soon afterwards, before the engagement was announced, Maud chose to travel. The season was ending, and she had time before the wedding to make a long-postponed excursion to Europe. Offended by her departure, Pauline let her resentment flourish. If Maud had stayed, even an angry sister might have noticed that she only wanted peace for herself. Instead, Maud allowed Pauline to turn her into a kind of witch. The happiness of Pauline's engagement, the publicity of her marriage, glittered against a dark background of indifference and betrayal.

Or, if Maud had stayed, Pauline might at least have been able to vent her resentment. Maud would have suffered and

survived, and Pauline's anger would have expired into acceptance, if not understanding. Maud left. For many years Pauline
saw as little of her as she could, altogether avoiding the famil-
iarity that had so long sustained her. Her indignation had
nowhere to go except into a sodden pit of recollection and
foreboding, where it lay, impotent and alive, year after year,
waiting to emerge on some marvelous day of wrath—a brooding existence, exuding ropy feelers of revenge.

Or, if Pauline's happiness with Oliver had lasted, her ran-
cor might have simply been forgotten. Pauline never interested Oliver except as a prize. He soon neglected her. He discouraged her from working, from having children—when he
learned the truth about her inheritance, he declared that in
such difficult times children cost more than they could comfortably afford.

So Pauline's resentment lived on, a ponderous beast dor-
mant in its gloomy trough. Twenty-five years after her marriage, her friend Owen Lewison told her one evening that
Allan and Maud, for reasons unknown to him, had sequestered
a valuable painting by Walter Trale, improbably claiming that
it had been stolen. He asked Pauline to find out if the picture
had been hidden in Allan's apartment. "High Heels" accepted,
with a vengeance, with no illusions about her task: she would
seduce Maud's husband and implicate her sister in a dubious
scheme. Her night with Allan, however, left her dissatisfied.
She liked him more than she wanted to; and this inexplicably
reawakened her age-old attachment to Maud. She was confused. She told herself that sleeping with Allan could not be
counted as revenge if her sister did not know about it.

She must pay her a visit and make sure she knew what had
happened.

The beast had come forth from its pit. In the light of day,
it looked less like a dragon than like a lost lamb.

Maud and Priscilla

1940-1963

MAUD, NO FOOL, did not regret that she had money to be liked for. She hoped, less shrewdly, that it might inspire in others tolerance for her ordinary self. She did not like talking about money, because the subject made her feel foolish, and her foolishness made her cringe for her father's sake. She had learned so little from him, and forgotten so much. Maud had tried managing the far from negligible sums her father had left her outright. She had even had conspicuous successes: in 1938, she added oil stocks to her portfolio after they had shrunk to half their value and before their precipitous rise. Her prescience, however, was invariably based on irrelevant facts. She had, for instance, no inkling of the oil industry's forthcoming boom, only observed that its stocks provided a higher yield than her other securities. She made costly mistakes, such as missing a chance to buy early into natural gas. After the third such mistake, she abandoned investment policy to her advisers.

Her withdrawal from finance sadly recalled to Maud her father's long efforts to train her. A difficult master, he had taught her by examples from which few rules could be drawn; and the prime rule read: in money matters, do not look for

rules. While she had believed everything he said, her belief was grounded in faith, not understanding. In resisting Pauline's demands, she had, exceptionally, acted with a reasonable conviction: she could accept as plain good sense her father's dictum that fortunes should be kept intact. Declaring this to sentimental Pauline would have sounded like rank hypocrisy; so Maud had taken refuge, with lesser hypocrisy, in the letter of her father's intentions.

In promising to carry out these intentions, Maud implicitly subjected her future offspring to the rule that had favored her over Pauline: one of them would inherit the bulk of her fortune. As it turned out, Maud had only one child.

When Priscilla came of age, Maud told herself, I know too much and too little about money, but at least I know something. I might have done worse. Priscilla should find out what money can do. Of course, Maud could not teach her. On the other hand, if efficient Priscilla had inherited her grandfather's flair, simply using money might be training enough.

Maud had mostly let Priscilla solve her own problems since, from infancy, she had proved so much better at it. All the same, Maud had looked after her conscientiously. Tempted though she may have been to leave her clever daughter to her own devices, she realized that even the cleverest child cannot foresee the measles or the injustice of lower mathematics. She provided Priscilla with the elements of a healthy life, she found good doctors to supervise her growth, at school she persuaded sympathetic teachers to monitor her progress. Otherwise, Maud simply kept herself available, although she hardly knew why. At eleven Priscilla had her appendix removed. Maud sat with her through her recovery, noticing ruefully that it was Priscilla who kept *her* cheered up.

Diffident Maud enjoyed having a bright, athletic, sociable daughter. She had what many parents strive for: a child who surpasses them. Maud's own successes always struck her as due

to luck, like her timely purchase of oil stock, or too secret to qualify as achievements. Her house, even her garden belonged to this domain of secrecy. Allan pleaded with her to show them to the world; Maud insisted on keeping them in the family.

Behind the house there had once stretched an acre and a half of lawn, conventionally hedged and planted with a few unsurprising trees. Within this space Maud plotted an arrangement of outdoor rooms, cunningly varied and juxtaposed. One room was shaded for sunny days, its neighbor wide open to the skies; some were planted by color (white, blue, rose); others flowered according to the seasons, from the primrose-speckled spring oval walled with high rhododendrons to the autumn rectangle, which was bordered with a multitude of chrysanthemums set against severely clipped hedges of golden-leaving beech. She favored old-fashioned plants—lilies, dahlias, Portland roses; syringa, deutzia, sweet shrub—perhaps because at the heart of all her design lay a simple experience of her girlhood. One day in May, playing hide-and-seek at her Massachusetts cousins', she had concealed herself between two ancient lilac bushes in full bloom. For a long minute she saw the world through their sun-fretted clusters, half suffocating in their heady stench. At the farthest corner of her garden she raised a small room that to her justified the rest: a perfect square of lilac hedges, trimmed along their sides and growing freely at their tops, each May modulating around their perimeter through every imaginable gradation of blossom, from wine-red to palest mauve and back again, the transitions tempered by flowers of the white lilac with which the other bushes were interspersed. Only Allan and Priscilla ever accompanied Maud there; and, of course, John. John had come to work as handyman for her father and stayed on. Not because of loyalty to the family or a predilection for gardening: the intensity Maud brought to her tasks inspired him with a lasting enthusiasm of his own. Except for Allan, no one knew her as he did.

Outside her private world, Maud had rarely experienced the special satisfaction of seeing what she wanted and getting it. Weather permitting, Priscilla did nothing else. One day her fourth-grade teacher called her a dunce; two weeks later she moved to the top of her class. At eleven she saw a movie with Sonja Henie; by the end of the winter she was competing as a figure skater. She successfully pursued popularity, even at boarding school, where she showed a tendency to collect boyfriends. Her classmates forgave her because hers were too old for them.

Any parents would have taken pride in her. For Allan, with his busy career, pride sufficed. Maud, with much less to do, wished she'd had a live mother whose example she could follow. While Priscilla's successes reassured her, Maud suspected that whatever her upbringing Priscilla would have become a prodigious achiever. A pang of regret sometimes transfixed her when she thought of her daughter: had she ever been truly useful to her?

Priscilla showed self-reliance from the time she could crawl. She saw the world as a nest of probable satisfactions. Obstacles like her fourth-grade teacher pointed towards bigger opportunities. Only once had she known complete helplessness. When she was fourteen, during her summer vacation, she had made friends with Lewis Lewison. Drawn to him by his unlikeness to other boys and by a shyness close to surliness, she had given up her hefty eighteen-year-olds to pursue him. At last he kissed her, and on one hot afternoon took her into the empty barn behind his parents' house, where he came to grips with her strong, skinny body, and with his own. Her resistance to his assault enraged him less than his inability to carry it through, which made him wild as he lay on her, rubbing against her flesh like a child trapped in a closet and banging the door. She had been terrified and, finding herself trapped, had lost control of herself.

Lewis ran off. Louisa found, washed, and consoled her. She promised to attend to Lewis and urged Priscilla to speak to her mother. Priscilla agreed. Maud would certainly show compassion, and Priscilla's "accident," if childish, had been provoked by grown-up business. She could talk to Maud as an equal.

Priscilla was less sure of this when she saw her mother. Maud appeared in the door of the house and looked at Priscilla with a not unfamiliar, not unaffectionate, not unwary look: Tell me everything is fine, it said, and I'll go away.

Priscilla was sitting alone in the front room. She had never done this. Perplexed, Maud stood still in the doorway: "I think I'll have some tea."

"Want me to make it?"

"That would be lovely. Darjeeling, please."

"I saw Lewis this afternoon."

"What a lucky boy! How does Gene feel about your leaving him for a fifteen-year-old? *I* saw Phoebe. As far as I could tell, she was teaching her counselors knots."

"I'd have done better going on that trip with her."

Maud put down two teacups and closed the cabinet doors. She groped for words that would invite Priscilla to go on, and succeeded in not finding them. Irritation with what she could not say made her voice tremble: "You should have a brand-new sleeping bag, at least." She laughed foolishly to cover the tremor.

Priscilla laughed too and squeezed Maud's arm. "It's no problem. The other guys will take me whenever I want. Show me what you're wearing tonight?"

They drank their tea. Maud never heard about Lewis in the barn.

As a rule, Priscilla confided in Maud. She told her all a mother might want to know. In delicate matters she often spoke after the fact, leaving Maud with foregone conclusions. When, a few months after her college graduation, Priscilla

announced her liaison with Walter, Maud was not surprised that she had already moved in with him. As usual, she had to like it or lump it.

Maud missed Priscilla during the following winter. She missed what they had never had together. It seemed to Maud that her daughter had grown up in one brief flurry of yesterdays, while she was gazing out the window at an Adirondack sunset. Maud had borne her; Priscilla had grown up without her. She could do little about that now.

She could do something. She remembered her father (oh, with him things *had* happened, she had been mixed up with him, she had hung on his words and arms), she remembered her father's determination to train her. If nothing else, she could at least teach Priscilla that money was an opportunity to be mastered. Priscilla might then emerge from the blindness that afflicted Maud and Pauline. Maud knew that, like the moon in the sky or the trees in the woods, money surrounded them too naturally to ever be thought about. Maud could not blame Priscilla if she "didn't really care" about money—she never asked her to go out at night to make sure the moon was shining and the trees growing. Such things looked after themselves. Even Allan, who himself knew and cared about money, showed no anxiety concerning Priscilla: "She's fortunate *not* to have to worry. That's what 'fortune' means. She'll learn when the time comes."

Allan's opinion was wasted on Maud. She brooded over the problem on melancholy winter days. She finally came up with a scheme. She could hardly influence Priscilla directly. She must create a foregone conclusion of her own: a situation where Priscilla would be obliged to use money and make decisions about it.

Maud conceived her project in early May, when spring was warming belatedly the upper reaches of the Hudson. Several weeks later, she went to her bank in the city and put it into

effect. She gave instructions to have twenty thousand dollars transferred yearly to Priscilla for the next ten years. Priscilla could spend the income; she could only invest the capital. She would *have* to invest it.

As she made these arrangements, Maud thought less and less about Priscilla and more and more intently of her dead father. When she had done her part, she asked the bank officials to inform Priscilla. The scheme should be presented to her as the working out of an old covenant. Maud told herself she should spare Priscilla the nuisance of feeling grateful. She had performed her duty in the manner of an invisible guardian, as an agent of impersonal benevolence.

These mildly insane precautions at once aroused Priscilla's suspicions. She recognized Maud's hand. Priscilla recalled that one afternoon when she was nine she had returned from school two hours late and found her mother conferring on the terrace with a policeman. The next day Maud had a television set (then new and rare) installed in Priscilla's bedroom: a bribe never to come home late again. Priscilla thought, I have now committed a bohemian cohabitation, and Mama is bribing me to give it up. That much Priscilla could understand. But the scale of the gesture! Giving away two hundred thousand dollars suggested motives less generous—a tax break, for instance. Priscilla did not mind. She simply wanted to know.

The early summer had been vexing to her. Dedicated to her partnership with Morris, she had not sold anything since his death—their paintings had all been impounded in the dead man's apartment. She hoped eventually to recover them, at least those by Walter; after all, no one else knew about them. With such a stock, and with Morris's life insurance as working capital, she could look forward to the future. Meanwhile, she had to abide the slow course of the law. She had little else to do. Walter spent his days hard at work. Most of her friends had gone away. When the bank told her of Maud's scheme, she decided to get out of the city and unearth her mother's

secret. She phoned Maud to announce her arrival on August first in time for lunch.

Priscilla's call surprised Maud only passingly. She had suspected that her precautions would prove wishful. Initially resigned to her visit, by the time Priscilla arrived Maud had come to resent it. Elizabeth had distressed her by leaving for the day. Later, Allan had called to make a disagreeable confession. Watching her daughter emerge from a taxi and stride buoyantly towards the house, she shuddered. My God, she's like Pauline.

On the shady west porch the women settled into upholstered white wicker armchairs. Declining a drink, noticing that her mother's glass was filled with green chartreuse, Priscilla tilted her chair forward, sat pertly upright, and declared her thanks: whatever Maud's reasons, Priscilla was stunned by her kindness. She spoke at length, underscoring her gratitude.

Maud did not respond. She appeared hardly to be listening. Something, Priscilla thought, is unusually wrong. She nevertheless kept up a cheerful monologue. She talked enthusiastically about her life with Walter. "I see, I see," Maud at last interrupted, only then referring to the pretext of her daughter's visit: "They made everything clear in the letter, didn't they? They put everything in the letter?"

"Yes, the letter was absolutely clear. They put everything in it, Mama, except you."

"Oh, me—" Maud sighed, waving to a ghost beyond the lawn.

"I came here for you."

"You're sweet, but you know, I only had to go through the motions—hardly worth taking credit for."

"But you deserve credit. As for going through the motions—Mama, isn't your elbow getting a little sore?"

"What do you mean?" Maud wrily answered. "It's only my seventeenth drink."

"Can you tell me one thing? Is it Allan?"

"He spoke to *you* about it?"

Allan had called Maud earlier. Fearful she would learn about the doomed gelding he had helped insure, he had described his part in the business. Although Maud did not fully understand him, Allan's discomfiture became painfully apparent to her.

"He didn't speak to me. Someone saw them," Priscilla explained. "I'm sorry, Mama. Who would have dreamed it of Aunt Paw?"

Even unwily Maud had the sense not to budge. She sipped her chartreuse and stared through the beetle-butted screen: "Tell me what you know."

"Oh, 'know'! When was it, the night before last, a friend driving across Sixty-third Street had to stop behind a taxi, and she saw Papa and Aunt Pauline get out together, outside the apartment. They were acting—" Maud had risen and started crossing the porch. She tripped over a board as smooth as any other. "Oh, Mama!"

Maud was stumbling with humiliation. Not because of what she was hearing: because she was hearing it from her daughter. She felt outraged by Priscilla's presence, and losing her balance didn't help. She kept silent.

"Mama! It's no fun, but it won't matter. Papa adores you and always will." She barely paused. "You don't have to drink brandy before lunch."

"It's not brandy. I was up at five, and I had my lunch at eleven," Maud declared. Her own anger bewildered her.

"OK, Mama."

Maud squeezed her crystal snifter so hard that it splintered. "Damn you!" she blurted, meaning to say, Damn it.

Priscilla stared at her eagerly. "It's awful seeing you—"

"So why bother coming? I've been so much better since— hah!" Maud chose to steam rather than explain.

"Mama," Priscilla went on, her voice dropping a minor third, "I can't enjoy your becoming a lush."

"Is that what you came here to tell me?"

"I came here, and it *is* a long ride, to tell you—I've already said it. Or maybe you weren't listening."

"Of course I was. I'm glad you're pleased."

"Aren't *you* pleased? I thought my coming up might mean something to you. I didn't know you'd just been 'going through the motions'—as usual."

"Anyway, enjoy the money." Maud had cut her left little finger.

"Mama, you're such a dope!"

"Is there something wrong with enjoying money?"

"Shit! Why do I sit here talking to this flop? Listen, I just inherited a hundred thousand dollars. Not to mention what I've made on my own, you'll be glad to know."

"I *am* pleased. You never said a word—"

"I've been selling paintings. I've been working with Morris Romsen—you know, the critic. Walter Trale gave us an option on his best paintings."

"Not all of them, surely. He didn't give you the portrait of Elizabeth."

"Oh, yes, he did."

"How funny. I bought it last month, and not from you, Miss Kahnweiler."

"What are you talking about?"

"I mean that I bought—that five or six weeks ago Allan and I bought Walter Trale's 'Portrait of Elizabeth' from Irene Kramer. I can't show it to you because your father's taken it elsewhere. Give him a call."

Wasting no time in conjectures as to how Irene had recovered the portrait (she was Morris's sister and heir, after all), Priscilla made silent calculations. She could get back to the city by six; that afternoon an opening was scheduled at the Kramer Gallery. Her father could wait. She had to see Irene.

"Mama, can you drive me to the station?"

"Ask John. He's out in back. I'm going to have a little lie-down."

At two-thirty Maud called her bank in the city to cancel her scheme. She had completed her new instructions and was about to hang up when unforeseen grief overcame her. She asked the bank official to wait and muffled the phone while her sobs subsided. She then said, "Disregard what I told you. Don't change anything, except for one thing. Change the name of the beneficiary. Please delete 'Priscilla Ludlam' and write in 'Pauline Pruell.' Née Dunlap. Send the papers for me to sign as soon as you can."

Maud and Elizabeth

JULY-SEPTEMBER 1963

"...ONE WEEK," MAUD was shouting precisely, "what's a week in a lifetime?"

No less loudly, no less deliberately, Elizabeth answered, "A lifetime? And you still want that milktoast?"

"That's for me to decide!" Maud cried (quickly whispering, "He's coming downstairs").

"(Nice going.) It's him or the portrait, you can't have both!"

"You're disgusting!"

"It's my portrait, isn't it?"

"*Of* you—hardly yours!"

"Cut the crap, Mrs. Miniver. I need something to show for my week. (Where *is* he?)"

"(I'll go look.)"

Tiptoeing out, Maud at once noticed that the portrait of Elizabeth was missing from the library, where for a week it had stood unpacked and unhung. After looking into the music room, the den, and the dining room—all empty—she rejoined Elizabeth. Together they watched Allan, encumbered with the painting, walking to the station wagon that he had parked on the public road.

"I was sure he'd come charging in."

"What was that phone call?" Maud asked.

Until today, Maud had not seen Elizabeth since the year before she married, and she had forgotten ever meeting her. She would not have recognized her name if, a year ago, she had not read her daughter's thesis on Walter Trale. Its account of his friendship with Elizabeth touched her because they had met in this very town, where Maud had been summering with her family. She vividly recalled the evening parties where men wore white double-breasted dinner jackets and women organdy and organza. She had gone swimming that summer in a new elastic, white-belted bathing suit, and she had become engaged to Allan (when he proposed, she had on high-waisted, pleated slacks, with a lawn kerchief over her hair). Her father was still alive, Pauline still her happy protégée. She remembered Walter, then only a boy, younger even than Pauline, his talent all the more glamorous for his youth, so that he was lionized by the horse-and-dog set. Maud felt less sure about Elizabeth. An image came back to her of someone beautiful and a little "wild," someone she could not place with certainty; someone in an older crowd who had disappeared after a few years; someone with the bright precarious youth of those not altogether young. What had that woman now become? (Like Maud, Elizabeth must be past fifty. What had she herself become? What had she done to attain this once-faraway age?)

During the months that followed her reading of Priscilla's account, Maud sometimes remembered to ask acquaintances about Elizabeth. Their answers whetted her curiosity. Elizabeth had married a Brazilian—or was it a Lebanese?—millionaire. She had married a carpet salesman from Topeka. She had remained single. No man could win her. No decent man would have her. She had turned into an alcoholic, or a drug addict, or a nymphomaniac. Hadn't she proclaimed herself a lesbian? Purest rumor—a rumor probably started by Elizabeth herself, after she had gone into business. Career women often

find it best not to marry. Elizabeth had had a brilliant career. Not as a businesswoman: as an actress. Or perhaps as an artist. Remember those banged bronze monsters in Brasilia, or were those the Brazilian's first wife's? Elizabeth had done none of those things. She had disappeared. She had come to nothing.

In June, on a visit to the city, Maud stopped at the Kramer Gallery. Irene, whom she had known for years, confided that she was offering rare paintings by Walter Trale to her best customers. Among them was the portrait of Elizabeth H.; Maud asked to see it and scrutinized it for the symptoms of Walter's fabled passion. She looked for Elizabeth as well, who only veiled herself in fresh mystery. Recognizing a windfall, Maud bought the painting on the spot. Her burgeoning fascination with Elizabeth left her, she felt, little choice. The fascination continued to grow.

It occurred to Maud, a few days later, to question Irene about Elizabeth herself. Irene said: ask Barrington Pruell. Louisa Lewison had once told her that he and Elizabeth kept in touch.

Maud thought that likely. Old Mr. Pruell had befriended Elizabeth in those early years. On the morning of July tenth she paid him a visit.

Maud and Mr. Pruell had a longstanding friendship. After her mother's death, Maud had turned to him for support. He knew her father well and understood, if he did not condone, his withdrawal from domestic life. He did his best to explain Mr. Dunlap's behavior to his young friend, and he encouraged her to keep up her grades and take good care of Pauline. Maud had trusted him. After her marriage they saw each other less. Maud frequented Allan's friends, city people, business people; publicly, at least, Mr. Pruell belonged to the horse-and-dog world. They now took each other for granted. When they met at parties, they hugged, exchanged "news," promised to meet privately, and never did.

When Maud announced the reason for her visit, Mr. Pruell

said, "It's your lucky day. No point my telling you about Elizabeth. She's coming to lunch."

"She's here?"

"She arrived last week. Stay and see for yourself."

Maud phoned Allan to tell him that she would be out for the day. She begged Mr. Pruell to talk to her about his friend: "I'd like to be the tiniest bit prepared."

Mr. Pruell laughed. "Ask *her*. You'll have more fun."

Elizabeth called to say she couldn't come after all.

Although Mr. Pruell promised to arrange another meeting, Maud felt a disappointment verging on anger. She felt betrayed. It was then that she realized she had been nourishing a small passion, one for which she could find no name. She knew that it included a trace of envy. What had made Elizabeth so different? How had she won friends like Walter Trale and Barrington Pruell and left in her wake the enticing confusion of her reputations? Elizabeth's failure to appear for lunch clinched Maud's obsession with her. She made up her mind that they would meet.

The next days brought Maud only frustration. She learned where Elizabeth was staying, what friends she saw, which parties she would attend. If Maud had called Elizabeth at her hotel, she could have met her in a day; but without a plausible excuse she was embarrassed to approach her. She did not hesitate, however, to get herself invited to every social event in town. And wherever Maud went, Elizabeth did not appear. After a while, Maud began wondering if the woman wasn't avoiding her. (She could imagine no reason for this. Elizabeth could hardly guess that she was being perversely pursued.) Without getting even a glimpse of her prey, Maud consumed a surfeit of olives and jellied ham and enough drinks to afflict even her seasoned metabolism.

After four days, she grew so discouraged that she actually gave up all hope of knowing Elizabeth. They were, she still

felt, linked by destiny: but their destiny was to never meet—"a conjunction of their minds, an opposition of their stars." One morning—the fifteenth of July—she picked up her phone and broke her engagements for the day. At eleven o'clock, after trotting into the driveway, dismounting, and tethering her bay mare to a convenient birch, an unfamiliar red-haired woman in riding cap and jodhpurs walked up to Maud's front door and rang the bell.

To Elizabeth, an hour later, watching Allan drive off, Maud declared, "If anything happens to that picture, I'll roast him."

"In the meantime, why not settle for the original?" Elizabeth slipped her arm into Maud's.

Maud took five seconds to understand. "You don't mean you want to *stay* here?"

"I'd love to. If you don't trust my friendly sentiments, I can honestly confess that I'm broke. Bone poor till September sixth. So it would also help."

"I do love to be useful—how did you guess?"

"Allan told me, of course."

"But you do see—"

"We can always finesse the drama. Although I'm pretty much stuck with it in any case."

"How come?"

"Allan was a discreet visitor but a frequent one. The help at the Adelphi are turning sort of frosty. It's hardly your problem, I know—"

"I suppose not. Then why *do* I feel responsible? I guess I'd rather be on your side than theirs."

"If it's not fun, I'll disappear. I promise. Instantly."

Maud surprised Elizabeth, who had called on her out of impulse, although not without a reason: she had heard that Maud was trying to meet her. Allan had described Maud to her misleadingly. Instead of a devoted homebody, Elizabeth discovered a woman whose clean-edged prettiness had been

sweetly softened by the faint wrinkling of years. Her discon-
solate politeness inspired Elizabeth with an intense longing to
make her giggle.

Until Allan's back-door entry, the two women had talked
like schoolmates making up for half a lifetime's separation.
Maud soon discovered what they had in common. When she
brought up Allan, Elizabeth could not help committing a
pause; which Maud of course noticed.

She had thought that Allan might be having an affair. For
a week he had acted towards her with distracted impatience;
he had also twice brought her home voluptuous masses of her
favorite Jeanne Charmet dahlias. What this behavior might
signify she had inferred from the solicitous phone calls of not-
very-dear friends. When Elizabeth brightly followed her pause
with talk of certain attractive men she'd just met, naming
names and detailing qualities, Maud interrupted: "Aha! *That's*
what my girlfriends haven't been telling me. There's another
woman, and it's you!"

Maud recognized something like relief in her voice: as if she
were thinking, If he had to cheat, better her than someone else.

Blushing wildly, Elizabeth said, "I won't say, 'If only I'd
known—.' I *am* glad we're talking to one another."

"But I've been chasing you for days!"

Elizabeth smiled. "You see why you never caught up?"

"You mean you were running away?"

"No. I was meeting Allan. I'd plan to go to the McCollums'
from five to seven, then Allan would call to say he could get
away from five to seven—"

"Because of course *I* was going to the McCollums' from
five to seven, because *you* were."

"So I would call Mrs. McCollum, or anyway not go."

"The first time was Barrington Pruell's lunch?"

"*You* were the dear old friend so anxious to meet me? Oh,
no! You do get it?"

"Yes, I do." Maud felt stupid. Elizabeth was overwhelming her.

Elizabeth leaned across the coffee table and took Maud's hands. "I *didn't* know. I only learned you were looking for me two days ago." Maud glanced up warily. "I never schedule things. Actually, coming here was my horse's idea."

Maud sighed. "I can see how funny it is, my making it possible . . ."

"What's funnier is us, right now." Elizabeth paused. "I'm sorry you wasted all that time. But so what? New game today." Maud smiled as if to say: You're very kind. "Look at it this way: thanks to Allan, we're friends."

Maud gazed into Elizabeth's eyes, thinking, What can I lose? They heard Allan treading carefully through the kitchen. Familiar with house sounds, Maud reported his movements. Elizabeth said she had to phone the stable—her mare was overdue. When she lifted the handset, she clapped her hand over the speaker and for several minutes kept the receiver at her ear. After hanging up, she said to Maud, "Let's blow his mind."

"You mean *shoot* him?"

"No, sweetie pie. Just wow him." Elizabeth proposed a portentous dialogue for Allan to overhear; they thereupon performed it with operatic gravity and gusto.

Maud told Elizabeth she was welcome to stay. Elizabeth thanked her with an embrace. Now she must ride her mare home. "She's probably girdled the birch."

"The 'ladies of the forest' grow like weeds here. It's expendable."

"I hope you like to ride."

Raising her eyes in woeful ecstasy, Maud answered, "Oh, Elizabeth, it's out of the question. Horses don't like me. Or I don't understand them."

"You never met the right horses. Come on out. This one's a dream."

Maud moaned and followed. On the lawn Elizabeth introduced her to the mare, Fatima. The two greeted each other
genteelly, if noncommittally. Elizabeth ambled away into summer haze.

She moved in the following day. She told Maud she had
everything she needed. "Enough for a week is enough for a
summer. Not that I'll stay *that* long." Maud didn't think she'd
mind. She had missed her already.

That morning Allan called Maud to ask her if Elizabeth
had said anything "about a horse." Maud cut the conversation
short. Allan had run away; he could stay away.

In the evening Elizabeth suggested that they go into town
for cocktails. Maud demurred: "How about drinks on the
porch? I recommend it highly. I do it all the time."

"You haven't been out in two days."

"But I love it here." Maud was reluctant to be seen with
her husband's lover.

"So do I. But soon? I've missed some promising bars."

Safe for the night, Maud acquiesced.

The previous morning, from the moment she began eaves-
dropping on the telephone, Elizabeth had been sure that Allan
knew she was listening. He had played the tough guy for her,
bringing their brief story to a pitiful end. She said to Maud, "I
couldn't quite make it out. He has a devious side, you know."

"You mean," Maud said belligerently, "last week was only
the tip of the Venusberg?"

"I don't think so. I've known womanizers (and they have
their attractions), but not Allan. Definitely not. He's had a
successful career, hasn't he?"

"Very." Perplexed, Maud dropped the subject.

Elizabeth asked, "Whose bedroom is the one next to mine?"

"My daughter Priscilla's. Or it used to be."

"Did I tell you I met her at Walter Trale's? She's sharp. She
knew so much about me I almost felt my age. Whatever that
may be."

Maud told Elizabeth about her recent largesse towards Priscilla, explaining, "So she'll know *something* about money." She reddened, remembering her friend's "bone-poorness."

"I bet she makes a fortune with it."

Maud drove Elizabeth to the stables the next morning. She had agreed to accompany her if she could just sit and watch. She enjoyed seeing Elizabeth take her mount through its paces: animal and rider looked equally content. After unsaddling, Elizabeth introduced Maud to a few more horses. Maud conceded that with Elizabeth next to her she might, someday, give one of them a try. As they were leaving, a man arrived from the racetrack with a depressing tale about a destroyed gelding.

That night, after dinner, they chose to read. Even though the light was weakening, they sat on the west piazza, their reading glasses perched on their nose tips, reluctant to forsake the evening sky behind the panoply of blackening hills. After ten minutes Maud heaved a sigh of delight. Elizabeth closed her book expectantly. "Well—" Maud said and read aloud:

An extreme languor had settled on him, he felt weakened with the cessation of her grasp. . . . He heard himself quote:

"'Since when we stand side by side!'" His voice trembled. "Ah yes!" came in her deep tones: "The beautiful lines . . . They're true. We must part. In this world . . ." They seemed to her lovely and mournful words to say; heavenly to have them to say, vibratingly, arousing all sorts of images. Macmaster, mournfully too, said:

"We must wait." He added fiercely: "But tonight, at dusk!"

He imagined the dusk under the yew hedge. A shining motor drew up in the sunlight under the window.

"Yes! Yes!" she said. "There's a little white gate from the lane." She imagined their interview of passion and mournfulness amongst dim objects half seen. So much of glamour she could allow herself.

Afterwards he must come to the house to ask after her health and they would walk side by side on the lawn, publicly, in the warm light, talking of indifferent but beautiful poetries, a little wearily, but with what currents electrifying and passing between their flesh. . . . And then: long, circumspect years. . . .

"Were the Edwardians ever more neatly skewered? Perhaps they were Georgians by then."

"It's dazzling. How about this?"

I finished my cigarette and lit another. The minutes dragged by. Horns tooted and grunted on the boulevard. A big red interurban car rumbled past. A traffic light gonged. The blonde leaned on her elbow and cupped a hand over her eyes and stared at me behind it. The partition door opened and the tall bird with the cane slid out. He had another wrapped parcel, the shape of a large book. He went over to the desk and paid money. He left as he had come, walking on the balls of his feet, breathing with his mouth open, giving me a sharp side glance as he passed.

I got to my feet, tipped my hat to the blonde and went out after him. He walked west, swinging his cane in a small tight arc just above his right shoe. He was easy to follow. His coat was cut from a rather loud piece of horse robe with shoulders so wide that his neck stuck up out of it like a celery stalk and his head wobbled on it as he walked. We went a block and a half. At the Highland Avenue traffic signal I pulled up beside him and let him see me. . . .

The western light had shrunk to a band of dark green. Maud asked, "What was in the parcel?"

A few days later, Maud consented to ride. At the stables, tucking her slacks into a pair of borrowed boots, she adjured Elizabeth, "You're responsible!"

"Tell that to the horse."

Faced with a beast like an overstuffed pony, Maud was driven to confess that she had once had "endless" riding lessons. Elizabeth chided her for a sneak. "I have the know-how," Maud explained, "it's the performance that gives me the willies. Jumping especially," she incautiously added.

Maud was then assigned a proper horse. For an hour and a half she walked, trotted, and cantered around the ring behind Elizabeth, who at last led her onto the infield grass, on which stood three jumps of whitewashed wood. Elizabeth dismounted and set the bar of the lowest jump at barely a foot above the ground. She led Maud over it at an easy lope. She repeated the procedure with the bar at two feet. Setting it at three, she saw Maud's knees clench on her saddle and thought, she's afraid of taking a spill.

Elizabeth decided to show Maud that she had no cause for fright. When she took the jump herself, she nonchalantly slipped out of her stirrups and slid off her mount onto the turf. Intent on making her fall look natural, she distractedly caught her right foot on the pommel and landed on her capless head. Maud, right behind her, was so unsettled by the mishap that she forgot her own anxiety and took the jump smoothly. Propped on one elbow, Elizabeth cheered.

On their way home, Elizabeth invited Maud to a bar on Broadway. Maud never went to bars. She would again have refused if surviving an hour on horseback hadn't drained her power to resist. Entering the P's-and-Q's, she nervously inquired, "You know this crowd?" She dreaded meeting people she knew, and not meeting people she knew, and meeting people she didn't know. She was reminded of childhood visits to her father's office, full of strange men in shirt-sleeves. She drank too fast and had to pee twice in half an hour. When they left she felt sweaty and sick.

Elizabeth ignored Maud's discomforts. At six-thirty the next evening, appearing in a pale-yellow voile blouse that

wreathed over a white sheath skirt, she proposed going back into town. Maud gazed at her admiringly and shook her head: "You go on without me."

"It wouldn't be the same."

"You saw what happened yesterday. I'd rather get sozzled at home."

"How come?"

"I don't like being stared at by strangers."

"It's half the fun. Especially if you give them something to stare at. What about that green Norell shift?"

"Why not a bathing suit?"

"You'd be surprised. Most of them never notice you—you 'one,' not you Maud."

"And the other half? You said 'half the fun'?"

"Staring, just like you said. Or anyway looking. It's pleasant to watch other people. That's what they invented bars for—pleasure."

As they drove to the Boots 'n' Saddles, Maud vowed to remember those words. It was true that, once seated, they attracted scant attention.

Maud talked about Allan: "He sounded eager to come home. I think he should stew in his juice. I have no desire to pass the sponge. Not right away."

"You mean me?"

"I'm glad it *was* you. I still don't like it."

"If you think he needs to squirm, he can manage that by himself."

"Tell me about his devious side."

"How should I know?"

"Why did you ask about his career?"

"I've come to a conclusion about men: they're usually nuts. I'm not sure about this horse business, but it sounds like he's playing dirty games. Don't ask me why. Maybe to prove he doesn't need your connections. Shall we try the neighboring

hole before going home? He'll come back when he really wants
to."

It was almost nine when they left the second bar. In her
kitchen, forgivably bumping into unclosed drawers and dropping an occasional fork, Maud assembled a meal. "May I leave
the garlic out of the salad dressing? You know the Italians do,
at least the ones in Italy." A Bibb lettuce in each hand, she
came to a stop in the middle of the kitchen and there uttered
a dreadful sigh.

"Baby!" clucked Elizabeth, "I thought you'd enjoyed yourself tonight." Glass in hand, she was leaning against a var-
nished-oak counter, swaying dancelike from side to side.

"Yes. But after you've gone—Allan, my friends, they're not
like you at all. The future looks, well, uninspiring."

"You have everything you need to be happy. You do know
that?"

"Ohhh, happiness . . ."

Maud walked over to the sink. Elizabeth followed her
and hugged her from behind. When Maud looked around,
Elizabeth kissed her mouth. The lettuces dropped into the
sink.

"It's nice of you not to resist."

Maud turned on the cold water. "Don't you think we'd
better eat something?"

"I love you, Maud."

"I was having such a good time!"

"You're a *glorious* woman."

"No. I'm not."

"I know. You've lived through forty-nine-and-a-half years
of minor disasters. How about joining the party?" Elizabeth
held her tight.

Maud kept shaking her head while she plucked a lettuce to
tatters. "You're kind, you're a marvelous friend, but you have
to accept me the way I am." She looked over her shoulder into

Elizabeth's face. "I'd love to love you. It's frightening, though. I've never been with a woman before."

"Look, kissing you was . . . 'I love you' means you inspire me." Maud's subsequent laugh recalled Saint Sebastian at the loosing of the arrows. "Can't you tell I'm happy being with you, 'the way you are'?"

"I have this recurrent impression that I'm a bust."

"No kidding? I admit that sometimes you make me feel sane and efficient, which doesn't happen often. Maybe you could turn into a genuine bust and I'd really be on top of things."

"I'm going on the wagon this second."

"Don't you dare! Anyway, it's too late to start today."

They watched television after dinner. Mandy Rice-Davies followed a newly crowned pope. Elizabeth switched to the Mets, only thirty-two games out of first place and showing progress.

"There goes the Duke."

"He's very graceful. If only I knew what he was doing."

"It doesn't matter. Do you think he could fancy an older woman?"

Maud glanced shyly at Elizabeth and did not answer.

Maud came to like pub-crawling. She enjoyed speculating with Elizabeth about the lives of other patrons. Sometimes, to settle disagreements, the women consulted the patrons themselves, making friends of them for an evening. Maud discovered the easy society flourishing in public places.

One such evening, sitting on a bar-stool next to Maud, Elizabeth said to her, "You know I originally came to see you because you were my lover's wife?"

"Of course."

"I bet you don't know why I liked you right away." Maud pertly tilted her head. Elizabeth pointed to their reflections in the mirror behind the embottled rear counter. "We have the same nose."

Later that night, the tenth since their meeting, Maud took Elizabeth into the music room, sat her down by the upright piano, and rendered Schumann's *Warum*.

"I haven't played since Priscilla graduated, heaven knows why. I never dared ask you—I've always longed to find somebody to accompany or play four hands with. You don't perchance play anything?"

"Just the one-holed flute, darling."

"Is that the baroque instrument?"

"It is if you treat it right. I'm a musical dunce."

"It really doesn't matter. I like playing alone. Just promise not to listen less than two rooms away."

The Mets tied the record for consecutive losses on the road. An earthquake wrecked Skopje, capital of Macedonia. Arlene Francis was arrested after a car accident. Priscilla called to announce her forthcoming visit.

Still later, Maud asked Elizabeth, "You know my bed's the size of a putting green—would you consider sharing it? It's when I'm drifting off that I recall what it was I wanted to talk about."

"I toss and turn like a seal, I'm told."

"And the morning after, they're vanished. I myself suffer from wakefulness in the dark hours. Can't we try?"

Maud was immediately cured of her insomnia, which Elizabeth immediately acquired. At four o'clock during their first night Maud opened her eyes to see her friend sitting cross-legged at her side. Since her fall in the riding ring, Elizabeth's neck sometimes stiffened painfully when she lay still.

Elizabeth woke up in the morning cradled in Maud's arms. She declared, "I need to get laid."

"I wish there was more I could do."

After breakfast Elizabeth made two phone calls. She told Maud she would be spending the next day and night in the city.

In the afternoon, while Maud was hoeing her herb garden (a task she delegated to no one), Elizabeth's voice streamed through opened windows into the steamy air:

> But this is wine that's all too strange and strong.
>   I'm full of foolish song,
>   And out my song must pour.
> So please forgive this helpless haze I'm in,
>   I've really never been
>   In love before.
>   Ba ba doobie,
>   Ba ba doobie,
>   Ba ba doobie
>   Ah bah.

Her clear tones had a seductive faint breathiness.

Maud told Elizabeth over dinner, "You could sing opera. Or at least operetta."

"Theater! Music! How I'd love it! Honey, I'm strictly bathwater pops."

For Maud, the following day bristled with event. Up with the sun, in the garden by seven, she drove Elizabeth to the bus station to catch the ten-o'clock southbound and came home in time for Allan's call. He confessed his role in insuring the lately destroyed gelding. Maud could not grasp the facts of his story, even after he repeated it, and she concluded by saying, "What a depressing business! Why tell *me* about it?"

(Allan drew two small consolations from talking to her. She did not mention the portrait, which two nights before he had shamefully surrendered to Owen Lewison. By confirming Elizabeth's presence, she lessened his pain at not being asked back.)

Soon afterwards Priscilla arrived. Maud then learned of Allan's night with Pauline. She fought with her daughter. Torn between anger and remorse, she decided to give Pauline the

money she had intended for Priscilla. At three in the afternoon Walter Trale called to tell her that the "Portrait of Elizabeth" she had bought was a copy. There had been a string of crazy misunderstandings. . . .

Maud believed him. Human communication was going to the bow-wows. Why today of all days had Elizabeth abandoned her? She thought of telling Allan about the painting, then remembered his fling with Pauline. She drove to the Boots 'n' Saddles. Finding the place empty in mid-afternoon, she drank two more solitary chartreuses. At home she was given a message from Elizabeth, with a number to call in the city, of which she did not avail herself.

The next day, Elizabeth arrived earlier than expected. In time for another free lunch, Maud told herself. She had difficulty responding to her boarder's embrace. Elizabeth seemed not to notice.

"Nice enough," she replied to Maud's polite inquiry. "I feel sort of dumb missing a day here."

"It's sweet of you to say so," Maud said, staring into her coffee cup.

"'Sweet'? Hey—this is *me*."

Maud pursed her lips. "I've been thinking there's something we really ought to discuss. It's been marvelous having you here, and I want it to go on being marvelous. So don't you think— don't you think it might be better if we decided exactly how long it is you expect to stay? Open-ended arrangements are so awfully . . ."

Unable to go on, Maud shut her eyes. Sneaking up on her, Elizabeth slid fingers under her dirty-blonde curls and took an emphatic grip on her ears. Maud was immobilized. Elizabeth said to her, "Little girl, you're jealous."

"Oh, really? Jealous of what? Of you?"

"It won't hurt to say so."

Maud began to cry. "You move in and take over as though

you'd been here all your life. All I know about you is that you spent a week putting out for my husband—"

Elizabeth squeezed Maud's ears to shut her up. "I implore you to forgive me. I'm an unfeeling jerk—"

"Everything's easy for you. You don't have a family to worry about. You don't have any money problems—you don't even have any money."

"My beloved, listen, please, I promise you that starting right now I will never again do *anything* without you—" She let go of Maud's ears.

"If you knew what I've gone through since you left!"

"I'll arrange something right now," Elizabeth said, walking across the veranda towards the front parlor. At the door she turned: "Think of it—our first double date!"

Maud, still snuffling, at these words looked up in astonishment. "What do you mean?"

"I'll find you somebody delectable."

"Elizabeth, stop it! That's not what I meant. I'm past fifty."

From the gloom beyond the door Elizabeth replied, "I'd never have guessed it. But you'll see: at our age, it's a picnic."

Over lunch Maud begged Elizabeth to revoke her good deed. Elizabeth could then play the offended party: "I got three dates broken to make sure you'd have the best." She ended the discussion by saying, "If you don't like him, you say no." Maud consented and began a recapitulation of the previous day.

In the afternoon they went for a ride, starting from a horse farm to the west of the house. Instead of climbing into the foothills as they had planned, they kept to the unpaved roads that ran between level fields of blossoming potatoes and newly harvested corn. Elizabeth questioned Maud about Pauline, and Maud told her about their childhood years, her foster-motherhood, the bitter falling-out over Pauline's engagement to Oliver. Her voice trembled, she spoke of "principles of money and responsibility."

Elizabeth remarked, "The two of you turning a million dollars into a problem—it's hilarious!"

"It didn't *feel* hilarious! Why are you stopping?"

Elizabeth was staring across broken cornstalks. "Did you see the lark? If that's what it was. Just like one, the way it fluttered into the stubble."

"I was stuck back in nineteen thirty-eight."

"I lived in Bavaria once. A romance. Skylarks came singing down out of the sky and settled into the wheat, same as these. That was summertime."

"I know that bird, but I don't know what it's called."

"Not lark, anyway."

"Well, they don't get eaten here, either. You must understand it *wasn't* both of us, only me. It took me a fortnight to ruin everything, and she never understood. Never." They rode through a stand of hefty cutleaf maples. "Hearing about her night with Allan . . . I told myself I deserved it."

"You sit a horse very gracefully, you know."

"And now I'll make it up to her."

Suppressing an impulsive Bronx cheer, Elizabeth replied in cold tones, "You make a mess, and you pay for it."

"And I'm happy to pay for it!" Maud explained that she was settling the money on Pauline, not Priscilla.

"That's great," Elizabeth said, "but why not forget about the Dark Ages? You can shoot a brand-new movie."

"You're a hopeless optimist. Twenty-five years aren't going to simply disappear."

Elizabeth vented her Bronx cheer and replied, "In the twinkling of an eye!"

Maud shrugged.

At dinner, Maud gave a confused account of Allan's phone call. Elizabeth made her understand (she herself had only now understood) that Allan had arranged insurance for an aging racehorse knowing that it would soon be killed. "But that's not

like him at all," Maud said. "That's ghastly."

"I've seen worse. But it's what I meant—"

"I'm glad he's not here. Especially after Pauline. I can understand *her*, but how could *he?* Twice in a month! What *did* you mean?"

"Funny-business like the gelding wouldn't happen out of the blue. As for Pauline: Allan's pushing sixty, he's suffering from multiple upset, and Pauline was familiar, attractive, and available."

"My God—I forgot to tell you about the painting."

Later still, the two sang songs from musicals. Elizabeth's snapping fingers perked up Maud's somewhat Schubertian accompaniment. Maud sang along as well as sight-reading allowed. They repeated numbers they liked, and one they rehearsed until they could sing it in duet:

> . . . I hope that things will go well with him,
>   I bear no hate.
> All I can say is, the hell with him,
>   He gets the gate.
>   So take my benediction,
>   Take my old Benedick, too.
>   Take him away,
>   It's too good to be true.

"Poor Allan!"

Elizabeth had made their date for the following evening. Maud remained dubious about it, but they set off in midafternoon, detouring to the city down the rural meanders of the Taconic Parkway. Near the first Poughkeepsie exit Maud again brought up Allan: "Should I divorce him?"

"No."

"He's been small comfort lately."

"So divorce him."

"Oh?"

"You have a problem."

"Once a day and twice on Sunday."

"You like him."

Maud sighed. "I know. We've always gotten along so well."

"What's he like in bed?"

"*You're* asking?"

"With me he had unusual difficulties. He isn't the first. Never mind why. I liked him."

"That's why you said he was no hardened cheater?"

"Exactly. I'd like to say he was a novice, except nobody can be expected to go twenty-five years—"

"*I* have. Elizabeth, why am I doing this? That's one reason it's hard to answer you."

"Look, once a month obviously scores low. So does always resorting to the same—"

"He treats me marvelously. He always has."

"By this time tomorrow you may have a broader basis—"

"I'm not listening."

They drove in silence along a half-empty reservoir. Elizabeth said, "I know you're no spendthrift—all the same, you do have your gardens and your 'conventional benevolences.' Are you sure what you're giving Pauline won't hurt?"

"Not really. In certain brackets the graduated income tax is a great leveler. Priscilla's the one who's losing out. If she hadn't talked the way she did the other day . . ."

"It was that bad?"

"She treated me like an old drunk."

"Children make stern disciplinarians."

"She told me about Allan and Pauline. I hated her for that."

They had stopped at a toll station. Elizabeth started briefing Maud on her date.

By ten the next morning they were on the Thruway north. Maud spoke little, apparently content. Elizabeth asked no questions. As they crossed the Tappanzee Bridge, Maud said,

"I've got to get into better shape. Riding's invigorating, but there are specific areas . . ."

"I believe you were a great hit."

"What do you mean?"

"George called to thank me. He also said you'd made it—"

"Hush! He might have let *me* tell you. In any case, that's to *his* credit, isn't it?"

"I know it's hard to accept—he found you *very* attractive."

"But imagine having to turn out so many lights. I didn't dare leave them on. I had a hard time being sure what was happening. If I can't tell what's making me feel so good, how can I ask for more?"

"You have a point."

"How do you keep so svelte?"

"Ballet basics."

"When do you dance?"

"I don't, just exercises. And riding. If no horses are available, I walk for hours."

"Well: the attic gets too hot in summer, and it's too damp in the cellar in any season—where do I put the barre and mirror? Now that I think of it, I'll skip the mirror."

"Don't. It's a necessary torment."

Glimpses of the Hudson revealed water bluer than the sky it reflected.

"I called Allan. I felt peculiarly fond of him this morning."

"You changed your mind about him?"

"He's not dying to come home. He's afraid the two of us will tear him to smithereens."

"But you're not getting rid of him?"

"That was yesterday."

"He'll make a loyal stud and gofer, provided you give him a hard time." Maud frowned. Elizabeth nudged her: "Think what you've got on him!"

"Don't even joke about it."

"He's not a bad man—even if he tries to be. Interesting, though. Not many wives of the gentility can claim bona fide criminals as husbands."

"If only I could be sure you weren't serious. When he comes home, I'm counting on him to help with Priscilla."

"She needs help?"

"You don't understand, I have no regrets about taking back the money—I only thought if Allan could set something up to take its place. Something small. . . ."

"You dodo, money's the last thing she needs. She just got a hundred thousand dollars in life insurance—"

"She did mention that."

"That's a fortune for somebody her age. You people . . . Sometimes I think they should make inheritance taxes total."

"She's going to hate me."

"So? You already tried buying her off. Please, darling, look at the road, not me. Your getting angry means she matters to you. Tell her that."

"She won't believe it."

"She doesn't believe you now."

"I simply can't phone her."

"Write a letter."

"All right."

"Promise?"

"All right."

"Today?"

"Today." Maud's promise recalled to her a childhood pledge to write a thank-you note—the first time she imagined someone actually reading what she wrote. That afternoon, when she sat down to her letter to Priscilla, she fell asleep. She needed another day to complete two handwritten pages fit to mail.

Benefit expositions of "The Horse in Contemporary Art" had opened at the Spa Music Theater and the Hall of Springs. Oliver La Farge died. Police brutality during a CORE march

was being "probed." At Kamp Kelly, Mr. Grimmis and Miss Crystal did their best to protect Ira and Arthur from the insidious Marcia Mason. Maud and Elizabeth lay in the sun, Maud deepening her tan, Elizabeth shielding her freckle-prone whiteness with a floppy hat and a gauzy, long-sleeved chemise.

Maud reported, "Mr. Pruell plans to journey on a sailing yacht from Cape Cod to Mount Desert. Tempted?"

Nothing appealed to her less, said Elizabeth, than cramped quarters amid infinite space. Perhaps the two of them might travel. . . .

They drove to town for misleading guidebooks and uninformative maps. They speculated about Mexico, Sweden, Afghanistan. They fancied an ocean liner followed by a panoramic train, rucksacking forays over exotic mountains—the Carpathians, the Kazakh Hills. They called Maud's travel agent, who proposed charter flights to Venice or Majorca. By evening their house had become the traveler's joy.

Maud posted her letter to Priscilla. Elizabeth asked, "What about Pauline?"

"Am I to have no peace?"

"If you're going to play Santa Claus . . ."

"But I'm Scrooge making amends! Did I tell you she's coming here in two days? She wants to talk."

"About the money?"

"She implied something darker."

"So—you can still make peace."

"I'm in a letting-the-chips-fall mood. But I'll think about it. It could hardly get worse, I suppose."

Maud avenged herself on Elizabeth by making her sing Blondchen's first aria in *The Abduction from the Seraglio.* Elizabeth labored to hold the long high notes. She afterwards described to Maud another Mozart aria she remembered—one that had falling in love with love as its theme and sailed along under a wind of pure desire. Maud found Cherubino's *Non so*

più, and Elizabeth, at her third try, learned to hold long notes out of pure desire. Maud wished sometimes that she had been born a man.

Priscilla had not responded to Maud's letter. Elizabeth pointed out that it had been mailed only yesterday. "But I sent it special delivery, and I went to the post office myself." Maud phoned Walter. The letter had arrived that morning.

"I'm so relieved. Is Priscilla all right?"

"As far as I know."

"What do you mean?"

"I haven't seen her lately."

"I still don't understand."

After a moment Walter said, "She's not living here anymore."

"Oh, dear—where's she gone?"

"She's at Phoebe Lewison's studio. I put your letter under the door."

Maud wrote down the telephone number. "I'm sorry, Walter."

"It's OK. And don't worry about her. If anybody can take care of herself, it's Priscilla."

Maud knew what he meant. She rang Phoebe's studio. At the sound of her voice, Priscilla hung up. "Oh, my God, what have I done?"

"Come on, you expected it. Anyway, you told me she thrives on obstacles."

"She's twenty-three."

"If she needs help, she'll ask. Concerned parents drive difficult children crazy. I'll go see her on our next date if you like."

"You're an angel. You wouldn't like to take care of Pauline, too? I know, I know. . . ."

"I want to meet her, though."

"Tomorrow, provided I survive. No, I'm glad she's coming. I'll tell her everything. And listen, too."

After Pauline's arrival the next day, Maud and Elizabeth had no chance to talk until evening. The sisters had settled after lunch in the lilac garden, each oppressed with her dissimilar, unspoken confession. Pauline had not yet heard from the bank. Learning from Maud of the provision made on her behalf filled Pauline with jubilation, soon followed by shame. ("She'd come to tell me about Allan," Maud later said to Elizabeth, "and she began worrying that I'd take back the money, then almost wishing I *would* take it back, since she'd behaved like such a skunk.") Sitting up very straight, Pauline at last informed Maud that she had slept with her husband. Maud said to her ("It made me feel proud, as though you were watching"), "How could you possibly do such a thing to me?" The coldhearted falseness of these words released in Pauline a twenty-five-year-old accumulation of rage. Maud endured her sister's vehemence, only nodding her head attentively, and at the end said to her, "I've never dared apologize. You'd be inhuman not to feel the way you do."

"When she saw I meant it," Maud told Elizabeth, "she started crying. She said to me, 'Maud, that's nonsense! You don't have a mean bone in your body.' So it became my turn to be pitiful and cry—I haven't cried like that since Mummy was buried." Tears were again running down Maud's cheeks: "Why did it take so long?" She glanced at Elizabeth, sitting on the floor next to the bed where she lay, with something like reproach. "Why did they raise us like that?"

Elizabeth got to her feet and embraced her friend. "I was lucky. I had a real-live, no-bullshit mother."

They heard a discreet knock. The door opened, and Pauline's head appeared. "Sorry!" she exclaimed at the prospect of these two women entwined. She saw Maud's tear-streaked face. "You OK?"

"Fine. I'm just debriefing. You don't mind?"

"Not a bit."

The three had planned to go riding the following morning. High Heels appeared in real boots. To Maud's consternation, Elizabeth backed out. Her neck was still sore, she had a persistent headache. . . . Maud scolded her for acting so irresponsibly. Her fall might have done her worse damage than she thought: "We have an ultramodern Medical Center in Albany. Use it."

Elizabeth agreed, Maud made an appointment, and the next day they stopped off on their way to the city. An orthopedist prescribed strong antispasmodics, forbade any kind of exercise, and gave Elizabeth an appointment for tests the following week. Pauline spoke of a wizard acupuncturist behind Carnegie Hall; they arrived too late to find him, too late as well for Elizabeth's promised visit to Priscilla.

Maud enjoyed her second night out, although she wished Elizabeth had let her date George again. Her friend had told her, "Knowing you, you'd only start getting attached. Anyway, you have a lifetime of monogamy to atone for." Driving home the day after, Maud asked Elizabeth, "How'd you get the way you are? Your no-bullshit mother? Was there a revelation that struck the scales from your eyes? I assume you once had scales, like us common mortals."

"My mother! She never let me imagine I wasn't a 'common mortal,' especially days when I wanted to be a dancer or a movie star." Elizabeth, at the wheel, accelerated through sparse midmorning traffic. "I thought she meant I should be like other people."

"Fat chance."

"I *sort* of had a revelation. You ever watch ladybugs?"

"Elizabeth, please—no nature stories."

"You asked, remember? OK. Let's say I came across a nameless creature of indeterminate size in my back yard—"

"I'm skeptical, all the same."

"—and after watching it doing namelessly insane things for

a while, I started laughing so hard that my—another, larger creature came out to see what was wrong with me. I can't really say what the first creature had to do with what came next—I'm only describing—"

"No *post hoc ergo propter hoc* for us!"

"—I saw the second creature standing there, not worrying, either, I mean about who she was or the way she looked. She stood there staring at me skeptically (just like you), and at the same time so obviously in love with me. I thought: That's the way I'm in love with her. I saw that what I most wanted out of life was to be her. And I was. *That* was what she meant about our all being 'common mortals.'"

"She was hardly common. She was special."

"So it doesn't make sense. Still, right then I stopped worrying about being *like* anybody else. 'Love came to Elizabeth'—it felt like going barefoot on the first day of summer. Maybe that's where the ladybug comes in. This happened forty years ago, about, and I gave up being anxious for the future, and I haven't lived a boring minute. You know I love you, Maud?"

"I hope you never stop!"

"You know that if I love other people, I don't love you any less? I love you totally, I don't know how to love somebody more—*and* I may meet some man and go love him for a while, or forever, and you'll know even if I don't talk to you for months that I love you the way I do now? Maud, Maud, if you could see how beautiful you are!"

"That's what doesn't make sense. I know why I love you, but who am I?"

After supper Elizabeth picked up a fat old biography she had unearthed from Maud's eclectic shelves and read from a letter by a certain Miss Savage:

> . . . I like the cherry-eating scene, too, because it reminded me of your eating cherries when 1 first knew you. One day when I was going to the gallery, a very hot

day I remember, I met you on the shady side of Berners Street, eating cherries out of a basket. Like your Italian friends, you were perfectly silent with content, and you handed the basket to me as I was passing, without a word. I pulled out a handful and went on my way rejoicing, not saying a word either. I had not before perceived you to be different from anyone else. I was like Peter Bell and the primrose with the yellow brim. As I went away to France a day or two after that, and did not see you again for months, the recollection of you as you were eating cherries in Berners Street abode with me and pleased me greatly, and it now pleases me greatly to have that incident brought to my recollection again. I shall hear from you someday soon, n'est-ce pas?

"What a start for a romance!"

"No romance. He refused, she died, he regretted."

"How could he resist? I was thinking of reading you a lovely bit from Hawthorne, but not after that. Not even on a night like this. Shouldn't we be outside?"

"Just one peek at the ball game. The Cards are playing. You know Stan the Man is retiring."

Halfway through the fourth inning, Maud went outdoors; as though the night were expecting her, and she it. Her unread words sang on her tongue—*So sweetly cool was the atmosphere, after all the feverish day, that the summer eve might be fancied as sprinkling dews and liquid moonlight, with a dash of icy temper in them, out of a silver vase*. . . . From the grass at her feet to the Pleiades, she read the night entire. A three-quarter moon was shining through a low thin stratum of haze onto deserted swards, onto geysers of leaf billowing about the stems they concealed. The warm air had coolness enough to be felt as a benign exhalation. The air carried no sound, none at least to be listened to; no night bird, no droning car. As Maud deciphered patterns she had learned by daylight, the imperturbable scene

expanded. Each recognition dissolved its object and invited
her awareness to claim what lay beyond, past this line of hedge
or that swerve of road. Maud went back to fetch Elizabeth;
glimpsing her crouched in front of the raw-colored screen, she
let her be. She walked around the house and stopped at its far
side. Looking up, she saw the looming gabled roof silhouetted
against the barely hidden moon: her house, her very own.
Towards the woods, where her low shrubs and ground cover
had run into entanglements of softer wildness, she sat down
on an old swing—she had sat there with Priscilla in her lap,
perhaps here her mother had swung her as a child. In Russia
they must have nights like this. Maud thought of Tatiana,
late on such a night, writing her letter to Onegin. Maud had
no letter to write, no longing for love. Her father's house had
been bequeathed to her: not a possession so much as a space
in which memory and dream escaped division. Inside it sat
Elizabeth, who loved her, knowing her as she might never
know herself, and there all her people would return: Pauline,
and Allan, and Priscilla. She would welcome them back into
her life. She would not let them settle for less.

She set apart her future for them, and this night for herself.
She looked up at the stars, prickles of longing, few tonight.
The light belonged to the moon as it displayed the summer
earth, irregularly suspended around hummocks and col-
umns of thickset silver leaves. Maud pushed her heels into
the ground, swinging back, then forward. Straightening and
bending her legs, she wondered if she could lift herself high
enough to catch sight of the moon. Above the roof's peak the
bright haze glowed stronger the higher she swung, as though
the house hid an immense city. The clogs had slipped from
her feet. For ten minutes air breezed mildly between her toes.

"I wish," she said back inside, "I wish summer would never
end. At least, not for another two months."

They discussed future dates. Elizabeth asked about local
resources.

"It's too small a town," Maud said. "I haven't got the nerve."

"How about the neighboring boondocks? I hear the bars in Hoosick Falls are bursting with trade."

They gave up the idea. "Men" seemed hardly worth the trouble.

Elizabeth woke up the next morning exhilarated by a dream. She had become a bird flying low over old countryside: villages of graying stone, irregular patchwork fields, clumps of deciduous woods. She had flown mile after mile; she was still filled with the elation of her flight. Sunlight penetrated her bedroom at the edges of its curtained windows, accumulating at its far upper corners in orange pools that generated a brightness of their own. Incoming beams formed luminous bridges between these glowing pools and the light outside, and across these beam-bridges crowds of larks now began to stream. In her dream she had been a skylark, and now her companions were following her home. Her room had become a gathering point for the larks of the earth. She imagined them rising in Bavaria out of yellow fields, from copses of English beech and ash, from shrubs on the edges of Eastern deserts, from reedy shores: skylarks, woodlarks, crested larks, and the nameless creatures she had seen with Maud in the stubble nearby. The birds did not sing, but their wings filled the room with an agreeable thrum.

In time she took a closer look at them. The swarming larks began separating from her awareness of them. She had recognized larger creatures between the birds and herself. Against the placid shadows of her room she noticed shadows that moved: people. She addressed herself to identifying them. The faint light made that hard. Curtains were opened, sunshine flooded the air, revealing close to her a body stretched out under a petrified sheet, on whose white ground was stamped, with what struck her as almost drunken obsessiveness, as though one might somehow miss its point, a pattern of blue whorls representing twined wildflowers: pinks, she guessed, counting the figures down her

legs, past her curled, upright toes. The pattern did not distract from her own grotesque sprawl in its midst.

A few skylarks fluttered around her fussily. The people or person came nearer.

After a while, which she estimated as only minutes, Elizabeth sensed that she was causing fearfulness in the people or person near her. She then saw clearly that not near but next to her sat her beloved Maud, holding one of her hands and clasping her shoulder. Her face showed undeniable fright. Elizabeth longed to comfort her. She could understand the fright of watching somebody inhabited by so large a number of birds.

Now calm, the latter had withdrawn to the upper reaches of the room, perching on moldings, skimming peacefully about the brass chandeliers. Elizabeth appreciated their discretion, as well as their presence, which recalled her to realities beyond her own feelings. The lessened wingbeats allowed her to distinguish other sounds. She had seen that Maud was speaking to her. She could now understand her words, so loving, so frantic: "Elizabeth? Elizabeth, please tell me what's happening. Are you all right? Tell me you're all right?"

Speaking struck Elizabeth as inappropriate for her, smiling no less so, much as she would have liked to gratify Maud with a smile. She found another solution. If her eyes could see Maud, Maud could see them (not only stare through them, as she was now doing). Elizabeth's eyes could communicate. She opened them wide to signify that, of course, she was all right.

Maud pressed a cheek against Elizabeth's before leaving the room.

She walked down the corridor in a state of furious apathy. She sat down at her desk and cracked her knuckles while she cried. She knew what to do and wanted to do nothing. She felt a fierce need to discuss this matter with Elizabeth. She had difficulty admitting that she yearned to take Elizabeth's head in her arms and stifle it.

Elizabeth had not looked at her like a doomed animal. Maud found her list of emergency numbers, called an ambulance, phoned the Medical Center.

She sat in the ambulance at Elizabeth's side. Elizabeth, who had fallen asleep in her bed, slept while being shifted to a stretcher and through the hot half-hour drive to Albany. At the Medical Center she was committed to waiting orderlies. Around noon, in a bright air-conditioned room, with a drip in a vein of her left forearm, she reopened her eyes.

To ward off teariness, Maud began speaking at once. She soon noticed that Elizabeth's eye movements were following a pattern. She was teaching Maud a small, sufficient vocabulary: a blink meant *yes*, looking left and right *no*, looking down *I don't know* (this took Maud longest to grasp). Looking up kept its primordial sense of *What will they think of next?* Maud forgot her urge to smother that inert, pretty head. Holding it in one hand, she brushed its thick red-gold hair until it glistened.

A neurologist told Maud that the stroke indicated subdural hematoma, caused perhaps by falling off the horse, more likely by an earlier shock. Options available included an exploratory operation to determine the extent of the damage. Treatment might also require surgery. In either case the results could not be guaranteed. He had little else to propose.

"How about doing nothing?"

"Speaking frankly, it's not a bad idea." The specialist had unintentionally lowered his voice. "Cases like hers usually result only in hemiparesis. Fairly soon she should be able to move on her left side. An operation *might* facilitate . . ."

When Maud mentioned the possibility of an operation, Elizabeth's eyes snapped upwards. Maud said, "I couldn't agree with you more. You'll come home with me?" Elizabeth hesitated before answering with a decisive blink.

Maud by now saw that regret and despondency would only exasperate their difficulties. She could not deny that a terrible

event had taken place. She could not deny that Elizabeth had survived it. For Maud, pretending that she hadn't—committing her to the hopeless and comforting isolation of the terminal case—would only signify that Elizabeth's existence no longer counted. It would invalidate the presence that for so few and so many days had suffused Maud's own life. Maud promised herself not to let the disaster, having ended her time with a healthy Elizabeth, put that time in question. She would confirm her promise by not renouncing the fullness of time to come. She declared to herself that her life with Elizabeth had only begun.

After two days of interviews, Maud engaged a permanent day nurse. She persuaded her housekeeper to reschedule her hours so as to come early and stay late. She bought an electric wheelchair that Elizabeth could later run with her good arm.

Two days after coming home, Elizabeth was taken out of bed, installed in her chair, and wheeled onto the veranda where, for the next two weeks, she was to spend her daylight hours. She often slept. When she woke up, she always found Maud at her side. Elizabeth soon made clear her dislike of Maud's unfailing presence. *She* was the invalid. The greatest solace Maud could provide was to live a busy life, for both their sakes.

So Maud went riding; called on Mr. Pruell; went to "their" bars. She set out on these excursions dreading the reminders of Elizabeth she was bound to meet on her way, and of the opportunities lost because Elizabeth had not accompanied her. The awareness of her friend only intensified her experiences and sharpened her powers of observation. The most trivial events now mattered, and Maud noticed them unremittingly: chance accumulations of clouds, traffic jams, silly remarks, the least of her feelings. She came back with too much to tell, and told it, so that the eyes in the stricken head would shine, flutter, and sometimes cry. Maud learned that tears stood for laughter as well as grief.

Maud began taking Elizabeth out. With the nurse in attendance, John, now chauffeur as well as gardener, lifted the patient into the front seat, then drove through the countryside: west through the Adirondacks, east to North Bennington, north to Lake George. Maud bought a second, collapsible wheelchair, small enough for the trunk. Elizabeth sat in woodland shade, surveyed the world from hilltops, went window-shopping. Maud proposed taking her along on her own outings; Elizabeth refused. She wanted to be seen only where no one knew her. She made an exception of the riding stables, where the well-bred horses ignored her infirmity. Maud would leave her by their stalls, or at the edge of the field where they were pastured, while she cantered around the ring, hoping Elizabeth was watching her jumps.

Maud came to understand that, if she lived her life completely, Elizabeth's would not be wanting; but she could not yet bring herself to make another date in the city.

In the last week of August, Walter Trale arrived, bringing Elizabeth's portrait. The confusion he had created with Phoebe's copy had cured him of his obsessive attachment to the original. He had decided that Maud deserved it—she had paid for it in good faith, and she would make a worthy custodian—and he was now putting the painting in her hands.

Walter planned to leave as soon as he had hung the portrait. He was frightened of seeing Elizabeth, whom his imagination had transformed into a freak. He needed only a few minutes to change his mind. After Maud taught him the eye code, he had his first conversation with Elizabeth; and soon afterwards, at Maud's invitation, he agreed to stay on.

On the evening of his arrival, when Maud quizzed him about Priscilla, he refused to discuss their breakup. "That's finished. Guess what she's doing now."

"Do I really have to guess?"

"She's working for Irene."

"I thought Irene was involved—"

"You're so right. It was Irene who zeroed in on her. Priscilla deserves an Emmy for chutzpah. She went to Irene and said, I behaved like a little punk, I apologize, please teach me the art business."

"And she hired her?"

"Priscilla knows how to lay it on. She told Irene about her basic training with Morris, nothing to what she could learn from her, she was the best in the business, etcetera. Priscilla promised to work for nothing, lick stamps, mop floors, just give her a chance. Irene called me up about it, I told her I couldn't care less, only don't ever leave her alone in the gallery. Sorry, Maud. Irene bought it. She told Priscilla she'd pay her what she was worth and promised to work her ass off."

"Walter, I'm terribly worried. You don't think she has the makings of a professional criminal?" Maud had been thinking that she had Allan's blood in her veins.

Walter set up a worktable on Elizabeth's veranda. He began a life of drawing, writing, and reading, sometimes interrupted for sketching out doors or visiting old friends. Once he drove as far as Peterborough to work on a set of prints. He liked Elizabeth's company, as she herself soon realized. She let him talk to her, read to her out loud (*Memoirs of a Midget*; books by Cornell Woolrich), or simply sit quietly nearby. In the evening they watched baseball together. One day, looking at her while she slept, he reflected that in spite of the pallor, the blankness of feature, the saliva trickling from her mouth, she had kept an unforeseeable beauty.

Walter had rehung the portrait on the veranda wall, close to where Elizabeth usually sat. The bright daylight lent its colors a forgotten vividness.

Maud took Elizabeth back to Albany for examination. Three specialists spoke of her condition with optimism.

Pauline returned. Maud went out to meet her on the front

lawn and brought her straight to see Elizabeth. But when Pauline spoke to her, Elizabeth shut her eyes tight, thus introducing a new idiom: *No small talk!* Elizabeth saw that Pauline was bursting with news and should be allowed to tell it. She batted her eyes in mimic excitement. Pauline understood, laughed, and announced her tidings: for several months Oliver had been having "a *very* serious affair. With a not-so-young thing. Yesterday he decided to confess. You would have thought he was doing me a favor. It's true he hardly knows anymore who he's taking for granted. He made one big mistake, though. In his best how-can-you-manage-without-me manner, he said he hoped I wasn't thinking about a divorce. I said right away I wouldn't settle for less and threw the creep out. Can I hide here while my lawyer gets a stranglehold on him?"

When she wasn't out, Pauline often joined Walter and Elizabeth on the veranda, reading magazines or doing crossword puzzles. Elizabeth was pleased to be at the center of the household.

Pauline paid little attention to Walter, whom she scarcely knew. Elizabeth saw Walter frequently staring askance at Pauline. Since her stroke, Elizabeth had been determined to ignore her incapacities, but they now filled her with impatience. An attractive couple freshly sprung from domesticity, the man drawn to the woman, the woman unawares. . . . Before, Elizabeth would have needed minutes to unite them. She wanted to unite them now, in one family—her own. Her family had become her passion. Mere callers, even old friends, were sent away.

She resigned herself to taking whatever time was necessary. At last her mischievous eyes caught Pauline's and pointed towards Walter, bent innocently over his work. If only she could have winked! But Pauline had understood. She blushed with understanding. Elizabeth watched her realizing that for the first time in twenty-five years she was accountable to no

one but herself. She could take any man she wanted, for as long as she wanted. And Walter, the affable, undangerous genius, had put himself at her disposal, under her sister's sheltering roof.

What happened next left Walter bewildered. He was not only seduced by Pauline, but doubly seduced: she unwittingly spiced her availability with the contempt for males that her marriage had taught her. For Walter, the mix was irresistible.

Early in September, Louisa Lewison called Maud to tell her that Phoebe had spent the last three weeks at the Medical Center, and that her condition was still critical. Maud drove to Albany the following day. Walter was hard put to accept the news. He knew how sick Phoebe had been—he had taken her to the hospital in June. He had assumed that since then she had been properly cared for.

He talked to Elizabeth about Phoebe, forgetting they had met. He described the genius with which she had reconstituted the portrait. "At the end, she knew more about it than I did. She would have loved you."

He made the trip to Albany two days later, early in the afternoon. Alone on the veranda, Elizabeth thought about Phoebe. She had heard all the others deplore sickness in one so young. For mortal illness, is one age better than another? The living die at all ages; a death sentence is handed down at our birth.

In May, when they'd met, Phoebe was so weak that Elizabeth expected her to crumple like a Raggedy Ann doll. Nevertheless, she had had all the time she needed to be "Phoebe." In her fearful thinness she was still beautiful, like a solitary water bird—a plover, perhaps (why not?) a prim shore lark, even if Elizabeth had never seen one.

She wished she could be with Phoebe now. Elizabeth considered that she herself might well be doomed. Anyway, she wouldn't sit on Maud's lap forever; and as for a home, she'd

go on a breathing strike first. Why not bring Phoebe here, or go back to Albany herself? Two dying women staring madly at each other . . . "There's holy communion for you!"

She'd rather get well. So many things to do again. Like going riding—not in the cards, she knows. Then what about one more man? Elizabeth remembers distant, silhouetted figures with inexplicable affection. Thinking of Maud and George, she laughs. She can't laugh. A growl is stifled in her chest, tears spring into her eyes and flow down her throat, making her gag or cough or suffer an unpleasantness of some sort. She thinks, my trachea is full of soap wrappers!

A wave glides across her eyes and up through the tip of her cranium. Larks once came streaming into her bedroom. She hears them returning. This time perhaps they might sing for her. The birds start uttering their long, liquid flourishes as they land on the upper story of the veranda, where she cannot see them, although she hears them clearly enough. She congratulates herself for having summoned once again the lark diaspora.

Now, what about that last man? She wishes the larks away. They go on singing as they alight above her head. She laughs again. From her belly she hears an unmistakable growl. Something new is happening inside her. She feels a nibble of lust.

Christ, how she'd carried on! And now? She'd settle, Maud willing, for another tumble with Allan. Not likely, though. Couldn't she at least touch herself, one more time? Her growl bubbles up into her throat as she relinquishes her vow not to struggle with her affliction. She concentrates her energies into a lurch that will flop her right hand onto her lap. She shudders. Shut *up!* she admonishes the incessant birds. She lets go. The larks are hushed.

She hears her bowels blurt. She sees through the ceiling of the veranda as though it had changed to glass. The speckling

of birds dissolves in a cloudless sky, early morning or late afternoon, she can't tell; the sky at first filmed with lavender, the color calmly drawing away (what a goofy place to lock up her life!) so that only brightness remains, white so faintly blued the blue makes it whiter, Maud in the middle of it, speaking from a recognizable and measurable distance, her voice a muffled enunciation of Elizabeth's rejoicing.

Maud's face almost touched Elizabeth's as she called to her. The nurse was saying, "She's soiled herself."

"I know," Maud replied. "Help me clean her up. Help me clean my darling up."

Pauline had followed Maud onto the veranda. "I'll phone the doctor."

The nurse shook her head. Maud said, "We'd better take her to her room. Please get John." Maud was holding Elizabeth in her arms, cheek against cheek. Elizabeth's eyes stared past her.

Pauline said, "Maud, my poor Maud! Perhaps it's better—"

"It isn't," Maud declared. Someone tapped discreetly at the screen door. "John? Could you give me a hand?"

Allan kept peering through the screen at the blurred figures beyond.

IN A NEW YORK movie theater, Oliver watched *Dr. No* with his friend Jollie; since Pauline's departure she had dwindled in his consideration. Leaving Priscilla in charge of the gallery, Irene was visiting a young painter in his studio. Phoebe lay alone in her hospital bed, while her parents waited in the visitors' room, Louisa in an armchair, Owen standing at a window.

In the morning Barrington Pruell and his party had weighed anchor in Harwichport for Mount Desert, rounding Monomoy Point in auspicious conditions. As they turned north, a strong following wind swelled their sails, a hot wind that drove them towards their destination with disagreeable speed. In glum inactivity the crew slouched at their stations, the helmsman hardly touching the tiller, neither they nor the passengers sweating or shivering in the warm, brisk air.

I myself was proceeding, on foot, to the railroad station. Although it lay a few miles from the center of Saratoga Springs, I carried no luggage, having come up from Albany for the day, and I had time to spare. I walked past houses and lawns of diminishing size until, with the town behind me, I found myself flanked on either side by an unkempt wood, a tangle of oak, maple, and birch, hedged with a stiff rank of staghorn. Spread out below and in front of me, fields of hay in rich second growth extended to a line of darker hills, the earth's wetness rising from them in steady vibrations. As I walked, I reflected on a question, virtually the only one of interest still unanswered: how had Allan's letter to Elizabeth come into the hands of strangers? At the station I bought my ticket and

walked through to the benches overlooking the tracks. About to sit down, I noticed a tall gentleman standing on the far platform. No one else was to be seen on this second Monday in September.

The man had dressed, as for an afternoon lawn party, in a costume of conventional perfection. A blazer of not-quite-navy blue followed the slope of his shoulder and the fall of his slack right arm with uncluttered smoothness. Above the flattened collar of the jacket appeared a neat ring of off-white crepe de chine shirting, its points drawn together with a glint of gold beneath a rep tie of plum and pewter stripes, whose mild bulge was nipped by a more visible clasp of gold above the open middle button of the blazer. From a gently cinched waist fell pleated trousers of dove-gray flannel—my mental fingertips fondled their imagined softness, confirmed by the delicacy with which they broke, an inch above their cuffs, against the insteps of brown-and-amber saddle shoes. To complete the array, the man in his left hand held a high-crowned, pale-yellow Panama hat, using it to fan—so solemnly I wondered any air was displaced—his sweatless head.

Tipped forward, turned a little to one side, the head looked strong and sleek, although, in its details, less than handsome: the aquiline nose was too thick at its tip, the space between the eyes too narrow, the lips too thin. These flaws hardly mattered.

It has been said that being perfectly dressed provides a satisfaction no religion can give; and from this man, even in our nondescript surroundings, such satisfaction emanated like light from a filament. The way he assumed his elegance implied an imperiously debonair attitude to the world around him. He seemed to be inventing his very presence here, imagining himself in some sublime farce staged for the amusement of knowing friends, and for his own.

This impression, as it turned out, contained an element of truth. A few days later, returning for the funerals, I learned

that the man I had seen in the station was a professional actor, not particularly well known or successful except in his secondary career: he appeared as a paid extra man at fashionable parties. He could supply a stylish presence, he spoke well (and not too well), he charged a reasonable fee. I had seen him at work, perhaps waiting for a lady due on the northbound train whom he had been hired to escort for the evening.

I was relieved to have this apparition explained. He had disturbed me more than I cared to admit. I was twenty years younger then, and no doubt my own uncertainty exaggerated the actor's effect. At the time, I still hoped that life naturally engendered life, that death, no matter how devastating its losses, could be overcome or circumvented by the living as long as they themselves remained alive. If I knew that Morris could never be replaced, I expected that his memory sooner or later would grow flat, surviving only as a reminder of a time that could be safely called the past.

I thought, in other words, that I could always recover. I was only beginning to learn that the dead stay everlastingly present among us, taking the form of palpable vacancies that only disappear when, as we must, we take them into ourselves. We take the dead inside us; we fill their voids with our own substance; we become them. The living dead do not belong to a race of fantasy, they constitute the inhabitants of our earth. The longer we live, the more numerous the inviting holes death opens in our lives and the more we add to the death inside us, until at last we embody nothing else. And when we in turn die, those who survive embody us, the whole of us, our individual selves and the crowd of dead men and women we have carried within us.

Your father dies: you hear his laugh resounding in your lungs. Your mother dies: in a store window you catch yourself walking with her huddled gait. A friend dies: you strike his pose in front of an expectant camera. Beyond these outward

signs, we take up the foibles, the gifts, the unrealized failures and successes of those we have watched and watched die.

Of course we do everything in our power to deny this. I shall deny it to you and to myself as long as I speak, still pretending that you are only you, and I I. In this way I can become altogether blind and go on groping my way through sunlight and darkness, with only my uncomprehending complaints to furnish names for the things I trip over and for the other sightless bodies I stumble against. In such circumstances, I sometimes think that only the residual strength of the dead beings inside me gives me power to survive at all. By that I mean both the accumulated weight of the generations succeeding one another and, as well, from the first of times, when names held their objects fast and light shone among us in miracles of discovery, the immortal presence of that original and heroic actor who saw that the world had been given him to play in without remorse or fear.

New York, January 27, 1987